To Gerald —

— the meets & the beets

who helps with the eats —

Henny

or is it the meats & the beats?

The Parade of Heroes

Also by Tristram Potter Coffin and Hennig Cohen:

FOLKLORE FROM THE WORKING FOLK OF AMERICA
    and
FOLKLORE IN AMERICA: Tales, Songs, Superstitions,
    Proverbs, Riddles, Games, Folk Drama and Folk Festivals

THE PARADE OF HEROES

Legendary Figures in American Lore

Selected and Edited by

TRISTRAM POTTER COFFIN

and

HENNIG COHEN

from journals and archives of American folklore and culture

Anchor Press/*Doubleday*

GARDEN CITY, NEW YORK

1978

Acknowledgments are made to the following for their kind permission to reprint copyrighted material; additional acknowledgments are included in the Notes:

"The Pigs of the Love Mad Lopez" by Frederick Morris, "The Greatest of the Grizzlies" by J. Frank Dobie, " 'Gassy' Thompson and His Mining Swindles" and "Pat Casey Who Struck It Rich" by Levette Jay Davidson, all originally appeared in the *California Folklore Quarterly*. Copyright 1942, 1944, 1946 by California Folklore Quarterly. Reprinted by permission.

"Why Students Call Pedro" by Archer Taylor, "Watkuese Saves Lewis and Clark" by Ella E. Clark, "The Gold Cap of Joaquin Murieta" by Mary Jean Kennedy, "George Washington in Texas" and "George Washington and the Outhouse" by George D. Hendricks, "Told at the Paul Bunyan Winter Carnival" by Richard M. Dorson, "Larry Gorman, 'The Man Who Makes the Songs' " by Edward D. Ives, "The Best Straight-edge Man in the World" by William M. Jones, "All or Nothing" by Carl Hartman, "Norbert Wiener, the Great Mathematician" by Bruce Jackson, all originally appeared in *Western Folklore*. Copyright 1947, 1953, 1954, © 1955, 1956, 1960, 1961, 1968, 1972 by *Western Folklore*. Reprinted by permission.

Advertisement of "Renegade Liqueur" appears as "The Renegade." Reprinted by permission of Heublein, Inc.

Material on "Napoleon's Battle Tunes" by Judith McCulloch. Copyright © 1975 by Mid-South Folklore; material on "Perry Martin's Moonshine" (1974) by William A. Sullivan. Reprinted by permission of *Mid-South Folklore*.

For Nancy and Maurice Johnson

CONTENTS

II. WORK, PLACES, PEOPLES

III. A PARADE OF HEROES

♩ INDICATES THAT MUSIC IS GIVEN IN TEXT.

LIST OF SOURCES

Publications

Arizona Friends of Folklore
Beloit Poetry Journal
Bureau of American Ethnology Bulletin
Bureau of Navigation Bulletin
California Folklore Quarterly
Century Magazine
Colorado Magazine
Ethnohistory
Folklore and Folk Music Archivist
Folklore Forum
Journal of American Folklore
Journal of English and Germanic Philology
Kentucky Folklore Record
Keystone Folklore Quarterly
Louisiana Folklore Miscellany
Mid-South Folklore
Midwest Folklore
Mississippi Folklore Register
Nebraska Folklore Pamphlet, Federal Writers' Project
New Mexico Folklore Record
New Monthly Magazine and Literary Journal
New York Folklore Quarterly
North Carolina Folklore Journal
Northeast Folklore
Northwest Folklore
Piscataquis County Historical Society Collections
Publications of the Texas Folk-Lore Society
Scribner's Magazine

Southern Folklore Quarterly
Southwest Review
Studies in the Literary Imagination
Tennessee Folklore Society Bulletin
West Virginia Folklore
Westchester Historian
Western Folklore

Collections

Archive of American Folk Song, Library of Congress
Collection of Shifra Epstein, YIVO Institute for Jewish
    Research
Collection of Toby Blum-Dobkin, Washington, D.C.
Louisiana Folklore Society
University of Arizona Folklore Archive
University of Pennsylvania Folklore Archive
Winona County Historical Society, Minnesota
YIVO Institute for Jewish Research, Yiddish Folksong Project

INTRODUCTION

The United States is a large, culturally diverse, and kinetic nation. People do not stay put in America. They travel about, switch occupations, marry into ethnic groups different from their own, move upward and downward into new social positions. In a relatively brief time, they have populated an immense geographical expanse. They made rapid agricultural and industrial advances, absorbed immigrants from all over the world, and achieved unprecedented improvements in education and communications. They have scarcely taken time to catch their breath. If there is one word that characterizes America, it is *change*, and when observing any aspect of American life, it is a good idea to keep this word *change* continually in mind. It is particularly important to do so when discussing American folklore and folk life.

Folklore is stable. Its purpose is to give permanence to peasant societies, to shut out disturbing elements, to provide coherence to life in an uncertain and ever-changing world. In America, folklore has been sorely tested. Immigrants to America, whether English Puritans in the seventeenth century, the Irish and Italians in the nineteenth, or the Puerto Ricans, Cubans, and Vietnamese in the twentieth, brought with them firmly established folk traditions and folkways, only to see them eroded and discarded as their children and grandchildren have been acculturated. Members of occupational groups—forest scouts and trappers, canallers, railroad section hands, lumbermen—have developed tales, songs, sayings, and beliefs to dramatize the behavior patterns demanded by their work, only to see the occupations disappear or become so modified by industrial change as to be unrecognizable. Members of regional groups—Cumberland mountaineers, Georgia coastal islanders, Pennsylvania Dutchmen—who cherished their isolation and the lore that goes with it have been forced into the mainstream of American life by the media of mass communications, highway construction programs, and the effects of the military draft laws.

Thus the history of folklore in America has been a story of people changing—giving up the old, embracing something new, then giving that up, in an endless (and ironical) search for the sense of permanence their less sophisticated ancestors had in the past and in the old countries. An Irish peasant leaves the stability of "the old sod" to become in succession a West Virginia lumberman, an Illinois railroad worker, a Montana cowhand. His son becomes an Oregon rancher and marries a French Canadian whose father was a professional hockey player and grandfather a Quebec farmer. Their son goes to college and becomes a prosperous lawyer. He marries the daughter of a banker whose ancestry goes back to the Amish immigrants from Germany who settled in Ohio. There is nothing folk, there is little specifically Irish, French, or German, little to show a lumbering or cowpoking background, little of West Virginia, Oregon, or Ohio left in the lives of members of a family such as this today. The family will be American, that's all, Americans with a typically complex and diverse background.

Nonetheless, as Americans this family will know a stability, not the stability of the old folk culture, perhaps, but a stability established out of the heritage of change itself. And this American stability will be reaffirmed by what is sometimes called popular lore: the mass media output, promotional matter, advertising copy, and magazine/newspaper subliterature that permeates the land, affecting everyone. The essence of the popular lore, a coherent tradition, speaks to Americans of braving a New World, of joining hands and developing the most free and powerful nation on earth. It is a tradition that posits a distinctively American way of believing and behaving. It is a tradition manifest in its heroes, its exemplary figures, in people singled out to be remembered and exalted and used as models.

This book is about the heroes of the United States—not just the heroes of folk tradition that have flourished and in many cases vanished; but also about the heroes of that popular lore that all Americans who go to school, listen to the radio, and watch television know. A folk hero, strictly defined, is a figure like the mythic Indian Gluskap* or Br'er Rabbit* or the pirate Jean Lafitte* about whom legends exist in oral tradition, owned by no one, transmitted from generation to generation by word of mouth. These legends of genuine heroes vary with the telling and change as people forget or misunderstand or embellish the versions that come down to them. A hero of popular lore, an imaginary being like Paul Bunyan* or Pecos Bill* or a celebrity like Babe Ruth,* is another matter because he may owe his fame largely to professional writers. Their magazine stories, verses, songs, plays, and movie and TV scripts are fixed by copyright, private property and presumably not to be tampered with. Furthermore, they do not evolve spontaneously or organically. They are designed in advance for calculated purposes, to publicize a cause or to turn a profit. The profit might well be intended for the professional writer, or the composer and the recording studio, or an advertising agency, or tourist bureau and the clientele it serves, or the heroic personage himself.

But in the nature of things, the distinctions between the two are hard to maintain. With little regard to their particular locale, occupation, or national origin, folk groups get to know about the brawn of John L. Sullivan* and the wisdom of Benjamin Franklin,* the lies of Baron Münchausen* and the truth as told by

---

* The asterisk indicates the first mention in the introduction of legendary figures who appear in subsequent selections in the text. See index for page references.

young George Washington,* the chivalry of King Arthur* and the stupidity of Foolish John.* Chicanos tell stories of Br'er Rabbit and Louisiana Cajuns sing songs about John Henry.* Writers find that the Rocky Mountain adventures of the celebrated scout Kit Carson* make good copy for dime novels published in the East, that faked Johnny Appleseed* stories are as well received as authentic ones, that it is easy to invent someone like Johnny Kaw* and convince readers that he is a genuine folk hero of the Kansas wheat fields.

The experts themselves often have difficulty with the problem of pedigree. Was the hero fathered by the folk or by a professional writer? Davy Crockett* was sired by both, a curious circumstance, yet not unusual for American heroes. But if the experts have trouble distinguishing between folk and popular heroes, and in identifying these genes within a single figure, their troubles are minor when compared to their attempts to put American heroes into categorical boxes. This mixed breed is as varied and complicated in its composition as the American setting itself. The matter of categories will arise again, but at the outset it should be noted that even the most suggestive classification systems tend to be either inflexibly precise, and hence too exclusive, or so relaxed and encompassing that they risk losing shape and significance. In either case—and the divisions of the present collection are typical in this respect—legendary figures often justify identification within several categories. For instance, Manabozho,* the Algonquin culture hero, creates the earth and preserves its inhabitants, but in other manifestations he is also a trickster. The slave Old John,* who largely through verbal agility outwits his master, is a trickster, but he is also a sharp operator; and while the tales of his tricks arise from regional and racial situations, at the same time he is akin to the archetypal figure of the witty servant. John Henry is essentially a prowess hero. However, his roles as an occupational hero and ethnic hero are of great importance, and underlying all of these roles is his emblematic position as a man of nature in conflict with the forces of technology, or in yet more abstract terms, man caught between the old ways and the new. Judge Bean,* "the law west of the Pecos," as he called himself, was primarily a local character who, unlike most, ultimately attained national repute. His localization on the frontier cannot be overlooked, nor can the touches of the sharp operator and the fantastic that contribute to his legend. Joaquin Murieta* was a bandit and a badman, but his region is California, his ethnic links profoundly Mexican, his setting frontier, his pattern of behavior closely parallel to the English folk hero Robin Hood,* and his fame due to folk tradition with more than a little bit of help from a San Francisco journalist. Peter Francisco,* a minor hero of the Revolutionary War, has risen in reputation in recent times largely as an ethnic hero of Portuguese descent. The known facts of his life and the stories that have grown out of them emphasize his physical strength and his vocation as a blacksmith. Hence he has a strong claim to a place as a prowess hero and a lesser one in the occupational category; and perhaps his ethnic claim should be discounted somewhat because it has been asserted mainly by the Portuguese-language press, and is of recent date, and his origin is actually uncertain. Joe Magarac* is complicated in another way. He is a hero of the steel industry, but his Hungarian background seems almost equally important. Yet his basic attractiveness in the present context resides in the fact that he is a literary creation passed off as an authentic folk hero. In sum, American heroes, like America itself, cannot be readily boxed in. The country is so large, the people so varied, the change so rapid.

All heroes are exaggerations, however, regardless of category or whether they originated in the folk or the popular culture. Like the representations of men on the Greek stage described by Aristotle, they are markedly larger than life or smaller. They are distinguished from ordinary men and women by such qualities as their unusual strength (e.g., Joe Call,* the wrestler; Zishe,* the circus strong man), skill (Hugo the barber;* Lamar Fontaine,* the Confederate sharpshooter), morality (Hiawatha,* the law-giver; Preacher Dow,* the thief catcher), guile ("Gassy" Thomp-son,* mining camp swindler; Jemima Wilkinson,* evangelist), or kindness to others (Grandma French,* nurse; Deluvina,* friend of Billy the Kid*). They are symbols, revealing through the songs, stories, and sayings based on their exemplary, if exaggerated, lives how ordinary people should behave. Since time immemorial they have served mankind well; without them it would have been much more difficult for a society to perpetuate the principles that enable it to survive. And almost incidentally, they are projections of ourselves.

Heroes develop at all levels of civilization and in all parts of the world. Some are divine, some are people who really lived, some are fictional. They range from mythological beings believed to have created the universe, through semihistorical personages who gained fame in the distant past to relatively little known figures whose modest distinctions are of recent date. In the advanced countries of the Western world formal religions like Christianity and Judaism predominate in the society. Such is the case in the United States. In this country, the most widely known mythologi-cal heroes, even at the folk level, are the divinities to be found in a literary work, the Bible, although mythological figures such as the Papago Elder Brother* survive in the origin tales and cere-monies of American Indians, some of whom still practice their traditional religions. Other mythological heroes remain only as vestiges in stories that have long since floated free from their origi-nal religious moorings. Of this sort are the fragments of myths about West African tricksters like the Rabbit that were spread by black slaves in the New World through their Br'er Rabbit stories. Of course, such narratives lost their religious significance as the blacks adopted Christianity, and they survive now as amusing animal stories told largely for their own sake, although they occasionally point a moral and, at another level, are significant cultural artifacts. Many of these tales, having lost their sacred character, mingled with similar stories told by American Indians about their animal tricksters, such as Ishjinki,* a hare, and were further augmented by medieval and Renaissance beast fables, such as the cycle of Renard the Fox, brought to the New World by early colonists, and sometimes also by African slaves who had learned them from Europeans before being transported to America.

The result is a memorable body of stories about small, clever animals who survive in a world of larger and stronger ones (foxes, wolves, buzzards) through guile and resourcefulness. It is characteristic of American diversity that the small and the weak as well as the strong emerge as heroic figures. This tendency in reverse is equally obvious in anecdotes, satiric jokes, and parodies that cut powerful public figures, especially politicians and mass media celebrities, down to size. The delight taken in this democratizing process is sometimes downright vicious.

Most American heroes are not gods, demigods, or former gods. Most are either known historical figures whose lives form a pattern others aspire to emulate or, as noted previously, manufactured personalities produced for a preconceived purpose but somehow likewise expressing an aspiration. In both instances they typify extremes of human behavior: in short, an ideal. They include King Arthur, imported from England; Hiawatha, an aboriginal who preceded the coming of the white man; George Washington, the American Founding Father. All of them came forward in a time of crisis, gained stature over the ages, and in retrospect seem semidivine. They are Cherry Tree Joe McCreery,* who rafted logs on the Susquehanna River, and whose ghost, according to the ballad, continues to do so; they are Charlie Glass,* a black ranch foreman in Colorado who was involved in a bitter range war; they are Perry Martin,* famous for his moonshine from the Mississippi Delta to Chicago; they are Millie Hull,* who ran a "Tattoo Emporium" in the Bowery. These are people of local distinction, notables who lived just up the road a piece, not very long ago, and whose exploits and personalities were such that people still talk about them. They are Charlie "Bird" Parker* and Babe Ruth, public figures of such fame that their careers were obscured in an artificial haze of mass media publicity, which they broke through by means of the sheer mastery of their performances and by the solid folkloristic substance they attracted. They are Febold Feboldson,* tall-tale hero of the Kansas prairies, and Annie Christmas,* female roustabout, gambler, and brawler from New Orleans—both brain children of prankish and inventive newspapermen. They are Peter Francisco, an unpromising foundling who grew up to become a Revolutionary War hero, and Alexander Turney Stewart,* an Irish immigrant lad who became a New York merchant prince. They represent a folk type that the scholars call the male Cinderella, and stories about them were told to encourage other Americans of modest station along the upward path of progress.

America has been an exceptionally fertile land for the production of fictitious heroes. This is understandable in terms of geography and history. Commensurate with the vast land itself has been the inclination toward expansiveness, toward magnitude, toward stretching the truth into the realm of fantasy. In part this fecundity is a compensation for a relative failure to generate authentic folk heroes, a failure that can be explained on the basis of lack of time. Compared with England or Germany or Spain, to say nothing of India, folklore in America has had insufficient time to germinate. But also important is the massive impact of the communications media: it has inhibited genuine folklore by the effectiveness with which it produces artificial substitutes. This process often starts with a historical figure about whom folk motifs are already beginning to cluster. To make him more attractive, more marketable, a better instrument of promotion, touches of color are added and new traits of character and new adventures are fabricated.

Daniel Boone* and Davy Crockett are classic examples of this phenomenon. In his own time Boone was transformed into a legendary character, initially as the result of a popular biography, for which he furnished information, and which was presumably of some advantage to its author, John Filson, a Kentucky pioneer. The legend-making process likewise served the interests of western land speculators, and land speculations from which Boone himself hoped to gain. Davy Crockett was also popularized by the mass media, in particular through a series of almanacs and autobiographies bearing his name, and stage skits, joke books, and newspaper sketches. Much of this was the handiwork of Whig political journalists who sought to exploit his attractiveness to backwoods voters. More recently Boone and Crockett have been used by the media mainly as entertainment—subjects for films, television series, and juvenile books of a simplistic, nostalgic sort. However, though their primary purpose is to make a profit for Hollywood, the networks, and the publishing houses, they also mildly purvey the traditional American verities.

Lesser notables like the Reverend Lorenzo Dow and Judge Roy Bean have undergone similar transformations. An independent preacher who traveled the southeast on horseback, Dow was nationally known for the eloquence of his sermons, but the quirks of his personality, and the mass media quality of the revivals and camp meetings he conducted, made him the subject of jokes and sketches in the press as well as a magnet that attracted folk motifs. His vocation was the exalted one of saving souls from perdition, and he was not unique in capitalizing on the media (or for that matter, folklore) in the service of his charismatic efforts. Judge Bean's life was mundane by comparison but it was sufficiently flamboyant to generate legends without the assistance of the media or folklore, though it eventually attracted them. As a frontier justice of the peace, Mexican trader, cattle rustler, Confederate guerrilla, gambler, and saloonkeeper, his life provided enough western color for the eastern writers in the truth alone, and little to belie their most lurid imaginative efforts. There were many legendary personalities like Judge Bean, among them Jim Bridger,* Strap Buckner,* and Mustang Gray.* They ended up as seriocomic figures, roistering and swaggering their way across the continent as the line of settlement moved westward, and leaving farfetched tales of outlandish exploits in their track. Behind the frontier, in the East and in Europe, there was an avid market for newspaper articles, cheap novels, wild West shows, and eventually films based on this material. In fact, because of this market, hack writers in the nineteenth century virtually appropriated the tall tale, an old European folk form, making it over into something typically American and making its hero into such an outrageously extravagant figure that the word *hero* itself shifted its meaning.

At the same time there are also in America many local characters known only in limited circles and little touched by the mass media or professional writers. They might well be the most original, distinctive, characteristic, and vital, and certainly are the most abounding collection of genuine folk heroes to emerge in this country. They are not figures of epic proportions. Rather, as to be expected in folk life, they exist quietly, a little off the beaten path and modestly on the social scale. They are tramps, river rats, raftsmen, coal miners, trappers, herb doctors, midwives, fiddlers, singers, liars, pranksters. They serve the needs of true folk communities. When one of them is taken over by the nation as a whole, when he "goes national," as it were, he will almost surely be warped to fit some wider purpose, and will likely lose his capacity to serve the needs of his original locale. The development of Paul Bunyan illustrates this. Paul Bunyan stories grew out of fragmentary references to workers in the logging industry known locally for their personality and physical strength: for example, the Bon Jean jokes of French Canadian lumbermen. In their initial state, they had a pragmatic function, initiating a greenhorn, or forcing a deviant back into line, or letting off steam. In the hands of copy writers of lumber advertisements or authors of children's books Paul Bunyan became the protagonist in a tale with a plot and his character was softened and sentimentalized. The Paul Bunyan and Blue Ox depicted on the post office mural or travel poster or float in a Thanksgiving parade are a far cry from the sweaty, swearing loggers in the forest. Still, the laundered Paul Bunyan does tell Americans what they like to believe: that the people who made America were friendly, happy, venturesome tinkerers who performed in exaggerated ways made necessary by the enormity of their task, which was to fashion a democracy in a wilderness. On the other hand, a local character like Jones Tracy,* who never went national, incarnates important traits of his subculture, the Maine coastal farmers, traits that loggers in the Midwest or Northwest, or other subcultures that are likewise repositories of American dreams, may well not be interested in.

Apart from Indian myth, autochthonous American heroes, undefiled by popular culture and approximating the scale of Old World counterparts, are a rare species. One of this precious breed is John Henry, the black strong man who drove steel to help build the Big Ben Tunnel in West Virginia. Splendid as he is, he cannot offset the reality that the bulk of legendary characters in this country are local eccentrics or local figures reshaped by the mass media and literary culture, or outright fictions. No disparagement is intended. To the contrary, there is much satisfaction to be found in the number, variety, dynamism, and hyperbolic quality of American heroic personages. And there is additional satisfaction when they are seen within a setting that at once delimited them and allowed them space for their expansive growth.

The present anthology is divided into three major parts, each with subdivisions. The first deals with heroes who are either involved in creating and ordering of the world or establishing codes whereby to live within it. Thus some of the heroes of the opening pages are gods or demigods: Manabozho, who made the earth; Pele,* goddess of the volcano; the Nephites* who are immortal but return to walk among men. Others are mortals who show what a mortal, living in a world that his gods created, should and should not do. They perform great feats: with bowie knife and pistol like Clay Allison;* with magic like Mejewedah,* the Ojibwa medicine man; with an alto sax like Charlie Parker. They illustrate ethical behavior: through politics like Franklin Delano Roosevelt;* through preaching and ministering like Lorenzo Dow. They are tricksters, some divine, some mortal, all demonstrating what to do and how to survive.

The second part is devoted to heroes of the occupations, ethnic groups, and localities. They are mortals, real or fictitious, and their function is to maintain the integrity of a well-defined subculture and transmit the qualities that give it identity. They are masters of their trade and proud of their work, like Hugo the barber, and Big Max,* the coal miner; and they reveal its characteristic oddities, such as Big Max's superstition. They embody ethnic stereotypes—for example, Pat Casey* in the Colorado gold fields, with his Irish luck and carefree bluster—or convey the special kind of ethnic pride that comes with a reversal of the stereotype, as in the instance of Zishe Breitbart, the Polish Jewish strong man; and they pass on to their children legends of their great poets and kings, the Arab Abu'n-Nuwâś,* Matthias, king of Hungary,* and their great rogues as well, like Stratouhotdas,* whose Greek-Turkish name means "priest of the streets." They are even figures from the great literature of the past, like King Arthur and the Wandering Jew,* their adventures reset in spots as unlikely as the Pennsylvania mountains and the Utah desert.

All are deeply rooted in their localities, like the "Leather Man,"* in his strange garb, tramping the back roads between the Connecticut and Hudson rivers for so long that he became part of the natural surroundings; like Bill Greenfield,* playing checkers and telling tales about how cold it gets in the Adirondacks; like Eel Olive* backsliding at a Baptist Church meeting in North Carolina; and Bone Mizell,* a cowboy on the savannas of South Florida, having his troubles with the constraints of religion, society, and the law. Bone Mizell happens to be of Irish descent like Pat Casey, but this seems less important than his rootedness in his locale; Big Max happens to be a black man but more significant is his work in the coal mine; Hugo is a German, and this is not unremarked, but his fame lies in his fast work with a razor. What these folk heroes give us is a sense of identity, and whether it derives from their work, or national origin, or place, or some combination of these, recedes into the background.

As the third part of this collection shows, the diversity of American heroes is such that they overflow the most reasonable of categories, whether they are classified by their genesis in folk or popular culture, their descent from gods who came down to earth or men who rose to godlike dimensions, or their association with region, race, and vocation. When examples of heroes are amassed, they incline almost organically into groupings. These groupings are discrete elements, each justified by its own inner logic and sometimes related to other elements, but they cannot be taken as units in a single, rationally ordered whole. Rather, the whole that they form is like a parade of the American species, and it excites wonder at his infinite variety.

They march across the continental landscape, frontiersmen like Thomas Fawcett,* who serves with General Braddock; titanic bear hunters like Hugh Glass;* mythic bears that defy hunters; Indian warriors like Tecumseh* and Black Hawk* who fight to preserve their land; Gulf Coast pirates like Jean Lafitte, and land pirates along the Natchez Trace like James Copeland,* bad men like Stagolee* who kill one day and give charity to widows the next; slick characters like Dan'l Stamps* who dodge honest labor, tell big lies, and bilk their neighbors; quick-witted backwoods travelers in Arkansas who garner hospitality with fiddle tunes; simpletons like "Boots" Van Steenburgh,* who falls in love with the "Swedish Nightingale"; fabulous storytellers like Len Henry* and Jones Tracy; song makers like Larry Gorman* who use their talent to poke fun at their friends and get even with their enemies, or like William Scott* and Aunt Molly Jackson,* to fight for justice. They are healers like Grandma French, who dressed the wounds of the construction workers, and Johnny Appleseed, who cured the hexed cow. They mourn their dead like Deluvina at the grave of Billy the Kid. They dispense justice like Kit Carson, who duels with a bully, and the Mexican padre* who cursed the town that bred the bushwhackers who defiled his church. They are wondrously insane like Love Mad Lopez,* from whom gushes dazzling fantasy, crack-brained like Sam Patch,* who makes proverbs and jumps over waterfalls, gently pixilated like Huckleberry Charlie* and Joe Root.* And as if all these were not enough to fill our needs and express our nature, we continue to create them: from public idols like Marilyn Monroe, Jack Kennedy,* and Malcolm X, whose lives seem to follow heroic patterns and whose activities are bathed in the radiance of hype; or we embrace fictions from advertising agencies and public relations firms because we see in them the substance of our dreams. We should remember that Americans, while priding themselves on their pragmatism, have always been great dreamers. We need dreams for the psychological truth, the spiritual truth, they contain.

Ultimately, it is out of a mixture of reality and a kind of world-dream that heroes arise. The student of heroes and their legends, regardless of whether the hero demonstrably lived or was fictional, soon learns that he is seldom working with unique material.

What he is dealing with is a formulaic personality with an archetypal life pattern about whom, for the moment, a number of appropriate motifs orbit. The psychoanalyst Otto Rank in *The Myth of the Birth of the Hero* (1914) and the folklorist Lord Raglan in *The Hero* (1936) discerned a complicated formula toward which the life stories of many ancient heroes curve. Similarly, Joseph Campbell in *The Hero With a Thousand Faces* (1949) posits a "monomyth" comprising "in the form of one composite adventure the tales of a number of the world's symbolic carriers of the destiny of Everyman." Without going into detail, it may be said that the life of the hero, mythological or historical, internationally revered or but locally known, Old World or American, will tend to conform to a common pattern.

The hero will have an unusual birth. In mythology he is frequently the offspring of a god or goddess who has had intercourse with a mortal. Zeus in the form of a swan couples with Leda, who gives birth to Helen of Troy. In a dream, a spotless white elephant with a white lotus in his trunk enters the womb of Mahamaya, who conceives the Buddha. The Whirlwind from the East blows into the daughter of the Woman Who Fell from the Sky and creates the four Winds, of which Manabozho, the East Wind, is the most powerful. In the Christian world, where the teacher Jesus is the son of one god and a mortal virgin, the birth of a lesser hero is often given in secularized terms. His unusual nature is presaged by the odd circumstances of his conception or delivery. King Arthur is the child of an incestuous union, for example; Julius Caesar is delivered unnaturally, by the surgical procedure that we know as the Caesarian section. Such births are apt to be accompanied by natural and supernatural manifestations to show their cosmic importance: thunder and lightning, stars that rise in the East, voices that speak from the depths, singing on high. This part of the pattern may be modified so that the birth of ordinary mortals is colored by suitably portentous detail.

Johnny Appleseed (John Chapman) is said to have been born during apple blossom time, though he was actually born in September. The frontier gunman Billy the Kid (William Bonney) was supposedly born in a covered wagon headed west, though in fact he was born in New York City.

Early in life the hero will manifest the power that is his. Sometimes, as in the case of Heracles, this demonstration is triggered by a jealous deity or the leader he is destined to displace. Hera, furious that Zeus has slept with the mortal Alcmene and that as a result she has born Heracles, sends a serpent to the infant's room where he lies beside his mortal twin, Iphicles, son of Amphitryon. Heracles strangles the serpent, a supernatural feat which, of course, reveals his divine parentage. Likewise, though for no apparent reason, the baby John Henry while sitting on his mammy's knee takes up a hammer and predicts it will be the cause of his death. According to the ballad, Zishe, the Yiddish strong man, was famous for his strength "in zane kinderyurn," in his childhood. The Shawnee chief Tecumseh as a youth was subjected to severe privations, including a fast of thirty days.

The conduct of the hero in his maturity exemplifies the ideals of the society. Jesus lives a life that is a model of ethical behavior. George Washington is the ideal Father of his Country—general, statesman, gentleman, farmer, and before that a frontiersman. Benjamin Franklin is the incarnation of the American success story, the apprentice boy who through diligence and frugality climbs to the top, and then spends the rest of his life serving his fellow man in a variety of practical ways. It doesn't matter, it is as it should be, that their lives are beclouded with legend. When a personality attains heroic stature, it is not what he was but what people need him to be and make him that is important. So Washington's austerity, his military confusions, his opportunism, give way to a benign patriarchal image. So, too, Judge Bean's wildly irregular life is forgotten and his colorful legal procedures stand; so, too, a psychopathic murderer like Billy the Kid becomes a sympathetic figure in tales of derring-do and sentimental songs.

When a mortal hero dies, as he must, the manner in which he dies is of great importance. Often he is treacherously slain at the height of his powers while he is serving his followers to the fullest. And the world hates the villain who has done the deed: the perfidious nephew, the member of the gang who has taken a bribe, the Judas. If a man's life is poised on the edge of becoming a legend, then there is little that will help it along so much as a treacherous ending. Robert Ford who gunned him down when he was unarmed helped to crystallize the legend of Jesse James.* A martyr's death or the aura of martyrdom—for example, the hanging of John Brown*—likewise spurs legendary process, as does a bold death in the face of great odds—Davy Crockett at the Alamo, John Henry up against the steam drill; and to some degree a comic daredevil like Sam Patch comes close to being dignified, and certainly does his legend no harm, by his last plunge over the waterfall. An authentic touch in the spurious folk tale of Joe Magarac is his immolation in the fiery steel furnace. Even if he has not died in a manner suitable to legend, the deficiency may be remedied. Daniel Boone, full of years, died peacefully at home in bed. He was hardly cold in his grave before a magazine writer improvised a scene that has him die alone in the wilderness as he aims his rifle at some distant mark on the horizon.

But heroes don't die, really. They depart to a heaven, a cave in the mountain, an Isle of Avalon, until the times once again become desperate, and they are needed. Christ will return to defend man on Judgment Day. Arthur, nursed back to health by Morgan le Fay, will return to fight once more; and indeed, hard-pressed British Tommies in the trenches at the Somme are said to have seen him by their side. Jesse James wasn't killed, but got away, to live out West somewhere. Hitler didn't really die. "He is alive and well and living in Argentina." The legend that produced the phrase is so well known that its momentum has set up a back current, and the phrase itself has become a jocular response to a ridiculous assertion.

Not all heroes conform to the pattern. The lives of some, like Jesus, fit it almost perfectly, others partially, and some, like Franklin Delano Roosevelt, not at all. Yet it is surprising how quickly folk and popular tradition push heroic biography toward this pattern. John F. Kennedy's death offers a modern instance. Kennedy, an idolized public figure, died in a Dallas hospital, shot by a man who, according to the Warren Commission, was alone responsible for his death. His body was taken to Washington and buried in a carefully prepared grave in Arlington Cemetery. These facts are as certain as facts can be. However, almost at once rumors began to spread that his assassin was part of a treacherous plot against American society, that Kennedy was not really dead, and even that he was removed alive but in a coma from a Dallas hospital to what was then Jackie Onassis' Greek island, where he remains in this state today—presumably waiting until the time is ripe for him to return and free America from the forces that attempted his death and the destruction of the American way. Heroes don't die, really.

Hero lore is essentially a record of people memorable for their exploits and extraordinary character. Their lives inspire or amuse. It follows that their lives are usually preserved in narrative and descriptive forms as myths, legends, tales, anecdotes, jokes, songs, ballads, and the like. These genres predominate here, though not to the exclusion of others. This anthology also includes descriptions of rituals in which heroic content is significant and examples of folk drama, verse, parody, riddles, proverbs and proverbial sayings, flights of verbal extravagance, and repartee that combines dialogue and music, such as the cante fable and the "Arkansas Traveler"* skit. Heroic elements are embedded in two interesting ways in these genre categories, one associated with rituals and the other with word play and other verbalizations. For example, the Papago Indians, at an annual ceremony timed by the position of the constellations, retell the story of Elder Brother, their mythic creator, and how he led them into their lands, died, and was reborn. The ritual telling features songs and incantations and is highly formal. Ritualistic observances honoring a tribal figure of a quite different cultural group invite comparison. It has long been the superstitious practice of midshipmen at the United States Naval Academy to salute and invoke the blessing of an old ship's figurehead in the shape of an Indian chief and generally known as Tecumseh. The decay of age made it necessary to replace the figurehead, and a bronze successor was designed. Solemn rituals over which naval officers of the highest rank presided took place when the figure was cast and when it was dedicated. Within the body of the bronze statue were placed relics taken from the original, including Tecumseh's tomahawk and pipe, and it literally embodied certain of his vital organs. The admirals in their ceremonial words took cognizance of the tradition among the midshipmen of invoking Tecumseh's blessing so that they would pass their examinations, but they made it clear that they saw Tecumseh as a kind of tutelary god whose higher purpose was to instill a sense of tribal continuity.

Calling Pedro,* a shout heard on the campus of the University of California at Berkeley during the examination period, is a verbalization that parallels the midshipmen's prayers to Tecumseh. Pedro, so it is said, is a mysterious figure who will somehow help students pass exams, and their noisy invocations of his supernatural aid are at least helpful relief from tension, as verbalization usually is. But this is not the only kind of verbalization involving heroic material. The sayings of a legendary figure serve to characterize him and to transmit lessons in conduct. Parson Weems's story of young George Washington and the cherry tree contributes to the shaping of a personification of integrity and inculcates moral behavior. It also produced a phrase, "I did it with my little hatchet," which became proverbial, and entering folk tradition, has had a range of functions from the serious to the parodic. The wisdom of Ben Franklin, which he borrowed from both literary and folk sources, characterizes the man himself. He reshaped it and popularized it through his almanacs, and some of his proverbs returned to folk tradition. The preposterous sayings of Sam Patch, popularized in the press of his day to the point that they became proverbial, were verbal equivalents to his fantastic behavior.

The editors of this anthology have selected their material from folklore journals, publications of folklore societies, and archives both public and private. These sources are listed on preceding pages. Local characters, legendary figures known only within limited areas, are especially important to this collection because they are not well known and are usually closer to folk tradition. In contrast, as we have argued, the mass media materials contain much fabrication, and because they are so widely disseminated, produced our national heroes.

Much of this fresh and diverse local matter was obtained from the publications of regional folklore societies. Some of them are quite informal, some had only a brief and casual existence and are rarely to be found in libraries. Others have had a long life under the guidance of careful, well-trained scholars. Our greatest debt is to the contributors and editors of these publications, and mostly to the people, the folk, whose heroes are recorded in them. Details about the informants and the circumstances under which material was collected were not always published with their lore. Hence our notes are sometimes incomplete in this respect. These notes are to be found in the back of the book. They also supply analogues, types, motifs, cross references, comment on obscure passages, and other relevant information.

Further readings and discussions concerning American heroes are plentiful. One should consult the bibliographical portions of Stith Thompson, *The Folktale* (New York, 1946) and Jan H. Brunvand, *The Study of American Folklore* (New York, 1978). Other works that might prove helpful are Tristram Potter Coffin, *The Female Hero in Folklore and Legend* (New York, 1975); Tristram Potter Coffin and Hennig Cohen, *Folklore from the Working Folk of America* (New York, 1973), "A Dozen Legendary Figures," pp. 373–418; Richard M. Dorson, *American Folklore* (Chicago, 1959); and Dixon Wecter, *The Hero in America* (New York, 1941).

ACKNOWLEDGMENTS

As indicated in the notes, Thomas Brothers of the University of Pennsylvania transcribed recordings of several songs. His intention was to make them readily accessible, and for this reason his transcriptions are close approximations rather than exact and detailed documents. He also corrected obvious typographical errors without so indicating. Musicologists may refer to the original publication of the song. Others to whom we are particularly indebted for scholarly assistance are Samuel Preston Bayard of Pennsylvania State University, Edward D. Ives of the University of Maine, Harry Oster of the University of Iowa, Keith Cunningham of Northern Arizona University, Wilson Heflin of the United States Naval Academy, Jan H. Brunvand of the University of Utah, George Reinecke of the University of New Orleans, and at our own institution, for assistance scholarly and otherwise, Anne Burson, Barbara Kirschenblatt-Gimblet, Kenneth Goldstein, Rochelle Goldstein, and Inez Jordan.

The Parade of Heroes

I. GODS, DEMIGODS, AND SUPERMEN

CULTURE HEROES

The culture hero stands at the beginning because it is his role to bring a way of life to an earth, and, if this earth does not yet exist when he begins his work, to create it. Starting with chaos, a few grains of sand lying on the bottom of a primeval ocean, a reed which he plants and which will grow from some subterranean world, he creates and regulates the earth as man comes to know it. His creative effort involves such details as arranging the topography; dividing time into night and day; hanging out the sun, moon, and stars; engendering or releasing human beings, then instructing them how to die, have sexual intercourse, conduct their rituals. The culture hero may steal fire for the benefit of man, indicate which animals are to prey on man and which he may eat, destroy ogres that ravage the lands. Often he produces a child, sometimes twins (one good and the other evil), who help him or succeed him in carrying out these complex duties. When all is done he vanishes from the earth, retiring to some resting place, some land beyond the waters, where he will await another demand on his time, a Judgment Day, a Second Coming. In short, the culture hero is a divinity.

As stated in the Introduction, genuine folk myths about culture heroes did not survive in the Judeo-Christian tradition of Western Europe and hence were not within the tradition of the first peoples who colonized America. Their functions had long before been taken over by the Bible. It is from the American Indians, and particularly from their pre-Christian legends and ceremonies, that most nonliterary American culture hero stories come, such as the tales of Manabozho, Gluskap, Elder Brother, and other gods of the aboriginal tribes.

They exist mainly as memories of the past, except to the extent that the old beliefs are still retained, and even then they often show obvious responses to white, Christian society. A case in point is the account of the contest between Gluskap and Christ presented below. Sometimes they reveal a remarkable capacity to adapt to modern times. The ancient Hawaiian volcano goddess, Pele, appears as a hitchhiker, and the Japanese taxi driver who gives her a lift has absorbed enough Hawaiian lore to recognize that her appearance is a warning of a volcanic eruption. The Three Nephites, who miraculously assist believers, are culture heroes of a relatively recent religious sect that originated in the United States, the Church of Jesus Christ of Latter-day Saints. Davy Crockett, the frontiersman, performed feats exceptional by any standard, but a sketch reprinted from a nineteenth-century almanac tells how he put the sun back on its course. This feat marks his kinship with primitive culture heroes. All peoples at one time explained the creation and ordering of the world by similar stories. Their survival, in pristine or much modified forms, demonstrates that the urge to explain life in this way remains.

MANABOZHO, CREATOR OF THE EARTH

We find in the "Travels and Adventures" of the old fur trader, Alexander Henry, an important reference to the national hero, or demi-god, Manabozho. In the year 1760 Henry joined the expedition under General Amherst and remained with it until Montreal was surrendered by the French. He then laid in a stock of goods, purchased mostly at Albany, returned to Montreal, and set out for the western Indian country.

The intrepid trader's adventures are related in his book printed and published by I. Riley, New York, in 1809.

He made his way to Michilimackinac in time to be a witness of the taking of that fort, then a Canadian outpost, by the Chippewas and Sacs on the 3d of June, 1763, and from his story Mr. [Francis] Parkman gathers the most of his narrative of that famous game of Bag-gat-iway, or Lacrosse, and of the massacre of the Canadian garrison of which it was the prelude.

Henry, having escaped, went up the lakes to Sault de Sainte Marie and thence passing easterly stopped at Michipocoton Bay on the north shore of Lake Superior, fifty leagues from the "Soo." Here he found several small islands, "under one of which, according to Indian tradition," he states, "is buried Nanibojou, a person of the most sacred memory." Nanibojou is, he remarks, also called Manibojou, Michabou, Messou, Shectac, and a variety of other names, but of all which the interpretation generally given appears to be, The Great Hare. "The traditions related are as varied as his name." "He was represented to me as the founder and indeed creator of the Indian nations of America." "He lived originally toward the going down of the Sun, where being warned in a dream that the inhabitants would be drowned by a general flood, produced by heavy rains, he built a raft on which he afterwards preserved his own family and all the animal world without exception." For many moons the raft drifted without finding land. The animals, who had been given the use of speech, like the crew of Columbus, murmured against him. At length he produced a new earth, placed his family and the animals upon it, and created a new race of men.

The use of speech was afterwards taken from the animals because of their entering into a conspiracy against the human race. Henry states that he had heard many other stories concerning Nanibojou and found that sacrifices were offered on the island, which is called his grave, by all who pass it. . . .

[In 1840] Francis, son of Interpreter Assikinack, had been selected for his intelligence by the superintendent and placed in school at Toronto. Here he developed his powers as a linguist and took high place in his classes in Upper Canada College, was afterwards appointed interpreter to the Indian Department, which he served until his untimely death. During this period and styling himself "a warrior of the Odahwahs," he read four able and critical papers before the Canadian Institute at Toronto, which were produced in the "Proceedings" of 1858 and 1860, under the direction of the editor, the late lamented Sir Daniel Wilson.

Young Francis explained that he had learned of the legends related by him from his father and other old men of the Ottawa nation. Among the myths related by him was one of the transformation of men from mere brute animals walking on four feet, until, from constant fighting and exercise, they learned to stand erect and walk upon their feet. The flood, with Nanahboozho for Noah, is a longer story. This demi-god made of a piece of mud a large island which he placed in the agitated waters, where it continued to increase until it formed the earth as it is now. He continued to reside with men for some time after the flood, instructing them in the use of many things necessary for their well-being. "He then told them he was going away from them, that he would fix his permanent residence in the north, and that he would never cease to take deep interest in their welfare. As a proof of his regard for mankind, he assured them that he would from time to time raise large fires, the reflection of which should be visible to them. Hence the northern lights are regarded by the Indians as the reflection of the great fire kindled occasionally for the purpose of reminding them of the assurance made to them by their benefactor."

GLUSKAP TESTED

One time when Gluskap [Micmac equivalent of Manabozho] had become the Indian's god, Christ wanted to try him to see if he was fit: so he took Gluskap to the ocean, and told him to close his eyes. Then Christ moved close to the shore an island which lay far out to sea. When Gluskap opened his eyes, he saw it. Christ asked him if he could do as much as that. Then Gluskap told Christ to close his eyes a while. When Christ opened his eyes, he found that Gluskap had moved it back to its place again.

SONGS OF ELDER BROTHER, THE "PAPAGO CHRIST"

The Papago watch the stars and when they see the Pleiades cross the sky in one night they say that the proper time for story telling has arrived. These nights are the longest of the year, and the Pleiades rise in the east at evening, cross the zenith, and set in the west just before sunrise, their setting being considered the end of the night. Comparatively few men are considered competent to tell the old tribal stories, and it is often necessary to send a long distance to secure their services. Two men go together, one telling the stories and the other assisting him. These men tell stories four nights and, in that time, can relate the entire series, beginning with the creation. There are said to be six divisions of the Papago tribe, each speaking a different dialect and having its own version of these stories. The words of the songs differ slightly in the several dialects but it is said that the melodies are always the same. The stories here presented are from the divisions of the tribe living at San Xavier and at Vomari. The more complete stories were related by Sivariano Garcia of San Xavier, who is not one of the regular story tellers but has been an attentive listener, thus learning the stories and their songs.

There are two classes of tribal stories. The first and most important class consists of stories that must be told in a prescribed order, while the stories in the second class may be combined in any desired order to form a night's story telling. To the first class [belongs the cycle of "The Ashes People"].

The principal character in these stories is Elder Brother (also called Montezuma and Ithoi), and the more important stories relate his adventures with Earth Magician (Tcivut makai), Coyote, Brown Buzzard, Beater Wind and other personages. In each story there are pauses at about equal intervals, the usual number being three, though some stories contain only two. These pauses always occur at the same places and are introduced at points of special interest. The story teller says, "Now we will smoke," or announces the pause in some similar phrase, and the people are at liberty to lie down, walk about, or go outside the lodge. During the telling of the story they are required to sit up and pay strict attention. There is no feast in connection with the stories, but tobacco is given the story tellers before they begin their work.

STORY OF THE ASHES PEOPLE

In the old times there was a flood that covered the whole earth. Elder Brother gathered gum from a certain bush (usabugum) and made a big olla [clay jar]. He took every sort of animal with him, and got into the olla. Last of all came Coyote and wanted to get in. Elder Brother told him there was some bamboo growing in the west. He told Coyote to get some of this bamboo. Coyote brought it. Then Elder Brother cut off the end and put Coyote inside, letting his tail hang out. The flood came while Elder Brother was doing this, and soon everything was afloat.

When the water subsided, Elder Brother came out of the olla and Coyote came out of the bamboo. They met four times as they were walking. Coyote was all muddy and could not walk very well because of the mud, but he sang the following song as he was walking toward Elder Brother.

Song of Coyote After the Flood

TRANSLATION
I can not walk, I am dragging along,
I cried! Ah, Ah!

Analysis.—This song contains all the tones of the octave and moves freely within its compass of eight tones.
The key is F minor but the song opens with the triad on
A flat, the relative major. This is followed by the triad
on F minor and does not reappear in the song. The tone
D is used effectively at the close. It is also interesting to
note the absence of the third (A flat) in these measures.
The fourth is the most frequent interval except the
whole tone which occurs often as a passing tone.

When they met the fourth time Elder Brother said, "Little
Brother." Coyote did not like this and said, "I was first."
Elder Brother said, "How much water was there when you
came out?" Coyote replied, "About 4 inches on my front leg."
Elder Brother said that when he came out the water was chest-
deep on him, and that showed that he came out first.
Then he sang this song about the olla in which he had floated.

Song of Elder Brother After the Flood

* The bar ⌐ placed above a series of notes indicates that these tone
constitute a rhythmic unit. [Densmore's note.]

Black refuge where I dwell.
I am going forth with it.
I am there.

Analysis.—The keynote of this song appears to be G, but the third above that tone does not occur. The seventh is also lacking and the tone material is that of the first five-toned scale, according to Helmholtz. The most prominent interval is the descending minor third. The phrases are clearly defined and usually comprise three measures.

After the flood, Elder Brother, Earth Magician, and Coyote began their work of creation, each creating things different from the other. Elder Brother created the spirits of men and gave to them the "red evening" which is regarded by the Papago as one of the most beautiful sights in that region. The sunset light is reflected on the mountains with a peculiar radiance.

Song of Elder Brother
After he had Created the Spirits of Men

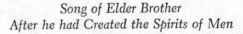

TRANSLATION

I have created you here, I have created you here.
The red evening I bring to you.

Analysis.—In this, as in the song next preceding, the third above the apparent keynote does not occur. Like the preceding song, it begins and ends on the same tone. More than half the progressions are whole tones.

Song of Elder Brother
After he had Created the Wind and the Clouds

TRANSLATION

I suffered to the bottom of my heart but at last I created a great deal of wind and at last I created many clouds, so now I am singing for joy.

Analysis.—This song is classified with E as its keynote, although C sharp is a particularly prominent tone. Except for the opening interval the melody progresses entirely by minor thirds and whole tones. Like several other songs of this series it ends with an ascending minor third. The phrases contain five, six, and seven measures, respectively, and each phrase has its individual rhythm.

Earth Magician had a bad temper. The things he made were criticized by the others and he became very angry. Then he began to sink into the earth. Elder Brother caught at him as he disappeared and became infected with a "cause of sickness." Endeavoring to shake this from his hands he disseminated sickness among men.

Song of Earth Magician when Disappearing in the Ground

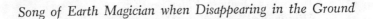

TRANSLATION

Here I sink, and I know all sorts of things.

Analysis.—There is a peculiar quality in this melody which may be regarded as wistful. The ascending fourth is a prominent and also the final progression. Two rhythmic units occur, each having the same count divisions in the opening measure. The tone material is that of the first five-toned scale which omits the third and seventh above the keynote.

Elder Brother had a rival named Brown Buzzard, whose power was so great that he could make boiling water bubble out of the ground near his house. He said that he would kill Elder Brother but that after some years he would come to life and then worse things would happen to the people. Four times the people tried to kill Elder Brother but he always came to life in four days. In their third attempt they boiled him in a big olla, but he put up his head and looked out of the boiling water. If the fire went out he got out of the olla, replenished the fire and got into the olla again. The fourth attempt to kill Elder Brother seemed to be successful. He was shot by Brown Buzzard, who went to him, after he was dead, and sang a song. In this song Brown Buzzard said he would not destroy all the things that Elder Brother had created, but would keep the wind and clouds for the benefit of the people.

Song of Brown Buzzard After Killing Elder Brother

TRANSLATION

I have done the worst thing now in killing you, my brother, but I am going to leave your wind and your clouds.

Analysis.—This melody is characterized by a descending trend. The phrases are short and the tone material is that of the fourth five-toned scale.

Elder Brother remained dead so long that children played with his bones and made bridges of his ribs. One day the children ran home and told their parents that Elder Brother was sitting there and fixing a clay canteen. As he worked he sang this song.

Song of Elder Brother After Returning to Life

TRANSLATION

There is an old man sitting down and fixing his vaäko (canteen), fixing his vaäko.

Analysis.—This is a melody of unusual beauty and bears some resemblance to oriental music. It is minor in tonality and contains a similar number of intervals in ascending and descending progressions. These intervals are 1 fourth, 4 minor thirds, 12 whole tones, and 8 half tones. The song is harmonic in structure and begins and ends on the keynote. The ascending fourth at the close is effective, also the frequent progression, D sharp-C sharp-D sharp.

The old people said to the children, "We told you not to disturb those bones or something bad would happen." Every one was afraid. Elder Brother said he had come back as he had promised and that he was going away but would return soon.

Elder Brother tried to walk but he staggered and in this way he started across the sky to find Brown Buzzard who killed him. Elder Brother rose up in the sky. In the middle of the sky was a "talking tree." When he reached the tree he broke off four branches and took them with him. The branches of the talking tree gave him power wherever he went in the world.

Song Concerning the Talking Tree

Analysis.—This song is classified as irregular in tonality. . . . These are melodies whose tones are not clearly referable to a keynote, and a majority are based upon the interval of a fourth. They are transcribed generally without signature, deviations from pitch being indicated by accidentals. The first half of this song is built upon descending fourths. The latter portion opens with two phrases on descending fifths, followed by a return to the interval of a fourth. The song is characterized by phrases with a descending trend, many having an upward progression at the close.

Elder Brother traveled four days until he reached the sun. Then he went across the sky with the sun and saw where he could find a man to help him kill Brown Buzzard. He went into Ashes Hill and found Earth Magician lying on a bed. When Elder Brother entered the room, he turned and said, "What sort of a traveler are you?"

Elder Brother answered, "I am here to talk with you." Earth Magician said, "I am in bed and have no time to talk."

Elder Brother waited. After a long time the other man said, "It is getting dark; you had better go. I have no time to talk."

Elder Brother stayed until the man had done this four times, then the man got up and sat by the fire. He directed Elder Brother to sit down. Elder Brother had brought tobacco, and they began to talk the matter over.

Elder Brother stayed there about 16 days, and they made plans for their journey to find the man who had killed him. Earth Magician directed his servants to prepare for the journey, making extra strong bows and arrows and preparing the food they would need. The servants went with them, and they started for the place where they would emerge from Ashes Hill. When they reached the place they sang this song.

Song Before Emerging from Ashes Hill

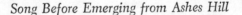

TRANSLATION

Now we are going to look over the world and see what is going on.

Analysis.—The intervals characterizing this song are the ascending fourth and the minor second, the latter comprising almost half the entire number of intervals. The song comprises three periods, each containing five measures and having an individual rhythm. The fourth and seventh degrees of the scale do not occur. . . . These are the scale degrees absent in the fourth five-toned scale, but the tonality of these songs is minor, the third and sixth being minor intervals, while the fourth five-toned scale is major in tonality, the corresponding intervals being major. This song was recorded on two occasions, and the records are identical in every respect.

After singing the song they selected four pure young men, who went first into the world, and after they had gone the others followed them. When the people came out of the mountain they saw a beautiful world with green grass and many flowers. Elder Brother looked about and then sang this song.

Song After Emerging from Ashes Hill

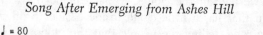

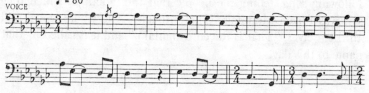

TRANSLATION

The world we have come into looks so grassy,
We come out to look over the world.

Analysis.—A downward gliding of the voice and a
nota legato characterize this interesting melody. The
progression C-B flat-C is used effectively; also the whole
tone between G flat and A flat. The tempo is slow and
the melody tones are those of the first five-toned scale.

The people emerged in the east and traveled toward the north,
then to the west, and south, some completing a great circle and
returning to the east. On this journey they continually fought the
earlier inhabitants of the land. From time to time groups of people left the company and settled down, the Papago remaining in
the Sacaton Valley. As they journeyed Elder Brother gave names
to the mountains. He would listen to the people as they talked
about the beautiful mountains, then he would tell them the name
of the mountain in a song.

It was said that the people saw a little cloud on top of a mountain and said, "We thought that we had everything with us. We
thought we had all the clouds. What can be the name of that
mountain that has a little cloud inside." Elder Brother sang the
following song, telling the people that the mountain which they
saw was Raven Mountain (Hawantohak). The whole crowd said
to themselves, "That is Raven Mountain," and it is called by that
name to this day.

"It is Raven Mountain"

TRANSLATION

Here we are on our way and see the distant mountain.
See, the mountain far from us that has the cloud is Raven
Mountain.

Analysis.—In this melody we find a peculiar haunting
quality suggesting oriental music. This has been noted in
other songs of this group. It is minor in tonality and
lacks the fourth and seventh tones of the octave. About
one-third of the progressions are whole tones. Next in
frequency is the major third. As in many of the songs of
this series the first and last tones are the same. Attention
is directed to the ascending minor third at the close of
the song.

THE THREE NEPHITES, MORMON IMMORTALS

Since Christianity had not spread beyond Europe and, except sporadically, beyond the fringes of Asia and Africa until after the great body of popular Christian lore had formed, legends of undying witnesses to Christ's ministry, like so many other oral Christian traditions, have been confined largely to the Eastern Hemisphere.

To legends of this kind, of which that of the Wandering Jew is perhaps the best embodiment, can be added a striking parallel from the Americas in person of the Three Nephites. Not wishing, like the remaining nine of Christ's Nephite disciples, to die at the end of the normal span of life (72 years), these three, according to the Book of Mormon account, desired at the hands of their Lord the privilege of continuing their ministry until His return.

Although the peregrinations and deeds of the Three Nephites must have lived in oral tradition, we cannot conjecture to what extent, since the scanty information we do have is gleaned wholly from canonical sources. Circumstances concerning their special appointment, the change wrought in their physical being, their investure with power to withstand the ordeals of prison, entombment, fire, and wild beasts, together with a brief summary of their early ministry, are set forth in the 28th chapter of III Nephi. This book in thirty chapters covers roughly the period of the Messianic dispensation. In the following book, IV Nephi, one finds only passing reference to the Three Nephites. These references contain, unfortunately, nothing but hints as to their *acta*. Mormon makes (ca. 325 A.D.) allusion to the three disciples in his own record, telling of having seen them before they were withdrawn because of the wickedness of the inhabitants of the land. In a final memorandum (ca. 400 A.D.) Moroni, son of Mormon, also avers having seen them before their withdrawal. . . .

From this meagre portrayal in Nephitish scripture there can scarcely have been preserved to adherents of Mormonism a well-defined picture of the Three Nephites, either as to their individuality or to the exact nature of their spiritual offices. This lack of information accounts in large part, no doubt, for the fanciful notions which many devotees of Mormonism have concerning them and their supposed present-day visitations among the living. It is little wonder that the folk, with only suggestions combed from historical record or lingering in folk reminiscence, but with no fixed pattern to direct its creative energies, should, when left to its own devices, have enlarged upon these suggestions in potentially as many ways as there are levels of folk thinking.

Stories about the Three Nephites run into the hundreds, and from a sampling of them I am able to make certain general observations. A characteristic vagueness beclouds the purpose of their visits, although they seem to come either as individual suppliants seeking food or respite or as benign ministrants to assist in times of sickness and crisis. As noted, the Three Nephites in most cases appear singly, and except for mysterious arrivals and disappearances deport themselves much as ordinary humans and are usually indistinguishable from them as to appearance and speech. Rarely, if ever, do they divulge their identity or reveal bits of information that would clearly stamp them as extra-mundane beings. As a typical example of these legends I cite a story supplied by a professional man, who heard it from a second party:

> "A stranger appeared at a humble home asking for food. He was given the last bit of food in the house and departed, after which the housewife noticed that the food was still there. Stepping to the door she saw no one and noticed that there were no tracks in the newly fallen snow."

Another one, told by an elderly lady, is a bit more vague, but is nevertheless typical:

"While walking along a country road on which there was no one in sight, I was accosted by a man who wanted to know the directions to —, a nearby settlement. He thanked me and vanished as mysteriously as he had come."

A third, related by a young rustic, emphasizes the superhuman speed with which the Three Nephites travel, and is but one of many such tales.

"A couple touring in Idaho picked up a hitch-hiker, who immediately began telling of the calamities about to befall the world. When he had finished they turned around, but he was no longer in the back seat. Later they picked him up again and were amazed that he could have traveled faster than they. . . ."

A story in some ways more reliable and more detailed than most stories dealing with these unusual characters was committed to writing and appeared serially in 1886 in a publication of the Latter-Day Saints. The article did not bear the imprimatur, editorially or otherwise, of the church and there is in the article itself no attempt at interpretation beyond a hint that the mysterious preacher might possibly be one of the Three Nephites. The layman, rummaging through his theology for a plausible explanation of this curious event might well suppose him to be one of the Three, or perchance, John the Beloved. At any rate, I think the comparison sufficiently striking to abridge the story and introduce it here as one pertinent to our discussion.

On a calm, sunny day of May, 1878, a clap of thunder resounded over the city of Lexington, Henderson county, Tennessee. The sound was heard distinctly for eight miles around and subsequent reports indicated that it had been heard as far as thirty miles. This phenomenon aroused much curiosity, since there was not a cloud in the sky and there was no storm after the thunder. On the afternoon of the same day there appeared near Lexington, the county seat, a strange man, of spare build, medium height, fair skin, dark brown curly hair, and a light beard of reddish cast. He was poorly clad. His appearance indicated that he was about thirty years of age. He announced a religious meeting to be held in the neighborhood that evening. Because of the unusual nature of his arrival, his apparent knowledge of roads and even paths in the fields, the meeting was well attended. He conducted the meeting alone, sang and preached in a manner unlike that of evangelistic preaching current at the time. At the conclusion of the meeting, when plied with questions, he said that his name was Robert Edge, and that he belonged to the Church of God. He refused to reveal whence he had come. At the solicitation of the congregation he appointed other meetings to be held in the vicinity, and soon his fame as a preacher had spread far and near. In due time, by an exchange of notes and gossip, it was discovered that no one had ever seen him any distance from a place of worship, and that he was never seen until he arrived in the crowd or had assumed his place in the pulpit. Persons appointed to watch him lost track of him before he had proceeded far. He never inquired directions from one place to another, and yet always arrived according to appointment. A case in point: At the close of a certain meeting a stranger asked Mr. Edge to speak at his house six miles distant the following Wednesday. The preacher accepted but, to the surprise of the host, did not ask him, nor anyone else, directions to his home. As usual he arrived at the appointed hour.

In his subsequent preaching Mr. Edge made allegations and attacks on various churches that brought him the ill will of many of his congregation and the animosity of the clergy. It was soon rumored that he might be a Mormon preacher. This he would neither confirm nor deny. More determined than ever to find out who he was, they commissioned one, Jones, a Baptist deacon, to find out the truth. Jones went to a house where Mr. Edge had eaten and proceeded at once to interrogate him.

Mr. Jones—"My friend, where are you from?"
Mr. Edge—"From about six miles" [meaning the next town where he had been].

Mr. J.—"What church do you belong to?"

Mr. E.—"The Church of God, sir."

Mr. J.—"Where is it?"

Mr. E.—"In the United States."

Mr. J.—"You have been speaking about one being ordained before he had the right to preach. By whom were you ordained?"

Mr. E.—"By Jesus Christ, sir."

Mr. J.—"Where?"

Mr. E.—"In Eternity."

Mr. J.—"How long have you been preaching?"

Mr. E.—"About eighteen hundred years."

"At this point," the article reads, "Mr. Jones sprang to his feet and walked away in disgust."

Mr. Edge gathered around himself a little flock of adherents, performed a number of healings, married couples and imposed his hands in blessings, but would not baptize the people. Harassed by a mob, Mr. Edge was forced to flee into Alabama, and later sent two letters of encouragement, one from Georgia and another from South Carolina, in which he mentioned plans of visiting England.

Almost two years later members of the congregation strangely came into contact with Mormon missionaries and joined the Mormon church. Among the first party of missionaries, who had heard this curious story, was Hyrum Belnap, author of the article who obtained, among other things, a deposition concerning Mr. Edge from Sireneous Reed and James Henderson Scott, which he reproduces in this article.

A Nephite Brings a Spiritual Message

I prayed for six years that I might have the privilege of a visit with one of those men (i.e., one of the Three Nephites), if not more. That's a long time, isn't it? We usually get pretty tired and give up before then. But my faith was that strong that that was possible.

On one winter evening just forty-nine years ago this winter (i.e., 1890) I was chopping wood out in the snow—snow about eighteen or twenty inches deep—and I saw that man coming up the street, and the impression come to me that that's one of the Three Nephites, so I watched him all up the street—kept on chopping but kept watching him. He come on up and come up to me and said, "Young man, I've come to talk with you. Come on in the house. I've got something to show you, and to have a talk with you." I didn't invite him in at all—he come right in my own home and opened the door for me. The house has been torn down, but that's a picture of it. (He showed us a picture of the house, and pointed out the room where he sat with the Nephite.)

I mustn't tell you all he told me; it would hit you too hard. I had around half an hour's conversation with that man. He talked about our temples. He talked about the disturbances that've come up in the Church, and he give me to understand that fact that the Almighty God, the Eternal Father, would never give us anything any more that surpassed or excelled that *Book of Mormon*. That was the greatest thing ever come to the people of this dispensation for our guide.

I pressed him hard to know what his name was. I didn't know then that prediction in the *Book of Mormon* that their names would never be known [III Nephi 28:25]. So when I asked him what his name was so I'd know which one he was he didn't tell me.

He was a fine looking man—the set of his eyes, so sweet and pretty—a fine head of hair—his nose, even and perfect—the finest complexion I ever saw on a human being. No child ever born had as fine a complexion as that man.

It wouldn't do for me to give you all our conversation. It would be too hard for you. I was never asked to make it known. Strange to say, you are the only people ever asked me that question (meaning, if he had ever seen one of the Three Nephites).

The disturbances I went through was outlined—the troubles which we went through. It wasn't long before this people was confronted with this question: "What shall we do about polygamy?"

He outlined those troubles then, the troubles coming to this people. I was wonderfully disturbed at that time. Things had taken place in this ward because I stood on an injustice when I was in the bishopric—I was out then—and consolation came through which I was reconciled fully, and also confirmed my conviction that I already had, that the *Book of Mormon* came actually from the only God and was a guide to these people.

When that man left me I questioned him hard where he was from. He was very pointed in not answering me or my questions. He didn't tell me his name, he didn't tell me just where he was going. He give me to understand he was from the north. When he left me he left me as sudden—he opened the door and shut it, and that's all. I opened the door but could not see my visitor. How he went and where he went I don't know. Perhaps he moved quicker than my eye—I couldn't say. It could be compared to sleight of hand.

He was the finest looking character there could possibly be. He was dressed like an ordinary man. Clothes of dark nature. His beard was just as white as—as the driven snow. And his hair—just as white as it could be. I said to him, "You have the appearance actually of being a young person, but your hair says that you are aged." All I got was a good big smile from that; he didn't say nothing at all. I can't give you all that conversation because I feel that it shouldn't go out. I witnessed it and I saw it all the way through—all he said about the troubles to come to us, and disturbances. He didn't give me any time for certain changes to take place.

He was well proportioned. He stood as straight as an Indian. In all his actions he was so pleasant, so nice looking, so young—in every way just as white as could be, his beard and hair. The prettiest hair I ever saw in my life was on that man's head. Such a lovely complexion. He fulfilled the "white and delightsome people" in every way. He told me of things relative to my own home.

PELE, GODDESS OF THE VOLCANO, AND THE FISHERMAN

On March 26th, 1926, there occurred an eruption of the volcano Mauna Loa, on the island of Hawaii, when the *a'a'* [slag] flow proceeded down the south slope of the mountain, destroying the village of Ho'opuloa. As is well known, the deity whose province extends over the volcanoes is known as Pele, the myths of whose origin, and the events of whose later life, have been fully recorded. She is known among the present inhabitants of the islands as "Madame Pele," and it is generally understood that she lives in the crater of Kilauea, on the slope of Mauna Loa. Outbreaks are said to be evidences of her wrath, and her revenge upon those who have disobeyed her.

The day preceding the flow of which we speak, a Japanese taxi-driver was on his way from Hilo to Ho'opuloa, when he noticed an old woman walking along the road. He stopped, asked her if she was going in his direction, and invited her to ride with him. According to this driver, she seated herself in the rear of the car, and he continued. Along the road, at various points, he came upon three stalled automobiles. At each, he stopped to inquire if he might help; but immediately the cars started. Soon after, he asked the old woman what her destination was; and not hearing any reply, he turned around to discover that she was no longer there. He at once realized that his passenger had been Madame Pele, and telephoned an American geologist, reporting what had happened. The geologist, acting perhaps on his observations of the preliminary rumblings of Mauna Loa, sent a party to observe the expected flow; for our purpose, it is sufficient to note that report on the island credits him with having sent his party *because* Madame Pele had been seen.

The next morning, a fisherman by the name of Ka'anana was

on the wharf at Ho'opuloa conditioning his boats for the day's catch. This man was a well-to-do fisherman, owning a rest-house on the south slope of Mauna Loa, a substantial house in the village, and two or three small fishing shacks at the water's edge. An old woman approached him, and requested that he bring her some fish of a kind that is rarely caught. He told her that he had not caught this fish for some time. She replied, however, that he would catch some that day, and that he should save some for her. In due time, he sailed for his fishing grounds, and the old woman went back into the village.

Next to his house in the village, and separated from it by a low stone wall, was another house. About noon, the woman who lived in it was busy cooking, when she heard a knock at the door. On answering it, she was asked by an old woman standing there what she was doing. When she replied that she was cooking dinner, the old woman wanted to know for whom it was being prepared. As the story goes, her answer was unpremeditated and unexplainable to her: "I am cooking for my husband, for my little boy, and for Madame Pele." At this, her visitor, with no further word, turned on her heel and left.

On his return with his catch, later in the afternoon, Ka'anana was met at the wharf where he docked his boat by a fish-broker, who bought his entire catch. As he was leaving the wharf, the old woman accosted him, and asked for her fish. Although he had caught the rare fish she had predicted he would get that day, he had neglected to save them for her when he had sold his catch in bulk. He told her he would be sure and remember the following day. But she answered that he would not catch any tomorrow, and left.

Near midnight Mauna Loa erupted. The flow was a slow one of the a'a' [slag] type, and made its way in two directions. One was toward the village of Ho'opuloa, the other, on the other side of the ridge, stopped before it did any damage. The first, however, made its way down the valley, threatening Ka'anana's mountain shelter. As soon as the first flare of the eruption took place, Ka'anana realized that the old woman toward whom he had been negligent must have been Madame Pele, and he immediately took steps to appease her. Luau, a pig roasted in the traditional manner, is something that Pele is reputed to enjoy. The fisherman killed his only pig, roasted it in a pit on hot stones, took it up the mountain, and laid it in the path of the flow, coming as close as he could approach it. It was to no purpose. His mountain shelter was devoured shortly thereafter.

He recognised that the situation was serious, for the flow steadily came on toward Ho'opuloa and his house during the day or more following the incident. And as the lava came closer, his alarm increased. He took all the money he had in the world, a little over twelve dollars, and placed it on the fence posts behind his house. The flow, keeping to the side of the stone wall on which Ka'anana's house was situated, swept relentlessly onward. As the account goes, there was only one place where its movement was arrested even for a moment. This happened when it reached the fence behind his house. At this point, it is said to have stopped for a moment, and then, with a mighty roar, to have come on, destroying his house, destroying a grocery store across the road, until it reached the edge of the water, where, continuing on its way into the bay, it ate up the rest of Ka'anana's property, his fishing smacks and his shacks. He was left utterly destitute. Not only this, but in creating a peninsula of lava, the fish were killed by the heat, and according to local tradition, it takes years before fish will again repopulate a bay where they have been exterminated in this way. Thus Ka'anana not only lost his property, but also the possibility of ever obtaining a livelihood at this spot.

It is told, however, that this flow did not cross the wall which separated Ka'anana's house from that of the woman who replied in so kindly a spirit to her old visitor, and that nothing belonging to her was harmed in any way.

DAVY CROCKETT AS DEMIGOD

One January morning it was so all screwen cold that the forest trees were stiff and they couldn't shake, and the very daybreak froze fast as it was trying to dawn. The tinder box in my cabin would no more ketch fire than a sunk raft at the bottom of the sea. Well, seein' daylight war so far behind time I thought creation war in a fair way for freezen fast: so, thinks I, I must strike a little fire from my fingers, light my pipe, an' travel out a few leagues, and see about it. Then I brought my knuckles together like two thunderclouds, but the sparks froze up afore I could begin to collect 'em, so out I walked, whistlin' "Fire in the mountains!" as I went along in three double quick time. Well, arter I had walked about twenty miles up the Peak O'Day and Daybreak Hill I soon discovered what war the matter. The airth had actually friz fast on her axes, and couldn't turn round; the sun had got jammed between two cakes o' ice under the wheels, an' thar he had been shinin' an' workin' to get loose till he friz fast in his cold sweat. C-r-e-a-t-i-o-n! thought I, this ar the toughest sort of suspension, an' it mustn't be endured. Somethin' must be done, or human creation is done for. It war then so anteluvian an' premature cold that my upper and lower teeth an' tongue war all collapsed together as tight as a friz oyster; but I took a fresh twenty-pound bear off my back that I'd picked up on my road, and beat the animal agin the ice till the hot ile began to walk out on him at all sides. I then took an' held him over the airth's axes an' squeezed him till I'd thawed 'em loose, poured about a ton on't over the sun's face, give the airth's cog-wheel one kick backward till I got the sun loose—whistled "Push along, keep movin'!" an' in about fifteen seconds the airth gave a grunt, an' began movin'. The sun walked up beautiful, salutin' me with sich a wind o' gratitude that it made me sneeze. I lit my pipe by the blaze o' his top-knot, shouldered my bear, an' walked home, introducin' people to the fresh daylight with a piece of sunrise in my pocket.

TRICKSTERS

The culture hero may be an awesome figure like the Olympian Zeus or he may be a trickster like Ishjinki, whose adventures are recounted below. As trickster, he may appear in human form like Manabozho and Gluskap or in animal form like Hare. Typically, he goes through a series of paradoxical adventures that demonstrate both the way to act and the way not to act. Thus the trickster is at once a deadly serious creator putting his world in order and at the same time a dupe or a deceiver, performing deeds that are foolish if not destructive to his community and himself. Roger Abrahams, a folklorist, characterizes the trickster in his clownish role as "the enemy of constraint," representing "the lawless, indeed anarchistic, aspect of ourselves" and serving "as a release valve for all of the anti-social desires repressed by the men who tell and listen to his stories." The anthropologist Paul Radin emphasizes his subservience to "his passions and appetites." When a trickster such as the Indian Ishjinki dupes others, we find in his energy and his counter-social action a vicarious release. When he dupes himself, we see him as a noodlehead and take satisfaction in our own superior control and social poise. When his self-deception becomes self-destructive, we regard his behavior as an object lesson and take warning from it. Though impulsive and amoral, the trickster acts within a moral framework and provides instruction in morality. The concept of the trickster is a difficult one for the modern mind. We are not used to having our gods play the fool, even for moral reasons.

Because we admire cleverness, resent restraints, and sympathize with the underdog, stories of the trickster or figures quite like him may be told long after their original religious significance has vanished. The Rabbit Trickster from African mythology became

the Br'er Rabbit of the American South. His pranks and tom-
fooleries in duping the bigger and stronger animals are not so
different from the relationship of the slave Old John to his
Master, or Konsti, the Finnish enchanter who beclouds men's
eyes, or even sharp operators like "Gassy" Thompson, who short-
changed silver-mine owners, and Dan'l Stamps, who peddled
watches that didn't work.

A TRICKSTER TRICKED

One day when he was alone Ishjinki saw a great many water-fowl. He went over towards them and the ducks said to one another, "Oh, old Ishjinki is coming."

"I say," said Ishjinki to the birds, "come on over where I am and I will sing for you, and you can dance." The fowls agreed to this and came where he was. As soon as they had gathered Ishjinki lay down and had them form a circle around him. He told them, "Shut your eyes and don't look, and I'll sing." So he commenced:

"Iya anastanaha istayijewi!"

(Whoever looks will have red eyes.)

As fast as the ducks passed around him dancing, he would reach out and catch them and wring their necks. He soon had a great many piled up before him. Every once in a while he would shout to encourage them, "Hau, good dancing!"

Finally one of the birds became suspicious and peeping saw that Ishjinki was wringing the birds' necks. "Look there," he shouted, "old Ishjinki is killing us!" All of the birds that were left alive then flew away. "Well," said Ishjinki, "I've enough to eat anyway."

The bird that peeped was the mud-hen, which still has red eyes to this day.

Ishjinki made a fire and put his ducks in the hot ashes to roast. While he was watching them, two trees which were close together began to rub in the wind. "Aaanh!" they creaked. "Ah shut up! you're too noisy!" cried Ishjinki. "Kwaa!" creaked the trees. "Shut up or I'll come and make you!" shouted Ishjinki. So the trees kept up their noise until Ishjinki climbed up and tried to hit the trees at the very place where they rubbed together. When he did this, the branches opened far enough to catch him by the wrist so that he was caught and unable to escape.

While Ishjinki was a prisoner, some wolves came by that way. "He!" cried Ishjinki. "Don't bother my cooking ducks!"

As soon as they heard this, the wolves stopped and talked it over and finally went to see if it were so. They took and ate all the birds, but stuck the feet back in the ashes. After they had gone, Ishjinki was released by the trees. When he got back and saw the feet of his birds sticking out of the ashes he was pleased, for he thought that they were still there, but he was disappointed when he found only the feet were left.

Hare Rides Coyote

There was once a village where an old woman lived alone in her hut near the outskirts. Every day she would go out to gather firewood, and one day she found a tiny rabbit. She picked him up and brought him home, and kept him until he grew to a good size and was very bright. This hare had a friend, a coyote, with whom he went about a great deal, although the old lady cautioned him not to go very far because there were so many evil things prowling around the world in those days. One day Hare and Coyote went to another village to look over the girls. They liked Coyote best because he had yellow eyes, a bushy tail, and a pointed nose, whereas Hare had big eyes, a stubby tail, and long ears. When they got back and their grandma asked where they had been, they just said that they had been visiting another town.

The very next day Coyote wanted to go again, and Hare said, "All right, you go, but I'll stay, for I feel sick." "Oh come on," said Coyote, "and I'll carry you." "No," answered Hare. "Well, I'll be your horse if you come. I'll take you right to the girls' door, then you'll only have to walk in." "All right," said Hare, "I'll go if you will let me put a bridle and an Indian saddle-pad on you so that I don't fall off."

Coyote agreed to this so they set out for the girls' place with Hare riding. When they got there they found the girls at home having a good time. Hare had put a cockle burr in the fur on one of his hind feet, and when they came to the lodge and Coyote said, "Now get off, my friend," Hare spurred him so that he bounded right into the wigwam.

"Well, girls," said Hare, "this is my horse that you liked so much."

The girls were ashamed and laughed and Hare rode home on Coyote.

BR'ER RABBIT AND HIS TRICKS

Br'er Rabbit Fools Br'er Buzzard

Once upon a time Br'er Rabbit an' Br'er Buzzard. Buzzard say he gonna shut up Rabbit five days until he starve to death. So he put him in a hole an' cover him up. Every day he come to him an' sing:

Br'er Rabbit he sing it after him. Did that five days. Every day Rabbit gittin' lower an' lower. B'rer Buzzard came 'round an' sing louder an' louder:

> Diddledum-diddledum-day-day
> Young man, I'm here.

De las' day Buzzard sing louder still; but Br'er Rabbit he very faint. He kin jes' barely say:

So Buzzard decide it is time to take Rabbit home to his little ones. As he was carryin' Rabbit to his little ones he said:

> Diddledum-diddledum-day-day
> Young man, here he.

All come 'round de table. Dey meant to eat him. Had knives an'
ever'thing, an' were jes' gonna cut him up when de father said:

> Diddledum-diddledum-day-day
> Young man, let's eat.

But jes' den ol' Br'er Rabbit jumped up from de table an' said:

Didd-le-dum didd-le-dum - day - day   Young man,   I'm gone.

> Stepped on a pin
> Hit bent
> That's the way he went.

No Tracks Coming Back

You know Br'er Rabbit said to be the wisest animal in the forest. So Br'er Rabbit was walkin' along one day when Br'er Fox
come along. "Say, Br'er Rabbit," Br'er Fox says, "ain't you goin'
to de big meetin'? Everybody goin'." "Zat so," says Br'er Rabbit,
"sure I'm goin'." So Br'er Fox went off an' Br'er Rabbit he take
an' look aroun'. Pretty soon he see hundreds o' footprints n' all
goin' in de sam direction. Den he see dey all rabbit tracks. "M-m-
m," says Br'er Rabbit, "all dem tracks goin' dat way, n' not a single one comin' dis way. Dat ain't no place fo' me."

Fox and the Dead Horse

Once Fox an' Rabbit had a crop together. So Rabbit wanted all
the crop an' Fox wanted all of it too. So Rabbit went out somewhere to study a plan to git all the crop. He was walkin' along the
road an' he found a horse. So he ran over to Fox an' said, "Guess
what I found,—a dead horse! Come on with me an' we'll carry

him off somewhere." So Fox went with Rabbit to the horse. So Rabbit said, "I'm gonna plait your tail to de horse's tail, an' you will pull while I push." So Rabbit had the whip. When he plaited the tails he whipped the horse an' the horse wasn't dead. When Rabbit beat him he ran aroun' pullin' poor Fox all over de fiel'. Fox cried out, "Neber min', Br'er Rabbit, I'll git you!" Br'er Rabbit say, "Git me now, git me now!"

Baby Rabbits

Once there was a rabbit an' a fox an' a bear an' a possum. They was goin' to build a home an' they had fixed it all except covering it. An' when they was coverin' it they had a can of cheese. Ol' Br'er Rabbit was sharp an' he acted like he had a wife. He would kneel a while an' whistle. Br'er Possum said, "What you whistlin' for?" Br'er Rabbit said, "I hear my wife callin' me." Then he went away an' eat the cheese. When he came back Br'er Possum said, "What did your wife want wid you?" Rabbit said, "She wanted me to name the baby." "What name did you give it?" Br'er Rabbit said, "Just Started." So a little while later he kneeled down an' started to whistle. He said he wasn't goin' no mo'. So he went up dah n' et out the cheese. So when he returned they asked him, "What did she want this time?" He said, "Oh, I had to christen another baby." They said, "What name did you give to this one?" He said, "Half Gone." So he went back kneelin' again. He heard his wife callin'. He said, "I ain't goin' no mo'.'" But he went just the same an' finished all the cheese. So when he came back they said, "What did your wife want wid you this time?" He said, "Had to christen another baby." They said, "What name you give this one?" He said, "All Gone." Then he went back kneelin' again. He said, "I hear my wife callin'. I'm goin' this time but no mo'.'" So he went up to the house an' licked the bottom of the dish. So when he came back they asked him the name of the baby. He said, "Lick the Bottom." So twelve o'clock came an' it was time to quit for lunch. Br'er Possum said, "Er-er-er, somebody done et the cheese." Br'er Bear said, "I know whut we do. We

will make fire an' put some bodies across the fire an' grease will
come out o' the one who et it." So they made a fire n' laid down
across it. So they was sleepy. So Br'er Rabbit slipped the grease
bowl under Br'er Fox. Pretty soon Br'er Rabbit jumped up cryin',
"Eh, heh, Br'er Fox done it, Br'er Fox done it."

Toad Loses His Tail

"Say Fox, you fond of chickens, aint you?" Fox say, "Yes, I sure
am." Rabbit say, "Go down to that hollow stump, there's a hen
an' five half-grown chickens down there." So Fox ran down, ll-ll-ll-
ll, on down he ran till he come to the hollow log. So it wasn't a
hen an' her chicks, but it was a dog an' her pups. The ol' hound
lit out after him an' the little ones ran after her. They yell,
"Yanny-go, yanny-go, yanny-go, yanny-go." Fox run past Rabbit.
Rabbit say, "Run, Fox, run!" Ol' Br'er Fox said, "Aw right, that's
a dirty trick. You wait, I'll pay you back." So Rabbit said, "Pay
me now, I aint got time." So one day he run up on Rabbit, got
him where there was a mud-hole. So Rabbit made into a hollow.
There was a small hole, so he gets in that. Just then Toad came
along. Fox said, "You watch him, Toad. I gonna git ax an' chop
him out." So he left Toad. Toad sits up, looks up. So Rabbit is a
great tobacco chewer. Rabbit took a big plug o' tobacco an'
chewed it up right good. He got plenty o' juice into it. Toad
jumped on the stump, lookin' straight up at the rabbit, his eyes
wide open. A big load of spit went b-r-r-r right into Toad's eyes.
Toad got busy then because all this stuff was burning his eyes.
Rabbit run, b-le-le-le-le-le. When he got away Fox come back,
ketch him wipin' his eyes. When Toad saw him comin' he jump
sidewise. Fox said, "Toad, is he in there?" So Toad said, "Yes." So
he commenced choppin'. Each chop Toad would take a hop sidewise. So Fox see Toad goin' through the mud-hole an' threw the
ax at him. The toad jumped an' before he jumped he said, "Shit!"
That's why every time you run on a toad but before he jumps in
water he says, "Shit!" an' in the water he goes.

Another Version

Once upon a time there was a rabbit an' a wolf, an' the rabbit an' the wolf was workin' for a man. They were drivin' oxens. So the wolf an' rabbit decided to steal one. The wolf had children an' the rabbit didn't. So they stole the ox an' they killed it. They skinned it an' they cleaned it. Then they cut it into four parts; that was to get it out of the way quick. So when they got it killed Rabbit asked Wolf what would he do if some ladies came an' asked him for some meat. Wolf said he wouldn't do anything, he'd just give the ladies some. Old Rabbit told Wolf to stay till he came back. The rabbit borrowed four suits an' the rabbit come back all dressed up as a lady an' asked the wolf would he sell her a piece of meat. The wolf said, "Oh no, lady, I'll give you a piece," as he gave her a hind quarter. The rabbit went back an' dressed again an' when he come back he asked for another hind quarter. But the wolf didn't known she carried that on her back. Rabbit came back. He asked the wolf to sell some meat. He give the rabbit a full quarter. He went back home an' dressed again and asked to sell some meat for her supper. Then he went back home an' stored it all. He came back as a man from work. He said to Wolf, "Oh, Mr. Wolf, where's all the meat?" Wolf said, "Oh, man, some ladies called to buy an' I give them the meat an' there is nothin' left but the head an' the guts. You take the head an' I'll take the guts." So the next day Wolf goes by the rabbit's house. Rabbit saw him comin' an' got his fiddle an' began to play:

Folly-rolly day,
You eat the meat an' I eat the guts,
Folly-rolly day,
You eat the meat an' I eat the guts,
Folly-rolly day.

An' the wolf asked Rabbit to play it again. Wolf began to run the rabbit. He runned him till he reached a hollow tree. When they reached the tree Rabbit run into the hollow part. The wolf couldn't git him out. He saw a frog an' asked the frog to watch the tree till he come back. Frog said, "What for?" He told him the rabbit was up there an' if he get the rabbit he kill him an' give him one half. He went home an' got his ax. He cut the tree down; limb by limb he split it. The rabbit was up in the hollow tree. He pretend as if he was eatin'. The frog heard him. The frog asked him what was he eating. Rabbit said, "Oh, man, good t'ing!" He asked him did he want some of it. He says, "Yes." The rabbit told him to look up de tree. He filled the frog's eyes full of pepper an' the frog began to git the pepper from his eyes. Rabbit got away. When the wolf couldn't git the rabbit he asked the frog had he been away. The frog told him no he hadn't closed his eyes an' neither been away. Frog began to get close to the water, an' when the frog began to leap the wolf cut the frog's tail off, an' the frog been bumpin' ever since and hasn't had no tail.

Br'er Rabbit Song

O Brer Rabbit! you look mighty good this mornin',
O Brer Rabbit! you look mighty good this mornin',
O Brer Rabbit! you look mighty good,
Yes, by God! you better take to de wood,
This mornin', this evenin', so soon.

O Brer Rabbit! yo' ears mighty long, this mornin',
O Brer Rabbit! yo' ears mighty long, this mornin',
O Brer Rabbit! yo' ears mighty long,
Yes, by God! dey's put in wrong,
This mornin', this evenin', so soon.

O Brer Rabbit! yo' tail mighty white, this mornin',
O Brer Rabbit! yo' tail mighty white, this mornin',
Rabbit! yo' tail mighty white,
Yes, by God! you better take to flight,
This mornin', this evenin', so soon.

KONSTI KOPONEN, THE EYETURNER

The most beloved eyeturner in Finnish American lore is *Konsti* (Trick) Koponen. . . . Tales of Konsti were told, particularly by immigrants from Savo [Finland], in the boarding houses and lumber camps of Michigan at the turn of the century, and are retold today by second and third generation Americans as well as their fathers.

My earliest recollection of these trick Koponen tales goes back thirty-five years, to a remark made by my grandfather. It had been a long, cold winter, and the farm fare of salted meat and potatoes had grown tiresome. "If only that boy, Koponen, were here," said grandfather, "he would fish us a perch from the floor cracks!"

"Did you see him do that?" we children asked.

"No, but everyone knows it's true," he answered with a chuckle that belied his statement. "Is that more wonderful than a pond he made on the dry cabin floor for the gypsies to swim in?"

Again and again the story emerges, sometimes with a lake of *piimä* (sour milk), sometimes of crystal clear water. Konsti Koponen, it seems, shared the true peasant's dislike of the roistering gypsy hordes that scoured the country-side. Once, when he was staying the night in a farm hut, a pack of gypsies came yelling loudly at the door for a bucket of milk.

"We have none! We have none!" moaned the farm wife.

"Come in! Come in!" cried Konsti. "Here you will find *piimä* aplenty. Enough to swim in!" And as the gypsies trooped into the hut, everyone there saw that the *tupa* (cabin) was filling with sour milk, to bench tops, to table tops. The gypsies scrambled to the highest ledges of the stove, and one fellow jumped into the pond, laughing loudly. His laughter changed to cries of woe, for suddenly the milk was gone, and the floor was dry as an old bone.

I repeated this tale, just as I remember it, to the family seated about the kitchen table in Gwinn, one warm evening in July, 1946. It gave rise to a spirited discussion. Aunt Hilja insisted that Grandfather had never called Koponen "Konsti." In Oulunlääni, where he came from, the trickster's name was "Kuippi." (None of us present knew exactly what this meant, but finally decided that it must be a colloquial term meaning "quick" or "clever.") Mother added that both her parents sometimes called him Aatu, and so his real name must have been Adam. Father, however, continued to call Koponen by his Savo nickname in the tale he then related, one which the others, even my younger brother, Robert, had heard before. He told the story in Finnish, and it was quite new to me.

Konsti Cures a Horse

Konsti was a healer who sold herbs, wandering around villages in Savo. Once he was walking along the road not far from Kuopio, when he met some gypsies. They had camped on the roadside, for one of their horses was sick, and knowing Konsti's fame as a healer, they stopped him. "Look at our horse and tell us what is wrong with it," they begged.

"Gladly," said Konsti. He went over to the horse, lifted up its tail, stared at it, then said, "I shall have to go inside the horse's belly to see what is wrong. Will you hold the tail for me?"

One of the gypsies hastened to be of help, and, so the story goes, Konsti pushed himself into the back end of the horse. The gypsies waited and waited, but Konsti did not reappear. At last a man came along the road and asked, "Why are you holding up that horse's tail?"

"Konsti Koponen is in the horse's belly, looking to see what is wrong with it," the gypsies answered.

"You're crazy," laughed the stranger. "I met Konsti on the road to Kuopio, not far from Tuovila's Bay."

"That reminds me of another one," said father, and went on with another old favorite.

Konsti Passes Through a Log

Once Koponen was passing the time of day with some friends in a village yard, when one of the men made a bet that he could not pass through a log, from end to end. Konsti took up the bet, and picked out a large, solid log nearby, put his head against one end, and pushed his way into the log.

Just then a man came along, driving a wagonload of hay. He stopped his horse, climbed out of the wagon, and went over to see what the crowd was gaping at. "Why are you watching a man crawl alongside a log?" he asked.

Koponen stood up at once, and was (or pretended to be) very angry. "I'll pay you for this," he said. "Look at your haywagon!"

At that, everyone turned to look. The haywagon was afire! Some of the men ran for water, others hastened to free the horse. Suddenly, in the midst of the confusion, they heard Konsti laughing. They turned to look again, and saw that the wagon and hay were standing as before, unharmed.

Konsti and the High-toned Miss

My mother then related in English the following story she had heard in her childhood, about 1900, in their Finnish boarding house at Bessemer, Michigan:

This time he was in a farmer's *tupa* (cabin) talking with menfolks when a rooster came strutting in through the open door.

"That is a powerful bird," said Konsti, "to be able to carry a big log." Everyone turned to look. Sure enough, the bird was balancing a log on his back.

Just then the young daughter of the house walked in, a *haituuni neiti*. "That is no log!" she cried. "The rooster is carrying a straw!"

"You will be sorry for this," said Konsti, "Have you no shame that you come here naked!"

Everyone turned to look at the girl, and burst out laughing. She glanced downward and ran screaming from the room. The laughter was even louder when they all saw that she was clothed as before.

My father had another ending for the story:

When the girl made fun of Konsti, he said, "I'll make you sorry for this."

The next day, being Sunday, the young woman was on her way to church. Just as she came near the threshold, she came upon a pond of water. The "high-toned miss" lifted her skirts daintily, but the water seemed deep, so her skirts went higher and higher. As she crossed the doorstep, she heard the laughter of people about her, and there she stood, with her skirts about her ears, on a dry doorstep.

Konsti Helps a Poor Farmer

I told the story of Kälmi of Varpus [a wizard] changing birch leaves into money, which served to remind father that this tale was also told of Konsti Koponen. "But it wasn't birch leaves, it was newspapers that Koponen changed," said father.

There was a poor farmer who owed a rich man some money. The rich man would not extend the poor man's note, so the court ordered an auction sale of the farmer's land and livestock to pay the thirty thousand marks.

The auction was ready to begin, and the *vallesmanni*, the sheriff, came to hold the sale. Koponen was there, and went in to see the old farmer. "Have you any old newspapers?" he asked. The farmer brought him old newspapers, and these Konsti tore into pieces. Then in full sight of the crowd that was there, he turned to the sheriff, handed him thirty-thousand marks, and asked, "Is the debt paid?"

"It is paid," said the sheriff, and give the farmer his receipt. Then he turned to the hard-hearted rich man and said, "Your debt is paid. Here is the money. Go your way."

But when the rich man got home, he found his pockets stuffed with torn newspapers.

OLD JOHN TRICKS THE MASTER

Old John liked onions and had been stealing them from the Master's garden at night. The Master became aware that somebody had been taking onions and asked John to catch the thief. John caught a skunk which he said was the thief. Old John further said that if Master didn't believe him, he could smell the skunk's breath.

The Master was fond of fishing and often took John with him on his fishing trips. One day while they were sitting on the bank of the river whiling away the time, John said that Master's walking cane had three ends, and he offered to show them to him. Master said that he was crazy and that if John could show him three ends to his walking cane he would set him free. John picked up one end and said, "That's one end." He picked up the other end of it and said, "That's the other end." Then he threw the cane in the middle of the river and said, "That's the last end."

Master's children went to a one-room country school near home. To reach the schoolhouse, they had to go through a wooded area where a panther was lurking and scaring them. Master told John to take his gun and kill the panther. John flushed the panther, shot and missed. When the panther started after John, he dropped his gun and ran for the schoolhouse nearby. John was running for dear life, but the panther was gaining. John ran up the doorstep just as the panther sprang. John slipped and fell, and the panther, which had overshot its mark, skidded into the schoolhouse. Quick as a flash, John jumped up and slammed the door shut. He had the panther trapped in the schoolhouse. When he went home and proudly told Master that he had caught the panther and put him in the schoolhouse, Master didn't believe him. John said, "If you go with me, I'll show you," and he took Master and showed him. The panther was looking through the windows as they approached the schoolhouse. Master said, "John, since you are a man so mighty as to be able to catch a panther with your bare hands, I want to see if you can take him out." John replied that that was not the agreement. "Getting him out is your job," John said.

Master liked to hunt and he frequently went with his friends. He told his friends of John's uncanny ability to identify any animal placed under a washpot. Master said that John could walk around the pot and tell what kind of animal was under the pot. So, one night on a hunting trip, they caught a coon and put it under the pot. The next morning they asked John to come out and tell what kind of animal was under the pot. John walked around the pot, kicked it, looked for hair, and so on. There was no clue. Master's young sons were playing nearby. John scratched his head and said, "Master, you got the old coon at last." One of the boys popped up and said, "John, how did you know?" John replied, "Yes, Master, you got the old coon at last."

Tom and the Master

There was once a Negro slave named Tom who was so smart that his Master told everyone in town not to make any bets with him. It so happened that another white man in town wanted to buy Tom. So the original Master told him, "OK, I'll let you buy Tom, but I must warn you never to make a bet with him." So the white man said, "Oh, I'm smarter than a nigger any day." He bought Tom and just as sure as life, Tom shortly thereafter propositioned the man. He said, "Master, I'll bet you anything that you're constipated." The white man said, "What? No, I'm not. I know I'm not constipated." Tom said, "Well, if you're not constipated I'll bet you a thousand dollars that by twelve o'clock you will be." So his Master said, "All right, you've got a bet."

At twelve o'clock Tom came back. He told his Master that he had to test to see if he was constipated. The Master asked, "How do you do this?" Tom explained that he would have to pull down his pants and let him stick his finger up his ass. The Master agreed to this. Tom did it, and said, "Well, you're not constipated." Master said, "Well, I guess that means you owe me a thousand dollars." Tom said, "All right." The Master went off happy because he had won the bet and outsmarted Tom. He happened to be bragging to a friend about this and his friend said, "What? Man, Tom had bet me *two* thousand dollars that by twelve o'clock today he'd have his finger up your ass."

PROWESS HEROES

Man, living in a world ordered by the culture hero, his impulsive, rebellious nature held in check or at least ventilated by the example of the trickster, still needs additional heroes to serve him as models. The values they embody reflect the standards, attitudes, and potentials of his society, and most of these heroes are historical. They may have been, like King Arthur, petty chieftains who defended their people against invaders and gained stature as they became enshrouded by the mists of time, so that eventually they seem almost godlike. Or again, as has also been said of King Arthur, they may have been gods in the forgotten cults of tribes that have long since passed from the scene. In either case, it is as the embodiment of a cultural ideal that they are significant.

The forms these heroes take are determined by the technology and beliefs of the society from which they arise. Among primitive, warlike peoples, the physical prowess of the hero is emphasized. His heroic position arises from his superior size, strength, skill with weapons and tools, speed, resistance to pain, beauty, and perhaps even clairvoyance. The hero of prowess may be correspondingly weak in other capacities. Such were Homer's Ajax and Achilles, and so are more recent prowess heroes like John Henry and Babe Ruth. Some heroines are simply female copies of powerful male heroes. John Henry's woman could drive steel like a man; Annie Christmas worked as a Mississippi roustabout. However, heroines are more often famous for their stunning beauty, like Helen of Troy. They are causes of wars, and prizes to be won, with little needed to commend them other than their physical attributes. A mass media celebrity like Marilyn Monroe is a contemporary counterpart of the Homeric idealization of physical beauty.

But the Prophet might as well have been male as female, her clairvoyance having nothing to do with her sex.

An ordinary man could hardly presume to measure himself against a culture hero who, after all, was divine, so he looked to the world about him for models and norms. Thus although the Indian hero Mejewedah exists in a misty realm between history and myth and from which of these he evolved is uncertain, it seems probable that he was a famous fighter and hunter who gathered a supernatural aura with the passage of time. The case of Joe Call is later and simpler. Where he was born and where he died is known. His fame as a wrestler, which is a matter of record, caused a number of folk motifs about the exploits of strong men to float in his direction. Much is also known about Clay Allison, the western gunfighter, who emerged as a folk hero in a similar way, and Lamar Fontaine, the Confederate marksman, whose evolution as a prowess hero was stimulated by newspaper exaggerations that he himself encouraged.

As we move forward in time, our prowess heroes seem increasingly secular. We have seen them in the limelight, which is another way of saying that the calculated effects of the mass media have superseded the magic of the folk process as the major factor in establishing their heroic status. When we could shake the hand that shook the hand of John L. Sullivan, when we saw him up close, we broke the spell. He may well have been a superman, but he could no longer be a god.

MEJEWEDAH, GIFTED IN MAGIC

There was once a time when in our tribe a great Ojibwa man lived who was called "Me-je-we-dah." He had many members in his tribe and frequently went to some other place when he was ready to fight. He went south once to fight the Flatheads, the Nebāgindibe.

One time this man told his braves that on the way to fight the Flatheads they would see an animal they had known, but not to say anything to it, because it could understand everything they would say. If they had any evil thoughts toward this animal it would know. There is always one foolish person in a company and there was one among Mejewedah's braves.

They were near where Chicago now is, but this side of it, near Battle Creek, and it was before the white people came here.

When noon came they saw this animal, and the foolish fellow said it was nothing to fear. He really was not afraid of the animal. It was a buffalo, and the buffalo knew in himself that this foolish fellow was not afraid of him. So after the braves knew this buffalo was angry they all stood in one row. The buffalo came up to the foolish brave, who then turned and fled, but the buffalo ran him down.

Then the foolish brave turned into a partridge, which flew and had every appearance of that bird. The buffalo also turned into a bird and continued the pursuit.

Then the foolish brave turned back into a man. The buffalo in the form of a bird immediately turned into a man too, and ran him down again.

After this brave was tired he jumped into a little lake and turned into a fish. Then the buffalo man took a spear and soon speared the fish and threw it to the party of great men. When the fish dropped, it was a man just the same as when he started out, only he was dead. The buffalo man then assumed his original animal form.

Then the leader, Mejewedah, became angry with the buffalo and the buffalo also was angry. When Mejewedah and the buffalo came together, Mejewedah took hold of the buffalo's horns and killed him by splitting his head open.

After this they went on to kill the Flatheads, just as they do in war. When they reached the enemies' country they saw a woman and a man walking in the woods. They caught the man, but they could not catch the woman, who went back to her village and called the people together.

Then her tribesmen went on horseback to where her husband had been killed by Mejewedah and his band. Mejewedah and his great men ran away. But they were finally surrounded and fought the Flatheads. One Flathead was as great as Mejewedah. In the fight the Flathead would hit Mejewedah with his war club, but Mejewedah was tough and could not be killed. Mejewedah killed the Flathead. After Mejewedah and his braves had killed all the Flatheads they turned and went home to their village.

Every time a young man married, Mejewedah would take the woman away for his own wife, and every one was afraid of him. But one time he went to do this and the young man was greater than he. So the young man killed Mejewedah.

Mejewedah was a sort of medicine man. He defeated a million people and killed many, but at last he met the young man that killed him. Mejewedah was more (Mide-wa-dis) gifted in magic than any of the others until he met this one.

GIANT JOE CALL

For well over a hundred years throughout the length and breadth of Essex County, New York, the newspapers and story tellers have spread the claim that Joe Call, the Lewis Giant, was in his day the strongest man in the United States, and until now no devil's advocate has arisen to confute them. If such did, he would have received short shrift, for Joe has become an ingrained and beloved legend among the mountains and hills of the Adirondacks.

When the real Joe died at Westport in 1834, probably no individual outside of a public figure or two like Commodore Macdonough was more widely known or better liked by the plain folk of northern New York and Vermont than he was. The common man of Essex County credited him not only with being double-jointed and having a double set of teeth but with being the champion wrestler of York State, Vermont, the Eastern Canadas, and many shadowy dominions beyond the seas. . . .

Today in Essex County, Joe is best remembered as the hero of the tale of the man who pointed the plow at his home. The story has variations and overtones but in the main is that a famous champion from across the water heard of Joe's remarkable feats as a wrestler and, fired with ambition to pit his strength against him, sought out the former at his home in Lewis. Seeing a man in the field plowing with an ox, he inquired the way. Without answering, the man merely lifted the plow and pointed toward a nearby house. The would-be champion just turned and headed straight for the Atlantic Ocean and has never been heard of since in these parts.

Joe Call's Sister

There was supposed to have been a very powerful Call sister who was hardly second to Joe in physical prowess. She is too fabulous for the Call genealogy, but among the Essex County story tellers she was a prime favorite and has had a long life.

Closest to their hearts is the tale of the champion—they were all champions who challenged Joe, according to his admirers—who came to Lewis or Woodstock to wrestle with him. Now, Joe was not at home and the man was terribly disappointed, so much so that he showed it. Finally, Joe's sister, seeing how badly he felt at not finding her brother home, volunteered to wrestle with him herself. They took hold and she picked him up and tossed him into the pig-pen. . . .

As told by a Chicagoan around 1900 as he heard it from Western New York, there is a slightly different twist to the powerful-sister angle. The girl was young and, of course, beautiful. The wrestler in this case came from a very distant State all the way to Lewis on horseback. Joe was not at home, and the fellow asked if he could wait for him. The girl told him that Joe would not return until late and that she usually did the wrestling while he was away, and then suddenly seizing the visitor by the slack of his pants, she threw him through the upper half of the open door out into the highway. The would-be wrestler arose, dusted himself off, made an obliging bow and at the same time remarked that if she would throw him his horse, he would start for home.

CLAY ALLISON, GUNFIGHTER

In the Old West there was an important distinction between these two types of the quick-shooting gentry of the frontier. The generic term was perhaps "killer", but between the two kinds of killers there was implied a certain degree of difference. The gunman was sneaking, murderous, and was always inclined to take every possible advantage of an enemy. He got the drop when his adversary was unarmed, or he killed from some safe covert, or he managed in some other way to evade the code of honorable shooting that existed in the days when "the six-shooter was the law of the land and every man stood his part". . . .

The gunfighter, on the other hand, was chivalrous, and always generous and sportsmanlike toward an opponent. Frequently he was compelled to kill by force of circumstance and altogether against his will, as when he might have to shoot himself out of some saloon imbroglio among men who, drunk on "tanglefoot" whiskey, had lost control of themselves. If the antagonist in a quarrel was not armed, the gunfighter was willing to allow his opponent time to procure the requisite shooting-iron. Sometimes indeed the gunfighter, realizing that his opponent was not so good at the game as himself, would contrive to allow some sort of odds in the fight. Admiration for fair play and a sportsmanlike spirit accounts for our being stirred by tales of these members of the hard-riding, quick-shooting chivalry of the plains. Though they may have left trails of blood in their wake, we stoutly refuse to classify them as murderers and perhaps feel resentment if the law eventually grips them and vindicates itself by sending them to the penitentiary or to the scaffold.

Clay Allison unquestionably belongs with the gunfighters. The universal testimony of those who knew his career is that, although

he killed many, he never killed stealthily. Usually to this assertion a bit of encomium is added to the effect that he never killed
any one whose death was not a relief and a boon to the frontier.
It is hard to determine with exactness how many Allison did kill.
Some old-timers have put the number as high as eighteen, and
one even lets it rise to twenty-one. But the majority are satisfied
to say twelve or thirteen. That is certainly a large enough score,
and appears reasonable, for the great tallies, such as that of
twenty or more for Ben Thompson, or of twenty-one for Billy the
Kid, always become considerably deflated when subjected to ex-
acting review. In the case of Clay Allison, I am inclined to give a
good deal of credence to the testimony of a certain man who
knew him in the days when he was an outstanding figure in northern New Mexico and neighboring parts of Colorado and Texas.
This man says unequivocally, "Clay never killed any one except in
self-defense, but he had about one dozen to his credit, all of
whom needed killing for the good of society."

A Duel in a Ditch

While Allison was working in the Brazos section and apparently was on the road to becoming in the course of time one of
the cattle kings of that section, he became involved in a serious
difficulty with a friend and neighbor. Allison himself never told
the cause of the difficulty, but the trouble was so grave it was impossible to settle it amicably. The two men therefore agreed to
fight it out.

Allison's grim originality showed itself in the details under
which the duel was to take place. It was agreed that a grave
should be prepared, of the usual length and width, but with the
exceptional depth of seven or eight feet. The two men were to
strip themselves to the waist and then seat themselves inside the
grave at the two ends, each grasping in his right hand a bowie
knife of a stated size. At a given signal, they were to arise and
start fighting. This they were to keep up until one or the other
was dead. A final stipulation required the survivor then and there

to cover the dead one with the earth removed in digging the grave. The story gives Allison the victory, but it also attributes to him such a high degree of remorse that it was impossible for him to remain in that vicinity. Therefore he sold out his interests and moved to Colfax County in New Mexico.

A Duel Called Off

There are some who contend that Allison's move across the state line into Colorado was not altogether voluntary. They hold that by that time he had killed several men in New Mexico, and was in danger of being apprehended for his crimes. However that may be, it is certain that Allison had succeeded in making a name for himself in New Mexico for quick and fully effective shooting. His famous encounter with Bill Chunk was enough in itself to give him a niche in the gunfighter's hall of fame. . . .

The cause of the encounter seems to have been Chunk's consuming envy and jealousy of Allison's growing fame as a gunfighter. Chunk belonged rather to the other class—the gunmen; he usually shot for the fun of seeing his victims fall. He claimed at that time that his tally was fourteen, and he announced publicly that he would round it out to fifteen by getting Clay Allison next. It was in this mood and temper that he came into Allison's vicinity.

When Allison heard of Chunk's boast, he tacitly accepted the challenge by continuing to go about his business without trying in the least to keep out of Chunk's way. In those days the Clifton House, a large, two-story adobe building near the present site of Raton, New Mexico, was a famous hostelry, and the general gathering place for persons, good and bad, who might be travelling through Colfax County. It was there that Bill Chunk and Clay Allison, naturally enough in the course of events, happened to meet. No one would have suspected that one was a deadly foe of the other, or that the other man knew his life had been threatened. For a day and a night, they drank and caroused together, apparently in the utmost good fellowship, neither one being willing to take the initiative in bringing on the affray that was bound to come.

The next day Chunk commented on the fine-looking horse Allison was riding and proposed a horse race to see which had the better animal. Allison accepted the challenge, for his confidence in his horse was unbounded, and they repaired to a race track somewhere in the vicinity of the Clifton House. Of the race itself, all that is known is that Chunk's horse beat Allison's, to Allison's great chagrin. Violent words followed, and Allison completely lost his temper. The upshot was that he slapped Chunk in the face for some remark, and there was imminent danger that hostilities were to commence immediately. But for some cause, never satisfactorily explained, Chunk and Allison both delayed the onset and held a discussion of the terms of the fight after they went back to the Clifton House. Allison, with his flair for the unusual, contended for an agreement to mount their horses and face each other at a distance of one hundred yards; then, at a signal, they were to run their horses toward each other, firing at will until one or both dropped to the ground.

They were engrossed in this discussion when the dinner bell rang. Chunk suggested that they eat first and fight afterwards, clenching his proposal with the remark, "We ought to see that the dead one goes to hell with a full stomach". Into the dining room the two went, taking their places at opposite ends of the dinner table, but with their drawn six-shooters resting on their laps under the table. During the meal Chunk casually dropped one hand below the table, as if to get his napkin, but in reality he seized his pistol and tried to lift it so as to fire at Allison. The barrel of the revolver, however, happened to strike the edge of the table, so that Chunk's aim was untrue. Allison fired immediately after. A red spot just above Chunk's eye showed where the bullet had struck. The dead man's head dropped sluggishly forward and fell face downward into the plate from which he had been eating.

Clay Allison coolly replaced his pistol in its holster and went on with his meal, requiring all the others at the table likewise to go on with their eating as though nothing unusual had taken place.

When he had taken all the time needful for a complete meal, he arose, and taking the dinner bell from a shelf, he went to the window and began to ring it vigorously, announcing to those present inside and outside the building, "Gentlemen, the proposed fight is now off, owing to an accident to one of the principals."

LAMAR FONTAINE, CONFEDERATE SHARPSHOOTER

Fontaine began military service as chief of scouts and courier for Gen. Stonewall Jackson. He served in the same capacity with Gens. [J. E. B.] Stuart and [Joseph E.] Johnston, and for a short time with [Robert E.] Lee. He took part in twenty-seven battles and more than one hundred skirmishes in which blood was shed. Although he was only a private in the ranks, he was once entrusted with a carte blanche order on the treasury of the Confederate States. He was known as the best marksman with rifle or revolver in either army. He was wounded sixty[-]seven times, and thirteen times his lungs were grazed. Five times during the war he was reported as dead. . . .

"Have you any idea of the number of men you killed in the course of your war career?" he was asked.

"I could make no estimate, but on one occasion I shot sixty men in sixty minutes, and the record was kept and was vouched for by Gen. R. E. Lee himself. It occurred at Waterloo Bridge, near Warrenton Springs, on the Rappahannock, in August, 1862. That was about the first time I ever met Gen. Lee, though I had often seen him before and knew him by sight. I was then acting as courier for Gen. Jackson, who, it seems, had been telling Gen. Lee about my skill with a rifle. On this day I carried despatches to Gen. Lee from Gen. Jackson. When I had performed my duty, Gen. Lee expressed a desire to see if what he had heard about my ability as a marksman was true. I told him I would do my best to demonstrate it. Over across the valley was a ridge upon which was stationed a Federal battery that was pouring shot into the Confederates as fast as the guns could be loaded and discharged. Drawing forth and opening his watch, Gen. Lee ordered me to proceed. I began to shoot.

"I would say, 'Now I'll shoot No. 3 on gun No. 1,' and the man would drop at the crack of my rifle; 'Now No. 1 on gun No. 4,' and that man would drop. And so the work continued. As fast as a man on the battery fell over another would take his place. Finally Gen. Lee closed his watch. 'That will do,' said he. 'Sixty men in sixty minutes is your record.'

"On a later occasion Gen. Lee asked me if my conscience did not trouble me.

"'What for?' said I.

"'Because of the people you have killed.'

"'General,' said I, 'does your conscience trouble you when you kill a rattlesnake?'

"'Why do you ask that?' he replied.

"'Because,' I answered, 'when I enlisted for the war I made up my mind that it was my duty to kill every Federal soldier I could, and I kill Federal soldiers from the same sense of duty that you would kill a rattlesnake.'"

Fontaine was asked how he acquired such a fine skill in the use of firearms.

"'Among the Indians in Texas,' he replied. '. . . I went to live among the Comanches, and for thirteen years I never saw the face of a white man.'"

The most remarkable feat accomplished by Fontaine from the point of view of the historian was the carrying of despatches and [musket] caps into the city of Vicksburg when that city was besieged by the Federals. At that time Memphis was in the hands of the enemy, and Fontaine, acting as a spy and under disguise, had been in this city [Memphis] for a month or so, picking up what information he could for the benefit of Gen. Joseph E. Johnston, who had his headquarters at Jackson, Miss. One day there came a summons for him to report to Gen. Johnston at once. Simultaneously, the Federals in this city [Memphis] got knowledge of Fontaine's orders and of his presence here. The desire to capture such a dangerous spy and redoubtable Confederate sharpshooter became so intense that a large reward was offered for him, dead or alive, and troops were sent to cover all of the roads leading southward [from Memphis]. He avoided them and reported on time to his General at Jackson for orders.

The orders were that he should carry despatches and 40,000 musket caps through the Federal lines into the city of Vicksburg. The difficulty of this undertaking may be judged from the fact that Vicksburg was beleaguered by 75,000 Federals, under Gen. Ulysses S. Grant. All the approaches to that city were controlled and guarded by the Federals and there was a reward of $20,000 for the head of Fontaine. He set out on his journey, avoiding all thoroughfares. Under cover of darkness, he passed through the Federal lines, and was about to make a run for the Confederate outposts when he found himself in a clump of brushwood, confronted by a half dozen soldiers, who appeared to know who he was, for on sight they opened fire on him. He rushed among them, revolver in each hand, and four of the men fell dead before him. The other two fled, and the spy ran into the city. When he presented himself before the officer in command, his despatches and musket caps intact, it was found that he had on his body the marks of seventeen bullets. This adventure is well authenticated.

ANTOINE BARADA AND THE PILE DRIVER

All in all, whether Antoine Barada the half-breed was Spanish-Indian as suggested by the name Barada which sounds Spanish, or French-Indian as suggested by Antoine, and whether the town [of Barada, Nebraska] was named after him or after Michael Barada, he seems to have been a real person, perhaps some one of unusual strength and of various adventures. In the legends about him he pulls out a big boat stranded in the sandbars, picks up a 400 pound boulder, and does similar feats. Miss Sandoz recalls of him:

> Antoine Barada was a hurry-up man, always rushing, rushing, can't wait for anything. One time he got tired of watching a pile driver working along the Missouri with the hammer making the up-down, up-down, the driver yelling "Git up! Git up! Whoa! Back! Back! Whoa!" and then all of it over again and the piling going down maybe a half inch. So Antoine he picked up the damned thing in his bare hand, throws it high and far so it lights clear over the Missouri where it bounce and bounce leaving ground tore up for miles and miles and making what the greenhorns call "Breaks of the Missouri." But at last it stop and if you dig down in them high ridges you find it is the damned pile driver with grass growing over him, a little poor soil, you understand, but it seems to satisfy them that ain't never crossed the Missouri and don't know better. When Antoine had disposed of the Johny Jumper hammer he sees that the piling that is left stands a mile higher than the rest, so he gives it a lick with his fist and it pop down into ground so deep it strike buried lake, the water flying

out like from bung hole fifty feet high and like to drown out the whole country if Antoine he did not sit on the hole first.

Miss Sandoz says that she "grew up on the Barada stories as told by half-breeds around Pine Ridge." They were brought there, she suspects by the Ruleaus and other families who used to live on what is called the Breed Strip in southeast Nebraska, and in the early 1900's still had relatives to visit there.

JOHN HENRY HAMMER SONGS

1.

If I could drive steel like John Henry,
  I'd go home, Baby, I'd go home.

This ole hammer killed John Henry,
  Drivin' steel, Baby, drivin' steel.

If I had forty-one dollars,
  I'd go home, Baby, I'd go home.

I'm goin' home, en' tell little Annie
  Uv my triuls, Baby, uv my triuls.

2.

Did you hear that rain-crow hollering?
  Sign of rain, Baby, sign of rain.

If I had forty-one dollars,
  I'd go home, Baby, I'd go home.

3.

This old hammer killed John Henry,
  Can't kill me; can't kill me!

This old hammer killed Bill Dooley,
  Can't kill me; can't kill me!

This old hammer weighs forty pounds, sah!
  Can't kill me; can't kill me!

Moe Stanley

Moe Stanley was a little boy
Sitting 'pon his daddy's knee
And Daddy said, "You know what, Moe?
You gots to be a steel-driving man like me."

Moe Stanley had a little wife
And the dress she wore was red.
He told her in case he should die,
"Sal," he said, "be true to me when I'm dead."

Moe's wife asked him for forty cents.
He didn't have more than a dime.
"If ya wait till the sun sets down
I'll be with the foreman in the mine."

Moe Stanley said to his foreman
"A man ain't nothin' but a man.
But I ain't lettin' that steam drill beat me down.
I'll die with this hamma in my hand."

Moe Stanley started in the left-hand side
And the steam drill started at the right.
Moe struck bottom at half past ten.
The steam drill didn't bottom till night.

Moe Stanley said to the pilot
"Why don't ya sing just a few more rounds?
And before the setting sun goes down,
You're gonna hear this hamma of mine sound!"

Moe Stanley hammered in the mill
As the whistle blew for half past two.
The last words he did say
"Lord, I've hamma-ed my insides in two."

"Sal, I've hamma-ed my insides in two
But I managed to win that bet.
So go see that foreman for me.
Tell him you've come to collect."

JOHN L. SULLIVAN AND JIM CORBETT

Come, lov-ers of the man-ly art an' lis-ten to my lay. I'll sing a - bout two come-ly lads__ who met in fist - ic fray; The bold John L. of Bos - ton, the cham-pion of his day, And spright-ly Jim-my Co'-bett of fair Cal-i - for-nia Bay. They met way down in New Or-leans, Sep-tem-ber the sev-enth at night, and thou - sands of the sport-ing blood were there to see the fight. The bet-ting was on

Sul - li - van, By man - y to be found. Some
said that he would fin-ish Jim be-fore the sec-ond round.

1. Come, lovers of the manly art
    An' listen to my lay.
I'll sing about two comely lads
    Who met in fistic fray,
The bold John L. of Boston,
    The champion of his day,
And sprightly Jimmy Co'bett
    Of fair California Bay.

2. They met way down in New Orleans
    September the seventh at night,
And thousands of the sporting blood
    Were there to see the fight.
The betting was on Sullivan,
    By many to be found.
Some said that he would finish Jim
    Before the second round.

3. These two men shook hands in the ring
    And Sullivan he led out.
But Jimmy was too smart for him
    And nimbly dodged about.
Two more blows from Sullivan's right
    The head of Jim did miss.
'Twas then the crowd looked on amazed
    And some began to hiss.

4. Round after round the Frisco Lad
    Came up with smiles so gay.

Every time that John L. banged at him
  He nimbly ducked away.
Right and left his anvil blows
  Upon our Champion fall.
First blood for Jimmy Corbett
  His friends so loud did call.

5.   At length came the last round of them all,
     John L. was much distressed,
Although his firm admirers
  All thought he'd fought his best,
When a blow from dauntless Jimmy sent him
  Reeling to the floor.
When time was called he knew it not,
  His champion days were o'er.

6.   Then up stepped Jimmy Corbett
    And took him by the hand,
For he knew that he had conquered
  The first fighter of our land.
Says he, 'I will acknowledge that
  I am a beaten man.
But I'm glad the championship was won
  By an American man.'

BABE RUTH: THE BODY BEHIND THE BAT

Certainly no name in baseball and very few in American culture share the heroic stature of "The Babe." . . .

The distance of his slams was often as impressive as the frequency. A 1926 issue of *The Sporting News* included this account:

> Babe Ruth hit what he declared to be the longest home run of his career during an exhibition game in Wilkes-Barre the other day. The ball cleared by more than 40', the right field fence, a distance of 400' from the plate and was still rising. It landed on the running track of an adjacent high school athletic field. Club officials said the ball traveled a distance of 650' on the fly.

This slugging came from a 6'2" body which weighed from 200 to 260 pounds, depending on the season and year of Babe's career. His arms were long and wiry although not heavily muscled. He did have strong wrists and large hands, thin legs and pigeon-toed feet. Babe's face was, perhaps, his most memorable physical feature: round and homely with a wide nose, thick lips, laughing eyes and a steady grin. Almost a caricature, itself, Babe's face and also his appetite became part of his image.

Stories tell that it was not unusual for Babe to consume at breakfast a pint of bourbon, quarts of ginger ale, four or five fried eggs, a plate of bacon, a pot of coffee and a stack of toast. A favorite midnight snack was half a dozen lobsters and plenty of beer. Babe also liked pickled eels, so Lou Gehrig's mother would bring a quart whenever the Yankees played a home double-header. Between games Babe would send out for a quart of chocolate ice cream to eat with the eels! Supposedly, when the team was on its way north from spring training in 1925, Babe visited an orphanage and proved what a heroic-sized appetite he really had. Back on the train after over a dozen hot dogs and three gallons of soda, Babe developed the worst stomach ache in history—so bad that the team had an extra layover while Babe's stomach was pumped out! To avoid indigestion in the future, Doc Woods, the Yankee Trainer, brought bicarbonate of soda to Babe before each game. Babe would measure out a mound of bicarb smaller than the Pyramid of Cheops, mix and gulp it down. "Then," Jim Cahn says, "he would belch. And all the loose water in the showers would fall down."

CHARLIE "BIRD" PARKER

Parker was also what Orrin E. Klapp calls a "Benefactor," or culture hero, as he, indeed, made "an important contribution to culture." No modern jazz musician has ever been more emulated than Charlie Parker, and his influence continues to remain a powerful force in jazz even though he has been dead for over fifteen years. The following tributes are typical:

Max Roach:	Bird was kind of like the sun, giving off the energy we drew from him. . . . . In any musical situation, his ideas just bounded out, and this inspired anyone who was around.
"Symphony Sid" Torin:	The whole scene of jazz should be built around Charlie Parker, because he was the character that made modern jazz possible. . . . Every musician I speak to, the young ones coming up today, they all say that Parker was the inspiration to the whole jazz scene.
Walter Bishop, Jr.:	The man was so influential in his field that he gave happiness to thousands. Thousands live and breathe Bird.
Robert Reisner:	Bird drove and inspired average musicians to excellencies they themselves never dreamed

	they could reach. . . . Almost singlehanded he saved jazz from "riffitis monotonous" or death due to oversimplicity and made it into an art form, giving it new dimensions of structure and feeling.
Teddy Blume:	Some say he invented the bent spoon routine [of narcotic ingestion].
Jay McShann:	Bird was the man.

The Feats of Charlie Parker

Many folk heroes are, or, more importantly, are believed to be extraordinary, if not superhuman. Parker is no exception. He was considered "unearthly," as "no one could ever come near him musically." Musicians often referred to him as "God." Chas Ellison remarked that "when serious musicians talk about Bird it's like they're in church." Trumpeter Howard McGhee complains that, "Whoever the musician is who plays with Bird, he feels he's playing shit next to what Bird is putting down." He could play beautifully on any instrument, even if held together with a "spoon, chewing gum, and tape." In Chicago, in 1942, he "couldn't get jobs because he was too good. Guys didn't like him; they were scared." And "in 1950 he started to deteriorate fast, and with all that he could still play more than anybody else." Howard McGhee reports that Bird "used to line up eight doubles of whiskey and down them before he hit a note on the job. . . . What I saw him take would kill an average man; the average man couldn't stand up under that." Buddy Jones states: "People believed him to have a superhuman constitution, and with good reason. I have seen him take several benzedrine wrappers, wad them into a ball, and swallow it."

As can be seen, these anecdotes are closely related to what Orrin Klapp calls "Feats" (extraordinary powers and/or capacity)

which set folk heroes apart from other men. Indeed, many of the
things said about Parker are simply not said about ordinary men.
Clusters of superlatives and hyperboles are characteristic:

> Parker "ate like a horse, drank like a fish, and was sexy as
> a rabbit."
> "He could eat four times to your one."
> "He was the only man I knew who could drink white
> heroin."
> He was often hit but "nobody ever knocked him out."
> "Charlie never slept."
> "He never knew night from day."
> "Bird never stopped, never, never."

According to Gigi Gryce, Bird would go into a music store and
memorize sheet music, therefore never having to buy it. Others report that he could master intricate and complex scores and arrangements at a glance. "Bird's memory was uncanny . . . his in-
tellect prodigious." Gryce believes Bird "was born a genius."

Apparently Bird also had an enormous sexual appetite. Teddy
Blume, Bird's former manager, told Reisner that Bird "had sex
three or four times a day with three or four different women. He
had more white women than you will ever have. . . . I marveled
at the extent of his sexual powers." Chas Ellison related a story involving Bird's sexual prowess which was told to him by a friend of
Parker's named "Little Bird," a non-musician who so idolized
Parker that he could sing from memory many of Bird's alto sax
solos:

> When one is strung on heroin, and one is high, you
> know, one normally doesn't have much interest in
> sex. . . . [Little Bird] mentioned an occasion where he
> and Bird *really* were strung . . . in Chicago one time.
> They had *more* than enough to keep them cool for two
> or three months. You know, they were *really* nice. This
> guy [Little Bird "represented" six or seven prostitutes]

had all of his ladies up in the room with him. And
. . . Bird got into his thing, you know. Little Bird
wasn't capable, and he just talked and talked about how
they stayed there for, like, three days, and Bird was taking care of business for three days.

How "Bird" Got His Nickname

A good example of the kind of traditional lore that has arisen
concerning Parker can be found when some of the many versions
of the origin of his nickname, Bird, are examined. Jazz singer Car-
men McRae states that the "nickname 'Bird' comes from yardbird. He did a short stint in the army, and yardbird is what they
call a recruit." According to Jay McShann, "Bird got his name
when we were going to Lincoln, Nebraska. Whenever he saw
some chicken on the menu, he'd say, 'Give me some of the yardbird over there'." Gigi Gryce reports that "Goon [Andrew Gard-
ner] used to call him yardbird, because he was such a relaxed cat."
Marshall Stearns, in *The Story of Jazz*, writes that Yardbird was
"a nickname borrowed from a comic strip." Frank Gillis, Associate Director of the Archives of Traditional Music at Indiana University, states that he has heard a variety of stories concerning the
origin of Parker's nickname:

One was that he sort of resembled a sparrow or a bird,
you know, in that he had a sort of barrel-type chest and
then slimmed down to a small waist. . . . Some people
say that because of the soaring melodic line of his that
he was called Bird.

Ellison, who refers to himself as a "stone Bird freak," also believes
that the nickname may have originated when Parker was first attempting to play unusually high notes on his horn:

[The nickname] is in reference to all the high tones
which he was attempting initially but couldn't bring off

successfully, you know. The guys around him started calling him Bird. They said he was whistling and chirping like birds.

According to Michael Levin and John S. Wilson, Parker's own version of how his nickname originated differs considerably from the other versions, and is far less romantic:

It was back in his school days, he [Parker] says, that his name started going through a series of mutations which finally resulted in Bird. As Charlie reconstructs it, it went from Charlie to Yarlie to Yarl to Yard to Yardbird to Bird.

THE PROPHET OF POND RIVER BOTTOMS

No one seemed to know when she came to the Pond river bottom country, where she came from or what her name was. I never heard her referred to as anything but the Prophet. It would have been grammatically correct to have referred to her as "the Prophetess," but no one ever did. Pond river is a tributary of Green river and is a dividing boundary between McLean and Hopkins counties [Kentucky]. It is really more of a creek than a river but the rich, black land adjacent to it is highly esteemed for farming.

I lived in this bottom country until I was ten years old. We lived on my grandfather's farm during the depression years of the thirties. In my earliest memories, I can remember people discussing the Prophet. Usually it concerned her latest prediction or where she was staying at the time. So far as anyone knew, she had no income. She never asked for money, only food and a place to sleep. There were a lot of conflicting tales about the Prophet. Most people regarded her as harmless and maybe with awe. There were others who swore she cast evil spells on those who offended her. There was one facet of her character everyone seemed to agree on. She was scrupulously clean. Her personal appearance was immaculate and her table manners would do credit to the standards of Emily Post. The Prophet was a middle-age woman, probably in her early fifties.

When she would arrive at a home, she followed a prescribed ritual from which she never deviated. After asking and gaining admittance to a home, she would start to harangue and go through her sermon. This consisted primarily of quotations of Bible scripture, but a lot of the spiel appeared to be disoriented gibberish. After she had finished with her message, she would ask if she might be given food and lodging. She would never ask to stay for a certain length of time. She might stay a week or more or maybe just a few hours. After receiving permission to stay in a home, she would occasionally take part in whatever subject was being discussed by members of the family, but more often she would sit apart and seem to meditate. She was not a loquacious person by any stretch of the imagination. It was during these moments of meditation that she would predict future events. Usually they were of an ominous nature. It was during one of these moments that she predicted the death of Vida Woosley. She was staying at the home of Hamilton Woosley at the time. Hamilton was Vida's son. It was during a winter cold spell and Vida had come down with what was considered a mild case of flu. The family had eaten an early supper and Vida had gone to bed early. Hamilton's wife and daughter were putting away the supper dishes and the Prophet was sitting in front of the fireplace with Hamilton. She had been staring at the fire for some time when she said, "I see a V in the fire and the V is for Vida, she will die before morning." The prognostication was very true for Vida was dead before morning.

On another occasion, one summer afternoon she was passing a field where a group of men were working in hay. She stopped for a while in the road and watched the men. After a while some of the men came over to talk to her. After talking for a few minutes she stopped and gazed up into the sky, and said, "this afternoon one of you men will die." The men laughed nervously and returned to their work. One of these men was Tom Cowens. Later that afternoon, while riding a wagon load of hay to the barn, Cowens fell from the top of the load and was killed. One would have to wonder if Cowens didn't have the dire prediction on his mind, causing him to be careless, which could have precipitated his fall.

My first meeting with the Prophet came one afternoon when I was playing in the yard with some friends. We were so engrossed in our play that we were totally unaware of anyone approaching. Suddenly a clear, sweet voice said, "good afternoon children." I had no idea about who this lady was. I had heard many unkind things said about her; and if I had been aware of her identity, I would probably have been paralyzed with fear. Instead I would have liked her to stay and talk some more. After delivering her message she left our house. She never asked for lodging or food. It was early in the afternoon and I suppose she had other places she wished to visit.

In 1939 we moved away from the bottoms and I never saw her again. We heard later that she had been placed in the state mental institution at Hopkinsville. I never found out why. I can only assume it happened because after the war began people became less tolerant of itinerants or people who didn't produce for the war effort.

ETHICAL HEROES

In the primitive struggle for survival, physical traits were of basic importance, and at this stage physical prowess was the outstanding characteristic of the tribal heroes. But as societies became more sophisticated, intellectual accomplishments and ethical behavior also came to be prized. Homer's Odysseus is primarily characterized as wise and eloquent, though capable of trickery in word and deed. These are nonphysical traits. Yet he retains his physical prowess, exemplified by his mighty bow, which only he could bend. His wife, Penelope, was known for her physical beauty, which attracted suitors during his absence. But she is best remembered for her fidelity, that is, her ethical behavior, and the wiles she employed to fend off her suitors. Eventually the balance will shift to the point where physical prowess is ignored. Among highly educated groups, or in a scientific age, or in a culture that exalts mind and spirit over matter, heroes and heroines with inferior bodies may be common. The sociologist Max Weber identified Benjamin Franklin as an ideal type of what he called "the Protestant ethic," and our regard for Franklin stems from his civic and scientific leadership, and from what he taught us about how to live together and how to get ahead. The physical image of Franklin, which comes to us largely from his portraits and his autobiography, is unimpressive, the lumpiness of an awkward youth and a gouty old age.

Though the gods have been displaced by men, and men turn to other men to learn how to make their way in the world, vestiges of the supernatural remain. The department store magnate A. T. Stewart was honest, thrifty, and hard-working, but he does not attribute his success to Franklin's precepts alone. It also involves a little bit of luck, in other words, divine intervention. The miracles performed by Preacher Dow are a more complicated example of the persistence in a rational age of belief. Preacher Dow uses his Yankee wits to discover a thief and to preserve the sanctity of wedlock, and, incidentally, to maintain the power of his priesthood. He survives as an ethical hero because he can adapt to the times. On the other hand, a political leader like Franklin Delano Roosevelt may, upon his death, be enshrined in popular memory because he conveyed to simple people who felt themselves forgotten or ignored a compassion that seemed to them almost saintly.

The point should be made that within America there exist enclaves that cling to their religious beliefs. For the Hassidic community in Brooklyn that performs a traditional play based on Abraham's offering up his son Isaac as a sacrifice, there is no wavering on the subject of man's submission to the word of Jehovah, though the play is enlivened by topical reference and comic capering, and though Jehovah's word blares forth from a somewhat uncertain public address system.

In their way these figures are all ethical heroes because they teach man by example and by their works moral behavior and social conduct, and help him to achieve his goals and to improve the physical conditions of his existence.

HIAWATHA FOUNDS THE IROQUOIS CONFEDERACY

As early as 1815, Ephraim Webster related a simple story of Hiawatha, resembling that given by Horatio Hale, but with much less detail, and a change of the chief's name. This is the oldest published form of the tale, the chief being O-We-ko, according to the recollection of the one to whom Webster told the story. Webster probably gave the usual name. . . .

He said that the happy thought of union for defense originated with an inferior chief of the Onondagas, who perceiving that although the five tribes were alike in language, and had by cooperation conquered a great extent of country, yet that they had frequent quarrels and no head, or great council, to reconcile them; and that while divided the western Indians attacked and destroyed them; seeing this, he conceived the bright idea of union, and of a great council of the chiefs of the Five Nations; this, he said, and perhaps thought, came to him in a dream; and it was afterwards considered as coming from the Great Spirit. He proposed this plan in a council of his tribe, but the principal chief opposed it. He was a great warrior, and feared to lose his influence as head man of the Onondagas. This was a selfish man. The younger chief, whom we will call *Oweko*, was silenced; but he determined in secret to attempt the great political work. This was a man who loved the welfare of others. To make long journeys and be absent for several days while hunting would cause no suspicion, because it was common. He left home as if to hunt; by taking a circuitous path through the woods, for all this great country was then a wilderness, he made his way to the village or castle of the Mohawks. He consulted some of the leaders of that tribe, and they received the scheme favorably; he visited the Oneidas, and gained the assent of their chief; he then returned home. After a time he made another pretended hunt, and another; thus by degrees visiting the Cayugas and Senecas, and gained the assent of all to a great council to be held at Onondaga. With consummate art he then gained over his own chief, by convincing him of the advantages of the confederacy, and agreeing that he should be considered as the author of the plan. The great council met, and the chief of the Onondagas made use of a figurative argument, taught him by Oweko, which was the same that we read of in the fable, where a father teaches his sons the value of union, by taking one stick from a bundle, and showing how feeble it was, and easily broken, and that when bound together the bundle resisted his utmost strength.

A DRUNKEN GOD AND A PIOUS KING

Mele

Ua ona o Kane i ka awa;
Ua kau ke kéha i ka uluna;
Ua hi'o-lani i ka moena.
Kipú mai la i ke kapa o ka noe.
Noe-noe na hokú o ka lani—
Imo-imo mai la i ka po a'e-a'e.
Mahana-lua na kukui a Lani-kaula.
He kaula no Kane.
Meha na pali o Wai-pi'o
I ke kani mau o Kiha-pú;
A ono ole ka awa a ke alii
I ke kani mau o Kiha-pú;
Moe ole kona po o ka Hooilo;
Uluhua, a uluhua,
I ka mea nana e huli a loaa
I kela kupua ino i ka pali,
Olali la, a olali.

Song

Kane is drunken with awa;
His head is laid on the pillow;
His body stretched on the mat.
A trumpet sounds through the fog,
Dimmed are the stars in the sky;
When the night is clear, how they twinkle!
Lani-kaula's torches look double,

The torches that burn for Kane.
Ghostly and drear the walls of Wai-pi'o
At the endless blasts of Kiha-pú.
The king's awa fails to console him;
'Tis the all-night conching of Kiha-pú.
Broken his sleep the whole winter;
Downcast and sad, sad and downcast.
At loss to find a brave hunter
Shall steal the damned conch from the cliff.
Look, how it gleams [through the fog]!

Kane, the chief god of the Hawaiian pantheon, in company with other immortals, his boon companions, met in revelry on the heights bounding Wai-pi'o valley. With each potation of awa they sounded a blast upon their conch-shells, and the racket was almost continuous from the setting of the sun until drowsiness overcame them or the coming of day put an end to their revels.

The tumult of sound made it impossible for the priests to perform acceptably the offices of religion, and the pious king, Liloa, was distressed beyond measure. The whole valley was disturbed and troubled with forebodings at the suspension of divine worship.

The chief offender was Kane himself. The trumpet which he held to his lips was a conch of extraordinary size and credited with a divine origin and the possession of supernatural power; its note was heard above all the others. This shell, the famed Kiha-pú, had been stolen from the heiau of Paka'a-lána, Liloa's temple in Wai-pi'o valley, and after many adventures had come into the hands of god Kane, who used it, as we see, for the interruption of the very services that were intended for his honor.

The relief from this novel and unprecedented situation came from an unexpected quarter. King Liloa's awa-patches were found to be suffering from the nocturnal visits of a thief. A watch was set; the thief proved to be a dog, Puapua-lenalena, whose master was a confirmed awa-toper. When master and dog were brought into the presence of King Liloa, the shrewd monarch divined the

remarkable character of the animal, and at his suggestion the dog
was sent on the errand which resulted in the recovery by stealth of
the famed conch Kiha-pú. As a result of his loss of the conch,
Kane put an end to his revels, and the valley of Wai-pi'o again
had peace.

BENJAMIN FRANKLIN'S PROVERBIAL ETHICS

Franklin's *Way to Wealth* is replete with sententious sayings.
His material has undoubtedly been taken from all types of sources
where wit and wisdom may be found. Since a proverb contains
"shortness, sense and salt" according to C. H. Spurgeon, and since
one of its prime requisites according to Richard C. Trench and
others is currency among the people, whenever Franklin employed
proverbs he must have borrowed them from some source or
other. . . . Franklin himself had this to say, "These proverbs,
which contained the wisdom of many ages and nations, I assembled and form'd into a connected discourse prefix'd to the Al-
manack of 1757, as the harangue of a wise old man to the people
attending an auction." Franklin here, then, is saying that very few
proverbs, if any, actually originated with him. . . .

Some of the expressions Carl Van Doren felt revealed a flavor
characteristic of Franklin, and were supposedly his creations, are,
in fact, wordings found in authors before him. Others are Franklin's translations of foreign expressions. Still others are all that is
claimed for them, i.e., they have the Franklin touch. To illustrate,
Franklin wrote in the *Way to Wealth* (1758), *'Tis hard for an
empty Bag to stand upright*, but previously wrote in 1740, *An
empty Bag cannot stand upright* which with *sack* instead of *bag* is
the form encountered in Thomas Fuller and other older sources.
The *'tis-hard-for* addition has not become the standard part according to compilers of proverbs after Franklin. In this instance
Franklin did not improve the older version. On the other hand,
Van Doren is correct in calling Franklin's *The Cat in Gloves
catches no Mice* an improvement over the archaic *A cat gloued
catcheth no mice*. I am not convinced, however, that Franklin has

improved Cotgrave's *The sleepy fox hath seldome feathered break-fasts*, which is taken from the still better rhymed version in French, *Renard qui dort la matinée N'a pas la langue emplumée* (xv century) by rendering it *The sleeping Fox catches no Poultry*, other than having shortened it.

Another case in point is *A fat Kitchen makes a lean Will*. Cotgrave rendered it *A fat kitchin a leane will*, for which he probably used the French version, *Grand chere petit testament*. Bohn (1855) has listed *A fat kitchen, a lean will* twice under Ray's proverbs and as a translation of the Italian *Grassa cucina magro testamento*. A variant form also occurs in Ray and in Fuller, *A fat housekeeper makes lean executors*. Franklin's form is not more expressive than this variant of Ray's and Fuller's. It is, as Van Doren says, shorter. Franklin was studying Spanish and Italian at the time he used the expression. Since Franklin's form occurs in both languages, I believe that it is his own or Cotgrave's translation. In any event, the *kitchen* innovation is not original with him.

The wording of *While the used Key is always bright* certainly belongs to Franklin, the idea of metal shining through use is as old as Ovid's *Aera nitent usu*. *Little Strokes fell great Oaks* was believed by Van Doren to have been Franklin's improvement of the well known, old *Many strokes fell the oak*. It is indeed an improvement, but it is not Franklin's. It is Thomas Fuller's proverb number 6319. The contrast *little—great* is a good proverbial set-up and leaves a more forceful impression than does the old form. It is not an unusual, but rather a frequent, popular characteristic of proverbs to have this so-called element of contrast. The wording of *What maintains one Vice would bring up two Children* is graphic to say the least, but it is not more potent than its parent form, *The maintaining of one vice costeth more than ten virtues*, found in Fuller. Franklin's homelier version sacrifices the contrast provided by *vice* and *virtue*. Furthermore, Franklin's statement is not likely to be regarded too widely as an apparent truth. On the other hand, it seems to me, Fuller's version comes closer to the real truth. From all appearances *Three Removes is as bad as a*

Fire is either Franklin's or was a current expression Franklin put into print for the first time.

Additional evidence of Franklin's ability to alter expressions is given us in his rendition, *Experience keeps a dear School, but Fools will learn in no other, and scarce in that.* In all probability this is a distant relative of Thomas Fuller's *Experience teacheth fools: and he is a great one, that will not learn by it.*

A NEW YORK MERCHANT'S WAY TO WEALTH

Alexander Turney Stewart, the great New York merchant of the nineteenth century, was an enigma to many of his fellow-citizens. They could not understand how it was possible for a young Irish immigrant, with little capital and no training for the dry goods business, to have achieved such an outstanding success in the most competitive industry of the day that the women of the metropolis and the surrounding area flocked to his stores and made him a millionaire before he had reached his thirty-fifth birthday.

Stewart's own explanation—that his success was due wholly to rigid adherence to a few fundamental business policies, most of which were derived from the Golden Rule—was too simple to satisfy his contemporaries. They insisted upon finding some explanation for his success other than hard work and a constructive business policy, and a Parson Weems of the day rose to the occasion and developed a story which made it seem wholly fortuitous. Stewart never had intended to enter the dry goods business, according to this romancer, but had been forced into it by circumstances beyond his control at a time when he was ignorant of even the commonest trade terms. On the other hand, it also was claimed that the constructive policies for which Stewart's business later became noted were already formulated on September 1, 1923, the day on which the young merchant opened his little store at No. 283 Broadway, usually referred to as his first store. The contradictory nature of these statements was carefully ignored, and both became legends.

Honesty Is the Best Policy

One of the clerks stated to a customer that a piece of calico was of certain quality, that the colors were "fast" and would not wash out, and if not so, the article would be taken back and the money returned. The remarks were overheard by Mr. Stewart, and he called the clerk to him and spoke with indignation: "What do you mean by saying what you know to be untrue?" The clerk, perhaps astonished at being called to account, replied that the woman would not return the goods, and if she did she could easily be put off by stating that she must have been mistaken, and that the purchase must have been made at some other store.

But no; that was not the point. A lie had been told to induce a purchase; and no goods must be sold in his store or in his name under any misrepresentation whatever. The clerk could conform to that rule at once or vacate his place.

While he was still in his little Greenwich street shop he heard his salesman one day inform an old lady that the calico before her cost 25 cents a yard, but that he would sell it to her at 20 cents. Pleased . . . the old lady purchased the dress pattern and retired, whereupon Mr. Stewart said to the salesman, "Jeemes, is it necessary to lie to do our business?"

"Oh," said the salesman, "that is only the usage in dealing with the accomplished shoppers who are in the habit of beating down."

"Oh, yes, I know it," said Mr. Stewart, "but you must never practice that usage in my store again."

But Lady Luck Helps

Rightly or wrongly, many of Stewart's contemporaries were convinced that he held many superstitious beliefs, and among his contemporaries was another Parson Weems who, with deft imagination, found an explanation of Stewart's great success in the fact that his first customer on his first day in the No. 283 Broadway store had brought him luck. The merchant was so grateful that in later years he settled an annuity on this lady, according to this story. The anecdote, published during Stewart's lifetime and never denied, ran as follows:

A young lady whose acquaintance he had made said to him on the day preceding the opening of his store,

"You must not sell anything on the morrow till I come
and make the first purchase; for I will bring you luck."

True to her promise she drove up in her carriage early the next
day and purchased goods to nearly $200 in value, principally of
Irish laces. Long years passed, the lady married and moved with
her husband to an European city. Mr. Stewart was in that city on
business, and there learned that his first customer was still living,
but in very reduced circumstances. Her husband was dead, but before his death had squandered her fortune.

Procuring good apartments, he caused them to be furnished in
a style corresponding to her former position in life. Then calling
on her and renewing her acquaintance, after conversing on old
times and former friends, he asked her to take a drive around the
city in his carriage. After looking at some objects of interest, he
took her to the new residence, saying: "This, if it meets with your
approbation, is your new home."

He settled an annuity upon her, and during the residue of her
life she lived not only in comfort but in comparative affluence,
supported entirely by his bounty.

One of the most persistent stories concerning Stewart's alleged
superstition had to do with an old apple woman who took up her
stand outside the entrance of his third Broadway store at No. 257.
The merchant, reputedly, believed that she brought him luck, and
it is a fact that his first great success as a New York dry goods re-
tailer was achieved at this location. Therefore, when he opened
his magnificent Marble Palace at Broadway and Reade Street in
October, 1846, Stewart is said to have personally moved the old
lady's apple stand to the new store, to make certain that her lucky
influence continued in the new location.

This incident may have occurred, but the best evidence is that
it is part of the vast Stewart apocrypha, since neither James Gordon Bennett, who published copious descriptions of the opening
of the Marble Palace in his New York *Herald*, nor any other contemporary New York editor made any mention of it. But the

story had great appeal to newspaper editors and persisted as a recurrent bit of miscellany for a number of years. It was frequently embroidered and updated.

In 1886, for instance, the New York *Tribune* reprinted one of the updated versions from the Cleveland *Leader* of an unspecified date. According to it, Stewart also had personally moved the old apple woman and her stand from the Marble Palace to Tenth Street and Broadway, when he opened the first section of his Astor Place retail store there in November, 1862, sixteen years after the opening of the Marble Palace. On this occasion he is supposed to have given as his reason for so doing his belief that when she died or left the store his good luck would go with her.

Eventually she did die, apparently during the winter of 1875–76, according to this version, and Stewart's premonitions were realized. "Strange to say it was even so," the item concluded. "A few months after this Stewart began to decline, and the apple-woman was hardly forgotten before he was in his grave."

PREACHER DOW RAISES THE DEVIL

My grandfather, Milo Durand, had quite a large farm in Elizabethtown, and it seems to have been a stopping place for peddlers, tinkers, tramps, preachers, travelers on the underground railroad, and other itinerants. Lorenzo Dow, the famous preacher-hero, was one of the guests at Durand Farm when traveling through this part of Essex County. As they sat talking Grandfather told Dow that he had repeatedly heard that on at least one occasion Dow had raised the Devil, and he asked him to tell him the circumstances. Dow seemed willing enough to relate the facts, and this is his story.

"One late afternoon in early fall, after having traveled many weary miles, I arrived at a little log cabin in a clearing and begged a night's lodging. Although I had been a welcome guest there before, the woman of the house, while she granted my request, did not seem overanxious to entertain me. However, I was too tired to proceed farther that night, so I entered the humble abode. The good wife said that her husband was away, and that she did not expect him home until the next day, so I thought that was the reason she seemed reluctant to have me stay. She hastily prepared a simple meal for me, of which I gratefully partook. The house consisted of a rather large living room and a small bedroom. There was also a loft, reached by a rude ladder. The furniture was exceedingly crude. A homemade couch occupied one side of the room and the other articles of furniture were benches, and roughly constructed table and stand. The fireplace took up considerable space and was supplied with andirons, tongs, poker, and a crane upon which hung a large iron kettle. As usual, there was the very necessary brick bake-oven, in which the baking was done by heating the lower part of it with live coals. A small fire was burning on the brick heater, as the nights grow chilly very early in the north woods. In one corner of the room stood a hogshead nearly full of tow, and the small flax wheel near by would soon be called into action to convert the tow into thread.

"After I had finished my supper, I read a chapter in the little, worn Testament I always carry, then humbly knelt on the rough floor, and prayed that the peace of God might descend on the inmates of the home giving me shelter. After this I retired to rest in the small room behind a bearskin curtain. Being very weary, I immediately fell into a peaceful slumber, but for some strange reason awakened in a short time with a feeling of impending evil and heard the low murmur of voices in the adjoining room. I did not recognize the man's voice but knew it was not the voice of the master of the house and came to the disturbing and unwelcome conclusion that the visitor was no chance caller.

"In a few moments, the silence of the night was broken by the sound of heavy, stumbling footsteps, and a thick voice attempting to sing a ribald song. Immediately there was consternation in the next room. The woman said in a frenzied whisper: 'You can't escape; if you meet him he will kill you; if not now, later. Here, get into this hogshead and I'll cover you with the tow.' With quick movements this was accomplished, and the woman had just seated herself, when her husband staggered into the room.

" 'Didden 'spect me home so soon, did ye, my dear?'

" 'No,' she answered, 'how did you happen to come?'

" 'Got to thinkin', 'lil woman might get lonesome, thash reason. Ain't had no company, hev ye?' he added suspiciously.

" 'Yes,' she said, 'we have company now, for the great preacher, Lorenzo Dow, is sleeping in the next room, if he can sleep in all this racket. You don't mind his being here, do you?'

" 'No, shiree, thash alright; good man, Lorensho Dow; trush him anywhere. He's got big pull with Almighty, he's sho blamed good; but ef I'd found some other company here, I might hev comed to the pint ev killin'. Shay, I've heerd tell Preacher Dow kin raise the Devil an' I want to see him do it right now.'

"In spite of his wife's remonstrances, he requested me to come out and show what I could do, and almost immediately I appeared on the scene and answered the strange request and said: 'Yes, I have the power to raise the Devil, but not in the manner you are now demonstrating. I warn you, however, that it will be a terrifying sight and perhaps dangerous, because when he appears he will be clothed in a sheet of flame. Do you still wish it to be done?'

"He answered, 'Go ahead, Parshun, I ain't 'fraid uv man, beast, or devil. She that big b'arskin over there? I killed the critter with a club'—which statement could well be believed because the mountaineer was over six feet tall and weighed at least two hundred and forty pounds.

"'Very well,' I said, 'but take this poker to defend yourself and deal the Devil a hard blow as he goes past you.'

"Then, with the tongs I extracted a burning brand from the fireplace and with the loud command, 'Satan, come forth!' flung the brand into the hogshead. Immediately, the tow ignited, filling the room with smoke and flame, and out of the conflagration emerged a wild fire-bedecked figure who, emitting loud shrieks, darted frantically into the outer darkness. The fire was quickly quenched by a bucket of water which stood near.

"The participants in the affair were affected in different ways. The husband, almost sobered, believed he had witnessed a supernatural demonstration and resolved he would try to live in a manner to escape eternal fire. The wife thankfully realized that dire vengeance for herself and her admirer had been averted and concluded that the path of virtue was the only safe one to follow, while the evicted 'Devil' extinguished his burning garments in a stream, and painfully made his way to his shack to nurse his burns and meditate on his deliverance from a worse fate than had befallen him. I was well satisfied with my ruse, believing that a domestic tragedy had been prevented and trusting that the lesson would be lasting and salutary. And that was how I raised the Devil."

Preacher Dow Catches a Thief

A man came to Renzie Dow, telling him that his ax had been stolen. Renzie was preparing to go to the meeting house, so invited the fellow to accompany him. At the meeting, the preacher assured him, he would be able to settle his problem for him. Along the way to the meeting house, the man noticed that Renzie stooped down, picked up a sizable pebble and thrust it into his pocket.

At the meeting house Dow launched into his services. At the height of this he announced that an ax had been stolen, a deplorable act, and that he was going to apprehend the criminal. Drawing the pebble from his pocket, he called his congregation's attention to it. Suddenly he drew back his arm and cried, "If I throw this stone, it will hit the man who stole the ax!"

Renzie's arm went forward, but he did not release the stone in his hand. The gesture was enough. One man had ducked.

In the second tale Harve relates concerning him, the nature of the stolen item has been forgotten. But we find Renzie in a meeting house again, ready to uncover the culprit. On this occasion this required a live rooster and a large black pot. Renzie placed the pot over the rooster.

"Now," said Dow, "I should like every man present to walk past this pot and place the palm of his hand on its bottom. When the thief places his hand on the bottom of the pot, we expect the rooster to crow."

The men walked past and something seemed awry, for the rooster had failed to crow. However, the minister was now busy examining the hands of all who had been in the line. All palms were blackened by the bottom of the pot excepting one. He, Renzie proclaimed, was the thief.

MARIE LEVEAU, HOODOO QUEEN

Marie Leveau is the great name of Negro conjure in America. There were three Marie Leveaux, of whom the last, the daughter and granddaughter of the other two, was the most renowned. The first one is said to have been a small black Congo woman. The daughter was a mulatto of very handsome body and face. The granddaughter was an octoroon of great beauty. Her curly head is described as bandeaued with bright tignons clasped with expensive jewels.

This granddaughter became the greatest hoodoo queen of America. She was born February 2, 1827, according to the birth records in St. Louis Cathedral, New Orleans and studied hoodoo with one Alexander. She was the natural daughter of Marie Laveau and Christophe Glapion. She lived on St. Anne Street, between North Rampart and Burgundy, in the French Quarter, but also kept a home on Bayou St. John near Lake Pontchartrain.

There is very little contemporary record of her, but her glory has not suffered with the passing of time. She is traditionally said to have been consulted by Queen Victoria, who was so pleased with the results that she sent her a shawl and a large sum of money. An oil painting of her hangs in the Cabildo, the Museum of the State of Louisiana, and her fame extends far beyond the borders of hoodoo.

She is supposed to have been attended by a huge rattlesnake. The morning after her death he was seen crawling away to the woods about Lake Pontchartrain and was never seen again.

There is the story of the storm when she was at her home on the shore of Lake Pontchartrain. She refused to flee, in spite of urging. Finally the storm swept the cabin into the lake. She resisted rescue, saying that she wished to die there in the lake in

the storm. She was always the magnificent savage, and she perhaps felt that, being old, her end was near. She preferred an exit
with nature itself playing its most magnificent music than dry rotting in a bed. She was forcibly rescued, but it is said that neither
wind, water nor thunder ceased until she had set foot on land.

She held a dance on the first Friday in each month and a grand
annual dance on the eve of St. John's, June 24. The dance drums
were made by stretching cow-hide over a halfbarrel. They were
beaten with the jaw-bone or leg-bone of a jackass or some other
large animal. Some people called the dance the can-can. It is said
that when she held her dances on the shore of Lake Pontchartrain, every St. John's Eve she used to rise out of the lake with a
huge communion candle burning on top of her head and one in
each hand, all lighted and burning brightly as she rose from the
bosom of the lake and walked to the shore upon the water. When
the ceremony was over, she would go back upon the waters as she
had come and disappear in the lake.

People feared hoodoo in general and Marie Leveau in particular
to such an extent that one day some one saw a sizeable cloth
package lying in the mud in the street. No one would touch it. It
lay there so long that the cloth rotted and a buggy driving over it
tore it open and revealed a gold coin.

When she lived in St. Anne Street the police tried to raid her
place. One came and she confounded him. Two were sent and she
put them to running and barking like dogs. Four came and she
put them to beating each other over the head with their night
sticks. The whole station force came at last. They knocked at her
door. She knew who they were before she even went to the door.
So she did some work at her altar and put the whole force to sleep
on her steps.

A Gambler's Petition and a God's Reply

It is difficult to say how much of hoodoo in Louisiana today
stems from Marie Leveau. . . . There is one body of lore that
seems to be in comparative disuse, but which is associated with

her "works". This is a ritual consisting of a series of formal petitions with answering directions from the god. . . .

Supplicant: Great Goddess of Chance, I would ask your favor. I would ask for pieces of gold and pieces of silver from your hand for when I go to the race course the horse does not heed me or make efforts that I may be victor. And the driver of the chariot does not lash his steed that I may come in first line, but instead lags behind that I may lose my gold and silver. When I pray to you with the dice in my hand, you do not smile on me, neither do you guide the dice that they may show a smiling face to me; but instead you guide them that they may turn to the help of other players and I go home with my pockets empty and my heart heavy. So again when I set me down among the select men and play with them the game of cards, you do not put into my hand the card which will undo my opponents; but instead you put into my hand the low cards which will be my undoing and into the hands of the other players the high cards which will be my undoing. Tell me, O great Goddess of Chance, what can I do to appease your anger and win your approving smile; that I may wax fat and I may have into my purse the bright gold and jingling silver of the empire? I am your steadfast worshipper and would fain win your favor so that my horse will come to the victory line the first one, and so that the high cards shall burn to get in my hand, and so that the dice shall be friendly to me.

The God: My son, you have asked a great favor of me, but you have not burned any incense at my altar and have not made any offering to my spirit. For I look only on those who are my steadfast worshippers. For those who come for a day, I know them not, neither do I smile on them. But for those who worship, I smile on them; for those of good spirit, I love them. So if you wish to carry my favor, you will put into a small bag made of the skin of chamois the following holy articles: the grains of Paradise, the powder of the root called John the Conqueror, the powder of the Magnetic Stone, the Eye of the Eagle, the tooth of a shark. These you will close together tightly so that they cannot break out, and on the day you care to win, you will put on this bag the extract

Hasnohanna and keep it in your left hand pocket and let no one touch it except the money you will wager on the games, so that it will multiply and grow. And on your hands when you are playing with the dice and the cards you will put the Essence of the Three Knaves and the Two Kings. Pour of these essences in the palm of your hands and rub it dry and in your room you will burn the incense and the spices of Saturn, so that you will quickly get your wishes and the cards, the dice and the horses will break in your favor and do as you wish. But fail not to worship me and love me, for the day you cease to worship me will be your loss. And the day you cease to love me will be your doom, for all things I have given I will take away. For those who never cease to love, I am a true mistress and shower my favors on them; and for those who love me for a while and forsake me, I am a hard mistress and cause them deep sorrow and desolation.

So Be It.

A PUERTO RICAN DÉCIMA ON THE DEATH OF
FRANKLIN DELANO ROOSEVELT

♩ = 120

VOICE

GUITAR

El

dí - a do-ce de a - bril__   La no-ti -

(Guitar repeats previous 2 measures throughout.)

cia s'e-spar-ció El mun-do se Ex-tre-me-ció con pe-na y hon-do

sen-tir__   Frank-lin__ De-la-no mo-rir

De u - na muer-te in-es-per - a-da

y la Ti - er - r'A - mer-i - ca-na

In - mor-tal - i - za-rá su nom - bre Al per-der tan

gran-de hom - bre que llo-ra l'A - mer - i - ca His-pa - na.

1. El día doce de abril La noticia se esparció El mundo se extremeció Con pena y hondo sentir Franklin Delano morir De una muerte inesperada, Y la Tierra Americana Inmortalizará su nombre Al perder tan grande hombre Que llora la America Hispana.	On the twelfth day of April The news spread. The world shook With grief and deep feeling. Franklin Delano died Of an unexpected death, And the American Land Will immortalize his name On losing such a great man That Spanish America weeps.
2. El mundo de luto está Al saber la triste nueva En el curso de esta guerra Mucha falta nos hará Triste está la humanidad La pérdida de repente Del hombre que francamente Defendió la libertad. Hoy llora la humanidad Al querido Presidente.	The world is in mourning On knowing the new sadness. In the course of this war We will want him very much. Sad is humanity The loss, so sudden, Of the man who open-heartedly Defended liberty. Today humanity weeps For the beloved President.
3. Del líder del Nuevo Trato Que fué un gran conferencista Siempre ferviente estadista Solo nos queda un retrato Porque el destino tan ingrato Ya nos ha sellado su suerte. Al hombre que francamante Defendió la libertad Y hoy llora la humanidad Al querido Presidente. Y hoy llora la humanidad Al querido Presidente.	Of the leader of the New Deal Who was a great orator, Always the fervent statesman, All we keep is a portrait, Because destiny, so ungrateful, Already has sealed his fate for us. For the man who open-heartedly Defended liberty. And today humanity weeps For the beloved President. And today humanity weeps For the beloved President.
4. Un mensaje de su esposa A toda la humanidad Fué mensaje de bondad	A message from his wife To all humanity Was a message of kindness

En sus frases valerosas
Y la humanidad llorosa
Consuela a la Primera Dama
Que en le Tierra Americana
Defendió la libertad.
Triste está la humanidad,
Y llora la historia humana.
Triste está la humanidad,
Y llora la historia humana.

In her valorous phrases,
And humanity, weeping,
Consoles the First Lady,
Who, in the American Land,
Defended liberty.
Sad is humanity,
And human history weeps.
Sad is humanity,
And human history weeps.

THE PURIM *SHPIL* OF ABRAHAM AND ISAAC

Purim, a Jewish holiday celebrated usually at the end of February or the beginning of March, is the day Jews recall their threatened destruction by the Persian king Ahashverus and his vizier, Haman, and their deliverance from their fate by Mordecai and Esther. Purim shares several features of festival behavior with non-Jewish carnivals, including feasting, folk drama, masquerading, carousing, jesting, and burlesque.

The origin of the Purim play dates back to the buffooneries and the dramatizations of the ninth and tenth centuries. In the Jewish communities of Germany, for example, Purim plays were known to have been performed in the fifteenth century, although the oldest unpublished text we have is from the end of the seventeenth century. The central figures of the early Purim plays were biblical heroes from the story of Esther. Non-biblical themes were also incorporated into the Purim plays and emphasized ethics and religious behavior similar to the religious play of the medieval church. The motif of the sacrifice of Isaac has become a fertile device for the inculcation of Jewish religious and ethical values. Thus, for example, the motif is part of the Rosh ha-Shanah [New Year] Service as well as the subject of many hymns and legends.

The Bobover Hassidic community, where the folk drama described below was performed, is one of the few ultra-orthodox communities which continue this tradition. The Purim play celebrates the community's role as cultural connoisseur of Jewish tradition, by always depicting themes from the Bible or other Jewish sources and by exhibiting its members' abilities to generate artistic creativity despite their almost total lack of exposure to such experiences.

The play is in a Yiddish dialect, popularly known as "Polish

Yiddish" and with many Hebrew verses and words, pronounced with Ashkenazic accents. All the members of the cast are male students, teachers and workers in their Rabbinical School.

The Bobover Hassidic community originated in Galicia [southern Poland] more than one hundred and fifty years ago. The current *rebe* [the Hassidic leader] of the community, Shlomo Halberstam, is a direct descendant of Hayyim Halberstamm (1793–1876), the originator of the sect. After the Second World War, Shlomo found refuge in the United States, where he established a Hassidic center in Borough Park, Brooklyn, New York. Today, the sect is made up of more than 2,000 families in the United States and Canada. Most are in New York City and in a large community in Israel. The sect has very little cultural or social contact with the outside world. Following their interpretation of Jewish tradition, members do not attend movies, theater, or secular concerts.

Before the *Shpil*

The Purim *shpil* [play] is performed on Purim night approximately at midnight, but the preparations of the scenery start as early as 5 P.M. It takes place in the *besmedresh* [a house of study and a synagogue] on a small stage on the left side of the ark. The stage, approximately eight feet wide and five feet long, is brought from outside the *besmedresh* (see the sketch p. 116). The rehearsals begin not more than two weeks before Purim in the *yeshive* [rabbinical school] dining room. Mimeographed sheets are distributed to the prospective actors, a cast of no more than five, almost all veterans of earlier plays. Some actors go back twelve years to when the Bobover lived in Crown Heights, Brooklyn. On the mimeographed sheets the different roles are written, as well as the melodies which the roles require. The Purim *shpil* as performed is a genre of cantorial opera. Almost the entire play is sung.

The performance is entirely the responsibility of the *yeshive* students, and the theatrical setting has been, for the last several years, the domain of a *yeshive* student who is famous in the community for his artistic abilities. Some of the arrangements for the play take place in the *besmedresh* on the afternoon of the performance itself while the regular activities are going on. Thus, sometime after five o'clock when some people are praying the Evening Service and others are studying in the main *besmedresh*, lights are hooked up to the ceiling. The colors are blue, red, and white. A movable curtain is hung on poles and several backdrops are rolled up to the ceiling to be rolled down during the play.

Several hours before the Purim *shpil* a few women come to the women's section in order to reserve a place for themselves. Men do not come as early as women to reserve a place, since the men's section affords many more viewing places, but women are restricted to a special section which provides only a limited view, and no seats. Around midnight, when the *besmedresh* starts to fill, a group of people, not dressed like the Hassidim, but in business suits and wearing hats, arrive with musical instruments. This is the famous *Neginah* orchestra, a very popular wedding orchestra which plays for both Hassidic and non-Hassidic weddings in New York. They traditionally come to play before the performance of the Bobover Purim *shpil* and the Bobover are very proud that they do not charge them for this service. They are seated close to the ark and play, for more than half an hour, songs from the Bobover repertoire for Purim. There is no dancing while they play. Meanwhile the main *besmedresh* fills especially with people in Hassidic dress, but also others, including some in business suits and hats, and also young people in jeans and knitted skullcaps.

The *rebe* arrives with several men sometime after the orchestra. He is brought to a table close to the main area of the performance. One of the *rebe's* relatives tells one of the orchestra members to stop playing and the *rebe* then leads semi-liturgical songs, first from the Bobover repertoire for the Day of Atonement and later from the regular repertoire. This part lasts close to half an hour. Then the *Neginah* orchestra plays several other tunes.

A tall man in Hassidic clothing, including a *shtrayml* [fur-edged hat] stands in front of the closed curtain and thanks the people who prepared the evening, Purim 5736 [1976], but without mentioning any name in particular. Several men in the *besmedresh* applaud, the only such ovation during the entire play. Using a microphone, which will later be passed to the actors, he asks the permission of the *rebe* to perform what he calls "a very old play," not stating its name.

The Performance

At 1:20 A.M., the play (a prologue and six scenes) begins. An actor comes from behind the curtain. His long white robe is adorned with two wide black stripes on each side of the front, has long flowing sleeves, and has a white sash. He wears a Russian-style white curly lamb hat. Later he will be recognized as Abraham, the protagonist of the play. His introductory words have an ethical emphasis. He addresses the audience (singing solo, accompanied by violin and accordion). He sings of them, honoring them as pious men, Hassidim, teachers and Halakhic [religious law] experts, who have come to hear the righteous words, the secret words both clever and wise, of those who are always ready to execute God's command. (This part is entirely in Hebrew, in Ashkenazic pronunciation.) Then, singing again, as he puts it, "several words about the purpose of the play which is to put lots of emotion into the *Sacrifice of Isaac*," he introduces the first scene.

While the introductory tune is played, the curtain is opened and the paper backdrop is rolled down. It depicts hills covered with brown rocks. On the left side is a huge tree with a wide, green trunk. In front, in the center of the stage, is a small "house," a box approximately two yards wide and one yard high with dark brown paper glued on it to resemble stone. A blue painted entrance rectangle completes the house.

From behind the backdrop two men emerge; one, in a contemporary short suit and a knitted hat, is Eliezer. The other wears striped dark blue and gray pajamas, padded to make him appear extremely fat, and has a belt over his wide waist. He also wears a black-and-white-striped *kafiya* [an Arabic shawl] on his head. He is bare-foot. Like Eliezer he has a bushy beard but black, not red like Eliezer's. He asks Eliezer if he recognizes him and declares in Hebrew, accented according to Israeli practice, "I am Ishmael, I am an Arab." While Ishmael is introducing himself, Arabic music is played on a tape recorder behind the curtain and Ishmael dances a gross belly dance. The audience is very responsive to his act, many laughing aloud. Then the music stops and he comes close to Eliezer, complaining to him that his father likes to study but he would rather go hunting. He tells Eliezer a story about his adventures as a hunter: "I am a hero," says he. "Several months ago in the forest I saw a huge lion, but did not run away from him, but rather came closer and closer to him until I could see his eyes. When a smart-aleck asks me why I did not knock off the lion's head, I answer that his head was cut off already." People laugh again. He continues with a story about Abraham's strange customs. "This year he bought *matses* [unleavened bread eaten during Passover] from the *yeshive* bakery and they were so hard they were impossible to eat." The audience laughs. Eliezer stands frozen and unresponsive and Ishmael starts to perform his "belly dancing" movements, holding the microphone, singing, "I am of ancient origin" and that he will soon get an inheritance which will bring lots of pleasure; "everything," he sings, "will be mine. Oxen and fields, gold and silver, diamonds and brilliants of a thousand carats . . . and white horses with golden wagons . . . I will soon be very successful and I will have everything . . . well-fed kosher pigs (the audience laughs) . . . I will live like a count because I am the only heir." Eliezer is now somewhat relaxed, and he sings, "I do not have to worry. You can speak as long as you wish. Do not tell me stories that you will get the inheritance." Here Ishmael interrupts him, teasing him while touching him, saying: "No, you will not get it." Eliezer continues, "By what right do you deserve the inheritance? You are a savage." Ishmael at this point tells Eliezer that his father is coming. Both of them disappear. Abraham comes to center stage holding the microphone close to his mouth, and sings a moving monologue to God, almost crying, telling God that all his riches are nothing to him as long as he does not have a well-behaved son. Ishmael is not a good child, and so he and Sara do not have a child to pray for them when they die. He begs God, to whom he had devoted all his life, to fulfill his request. When he finishes his solo, several women in the women's section are holding handkerchiefs in their hands and wiping their eyes. Then from the ceiling (from a tape recorder), a "Heavenly Voice" speaks to Abraham in a cantillated melody, announcing to Abraham that his prayer had been accepted and that his people will be the chosen one of God. Abraham responds with a song of gratitude and with a moral injunction, "Trust in God." (The melody is a very popular melody from the Bobover repertoire—a composition by the *rebe*: "From the Diaspora I will gather you.") When the curtain is closed everyone joins in the singing while clapping hands, to the accompaniment of the accordion and violin.

The second scene has the same backdrop as the first, but a table and chair replace the rustic house. The curtain opens to reveal Isaac, dressed as a little Hassidic man. He sits and reads in the special intonation reserved for it, a passage from an open *Talmud* [compilation of law, with commentary]. His body sways back and forth. Ishmael comes in with a huge bow and arrow and starts laughing at him. Isaac tells him to leave him alone and to let him study. Ishmael says to him, "If you want to study, study—if you want, go on as you wish." He imitates the boy's movements. The audience enjoys it and laughs, because his movements are indelicate due to the cushion inside his clothing. Then Ishmael says to Isaac: "Leave the *Talmud* and come to me. I like to talk to you." Isaac comes closer and Ishmael sings a joyful song on how to use the bow and suggests that he learn how to hunt. Ishmael gives Isaac the bow and arrow and Isaac directs it towards him. Ishmael, worried, cries: "No! No!" The audience laughs. While Isaac holds the bow and arrow a man dressed as Sara enters. Sara wears a yellow gown, a kerchief which covers her hair, and men's shoes, and her beard has been knotted up. Her hands hold the ends of the kerchief to hide the beard. When she asks Isaac where he got the bow and arrow, she speaks in falsetto. When Isaac answers that Ishmael gave it to him, she asks him to come closer to her. Then Abraham enters, singing to Isaac, telling him that Ishmael is not a type for him to emulate and that if he associates with Ishmael he will become an Arab. While he sings, Ishmael sits on the chair where Isaac sat before and poses as if he is studying the *Talmud*. Then he stands and does his belly dance. Sara sings to Abraham, telling him that Ishmael has a bad influence on Isaac and might destroy him; therefore he must send Ishmael away. Hagar enters. She is dressed in a woman's dark robe with a kerchief covering her head and beard. Abraham sings that to please Sara, to whom he refers as "strong Sara," he is sending them away. He will give them a piece of bread and some water for the journey. This is their destiny, says he, and he wishes them all the best in the world, as it is written, "and you will go from here to the Paran desert." Hagar then sings that she accepts her destiny. The curtains close.

The third scene takes place in a desert. The drop is painted with Arizona cactuses of various sizes and shapes, as well as some small bushes. Ishmael and his mother are walking on the stage, his arm on her shoulders. They walk back and forth singing together about how miserable they are. Ishmael says to his mother, "We have been wandering here for a long time since Abraham sent us away, but it is not as bad as might be expected. I am an astrologer," continues he, "and can see what this land will look like many years from now. Now maybe there is no water but I can see a kind of *mashke* [intoxicating drink]. One cannot drink it, it smells terrible, for what it can be used I do not know. [The reference is to petroleum.] I can see how many nations will exchange 'greens' [dollars] for 'black' [oil]." The audience laughs again. "An old story," says he, "I do not understand people . . . I see there also somebody, he looks like one of Abraham's children . . . now I see him clearly . . . he is called Hershel Kis-Kis-Kissinger. . . . And I see my grandchildren all looking at an Island. . . . I see all that will happen in the future, and they say that today the world is crazy" (the audience laughs). . . . "But meanwhile I have nothing."

Then he sits on the floor and cries several times like a baby, "Mother, water." In the background cries of a jackass are heard, accompanied by the playing of an accordion, as well as an imitation of unidentified animal voices. Hagar sings. Her voice, like Sara's, is a male voice. She sits next to Ishmael, putting her arm around his shoulders, and talks about how life was different before Abraham sent them away. Ishmael then sings a happy song about how with his hunting skills and his wealth he is going to take over the world one day. He is going to rob people. The melody is the same as in the prologue and people join in as the curtain closes.

The fourth scene has the same setting as the first one. The "Heavenly Voice" is heard from the tape recorder in the ceiling. A singing dialogue begins when the voice calls for Abraham and Abraham answers, "Here I am." Then the "Heavenly Voice" asks him to sacrifice his son, and Abraham answers that he is ready to obey but asks the "Heavenly Voice" to tell him which one of his sons. The "Heavenly Voice" replies, "Your son whom you love." When Abraham says that he loves them both the voice tells him he means Isaac. Then Abraham talks to himself: "What shall I tell Sara. . . . I cannot tell her that I am going to sacrifice Isaac to the Father. . . . I will tell her I need to send Isaac away to study." He calls to Sara and when she arrives he continues to sing, telling her his plan to send Isaac away from home. He then calls for Isaac. Sara puts her arm on Isaac's shoulders, singing to him about how hard her life will be without him. (In the women's section there is crying.)

The fifth scene has a new backdrop, a desert with a valley between a rocky chain of hills. The sky is blue. There are some small bushes. Abraham calls for Ishmael and Eliezer. They appear and he sings that they should prepare themselves for a long journey. As they walk on their way (pacing back and forth on the stage), Isaac and Ishmael carry branches. Abraham stands close to Isaac at the center of the stage and they sing a dialogue, Abraham explaining that God asked him to sacrifice Isaac. Isaac does not complain but later in the song he laments his fate. Abraham starts each stanza affectionately, with the words *"Yitskhokl"* [*Yitskhok,*

Hebrew for Isaac; *l*, Yiddish diminutive]. When Isaac sings he does not look directly at Abraham but rather at Abraham's shoulder. During the dialogue Isaac continues to hold the branches. The lights are red and white. Then from behind the curtain comes a man in a long black gabardine robe with flowing sleeves trimmed with two wide red stripes on each side of the front. In his hand he holds a shepherd's crook. He wears a wig of long hair with a bald spot and is hatless. The lights are focussed towards him. Some people in the audience recognizing him, say, "Satan, Satan." He approaches Abraham, who meanwhile has arranged the branches on the floor with Eliezer's help. Satan greets Abraham, asking him what he is doing with branches and his son. Abraham recognizes him, but asks him to identify himself. Satan tries to avoid revealing his identity and asks Abraham if he is the owner of the restaurant in the desert with four entrances and a big shield on which is written, "No Satan is allowed." [The allusion is to Genesis 18:1–9, in which Abraham entertains the angels.] The audience laughs again. Satan continues, "I would like to know when I can have a conversation with you." Abraham shouts, "Go away, leave me alone." Satan responds, "Maybe I can talk to you on the Sabbath, during the Torah readings?" The audience laughs. Abraham sings a duet with Satan. He sings that he is not afraid of Satan. Satan sings that he cannot be got rid of, and that yesterday he heard that Abraham intended to slaughter Isaac. "How can you use your own son as a scapegoat?" he asks. Abraham again asks him to leave, while Satan sings to Isaac, telling him to think about his poor mother and how she will feel when she finds out what has happened to him. The scene ends with Isaac singing a song of support to his father: Abraham should do what God has asked of him.

The sixth scene has the same backdrop as the first. The house is brought back, but this time without the blue door. Abraham lifts Isaac and places him prone on the house, facing the ceiling. Holding the microphone in his hand, Isaac sings a solo in which he asks Abraham to bind him tightly so he will not flinch when he is slaughtered and reminds him to use a kosher [ritually approved]

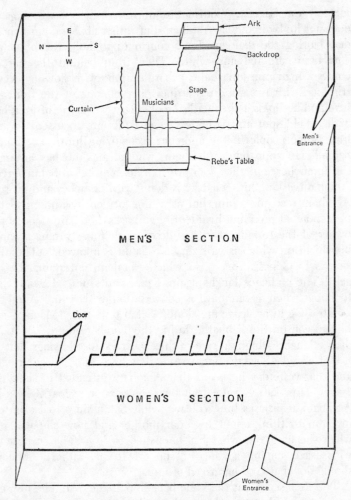

knife. Meanwhile Abraham ties him with a long rope. Isaac continues to sing, asking Abraham to take one of his bones to Sara. When Isaac is completely bound, Abraham takes a huge silver-painted wooden knife, and while the violin plays, he tests the edge of the blade with his fingers. He does so for two or three minutes; Isaac lies still. The audience is very quiet. Then Abraham says: "I am ready to perform the sacrificial duty." Immediately, the "Heavenly Voice" resounds from the ceiling saying, "Don't touch the boy!" It suggests that instead of Isaac a ram be sacrificed. The prompter, who sits on the side, moves a piece of the backdrop and a painted ram is seen. Abraham releases Isaac from his bonds and the "Heavenly Voice" is heard again, praising Abraham for his obedience. Many of the men in the audience join in the singing of the last song. The curtain is closed, people move, but there is no clapping of hands or shouting of "bravo." The time is 3:00 A.M.

II. WORK, PLACES, PEOPLES

There is very little that might rightly be called an American folklore, that is, an oral tradition that is known generally across the country. What actually exists in the United States is a number of lores that have developed from the homogeneities of occupational, regional, and ethnic groupings. The truly pan-American lore is popular lore. It is more closely associated with literacy and is the creation of professional writers who have distributed it through the media of print, recordings, radio, films, and television. This popular lore, rather than genuine folklore, provides the symbols of our national heritage, contributes to the oneness of our country as a national entity, and tells us all what it means, broadly speaking, to be an American. Popular lore unifies the nation. Folklore fosters diversity within the nation.

The occupational, regional, and ethnic lores that exist among the less literate groups in America, the true folklores, serve to maintain the coherence of various minority cultures within the national culture as a whole, which continually threatens to engulf them. They offer stability and means of survival to threatened peoples.

Of course, vocation, race, and locale overlap. For example, lumbermen become cowpokes, miners, truck drivers. Forests are stripped in Maine and the industry moves on to Michigan and the Pacific Northwest. French Canadian loggers give way to Scotch-Irish, Finns, and Russians. Industrialization takes place, and with the coming of steam, the diesel engine, and radio the old isolation is broken and lumbering loses its intense homogeneity. Nonetheless, at the folk level, one element—the vocation, the locale, or the ethnic background—will be pre-eminent. The heroic figures in the selections immediately following are defined by the work they do: Cherry Tree Joe McCreery with rafting lumber down rivers, although he was a Pennsylvania Irishman; Charlie Glass with western cattlemen in their range wars and Big Max with West Virginia coal miners, although both of them happen to be black; Perry Martin with his superlative skill making moonshine whiskey, although he was a memorable local character and closely associated with the life of the Mississippi Delta "river rats."

The heroes who developed artificially, at the level of popular culture, have likewise tended to represent specific occupations, regions, or ethnic groups. The giant of them all, Paul Bunyan, is in origin and throughout his tale cycle a super-lumberman. His ethnic identity is insignificant, and his geographical links are slight. He moved about as the industry moved in search of new timberlands. Even when he turns up as an oil field worker, stress is on his superhuman ability as a worker, and ethnic origins and the locations of the oil fields of minor importance. As will be seen, however, with other heroes ethnic or regional roots are primary considerations.

JAMES BIRD, HERO SHOT AS A DESERTER

The ballad, "James Bird," was written by Charles Miner and first published in his newspaper, *The Gleaner*, at Wilkes-Barre, in 1814. Unlike many American traditional ballads, it did not spring from the folk, but was the composition of an educated man, [a city dweller], who was a newspaper editor and publisher, and later in his career, a local historian, and a Congressman. Regardless of its origin, "James Bird" long ago was accepted by folklore scholars as an authentic, traditional and widely popular American ballad. After the passage of almost a century and a half it is still current among the common people, especially in rural parts. . . .

What does history say of James Bird, the man and soldier, and the hero of the famous ballad? Perhaps we should say the history as it has been preserved in Luzerne County, his native home.

James Bird was born on December 21, 1785, the eldest son of John and Rebecca (Montayne) Bird. His father, a veteran of three years' service in the Revolutionary War, had migrated to the Wyoming Valley in Northeastern Pennsylvania, locating his home at a site near the present intersection of West Eighth Street and Hollow Road in West Wyoming Borough, Luzerne County. There James Bird is presumed to have been born. . . . After an apprenticeship, he followed his father's trade as a weaver. It was while engaged in this trade that he volunteered for military duty in the War of 1812 as a substitute for another man. He was accepted as a member of the Maltross Artillery Company of Kingston, Luzerne County, commanded by Captain Samuel Thomas.

On April 13, 1813 he entered active duty and was assigned to the U.S. brig *Niagara* as a member of the Marine Detachment under command of Lieutenant Benjamin Hyde. At the time Bird was described as being five feet and 11 inches tall, with blue eyes, sandy hair and light complexion.

Early in the fighting of the Battle of Lake Erie, on September 10, 1813, the flagship *Saint Lawrence* was put out of commission, and Commodore Oliver Hazard Perry, its commander, transferred to the *Niagara*, where Bird fought throughout the battle. . . .

After the Battle of Lake Erie, the Maltross Artillery Company was detailed to the city of Detroit where it remained until November, 1813. The English having been driven from the lakes, the Kingston unit returned to its home station. James Bird, however, remained behind with the fleet.

News of the impending battle of New Orleans reached the fleet at Lake Erie. An opportunity for action proved too tempting to James Bird. On the night of June 4, 1814 he was in charge of a detail guarding military supplies. Leaving his post, he marched away with several of his men to join General Andrew Jackson at New Orleans.

Bird was pursued. Six days later he was arrested at Pittsburgh from where he was to have embarked with a group of volunteers for the Crescent City. He was brought back to Erie on June 22, and confined aboard the *Niagara* where he was arraigned before a court martial on September 12. He pleaded guilty to a charge of desertion, and was sentenced to death before a firing squad. After approval by President James Madison, the sentence was executed on board the *Niagara* on November 11, 1814.

The Ballad of James Bird

Sons   of   free - dom,   lis - ten___ to   me,

And ye daugh - ters too___ give ear,

You a sad___ and mourn - ful___ sto - ry

As was ev - er told___ shall hear.

Hull,___ you___ know, his troops sur - ren - dered

And___ de - fense - less left the west;

Sons of freedom, listen to me,
　And ye daughters too give ear,
You a sad and mournful story
　As was ever told shall hear.

Hull, you know, his troops surrendered
　And defenseless left the west;
Then our forces quick assembled
　The invaders to resist.

Amongst the troops that marched to war,
　Were the Kingston Volunteers;
Captain Thomas them commanded,
　To protect our west frontiers.

Tender were the scenes of parting,
　Mothers wrung their hands and cried,
Maidens wept their swains in secret,
　Fathers strove their tears to hide.

There is one among the number,
　Tall and graceful is his mien,
Firm his step, his look undaunted,
　Scarce a nobler youth was seen.

One sweet kiss he snatched from Mary,
　　Craved his mother's prayer, and more,
Pressed his father's hand, and left them
　　For Lake Erie's distant shore.

Mary tried to say "Farewell, James,"
　　Waved her hand, but nothing spoke,
"Good-bye, Bird, may Heaven preserve you,"
　　From the rest at parting broke.

Soon they came where noble Perry
　　Had assembled all his fleet;
Then the Gallant Bird enlisted,
　　Hoping soon the foe to meet.

Where is Bird? The battle rages;
　　Is he in the strife or no?
Now the cannon roars tremendous;
　　Dare he meet the hostile foe?

Aye! behold him! see him, Perry!
　　In the selfsame ship they fight;
Though his messmates fall around him
　　Nothing can his soul affright.

But behold! A ball has struck him;
　　See the crimson current flow;
"Leave the deck!" exclaimed brave Perry;
　　"No!" cried Bird, "I will not go."

"Here on deck I took my station,
　　Here will Bird his cutlass ply;
I'll stand by you, gallant captain,
　　Till we conquer or we die."

Still he fought, though faint and bleeding,
　　Till our stars and stripes waved o'er us,
Victory having crowned our efforts,
　　All triumphant o'er our foes.

And did Bird receive a pension?
　　Was he to his friends restored?
No; nor never to his bosom
　　Clasped the maid his heart adored.

But there came most dismal tidings
　　From Lake Erie's distant shore;
Better far if Bird had perished
　　Midst the battle's awful roar.

"Dearest parents," said the letter,
　　"This will bring sad news to you;
Do not mourn your first beloved,
　　Though this brings his last adieu."

"I must suffer for deserting
　　From the brig *Niagara:*
Read this letter, brothers, sisters,
　　'Tis the last you'll hear from me."

Sad and gloomy was the morning
　　Bird was ordered out to die;
Where's the breast not dead to pity
　　But for him would heave a sigh?

Lo! he fought so brave at Erie,
　　Freely bled and nobly dared;
Let his courage plead for mercy,
　　Let his precious life be spared.

See him march and bear his fetters;
　　Hark! they clank upon the ear;
But his step is firm and manly,
　　For his heart ne'er harbored fear.

See him kneel upon his coffin,
　　Sure his death can do no good;
Spare him! spare! O God, they shoot him!
　　Oh! his bosom streams with blood.

Farewell, Bird! farewell forever;
   Friends and home he'll see no more;
But his mangled corpse lies buried
   On Lake Erie's distant shore.

CHERRY TREE JOE, RAFTSMAN

Cherry Tree Joe was the Pennsylvania Paul Bunyan, long before an advertising campaign crystallized around the Wisconsin figure of Bunyan all the legends that had been told for many years through the lumber industry from Maine to Washington. But while books aplenty had been written about Bunyan, the only thing I could find in print about McCreery was a ballad with a few lines of introduction, printed in J. Dudley Tonkin's "The Last Raft," from a broadside and copied in "Pennsylvania Songs and Legends."

Inquiry among folklorists, historians and "old residenters" brought little help. There were plenty of tales about Cherry Tree Joe, but little unity of tradition. While there was a general feeling that McCreery, like Mike Fink, was a real person, no two people seemed to agree on whether he was from Cherry Tree, on French Creek in Venango County, or from Cherry Tree in Indiana County, on the West Branch of the Susquehanna. [According to folk tradition he] was a giant of a man, his size varying from a mere six and a half or seven feet in some stories, to such a figure as could wear a raft on each foot and skate down the river. He was supposed to have a cabin somewhere back in the woods, where he kept moose for milk cows and a panther for a house-cat. His wife cooked on a griddle six feet square, and used a barrel of flour every morning to make flapjacks. . . .

There were other stories, too. He was so strong he could shoulder five bushels of shot, but when he tried to carry the load on a bet he mired up to his knees in a flint rock. He was so tough that when he spit on the ground, it would bounce.

When a raft would get tied up on a rock, snag or dam, instead of using dynamite, rivermen would just call for Cherry Tree Joe. But one time the result was unexpected, to say the least.

That was a bad jam, and the whole raft was made of birch logs. While he studied just how to get the matter straightened out, Joe pulled out his knife and began whittling. Before he realized what had happened, he had whittled the whole raft into tooth-picks. . . .

It was not until the autumn of 1955 that I found opportunity to press the search further, when I was drawn to Cherry Tree, in Indiana County, by the final meeting of the old Raftsmen's Association, whose few remaining members were dissolving the group.

After a monument had been dedicated to the raftsmen, and the service feelingly concluded with a paraphrase from the Cherry Tree Joe ballad:

> The cheery hail of "Land! Tie up!"
> To be heard no more, forever, upon these rivers.

I found time to make some inquiries about the folk hero. I dis-covered at once that I had found the right Cherry Tree.

Especially among the older raftsmen and townsfolk, many of whom could remember McCreery, there was no difficulty in get-ting information on either the man or the legend, although not all the statements about the man proved correct. . . .

Cherry Tree Joe, I learned, was born in 1805, near Muncy, Pa. For a man whose legend was to grow so fast he became a folk hero in his own lifetime, it seems appropriate that he should have been born in Lycoming County, where they used to say that the land was so rich that if you dropped a shingle nail on the ground at night, it would grow into a railroad spike before morning! . . .

Joe McCreery was big and husky as a youth, but he was agile and quick, too, as a logger had need to be, if he wanted to live long. Rain or shine, hot or cold, you had to be out when time and water enough for a drive came. And when a log turned under your feet it might be a question of jump quick or be crushed to death, instead of merely risking a bath in icy water. Rafts of planks, squared timber and logs were run down the West Branch at a fairly early period, and log driving became common after 1846.

Most of the early lumber for rafts was out of the old up-and-down "thundergust" sawmills, so called because they were on small streams where every thundershower was utilized for waterpower.

I published much of this matter in a newspaper story soon after the visit, quoting from the song, in hopes of finding someone who knew it in folk transmission. One reason was a nagging desire to know more about its tune. Many people say it was sung to "Yankee Doodle," and recent broadsides and some Indiana Countians say the tune was "Blue-Tail Fly." But neither would fit the words.

To my delight, a few days after publication of the story I received a letter from a woman in southern Washington County, who wrote that she had been much interested in the story. According to her letter, she was a great-granddaughter of Cherry Tree Joe, and remembered the song well.

Cherry Tree Joe McCreery

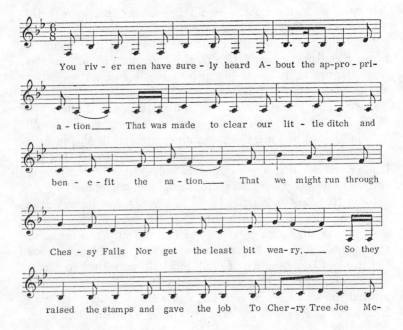

You riv-er men have sure-ly heard A-bout the ap-pro-pri-a-tion___ That was made to clear our lit-tle ditch and ben-e-fit the na-tion.___ That we might run through Ches-sy Falls Nor get the least bit wea-ry.___ So they raised the stamps and gave the job To Cher-ry Tree Joe Mc-

Cree - ry.____ Look - in' out for num - ber one, Spend - in'

all the mon - ey, and get - tin' noth - ing done.____

1. You rivermen have surely heard
      About the appropriation
    That was made to clear our little ditch
      And benefit the nation.
    That we might run through Chessy Falls
      Nor get the least bit weary,
    So they raised the stamps and gave the job
      To Cherry Tree Joe McCreery.

    REFRAIN
    Lookin' out for number one,
      Spendin' all the money, (boys,)
    And gettin' nothing done.

2. There's Bob McKeage and E. B. Camp
      Who held the ready ginger,
    Some men of sense said, "Build a dam,"
      But would not raise a finger.
    "We'll blow the rocks sky high," said they,
      "So Porter don't get skeery."
    "But let'er rip and she'll go through,"
      Said Cherry Tree Joe McCreery.

3. Now you all know and I can show
      That fate is a cruel master;
    When once you're going down the hill,
      He's sure to push you faster.
    And that's the way, mind what I say,
      And don't you see, my dearie?

That everything that happens now
  Is blamed on Joe McCreery.

4. One day last spring, as I came up,
      I met somebody's daughter,
    Who held her apron to her eyes
      To catch the salty water.
    "Dear girl," said I, "what makes you cry?
      You must feel very dreary."
    "Why, my daddy stoved in Chessy Falls,
      And I'm hunting Joe McCreery."

5. The other day they had a splash
      And jammed her tight as thunder,
    A circumstance that caused our folks
      To gaze around in wonder.
    They prayed and tore, ripped and swore,
      Until they all grew weary.
    Sheff cut his bill raft into sticks,
      And cursed Cherry Tree Joe McCreery.

6. Now Captain Dowler, the other day,
      He struck a raft of timber,
    That was hanging up to Sliding Point,
      And tore the rope asunder.
    The captain winked and scratched his head
      Saying, "This is kind of dreary,"
    Then jumped his oar, went on shore,
      And prayed for Joe McCreery.

7. Our Squire Riddle on the hill,
      Who deals out justice even,
    His head is very bald, you know,
      No hair 'twixt him and heaven.
    I asked how his hair came out,
      He answered sort of dreary.
    That it must have come out, thinking about
      Cherry Tree Joe McCreery.

8. In years to come, when no rafts run
      On our dear little river,
   And the cheery cry of "Land! Tie up!"
      Shall be heard no more—forever,
   Down Rocky Bend and through Chessy Falls,
      On winter nights so dreary
   You'll see phantom raftsmen chasing around
      The ghost of Joe McCreery.

CHARLIE GLASS AND THE SHEEPHERDERS

In the Fruita, Colorado, cemetery stands a large tombstone with the simple inscription "Charles Glass, Died February 22, 1937" carved upon it. Nearby are the markers for several members of the famous Turner and Young families whose cattle have roamed eastern Utah and western Colorado for many years. Glass spent much of his life working for these families, but he was generally known as the top foreman of the Lazy Y Cross ranch of Oscar L. Turner. These people lived and died believing that the men who worked with cattle were a Chosen People and that those who worked with sheep were among the lower breeds of men. It is not strange that a foreman was buried among the men he worked for, even if he was a Negro in an all-white society, but it would be unheard of to find a sheepherder buried close to a cattleman even if they were both white. However, the interment of Charlie Glass in the Fruita cemetery seems strange since the town charter prohibited the burial of Negroes there. The tombstone marks the dramatic ending of a lingering range war and stands as a permanent symbol of the legendary Charlie Glass, a Negro cowboy.

Each year on Memorial Day, an old cowhand who once rode with Charlie Glass brings flowers to the grave and stands humbly and respectfully in memory of his foreman. Charlie was probably three-fourths Negro and one-fourth Cherokee, but he always referred to himself as a black man. "When I was a lad learning to ride broncs," remembered this old friend, "he'd hit me across the fingers with his quirt when I pulled leather. I was afraid of Charlie Glass, but I always liked him."

In western Colorado and eastern Utah, the name of Charlie Glass is well-known in ranching circles, and in Grand Junction, Colorado, where he kept a permanent room for his few possessions, he was a legendary character in his own time. It is believed that he grew up in Indian Territory, and that he left his home range after he killed the man who shot his father. He first worked for the Thatcher cattle interests in southeastern Colorado and shifted to the Pinon Mesa country in western Colorado in 1909 where he worked for the S-Cross ranch. Whether this change was motivated by a desire to get farther away from the Indian Territory marshals or drifting cowhands who might want to even up an old score, or whether he was "imported" to do a killing job, is not known. However, the legend neither connects him with the range feud on Pinon Mesa nor explains why he moved north of the Colorado River in 1917 where he spent the rest of his days around Cisco and Thompson in Utah.

Everyone who will talk about Charlie—none will allow his name to be used for publication—says that he was silent about his past, but that upon occasion he did board the D&RGW for a two- or three-week trip believed to be "back home." When he left, he always checked his gun with the station agent, and this may indicate that the old wounds had healed or that the legend about his Oklahoma killing was unfounded. In the generation that he worked for cattle interests in the Utah-Colorado border areas, he was known to be fiercely loyal to his employers, enjoyed the confidence and respect of all who worked with him, and in after hours was devoted to poker as well as to wine, women, and song for recreation. In a day when rustling was so common that a rancher "had to have a cow with seven calves in order to have veal for Christmas," Charlie earned his keep as a range boss, a Negro in white society taking orders from and giving orders to whites who accepted him for what he was, a good man on a horse. The legend of Charlie Glass might well have grown out of this situation. However, the legend grew by leaps and bounds when he shot a sheepherder in the range "war" of 1921, and it exploded when he mysteriously died in 1937. . . .

Charlie began working for Oscar L. Turner, a highly respected cattleman, in 1917. The Lazy Y cattle roamed the Cottonwood district of eastern Utah, but the Turner-Young livestock grazed Mesa, Garfield, and Rio Blanco counties in western Colorado and

Grand and Uintah counties in Utah, plus some lands leased from the Indians and the federal government. There was little regulation of the range in these years. The few large ranches apparently agreed among themselves about the division of the range, and sought help from the state capital in drawing lines between themselves and the sheepmen. It was common practice for cowboys to homestead a quarter section at some strategic spot—waterhole or canyon entrance—and thus help the rancher control the range that he did not own. Charlie filed for a homestead for Turner and proved up on it. He became the foreman of the Turner ranching operation and proudly and effectively protected the range interests of his boss from marauding sheepmen. . . .

The sheep industry had been important in the Utah-Colorado borderlands for many years. Looked after by Basques imported from Spain, the herds fed on the high country grasses in the summer and spread over the desert areas in the winter. In Charlie Glass's day, flocks from western Colorado's high country moved into the range land above the Colorado River in Eastern Utah during the winter months. They did much as they pleased, paid little attention to range rights based on tradition or lease, and were a constant threat to the established cattle ranches. Charlie regarded himself as a protector of the cattle range, and no doubt his attitude toward sheepherders hardened in these years.

The Joe Taylor sheep outfit, during the winter migration, roamed over parts of the range above the Colorado River every year, and according to one old cowboy, they "sheeped" the Lazy Y range and others repeatedly. It was easy for a Basque who could not understand English very well, if at all, to misunderstand when told that he was trespassing on the Turner range. When pushed off the Lazy Y range, the Basques, often called "Greeks" by the cow country people, would move their herds peacefully, would not talk back, but would return another day.

When Glass became Turner's foreman, the migratory sheepmen appeared to be "plenty spooked," in the words of one who rode with him. Whenever Charlie came into their area, they might start shooting at some object or into the ground, but never at him, just to let him know that they carried guns. In so doing they would also put their dogs to work moving the sheep in the other direction, making it unnecessary for Glass to ride any closer. It seems apparent that the Basques understood that Charlie represented a new strength in the resistance to the migratory sheepmen, and besides, he had a reputation of having certain notches in his gun. Although the legend does not picture Charlie as a gunman brought in from Pinon Mesa to do a job, he does symbolize the traditional hatred of cattlemen for sheepmen, and represents the strength of the mounted cowboy with a gun. Perhaps the fact that Charlie was a Negro, who referred to himself as "this old black boy" and who always carried a gun in a shoulder holster and never buttoned his coat, may have contributed to his local reputation as a good man to put a stop to the wandering marauder wrapped in wool.

In the winter of 1920–1921, the Turner range was "sheeped" repeatedly despite the line that had been drawn by Sheep Inspector H. E. Herbert. A large number of sheep had been quarantined, apparently those from out of state, and a line had been established to protect the cattle from them. This was state government in action to protect Utah cattle interests. Despite this legal effort to keep the two ancient enemies apart, the Basques continued to trespass across the line.

On the morning of February 20, 1921, a Basque camp-mover named Gerrold Yaber, working for William Fitzpatrick, was stopped by Jimmy Warner and Glass fifteen miles west of the Turner ranch. Warner accused Yaber of moving his sheep right past his tent while he slept and into a canyon claimed by Warner. When Yaber threatened to cut Warner's bridle reins with his horseshoe hammer and knife, Warner pulled his gun. As Yaber ran toward the tent to get his gun, Glass beat him there and took possession of it, then suggested that they sit down and talk over this matter of trespass. Later, Yaber found his gun under his pillow.

Four days later, there was a confrontation between Glass and Felix Jesui, camp-mover for Fitzpatrick, which occurred one mile south of the Turner ranch. According to sworn testimony taken in court, Jesui was taking the place of the regular herder and was moving some sheep toward the canyon in which the Turner ranch was located. When Glass and one of his men saw him, Charlie moved toward the trespasser while his man moved up on a rim and sat there with his .30-30 across his saddle. Later, this associate said that he could not have covered Charlie completely but he could have got the man who shot at Charlie.

According to the court testimony, Charlie dismounted, shots were fired, and the Basque lay dead upon the desert floor. Charlie then remounted, rode to the Turner ranch, and reported to his boss that he had killed a Basque. Turner then rode to Cisco, phoned Sheriff J. S. Skewes at Green River, and reported that Glass had shot a sheepherder and would surrender peacefully. The sheriff went immediately to the Turner ranch, bringing with him Dr. J. W. Williams, County Attorney A. O. Tangren, and others. Charlie's "back-up" man rode to Cisco and back with him to view the body with the officers and doctor. Soon after that, the back-up man disappeared. Officials were told that he was the son of a preacher in Fruita and that the family had moved to California. Consequently, the only presumed witness to the shooting was not present at the inquest or trial when Glass was tried for murder. The only evidence that he was a witness is his own statement made under the cloak of anonymity in 1964. Why did he leave the country? Could it be that Charlie pulled his gun on a sheepherder and solved the range problem for the cattlemen for many years? It may be of passing interest to know that in the trial that followed, Turner footed the bill for the defense of his fore-man, and Charlie remained in the employ of the family long after Turner died. Certainly, the loyal foreman was treated as if he had the full support of his employer.

The coroner's inquest was held the following Saturday in Moab, Utah, and the jury brought in a verdict that Jesui came to his death from a gunshot wound inflicted feloniously by Glass. It was stated that there were no witnesses and that Glass had shot in self-defense. According to the Moab *Times-Independent*, March

3, 1921, the testimony disclosed this account of what happened at the incident one mile south of the Turner ranch: Jesui was a camp-mover in the employ of William Fitzpatrick, but on the morning of the killing he took the place of his herder, Eusebis Astegaraga, and was in charge of a herd of sheep which he had started to move up the canyon where the Oscar Turner ranch was situated. Glass, according to his story, had left the Turner ranch in search of a calf in close proximity to the ranch. He walked up to Jesui and told the herder to move the sheep back. Some words doubtless ensued. There were no eyewitnesses and only the Negro knew who shot first. The tracks of the men showed that they were perhaps fifty feet apart when the shooting took place. The herder had two guns, and an examination of the weapons after the shooting showed that one of the guns, a .25 Colt automatic, had been emptied. The other gun, a .30 caliber rifle, contained one empty shell and this gun was cocked. The Negro had a .38 Colt automatic and he fired four shots. The herder was still gripping one of the guns when his body was found, and the other weapon was lying by his side. The newspaper account concluded:

> The herder was shot once, the ball entering the head just above the right eye and penetrating the brain.
>
> The body of Jesui was buried in the Moab cemetery. The man was about 26 years of age, and was born at Navarro, Spain. He had been employed by William Fitzpatrick for some time.

After a brief inquest, Glass was arraigned and charged with second-degree murder. He was released on bond in the sum of $10,000 provided by Oscar Turner, W. E. Gordon, Don Taylor, Max H. Taylor, and Tom Taylor. It was later said that Turner "spent a small fortune out of his own pocket" in defending Glass and told his foreman that he wanted no reimbursement for the money spent. However, Glass said: "I want to pay my own freight" and deeded his homestead and its improvements to Turner and continued in his employ until his trial.

Shortly after the killing, around thirty-five horses belonging to the sheep outfit were found dead in the area of the Turner ranch, possibly on range claimed by Turner. Charlie Glass and his fellow cowboys were accused of killing these horses. One of the Turner cowpunchers has stated that though they were in the valley at the time they knew nothing of the affair until they read it in the newspapers. No charges were ever filed against anyone. Considering the high level of distrust or even hatred between cattlemen and sheepmen at the time, the charge could be true or highly exaggerated and the guilt, if any, placed upon any one cattleman and any one cowboy riding for him. Considering the testimony made privately by one of Glass's associates at a much later date, it is probable that Glass had nothing to do with the affair. Since this range lay across the main north-south "Robber's Roost" trail for stolen livestock, famous from the 1880's to the 1930's, the slaying of the horses may well have been done by the specialists in mayhem and murder.

When District Judge F. E. Woods convened court in Moab in April, 1921, District Attorney B. W. Dalton presented a motion for a change in venue in the Glass murder case. Affidavits were given to show that a feud existed between cattlemen and transient sheepmen which would mitigate against the state in the trial. Sheriff W. J. Bliss testified that such a feeling existed but on cross-examination he expressed a belief that "a fair and impartial trial could be secured in the county to try the case." The defense introduced affidavits from businessmen and other citizens stating that they had no knowledge of antagonisms between sheepmen and cattlemen in Grand County and "in their opinion an absolutely fair and impartial trial could be had in the county." In the end, the court overruled the motion, according to the Moab *Times-Independent*, April 14, 1921, saying that the state's showing "was rather weak as compared to the large number of defense affidavits which he stated came from men whom he knew to be representative citizens." . . .

On the witness stand, Glass told his story "in a straightforward manner." As the *Times-Independent* reported on December 1, 1921:

> According to Glass, for several days preceding the homicide the Basque shepherds had persisted in driving their herds across the line which had been established to protect a small nook of country surrounding the Turner ranch, which country had been reserved for weaner calves and poor cattle belonging to Oscar Turner, for whom Glass was working. On the morning of the killing, Glass had been going about his usual work when he discovered a herd of sheep about a half mile over the line; that he rode to within 25 feet of the herder, dismounted, and then advanced to meet the Basque, Felix Jesui, and talk the matter over with him; that Felix was armed with two guns, a rifle and a pistol, and was very defiant; that Glass said he wouldn't quarrel with the herder but would see his boss, and started to leave the scene; that he reached his horse about 25 feet distant, when the herder yelled and shot his rifle, the bullet whizzing past the cowboy's shoulder; that Glass whirled around, and drew his gun, which was in a shoulder scabbard under his coat and shirt; that by the time he got his gun into play Felix had shot at him two more times with his pistol; that both men fired at each other several times simultaneously before the herder fell; that Glass then returned to the ranch, told what had happened, and gave himself up to the sheriff.

The case went to the jury at 10 P.M. after a week of testimony and summary, and shortly after midnight the jury reached a verdict of acquittal on one ballot. . . .

Following the trial Charlie returned to his foreman's job and spent the next sixteen years working for ranchers in that borderland range country of eastern Utah. One of his old cowpuncher friends says that "all along all of us figured that the sheepmen—sheepherders—relatives—or someone would try to get even—no one said anything and Charlie never talked—Charlie did not want any one to help him or to look out for him—always contending that 'this ole black boy' can take care of Charlie." This perhaps explains why he wore a shoulder gun down to the end of his life. He continued to ride in the rodeos, make the rounds on the Barbary Coast, and play cards with his cronies in Cisco, Thompson, and Grand Junction. He had a passion for poker and enjoyed putting his wages on the line even when he played with the Basque friends of Felix Jesui. . . .

On the night of February 22, 1937, Charlie sat in a big game at Thompson. The bottle was passed again and again as the evening wore on. Someone proposed that they drive down to Cisco and get in the big game going on there. Charlie agreed, and three of them got into a pickup truck owned by one of the transient sheepmen and away they went. Their spirits were high as they left town.

Within an hour after the station agent went to work at midnight in the Thompson depot of the D&RGW, someone came into the telegraph office and asked the agent to call the doctor because Charlie was "bad hurt." When the doctor came to the depot, he was escorted to the shed behind the building by the agent who carried a lantern. There lay the legendary cowboy in the back of the pickup truck, dead of a broken neck. He had died with his boots on. The two Basques, Andre Sartan of Grand Junction and Joe Savorna of Montrose, transient sheepherders wintering their herds in eastern Utah, had suffered some minor scratches and bruises. They reported that the truck had upset one and a half miles west of Cisco, rolling over three times. . . .

The body was taken to the Stark Funeral Home in Fruita and buried in the Turner plot not far from the place where Charlie's old boss, who had died in 1929, lay. The inquest simply reported that he had died of a broken neck suffered in an automobile accident. However, his old cowboy friends still hold that the Basques killed him, turned the truck over to put some scratches on it, and then drove back to Thompson with the body in the back. The Basques were cousins of Felix Jesui, these friends point out, and had long planned the revenge that took the life of Charlie Glass. Otherwise, how can you explain why there was an upset on a straight road on a night when there was no sleet or ice and why the two Basques were unhurt?

THE BEST STRAIGHT-EDGE MAN IN THE WORLD

Where he came from and where he went no one knows. Those outside Rocheport, Missouri, in surrounding towns such as Columbia and Booneville remember him only as "Hugo of Rocheport" or "Old Rocheport," but some of the older people in Rocheport remember that he was Hugo Diederich, a German ("Dutchman") with thick, stuttering accent, which they enjoy imitating.

The most common stories about Hugo seem to combine the speed and technical skill that would interest a barber with the railroad schedule that is interesting to railroad men. When Hugo came to Rocheport, he was already past his prime. He set up his shop in a part of town now largely deserted, right across the street from the railroad track. The engineer used to jump off the engine and get a shave from Hugo in time to catch the caboose when it came along. An older barber in Columbia said that this was possible because the train stopped five minutes in Rocheport to pick up passengers. A young barber had heard that the train just slowed down to pass through town and since it was a freight with as many as eighty or ninety cars there was still plenty of time for the engineer to catch the caboose. All the barbers believe their own version of this story and regard other versions with smiling doubt.

This engineer story, probably the widest known of all, is backed up by another train story. One day a man rushed into Hugo's shop five minutes before train time. Could Hugo give him a shave in such a short time? Hugo could. "But I don't like any pulling or scratching," the customer said.

"Mister," Hugo replied, "if I give you one scratch, you get another shave free before the train comes."

The barbers are all interested in the technical aspects of Hugo's skill. One said that he did not even put a towel on his customers, but threw the shaving mug at them as they walked into the shop and had them shaved before they opened their eyes—without a single whisker pulled, of course. Another says, however, that he made a great ritual of putting the towels on and seemed to take a great deal of time in preparing his customer, but that with five swipes of the razor he could have a man clean-shaven.

Hugo was born to be a barber. His endurance was amazing. When the crews were in town he shaved for twenty-four hours straight; and, if he had a lull, he did not sit down but stood honing and sharpening one of the 1,000 razors that he always had ready for use. He also was endowed with fingernails that did not grow out to the ends of his fingers, but were covered at the top with a thick layer of skin, so that in massaging his customers he could not possibly scratch them.

Hugo's skill was finally recognized internationally when he entered a competition at a world's fair and received a medal as the best straight-edge man in the entire world. The younger barbers say this was the New York World's Fair, an older man is certain that he got the medal in Chicago, but an old railroad man in Rocheport remembers that it was in St. Louis in 1904. According to the railroad man's own birth date, however, he would have been only six at the time and not in Rocheport at all.

Although everyone believes completely in Hugo, only one man is reported so far that really saw him in action. There was always another barber in town whose work, though much slower, was preferred by the permanent residents. But one day, when the regular man was extremely busy, a native went to Hugo's shop, which was then in the local hotel. Hugo went through an elaborate routine of preparing the lather and towelling the man. Then he took a razor and with one stroke shaved the whiskers off the entire right side of the customer's face. The resident leaped from the chair as Hugo turned to wipe his razor on the paper which he kept behind him.

"What's the matter," cried Hugo, "I will shave you quickly, I will shave you."

"I know you will," said the customer, "but if your razor slipped my head would fall off." And he threw down the towels and went across the street to be finished by the other barber.

THE TATTOO LADY OF THE BOWERY

I first met golden-haired Millie Hull on this street, under the Elevated in her musty, cluttered "Tattoo Emporium." She was tattooing a facsimile of Mickey Mouse on a young girl's thigh. I peeked through her storefront window intrigued by the dexterity with which she manipulated the needle. Finally, I entered the store. "You'll have to wait your turn," she said. She didn't look up.

"This gal has a lot of moxie." She pointed her thumb towards her pretty subject. "She wasn't even nervous. Her leg will be sore for a week, that's all. I did a beautiful job on her.

"She got tattooed on the thigh as you can see. Other gals get tattooed elsewhere. I won't tell you where. I do those jobs behind curtains. Most want Mickey Mouse. That's the rage now. Other gals want other things tattooed. Some of the things they ask for would open your eyes."

Millie's eyes took on a soft, faraway look. She reminisced "When I was this girl's age, I was like her, except I didn't go to school. I was a dancer in a 'hootchie kootchie' show. I drifted into this work pretty naturally. My boy friend was a tattoo specialist. When we had nothing better to do, he'd tattoo me.

"I had so many tattoos put on me that when I first tried my hand on the machine I took to it right away. I gave up my dancing career and stuck to this. I meet a lot of interesting people this way.

"I'm known as Queen of the Bowery. My people were just ordinary folks, not nobility or anything like that. I was born and raised right here on the Bowery. I really can't account for my special ability except that maybe art runs in my family. My two brothers are famous artists. Maybe you've seen some of their works. One is a quick sketch artist in Central Park. The other is a sand sculpturer in Atlantic City during the summer. As for myself," she modestly admitted, "I'm the most famous woman tattoo artist in the whole world.

"Tattooing is a hobby with a lot of people. The late King George of England had a British coat of arms tattooed on his chest. Most people come here on a dare. Once you have a tattoo put on you can never take it off. Not really.

"I have three hundred designs on my body," she said proudly. "I have room for plenty more. The American eagle is on my neck. I have fourteen angels on my back. The Madonna and the Baby are on my instep." She coyly lifted her dress, revealing dimpled knees. "Twelve Japanese geisha girls are tattooed on my legs. See?

"Last summer I wasn't able to go without stockings because of those geisha girls. (The war between China and Japan had recently started.) The Chinese around here might be offended. They are good fellows to do business with even though the only thing they ever get tattooed on them are the Chinese and American flags crossing each other.

"In my business, I do a lot of good for people. Just the other day, I tattooed hair on a bald man's head. In the dark, it looks almost like the real thing. I'm working on an invention, too. I'm trying to make a flesh colored ink so that I'll be able to tattoo birthmarks and scars off people."

She refilled the coffee cups, then continued.

"I thought you were a doctor when you first came in here smoking a pipe and all that. I get a lot of doctors in here, especially skin specialists who talk to me about the seven layers of epidermis —something or other on the arms and legs and three of the same stuff on the body; and about nerves and bones. I didn't ever learn any of that at a medical school like they did. I found that all out myself, from experience.

"You should see how some bellies twitch when I tattoo them, especially when I hit a nerve. If I didn't know how to handle these complications, it would interfere with my artistry.

"I don't know why, but like I told you, Mickey Mouse is my

most called for design among the girls right now. It takes only a few minutes for a job like you just saw me do. There are some four color jobs which take a month to do. Though I do most of my work from a stencil, I can do it freehand, too.

"People come to me from all over the country. They even come in on freight trains to have me tattoo them. I'm famous like the Mayo Brothers. They help people, too.

"The only people I won't work on are drunks. They're pretty tough to handle. They're always trying to make a pass at me or get a free feel. That's why my partner, Tommy Lee, hangs around. We've been together for twenty years. Tommy's a great guy. He's got three hundred and sixty-eight designs on him. There's no more room left on him. Not anywhere.

"Last year I had a tough job making him stay here with me. He wanted to go to the South Seas and get caught by a cannibal tribe. Some sailor who was in here convinced Tommy that the cannibals would make a God out of him because he has so many beautiful pictures on him.

"If you come around sometime when I'm not too busy," she offered, "I'll be glad to show you all my tattoos."

BIG MAX

The other day I had the pleasure of meeting an old lifetime friend of the family, "Big Max". Big Max, as he is called by his friends, is a medium-brown-skinned Negro, who is six feet five and one-half inches tall, and weighs two hundred and forty-five pounds. So you can easily see why he is called Big Max, and wherever he goes, it is not long before his name follows him.

Big Max is foreman for a big construction company in Cleveland, Ohio. On his vacation he decided to come and visit his old neighborhood, which incidentally is Jackson Addition. He came by the house to see his old friend and working buddy, my dad, and as the two were sitting around laughing and talking about old times, they told me some old stories about Big Max. My dad said that Big Max would run from home to work, and after work he would run home again. The strange thing about this was that the mine in which he worked (Osage) was ten miles away.

Big Max was as strong as a team of oxen. One time a motor car fell over on a man and pinned him from the waist down. Three or four men tried to lift the load off the man, but they couldn't do it. They were just about to send back for a bar so they could pry the weight off, when Big Max came by and lifted it himself, thus saving the man's life.

He could load more coal than six men, and it was thought that he was invincible. One day there was a terrible "cave in" in the mine. Everyone in the section was killed except Max, and when he was found, he had dug himself half-way out.

His stamina was unbelievable. He had a record (and still has) for staying in the mine; he would sometimes stay in the mine, day and night, for a week. His food was brought in to him. Some of the fellows actually thought of him as God of the mines.

When my dad asked him why he had quit the mining profession, he said, "Do you remember the bad explosion that closed off Section Number Five on the main run?"

My dad said that he did.

"Do you remember the story of the man who was never found, and how the mining officials were doing his wife and six children?"

Dad nodded, but I said, "Wait a minute! What about this story?"

Big Max turned to me. "All the men who were in Section Five were either killed or accounted for except one. He was never found. His time card wasn't punched 'in' or 'out'. The mine officials would not pay his wife the miner's welfare money because they thought he had deserted her. Well, anyway, I opened up the section and went in first to check and see if it was still hot. Now, when I say 'hot', I mean if it has a high content of combustible gases. Our main job was to set in new beams and clean up the sections so new track could be laid. After I had checked the place completely for the gas, I started helping the other men set beams.

"In one of the sub-sections was a bad place, and since none of the other fellows wanted to chance putting in the new beams, I said I would go ahead and set in the first one for them. I went back into this dark section and started to make preparations to put in the first beam, when one of the fellows came back to help. I said, 'So you are not afraid, after all?' and he said 'No'.

"It was then that I noticed that I had never seen him before. He did not look like a miner—at least, not like a well-nourished, healthy miner. His skin, even though it was covered with black, thick coal-dust, was milkish-white. His eyes were set deep in his head like deep wells. And, although he could do as much work as me, he was just a bag of bones.

"After we had put up the first beam I started cleaning a place for the second beam. The man who was helping me grabbed the shovel and said, 'Don't put that post there; put it here!' He said it real mad-like, so to keep down an argument, I started doing as I was told.

"I had cleaned about a foot of loose coal and slate when I hit something. It looked like a boot, like a man's boot. Just as I turned around to tell my friend that I had found the remains of a man, he disappeared. I didn't particularly think anything of it because I thought my eyes were playing tricks on me, since I hadn't been to bed in three days. And then, too, I thought he might have gotten scared, and gone back. Well, anyway, I reported the body to the authorities and went home.

"In the middle of the next night, I was sleeping soundly when I was awakened by a knock at the door. I went and opened it, and discovered it was the fellow at the mine who had been helping me. He said, 'Thank you for helping me. Now my wife will get what is coming to her.' He disappeared again. I got dressed and went immediately to the mine to see just who this fellow was that I had discovered. He was the man who had been missing. They could tell by his miner's tags. I left the mine and have never, and shall never set foot in a mine again."

WHY STUDENTS CALL PEDRO

The following versions of tales and explanations connected with the call "Pedro!" which is heard on the University of California campus at Berkeley, were collected by a class in folklore. . . . [One informant reports that] between 1938 and 1941, in the vicinity of Dana Street and Channing Way (south of the campus), the cry "Pedro!" was heard only at night, and usually between 11:00 and 12:00. It was definitely associated with examination weeks—midterms and more especially finals—and seemed to be a method of relaxation from studying. The reply to it, when started, was either "Pedro!" repeated or else "Shut up!"

1. Pedro was a student at the University of California. He had not studied all term, so when finals came he had to cram very hard. When the grades came out, and he discovered that he had gotten all A's, he dropped dead from the shock. Ever since that time students all yell "Pedro!" during finals, hoping that his ghost will come and help them through examinations.

2. Pedro used to go to "Cal." During exam week he suddenly walked out of his room one day. No one has seen him since. Therefore, people call him during exam week or midterms.

3. Pedro is a little man with a dog. If he answers when you call him, you'll pass your exam.

4. If you yell loud enough, Pedro will come down out of the hills and help you study for your finals. It usually requires a masculine voice.

5. There is an unknown being or thing, which when found will bring an A in a course from the professor to whom it is presented. Hence, students are always looking for it.

PERRY MARTIN'S MOONSHINE

Charlie Crawford is seventy-three and the retired town marshal of Rosedale, Mississippi, after fifty-three years of service. He has the distinction of having been the first person in town to see Perry Martin. On a hot summer afternoon in 1918, Crawford drove out to River Landing to see the *Kate Adams* come in. While he was waiting, the *Keen Kutter* put in, and off the boat stepped a small, lean man of about forty, carrying a Winchester rifle on his shoulder and a forty-five in his belt. "You take me to town?" the man asked Crawford. The lawman thought that he should and answered, "Yes." Driving to town, neither man spoke. When they reached Rosedale, some four or five miles from River Landing, Crawford took the man to the courthouse in the center of town. The stranger got out of Crawford's roadster, and Crawford started to leave. However, the stranger said, "Hey, where are you going? I thought the sheriff sent you to pick me up and take me in. I'm Perry Martin and I just killed five men over on the river. Would you take me to the sheriff's office?" Crawford led Martin to Sheriff Lacy's office and thus gained the unwanted reputation for having "brought in" Perry Martin. Lacy called the sheriff of Desha County, across the Mississippi River in Arkansas. Martin talked to the Arkansas sheriff, saying that he would have to complete some business matters before he could come in. They agreed to meet three days later in Arkansas City, the seat of Desha County, and both men kept the appointment. The men Martin had killed had attempted to steal some timber he had felled and was floating downriver to a mill. Martin was simply protecting his property.

In 1929, eleven years after this incident, Martin pulled his river club boat out of the water and set it on blocks in a cypress grove on the river side of the levee in Rosedale. He remained at that spot until his death on 9 September 1968, spending only one night away from his boat. That was in 1950 when Martin let his wife, Lou, buy a house on the Rosedale side of the levee. They spent the first night together in the new house, but Perry got sick and could not sleep. Thereafter, Perry slept on his boat while Lou stayed in her house. They maintained a genial marital relationship, however, and always took their meals together.

During the eleven years between 1918 and 1929, two important things happened to Perry Martin. He killed a man and had to serve a sentence in the Arkansas state penitentiary, and he quit the timber business for moonshining. Martin's term in the penitentiary was the ultimate result of Ed LaGrue's penning a hog which Perry claimed was his. When LaGrue refused to surrender the hog, Martin had him arraigned by a justice of the peace who secured the property for him. Martin got word that LaGrue had threatened to kill him on sight. Fortunately, though, he saw LaGrue first. Martin was on the east side of the White River where it flows into the Mississippi northwest of Rosedale. LaGrue stepped out of the woods on the west bank. Martin shot across the river at LaGrue, hitting him right between the eyes. A trial for manslaughter ended in Martin's conviction and a sentence of ten years in prison.

Martin served only a year. When he was released, his life took a new course. The son of a wealthy rice farmer, he had been educated for the ministry and was interested in Arkansas politics on both state and local levels. However, in 1920 he left the rice farm and a family of a wife and two children and settled on Big Island, Arkansas, an island of about 121,000 acres located about eight miles northwest of Rosedale. During the prohibition years Big Island was reportedly one of the biggest whiskey-producing areas in the United States. Its population consisted exclusively of fugitives from the law—particularly moonshiners. Earl Drury, a retired moonshiner and former constable of Rosedale, operated a still on Big Island at the same time as Perry Martin. He said that when sitting in front of his still, he could see an additional twenty-one stills in operation. I asked Drury if life was dangerous on Big Island. "No," he said. "On Big Island there was lots of law and order—more than there ever was or ever will be in Rosedale. If there was an argument, somebody got killed." According to Drury, the major figure in the enforcement of order was Perry Martin, who wore a deputy sheriff's badge from Desha County.

More important than Martin's role as a lawman among outlaws was the fact that he was the best among many good moonshiners. His still was acknowledged by his peers and lauded by his customers. An indication of the care with which Martin made moonshine came from an interview I had with a former moonshiner, himself known for having produced high quality corn whiskey. He told me he was running a very large still when Perry Martin came by and told him he was cooking it off too fast. The moonshiner tried to explain to Martin that the size of the still affected the rate of cooking. Martin said that still size did not matter; good whiskey had to be cooked off very slowly. Martin's moonshine gained him a national reputation. One informant told me, "People who weren't even whiskey drinkers drank P.M. when they could." I have been told that even today moonshine sold in New Orleans frequently carries the Perry Martin label, a label which used to signify the very best. When a Rosedale native made a purchase in a Pittsburgh drugstore recently, the proprietor recognized the accent and asked what part of the South he came from. Upon hearing the Mississippian's answer, the proprietor replied, "I know Rosedale well. I bought moonshine whiskey from Perry Martin and others there in Rosedale by the boxcar load during the depression." The range of the reputation and market of P.M. lasted many years after the depression era. Junebug Holloway, manager of a restaurant in Cleveland, Mississippi, said that while he was a soldier stationed near New York City in the 1940's, he found P.M. in all the higher class bars. Bolivar County Deputy Sheriff Sibley told me that in 1964 he had seen a sign over a bar in a tavern in northwest Chicago which read, "Perry Martin Special—35¢ a shot." Naturally the reputation of P.M. was greatest in the local community. Perry Martin's son reports that he has had escorts from the state police when he delivered kegs of P.M. to Jackson for governors' inaugural balls. Recently I visited a friend's new house in Cleveland, Mississippi, about fifteen miles east of Rosedale, and he bragged that an Old Hickory bottle in his den contained some of the very last Perry Martin moonshine. To my knowledge it is the only P.M. left. A man in Rosedale remembered P.M. as "so good and so strong it would make a little rabbit walk right up and spit in a bulldog's face." Perry Martin at ninety ran his last batch of moonshine in the summer of 1967, only a year before he suffered a fatal stroke. He was raided and fined, and his still was destroyed. He had made only one run on his new still, and in a moment of frustration he abandoned the craft which had made him famous.

There are four reasons given for the high quality of Perry Martin's moonshine. Firstly, he used the basic Kentucky recipe—one part corn to one part sugar, sometimes cutting the corn by as much as half by mixing in rye malt. Also he had the advantage of using water from the Mississippi. Secondly, Martin was always meticulous in regard to cleanliness and sanitation. People who saw his stills were impressed by the immaculate and brilliant sheen of the copper parts. Thirdly, Martin always cooked his product slowly and in small batches. Finally—and some say most important—Perry Martin's moonshine was rocked under willow trees by the ebb and flow of the Mississippi along its banks.

Reactions to Perry Martin by his admirers are of two varieties. The first was summarized well by Russ Quentin, manager of the Conservation League Restaurant at Beulah Lake which lies along the Mississippi just south of Rosedale. Quentin knew Perry Martin because of a friendship with a stepson of the moonshiner. Quentin told me, "I knew the roughest man in Rosedale—so rough didn't *nobody* mess with him. Well, this man wouldn't even mess with Perry Martin." This image of Perry Martin is supported by those who remember the men Martin killed. The number varies from seven to nine to eleven. I have verified only seven killings, one of which was that of Martin's own stepson. Mrs. Myron Martin, a daughter-in-law, who lives across the gravel road from the ruins of

Perry Martin's club boat, told me that she had never been near the location before she married: "These were Perry Martin's woods. Nobody came here that didn't have business here." To Mrs. Martin one of the most frightening things about her father-in-law was that one never heard him in the woods until he was face-to-face with him. Russ Quentin, however, tells of the time he was going through the woods looking for Martin's stepson and didn't come face-to-face with anyone. Instead, a gun barrel between the shoulder blades surprised him. When Quentin revealed the nature of his mission, he was given detailed directions for finding his friend but was advised not to turn around.

The other view of Martin stresses his popularity, generosity, and humor. It is said that Perry Martin entertained the most eminent Mississippi politicians on his club boat. His greatest popularity—surprisingly perhaps—has been among those who are responsible for local law enforcement. Martin was not unique among moonshiners in enjoying a good relationship with lawmen. I asked a retired moonshiner if he were ever bothered by lawmen. He replied, "Only trouble with local law was them drinking up my whiskey." Unlike most counties in Mississippi, Bolivar County has never offered a bounty for locating and destroying stills. The local lawman was viewed as a defender from the revenuer, a foreigner minding what was not his business. One Rosedale lawman told me, "We were all in moonshine then, either making, selling, or drinking it." Charles Crawford said, "Perry Martin had a reputation for being dangerous, but he was the most honest man I ever knew. He tended to his own business—let everybody else's alone." Crawford said he always tried to give Martin warning if he knew his still was going to be raided. When Crawford himself had to raid one of Martin's stills, the moonshiner again had adequate warning. Billy Joe Estes, Rosedale police chief during Martin's heyday, told me that Perry Martin was not bothered by the law because he was as good a man as he was a moonshiner. He ran his business on the river side of the levee; he stayed away from Rosedale except to get haircuts and to vote.

A natural question about Perry Martin is, "What happened to

the money he made?" The answer is, "He gave it away." In addition to his own family, he took in a girl deserted in a river boat, raised her, and sent her to college. He also took in a boy, who now lives in Rosedale, and raised him. He was a ready and effective host, happy to entertain customers and visitors. In addition to refreshments, Perry Martin served his guests humor. He liked to tell about the time he was raided by a bald-headed revenuer who turned up each broken bottle of moonshine and poured it on his head. The revenuer said he hoped it would make his hair grow. Martin said he knew better; the man just wanted the chance to drink what dripped past his outstretched tongue. Martin's favorite anecdote was one about Ned Filch. Ned loved the beer which formed in barrels of fermenting mash. He always carried a slop jar when he visited a still so that he could taste and test the beer. A revenuer surprised him drinking the beer and assumed that he was operating the still. The revenuer told Ned to raise his hands. Ned Filch finished his beer and smacked his lips. Then he turned to his assailant, respectfully saluted with his right index finger, and said: "Well, sir, if you kill me right now, you'll never kill me when I feel no better."

America has not produced mythic, epic heroes like England's Beowulf, Ireland's Cuchulainn, France's Roland, or Spain's Cid Compeador. Such heroes, whether they originate in the deeds of warrior kings from the early ages of European history, as one theory has it, or whether, in accord with the opposite theory, they arise from a race memory of archetypal figures, are not typical of what happened in America. The historical soil was too thin to grow a Beowulf, the racial elements too varied to form a national psyche, and besides, there has not been time enough. But most of all, the land is too big. Its spaciousness permits constant moving about and perpetual change.

Instead of traditional heroes who would engender national coherence and project national attitudes, countless local characters emerged. Though genuine folk personalities, they were known only to the people of a small geographical area. Early settlers who survived the hazards of the frontier and lived to tell about it and whose stories were fancied up in the retelling; backwoods judges who handed down extralegal decisions; farmers renowned for their pranks rather than their crops; eccentrics who wandered the countryside—they spoke in their rich and peculiar dialects for the diversity of the continent. Not always heroes exactly, they yet gave Americans a sense of local identity, pride in their individuality and in the immediate experiences and ways of doing things shared with neighbors. Localization prevented Americans from being overwhelmed by the immensity of the land by rooting them to a particular part of it.

In contrast, American national heroes, generally speaking, were created by the media of mass communications, for the birth of the nation took place in a literate age. George Washington may well have been first in war and first in peace, but he was not first in hearts of his countrymen until Parson Weems contrived the beloved tale of the cherry tree. The parson's purpose was only in part patriotic; he made his living by writing and peddling religious tracts and biographical booklets. Thus was the first President sold.

The media tend to smooth away differences and to fix the way tales are told, though at the same time they whet appetites for new faces and new styles. This contaminates the seedbed of folklore. But the media are responsive and inventive, and it is hard to argue that they have not given Americans, or at least fed back, the kinds of heroes Americans wanted. The process took a while to develop. It helped to make Davy Crockett, whose genuine exploits contain the stuff of legend, into a massively popular figure. Today there appear to be categories of heroes that simply could not have come into being without the media. Could Elvis Presley have existed as a national hero without them?

The play-off between folkloristic local characters and the national figures, generated by the media, who represent national aspirations and attitudes has a democratic fitness about it. It suggests that while Americans lack the tradition that the presence of a mythic hero like Beowulf would indicate, they are challenged to exact affirmative qualities from both the individualism of the local character and the socializing influence of the mass-culture hero.

THE CHARACTER OF STRAP BUCKNER

Strap Buckner when a youth came to Texas as one of the "original three hundred colonists." His origin no one knows, and his name "Strap" is unexplained, unless his giant stature is its explanation. He possessed the strength of ten lions, he had heavy hair as red as a flame, and he had freckles. Like many giants he was good-humored, but he had in his strength a pride that gradually became insufferable.

To give expression to this strength and pride, Strap good-naturedly went about knocking men down. If, perchance, he injured his victims, he carried them to his cabin and nursed them back to health—so that he might knock them down again. He knocked down Austin's whole Colony at least three times, including Austin himself. It is said that he had a "genius" within him, and the "genius" was to knock men down.

Strap and the Black Bull

In the early days of the Austin Colony, a black bull, known as Noche [Night], mysteriously came and went, causing fear whenever he appeared and anxiety as to his return whenever he left. Strap, exercising his "genius" in a new way, challenged the bull to single-handed combat. Noche accepted the challenge. On the appointed day, the entire colony looked fearfully out from its windows wondering what would happen when Strap and Noche came together. With a red blanket tossed over his shoulder and with no weapons, Strap strode on to the prairie where Noche twisted his tail, pawed the earth, and bellowed mightily.

Strap, by way of imitation, pawed and roared also. Noche

disliked the gesture of mockery and came at Strap "like a thunder-bolt clothed in tempest and terror." Strap held his own ground and met Noche with a resounding blow on his frontlet. Blood spurted from Noche's flaming nostrils, and Noche himself turned tail and fled, bellowing. Never more was Noche seen in the Colony!

Furthermore, as a great and successful hunter, Strap with no weapon other than his bare fist and an iron pestle, which he threw with deadly accuracy, obtained any game he attempted. Consequently, the wild cat, the bear, and the buffalo moved out of that region.

Strap and the Indians

After many adventures Strap arrived at the trading-post presided over by Bob Turket and Bill Smotherall, who exchanged beads, trinkets, and liquor with the Indians for skins and furs and horses. As Strap liked the country and the liquor, he proceeded to build himself a cabin in the cedar brake and settle down. On the first day, his "genius" impelled him to knock down Bob Turket and Bill Smotherall, but they recognized his great "genius" and took his blows kindly. Within a week he had knocked down all the Indian warriors within a radius of ten miles. They also revered his "genius," and instead of scalping him praised him highly. They named him Kokulblothetopoff, meaning the Red Son of Blue Thunder; and the king gave him the swiftest horse in the world, a grey bob-tailed nag. The king also offered in marriage to Strap the princess Tulipita; but Strap, with the wisdom that Samson did not have, refused to have his powers weakened by a woman. Of course Tulipita pined away in silent grief.

Strap loved this free new life where the jug was ever ready to quench his thirst and the Indians were ever ready to accommodate his "genius." But gradually the Indians wearied of Strap's friendly blows; and one dark night they stole away, never to return to his immediate neighborhood.

Strap Fights the Devil

In the morning, when Strap could not find his Indian friends, he mourned much as he had when he left San Felipe: "Other friends have left me before. Such is the common penalty of greatness." After weeping and fasting for two days, Strap reached for the jug—it was empty. He called his grey bob-tailed nag, mounted with jug held aloft in one hand, and rode away to the trading-post, his long red hair streaming behind him. On the way he found twenty-two Indian braves in the midst of a revelry under an oak tree. Sweetly he smiled, benignantly he laughed and dismounted—and knocked them down. At the trading post he knocked down Bob Turket and Bill Smotherall. By this time his eye was sparkling, his cheeks were flushed, and his hands were alive with desire. He drank a quart of liquor from his replenished jug, and his "genius" became vastly inspired. Having knocked down all living things, Strap began on the inanimate and knocked into a hundred pieces a clock fashioned in the shape of a portly knight. Finally, he so far forgot himself and the dignity of his "genius" as to hop up on the counter, flap his arms as a rooster flaps his wings, and crow in triumph.

A new spirit of defiance that eventually proved his downfall moved him. He called himself the champion of the world, defied all that lived, and then three times challenged the Devil. At once a deep rumbling and roaring came from the earth. The rumbling was Noche's answer to the challenge. Noche had not forgotten his defeat. Strap rode away to meet the issue. As he left the trembling Bob Turket and Bill Smotherall, a red monkey swung up unseen behind him; and when Strap dismounted, he noticed scratches and bloody marks on the horse's haunches, but he did not know their cause.

Night came on, and with it a violent storm that shook Strap's cabin with threats of destruction. But Strap barred windows and doors and calmly prepared his supper of bacon and hoe-cake. As he was saying grace to the inventor of delicious bacon and brown hoe-cake, an unusual blast of wind blew open one of his windows;

and Strap looked up to encounter two flaming eyes glaring at him through the opened window. Strap addressed the creature as Ocelot, wild cat, and followed his insults with a stone that missed its mark. The fiery eyes continued to stare. Next he hurled his iron pestle, but it hit only the window-sill and buried itself half through the oaken barrier. The eyes and their owner disappeared; Strap barred the window more tightly than before and went on with his supper.

Suddenly a blinding sheet of lightning and the simultaneous crash of thunder startled Strap into violent expression. When he recovered from his alarm, he saw in the middle of his floor, a black figure, with a thin face and eagle-like nose, two red horns on its head, cloven feet, and fiery eyes. Its visage expressed unspeakable mischief and villainy. By way of introduction it thumbed its nose at Strap in derision. Next it drew from behind, its long tail ending in a sharpened point, and threw it upon Strap's knee. Strap, surprised and disgusted, knocked off the tail and told his strange guest to keep his tail to himself.

The figure answered only, "Skin for skin," and tossed his tail toward the fire-place, where it caught in the mantel-piece. Strap impatiently demanded more information, and the creature answered that he had come in reply to Strap's challenges to the Devil, and that he would meet Strap in mortal combat at nine o'clock the following morning. Then he departed through the key-hole, leaving behind him a nauseating odor of brimstone.

Strap spent some time in meditation that evening; and, having put himself in the mood of calm philosophy, he went to bed and to sound sleep.

At nine o'clock the next morning the Devil appeared in the form of a skinny, ugly dwarf dancing a jig. He politely saluted Strap as a man of honor and of his word; and then together they went out into the raging storm. In the glare of an especially vivid flash of lightning the dwarf disappeared, and in his place appeared a long black cat that mewed as it trotted by Strap's side. And then in succession, as the lightning flashed and the thunder roared, the Devil changed his form from cat to sky terrier, to black bear, to the black bull Noche, and to the black imp.

Side by side these two strange kings climbed to a knoll covered by oaks. The Devil suddenly began to expand until he was one hundred and ninety feet tall and eighty feet around, with his tail increased in proportion. As he tossed his tail into the air, it caught in a black cloud and stuck there. Strap naturally objected to this latest transformation of the Devil and complained aloud of the discrepancy in their statures and might. The Devil agreed, therefore, to reduce to normal size if Strap would throw away his iron pestle. Obligingly Strap discarded his one weapon. Quickly the Devil shrank, all except his tail, which was still lodged in the black cloud.

The contest began in the likeness of a boxing affray, but suddenly the black cloud moved on, carrying the Devil's tail farther away and causing the infernal imp much pain. Strap, always the gentleman, instead of taking advantage of the situation to crush the Devil forever, volunteered to climb up and unhitch the tail. But the Devil merely rolled himself up in the coil of his tail until he reached the cloud; then, having loosened his appendage, he jumped back to meet Strap at the place of combat.

All day the battle raged, with varying fortunes until the Devil finally overcame Strap by assuming a monstrous size that gave him the advantage. Bob Turket and Bill Smotherall, with forty Indian braves, stood on the river bank and listened to the hideous sounds of battle. As night descended, they saw a great grey horse riding through the air carrying a red monkey and the limp form of a man.

The next morning, the two traders and one thousand Indian braves went to Strap's cabin, which they found closed and deserted. They went on until they came to the place of battle, a place which showed evidences of the terrific conflict, and which from that time has remained barren and bleak.

The Return of Strap Buckner

It was three months after his defeat by the Devil that Strap returned on his swift grey bob-tailed nag, appearing unexpectedly at the trading post while Bob Turket and Bill Smotherall were counting skins. His face bore a sad, far-away look; and his only words were "Skin for skin."

In fear the traders told him that he might have all their skins if he would only depart. He answered only, "Skin for skin," and went sadly to his cabin in the cedars. There he remained for three months. Three times a week he visited the trading house, where he wandered sadly about, uttering only the words "Skin for skin." He drank no whiskey. His "genius" had departed from him; and yet the traders and Indians were more afraid of him than ever; he bore the marks of another-world experience. The Medicine Man invariably sounded his big bongooree after Strap had passed by.

One night, at the end of three months, Bob Turket and Bill Smotherall and ninety Indian braves saw a blue flame across the valley in the direction of Strap's cabin. Out of the blue flame there arose a grey horse carrying on his back a gigantic man waving an iron pestle over the cowering form of a red monkey. In the morning the two traders and eleven hundred Indian warriors marched across the river to Strap's land. There they found the ashes of his cabin. In solemn circle they wept over the sad ending of Strap Buckner, and the Medicine Man sounded his big bongooree.

Strap Meets His Match

Many years ago a strange man, easily identified as Strap Buckner, built a cabin on the headwaters of one of the ravines running into Little River northeast of Taylor. He was a bully who took particular delight in driving off other trappers. Whenever there was a fur buyer or trader in the neighborhood, Strap appeared on the scene to "boss" proceedings and to pick a scrap if possible. Usually he was victor in these encounters. On one occasion, when several buyers, traders, and settlers had assembled, some man told of a swarm of bees which he had seen in a split between the branches of a large pecan tree on the banks of Little River.

Strap Buckner immediately led a party of several men, one of whom was named Robinson, to the tree, which he proposed to climb in order to get the honey. In climbing, Strap made so much noise that he aroused the bees. Infuriated, they swarmed about him. Strap's easily inflamed temper flared into action. Locking his legs around the trunk and holding to a limb of the tree with his left hand, he struck out furiously with his right hand and hit the fork of the tree so hard that one-half of it crashed to the ground. Buckner continued to battle with the bees until his eyes were swelled shut. Then he dropped fifty feet to the ground and was given first aid by the men who had accompanied him. Strap soon recovered, but he vowed vengeance on any bees that should thereafter be found in his region.

One spring day Strap Buckner was riding along on his famous pitching horse en route to a small trading post near Pflugerville, on the headwaters of Brushy Creek. Suddenly, as he came over the crest of a limestone ridge, he rode into the midst of a swarm of bees looking for a new home. The bees at once began to light on Buckner and his horse; and the battle lasted all the way from the trading post to Walnut Creek, where the horse became so maddened that he threw Strap from his back. After hours of fighting, Strap drove off the bees. Blinded from the stings, he made his way to the creek, where he spent three days in soaking his eyes to relieve the pain and to restore his sight.

Now, Strap Buckner announced when he went into the Little River country that he would allow no one to settle in his territory. One day he heard that a family had "located" a homestead in the region and was planning to put in a field. At once Strap went off to oust the settler. When he arrived at the enclosure around the house, he dismounted, kicked down the gate, and stalked around the house to the back. There he found the settler, a man taller and stronger than himself, busily engaged in removing honey from the gum made from a hollow log. The bees were not pleased with the proceedings, but the settler knew his bees and refused to allow them to get the upper hand. Strap stopped in amazement. Then he held out his hand to the settler and said: "Howdy, stranger, shake. If you can handle those bugs, you're a better man than Strap Buckner."

JUDGE BEAN SERVES AS CORONER

This incident actually occurred in 1882, when the Galveston, Harrisburg and San Antonio, more generally known as the Southern Pacific railroad, was building west from San Antonio to El Paso. The building of that road in the exceedingly rough, canyon-cut country west of Del Rio called for great engineering skill. When the Pecos river was reached, it was spanned by a great cantilever bridge, 320 feet above the river bed. There were draws and canyons to cross, cuts and fills to make, and the construction of the road proved to be very expensive. A Philadelphia bridge company had the contract to put in all steel bridges, while another company erected the falseworks.

One day while the bridge carpenters were erecting the falsework for an iron span across a deep, rocky canyon, the structure fell. Seven men were killed outright, and three were injured fatally.

It was thirty miles over to Langtry, where Roy Bean was justice of the peace and saloon keeper. As the nearest coroner, he was summoned to hold an inquest. Mounted on a mule, he hastened to the scene of the accident. When he arrived, he found the seven dead men laid out side by side on the bottom of the canyon, and alongside the corpses lay the three injured men, so near to death that they were scarcely breathing.

Bean immediately selected a jury from the crew of workmen, and, calling them together, viewed the ten silent figures lying in the blistering sun of the hot afternoon. Then he proceeded to examine the bridge timbers, remarking on the size and length of the heavy beams.

Approaching the corpses once more, he examined each one, and remarked, "No doubt but that this man came to his death by them big timbers falling on him." When he came to the dying men, he made the same remark.

At this, one of the jurymen called Bean's attention to the fact that the last three men in the row were not dead.

Bean silenced him. "Say, you gander-eyed galoot," he said, "who's running this hyar inquest? Don't you see them three fellers is bound to die? Do you think I am damn fool enough to ride thirty miles on a sore-backed mule again to hold another inquest? Officially and legally them fellers is dead, and so I pronounce them dead, every mother's son of 'em, and you will accordingly render your verdict that they came to their deaths by them big bridge timbers a-falling on 'em."

The last of the injured men did not die for three days.

"BIG SHOT" BILL GREENFIELD, ADIRONDACK MÜNCHAUSEN

It has been frequently affirmed in that locality that Bill Greenfield had owned a dog that was so smart that it could teach school and that he had possessed some turkeys that were so tall that they could pick beechnuts off trees. In true *Baron Münchausen* tradition Bill had experienced the misfortune of having his best hunting dog split in two by a sapling while chasing a rabbit at full speed. Bill had hastily picked up the two sections of the dog and had slapped them together so quickly that two legs went up while the other two went down. After that, Bill's dog was obliged to chase rabbits by running along on two feet until he tired. Then, without lessening his speed, he flopped over on the other two feet and kept right on going. . . .

Walter Edwards supplied other tales, however, of which I was not so familiar. As I adjusted my spectacles before jotting down a few notes, Mr. Edwards asked me if I had heard about Bill's famous glasses. No? Well, it seems that Bill Greenfield had pretty good eyes but whenever he found himself in very dark places, he had a special pair of glasses to put on. These glasses were so powerful that with them he could see into a rock ten feet thick.

Cold Winter

Winters were generally pretty severe in that Adirondack community. It was so cold around Tenantville one winter that when the Greenfields had to go out to the barn to look after the stock they got chilled through and through. So when they got back to the house and were before the blazing fireplace again, Bill said to his father, Abner, "Pa, I'm sick of this cold." And sure enough, before Abner could reach his son, Bill had vomited an icicle ten feet long.

Swapping Work

"Big Shot" Bill had been particularly remembered as the best checker player in the neighboring counties of Saratoga, Fulton and Hamilton. He carefully guarded two sets of checkers with which he often played with anyone who did not mind taking a beating. One set of checkers consisted of $5 gold pieces and the other set of $10 gold pieces. . . .

Swapping chores was also in keeping with local tradition because neighbors were few and help was scarce. One of Greenfield's neighbors asked Bill to assist him on his farm for a week. In return for the favor the friend was expected to work for Greenfield during the following week. Bill kept his word by faithfully hoeing the garden and raking the hay. The next Monday morning the neighbor arrived at Bill's humble dwelling and was ready and willing to do his share. Greenfield called him into the house, fetched out the checker board and gold pieces, seated his friend in a chair across the table, and started his favorite game.

They played checkers all morning. At noon Greenfield got together a lunch of sorts. But as soon as the table had been cleared, Bill set up the checkers again and went "to work" at it. The game continued until supper time. After supper was cleared they played checkers until bed-time. Throughout the entire week the same routine was followed. When consulted about it later, Bill's neighbor claimed that he had never worked so hard in his life.

It was Mr. Tenant who recalled that Bill Greenfield's house-furnishings consisted mainly of the table and chairs arranged for the convenience of eating and for playing checkers. There had also been a useful stove and a sturdy bed. The principal room, however, was amply festooned with chicken wishbones that had been strung up in all conceivable places. Bill often boasted that he had eaten every one of the chickens from which the wishbones had come.

EEL OLIVE'S FALL FROM GRACE

One of Eel Olive's pranks is said to have occurred at Middle Creek Baptist Church about 15 miles south of Raleigh [North Carolina].

One day when Eel arrived at the church he proclaimed that he had "religion in his bones" and that day he would take the great step. After three or four sermons, each lasting about an hour, the pastor announced that Eel Olive was prepared to tell the experience which had led him to desire to unite with the church.

In a very solemn mood, Eel went forward and faced the congregation. He talked in a very soft voice.

"Brethren and sistren, last night as I lay on my bed I had a most unusual dream. I dreamt that the pearly gates of Heaven were thrown wide open before my eyes, and there sat God on his white throne inviting me to come up and join Him. A long ladder was placed at the foot of my bed, reaching all the way up to Heaven. I accepted God's invitation and started up the ladder. The steps seemed farther apart the farther up I went. I managed to get along all right until I reached the last step. When I tried to take the last step my foot slipped—." Here he paused. Then in a clear, loud voice he said, "I took the damndest fall I ever took in my life!"

NICK THE FIDDLER

In a lowly grave in the old Arsenal Street Cemetery lie the ashes of one of the greatest violinists that the world has ever known—Nick Goodall. Proclaimed by musicians of his day to be a genius, his fame would have become as great as that of Paganini or Ole Bull, had it not been for a queer twist in his brain. Instead of gathering riches with his magic bow, he ended his days in the Jefferson County Almshouse.

One of the best-known stories about Nick is the one entitled "the sacred concert." One of the village pastors had induced Nick to play at a church concert, with the warning that he must not play anything but sacred tunes. When the time came for Nick to play, as usual he had decided not to perform. Everyone had become very restless, and suddenly he raised his violin and began to play "The Girl I Left Behind Me," "Pop Goes the Weasel," and other secular melodies, greatly to the consternation of the staid church people. The pastor accompanied Nick to the main auditorium of the church. The change in environment changed Nick's playing completely. This time his violin began to breathe the songs of birds. The church people soon became entranced with the beautiful music. . . .

Ole Bull, the famous Scandinavian violinist, was once playing in Elmira where Nick was then living. He was told of the wonderful genius of the eccentric violinist, and a meeting was brought about. Bull seated himself in the empty theatre, while Goodall sat on the stage, silently gazing into space. Bull was impatient to get back to his hotel and was about to leave when Nick drew his magic bow across the strings. Nick buried himself in his playing and forgot that he was performing before the world's greatest violinist. For three hours Bull sat there entranced with the melody of the fiddler. "The man's a genius!" he exclaimed. . . .

After this incident, "Jack Nichols," a young man interested in theatrical affairs, conceived the idea of starring Goodall as he appeared in everyday life. Goodall consented to the scheme and opened in Troy to a packed house. All went well for a time, and Goodall played as he had never played before, holding the audience spellbound. After two hours of music, the manager wanted to close the concert, but Goodall wouldn't have it that way. He had been hired to play, and play he would. His audience left by twos and threes, and none was left but the night watchman, who soon fell asleep. All night long the strains of music sounded through the empty auditorium, and when daylight came, Nick tucked his fiddle under his arm and set out over the hills for Elmira. His starring tour lasted but one night.

He was a genius in many ways. He could play one piece on a piano with one hand, another with the other hand, and whistle or sing a third.

THE LEATHER MAN

. . . Tramps were so common that they aroused no curiosity in the villages through which they passed. Nor did they leave any imprint upon the life of those days.

But there was one vagabond who did arouse curiosity and interest because of his unusual costume, the regularity of his appearance at the same houses, and the fact that he never spoke to anyone. Known only as "The Leather Man" because he wore a leather cap and a heavy suit made by hand out of small patches of leather and carried a bag also made of leather in which he carried a few handmade tools, odd pieces of leather, and old boot-tops, he tramped through Westchester and Putnam counties in New York, and through western Connecticut in the years 1858–1889. The Hudson and Connecticut rivers were his borders. He was not a peddlar, nor an ordinary tramp. He offered nothing for sale, and slept in caves or rock shelters, not in barns or meadows. People became so interested in this character that they kept records of the dates upon which he appeared, and we know from these accounts that he would appear at the same time of day every thirty-four days at the same house. He never knocked upon a door nor rang a doorbell, but simply approached a door, and stood there until he was noticed and food was handed him. He would then nod his head in thanks, give a grunt, and depart. Sometimes he would sit in the yard to eat this food. Sometimes he would take it away to eat later on in one of his rock shelters. Just one instance is recorded where he is known to have entered a house to eat a bowl of bread and milk. This was at the James Moriarity place in Wilton, Connecticut, and occurred only a short time before "The Leather Man" died, when he was becoming weak and regular walking was hard for him.

For overnight stops "The Leather Man" had a series of shelters, approximately ten miles apart. These shelters he kept neat, leaving them in readiness for his next visit. A few empty tin cans were left in all of them for cooking supper and breakfast. Upon his departure in the morning, "The Leather Man" always cleaned out these cans, tipping them upside down onto wooden sticks which he placed in the ground. Dry firewood was always left by "The Leather Man" in these shelters in readiness for his next stop there. On cold nights he would make a small fire upon a flat rock; then, when the rock was heated through, would sweep out the coals, and lie down upon the rock. Evergreen branches, held in place by strong pieces of wood, were his mattress, probably placed around the warm stone. In front of the shelters, it was his custom to prop up poles or tree branches (sometimes railroad ties), and, because of this, the shelters are sometimes referred to as "huts." . . .

The above facts about the housekeeping of "The Leather Man" were discovered by small boys of those years when he was wandering around New York and Connecticut. They were naturally curious about anyone whose mode of life was so out of the ordinary, and they investigated his shelters when he was not in them. One of these small boys, now a gentleman ninety-one years old, tells me that a group of boys of his acquaintance, armed with guns, once surprised "The Leather Man" in a shelter, and tried to frighten him into talking, but were unsuccessful. The writer's father, as a boy, went to a shelter on Good Hill, near Woodbury, Connecticut, when "The Leather Man" was there. He did not drive away the boys, but, according to what I was told, "did not make us welcome." . . .

[The] name of "Jules Bourglay" has been associated with "The Leather Man," rightly or wrongly, for many years. . . . A legend has come down to this day that "The Leather Man" fell in love with a French girl by the name of Marguerite Laron, whose father was a wealthy leather manufacturer in Lyons, and who frowned upon this marriage because Jules Bourglay was of too low a social level. He was finally persuaded to take the young man into his firm to see if he would amount to something. Evidently the young man advanced quickly, and was allowed charge of the firm's funds. Wanting to make good quickly, he speculated with these funds, was caught in a drop in the leather market, and ruined the firm completely. So incensed was Laron at this turn of events that he not only forbade the marriage, but banished Jules Bourglay from France. This affected the young man's mind, and he is said to have been confined to some mental institution for two years, then to have escaped and come to New York. Another legend is that "The Leather Man" was a murderer doing penance for his crime. Still another tale is that he was a veteran of the Napoleonic Wars. Still another states he was one of a band of Negro robbers never caught after a burglary in Connecticut. All of these stories need to be taken with the proverbial "grain of salt", being told and re-told by so many people over so many years. None of them has a basis in fact that can be proved. The story of "The Leather Man" is part of our folklore.

. . . Boy and Girl Scout troops are taken each year on hikes to "Leather Man" caves, and his story is told, and elaborated upon, around many a Scout campfire. Many a school composition has been written about him. The novelist, Lawrence Treat, has done a mystery story on this subject entitled *The Leather Man*. Local libraries in New York and Connecticut along his old route usually have a "Leather Man" file of newspaper clippings about him. During the years he wandered about in his methodical manner, "The Leather Man" posed for several photographs by professional photographers who probably waited for him at some of his regular stopping places. The New Haven *Register* once had a picture made for the paper's use, and ran it as late as November 24, 1918. One of these photographs was reproduced on postal cards, and widely sold locally, but these are out of print now. Many people bought one for their family albums.

Death came to "The Leather Man" in March, 1889, alone in one of his rock shelters near Briarcliff, New York, on the farm of the late George Dell. . . . After a coroner's inquest had proved that the death came from natural reasons, he was buried in a pauper's grave of Sparta Cemetery on the present Route 9 between Briarcliff and Ossining. The grave was marked by only an iron pipe stuck into the ground. The leather suit was on exhibit for a time afterward in the Eden Musée in New York City. His leather bag was sent to Hartford, and is still there in possession of the Connecticut Historical Society, though not on exhibit at present.

Who Was the Leather Man?

His Itinerary

Eighteen eighty-five seems to mark the date when the late Mr. Chauncey L. Hotchkiss of Forrestville, Connecticut, first made known the results of his research on the Leather Man's itinerant regularities. Two or three years before, his attention had been caught by the realization that, for a notably long period, the strange fellow had appeared for his meal at the I. W. Beach home in Forrestville exactly every thirty-fourth day at two o'clock in the afternoon. Determined to discover where he came from, where he went and if his habits were equally regular throughout his journey, Mr. Hotchkiss traced the Leather Man from town to town until he had chained him into a definite circle of systematic halts.

Based on information thus compiled, the front page of the Hartford *Globe* for July 12, 1885 carried a time table chart of the Leather Man's course, which other Connecticut newspapers outlined carefully in articles published around the same time. Why this schedule was not publicized even more widely is odd, for who, knowing the funny old character, would not have been interested to read how he trudged over at least three hundred and sixty-six miles every thirty-four days, year in and year out? This mileage included digressions made to reach hideouts—often some distance from the direct line of march. Approximately calculated, twenty-two days were spent in Connecticut and represented about two hundred and forty miles; the remaining twelve days were used to cover about one hundred and twenty miles in New York State.

Briefly outlining the route indicated by Mr. Hotchkiss, the Leather Man entered Connecticut at Balls Pond, some seven miles north of Danbury and directly opposite Putnam Lake in New York. Going west [northeast?] to New Milford, he changed his direction, passed through towns to the east until he reached Waterbury, where he headed north for Harwinton. From here, taking a zig zag course southeast to Haddam on the Connecticut River, he followed the towns along the River to Long Island Sound (or Saybrook) and started west. Except to detour widely around New Haven and skirt Bridgeport, he went from town to town along the shore, as far as Norwalk. Here, he turned northwest, heading for New York State by way of New Canaan and Wilton. Taking the Leather Man across the State line apparently somewhere south of Ridgefield, Mr. Hotchkiss found him immediately in Purdys; then Kensico Village (now buried under the southern end of Kensico Reservoir); back at Croton Falls, Doanesville, the southeastern part of Brewster, southeastern Peekskill, Yorktown, Shrub Oak and, again, at Balls Pond. Mr. Hotchkiss stated that if anything happened to delay the Leather Man along his way, he cut short his New York trip in order to re-enter Connecitcut on schedule.

His Youth

As for the tales of his youth, they range from "it was whispered he was a favorite officer in the last Napoleon court but was banished for a military error in the Crimean War," to two quite different stories apparently emanating from a single person, the aged Frenchman in Bridgeport, more definitely designated by some as Jules Martins.

One of these is substantially the same as the commonly accepted story in theme but differs in certain details. As recounted by the *Highland Democrat*, presumably early in 1889, it tells "that Bourglay, when a young man, was connected with a large mercantile establishment in an interior city of France, and that he advanced rapidly in the business there, showing such remarkable aptitude and capabilities that he finally assumed the charge of his employer's extensive interests, the latter retiring from active labor. About this time Bourglay became engaged to the young, beautiful and accomplished daughter of his employer, and the preparations for the wedding were already well advanced when a financial crash came that swept away his employer's capital and separated Jules from his loved one."

The second, although claiming to be the story "commonly accepted," is rather unique. Related in *The New York Times*, March 26, 1889, as coming partly from "words told a Yale professor who got him to talk," it reads: "When a young man he fell in love with a girl employed in a leather manufactory near Marseilles and owned by his father. The father opposed the match. The girl rejected the proposals of a dishonorable alliance with the son made by the parents. The girl disappeared. The young man became convinced there had been foul play and eventually that the girl had been murdered through the machinations of his parents. He then left home and his country and never let his friends hear from him. Frequent publications of his regular route and punctual appearance at designated points came to the attention of his brothers. His identity was absolutely established. He would not quit his vagrant life that he followed so persistently as a sort of expiation for the crime he believed his father had [committed] or had someone else comit."

Was the Leather Man's identity "absolutely established"? If so, when, where and how was it done? To be sure, none of the sources from which the newspapers claimed their information are improbable. Yet they do have a hollow ring and one is inclined to believe they were repeated largely from hearsay.

His Death and After

Shortly before his death, newspapers carried a story concerning an aged Frenchman named Jules Martins who appeared in Bridgeport, Connecticut. He had come directly from France hoping to determine that the Leather Man was Jules Bourglay, for whose discovery and return to France he would receive a ten thousand dollar reward. Jules Bourglay's father had died, Jules Martins said, leaving fifty thousand dollars which had been a public charge ever since, and it was hoped Bourglay could be persuaded to return and take possession of the fortune. Washington Bridge near Bridgeport was the point selected by Jules Martins to intercept the Leather Man. If, as some say, the two met, it appears odd that no account of the meeting followed, for the outcome of the event was awaited with much interest and anything spotlighting the Leather Man in 1889 was valuable, general news. The adverse opinion, that Jules Martins waited in vain at the bridge because the Leather Man had died in the meantime, seems more likely. . . .

Needless to say, the Leather Man's death and the inquest were thoroughly covered by the usual run of newspapers and a few more besides. The suspicion of murder, adequately played up, resulted in establishing a belief that the Leather Man's so-called fortune had been buried in the leather bag near one of his hideouts. Subsequently, a feverish hunt for the treasure began. Great numbers of strange people came to the Dell farm, it is said, to search the woods in the vicinity of the hut with enthusiastic thoroughness. Probably several other hideouts were searched likewise. But no one found anything.

One incident in this regard was widely written up around the first of April and dealt with the Saw Mill Woods cave near Shrub Oak. In the *New York Daily News,* under the headline "Saw the Leather Man's Ghost," the story ran: "Last night after Farmer Clematis Sorrel had finished his day's work he started, with a lighted torch in his hand, for the big Saw Mill Woods in quest of treasure. Soon after midnight the farmer returned to his family and related a story of his narrow escape from the clutches of the Leather Man's ghost. He said that while he was making his way out of the cave his torch was extinguished. Having no matches, he endeavored to get out without a light. He was soon confronted by the Leather Man, who lit a pile of dry sticks and beckoned to Sorrel to leave at once, which he did with all possible rapidity, running all the way home . . . Mr. Sorrel is not a drinking man. He thinks the Leather Man has a double, or he has seen his ghost . . ." Farmer Clematis Sorrel seems to have been Clemence Sarles, known locally as a lover of tall tales and quaint pranks.

"COXEY" BIVENS LIVED IN A CAVE

No one in the vicinity of Narrowsburg, New York, was ever exactly sure why "Coxey" Bivens went to live in a cave on the shore of the Delaware River, when he could have lived in a comfortable house. His father was killed on the Erie Railroad, and soon after his mother died. And without his parents, it could have been that "Coxey" preferred to be near his beloved river.

The "cave" he selected as his abode was not a real cave but more like a huge over-hanging rock which faced the broad expanse of the Upper Eddy. It was located upstream, a short distance from the Big Eddy, the widest, narrowest and deepest part of the Delaware River above tide. Paradoxically, the river narrows down to 250 feet, then widens out to about three quarters of a mile and there reaches its greatest depth, about 106 feet. The Delaware here is said to afford the best bass and pickerel fishing in the east. It is also a good place for "set lines."

"Coxey" was a "river rat," a local name for river guide. Wealthy fishermen would come to these parts, and "Coxey" would guide them, show them where the "biggest" ones were biting, row the boat, and perform other duties. They paid well and, for a good catch, gave liberal tips. Sometimes they had a bottle with them! At the end of the fishing trip, they would proceed to the nearby tavern. The sportsmen always bought the drinks. The man behind the bar knew "Coxey's" brand as he was a frequent visitor.

Along the sandy shores of the river, "Coxey" could gather bait, such as helgramites, the larva of the dobson fly, and lamprey eels, excellent for catching bass. Fishermen would pay a few cents each for their bait, so this, along with his income for an occasional day's work as a handy man and, of course, Coxey's river work provided his income. . . .

It has been said that Tom Quick, the Delaware Valley Indian slayer, used to stand on the roof of the cave and shoot Indians as they passed in their canoes. There is, however, no historical evidence to substantiate this local legend. In the past few years, an indigent family made their residence in the cave but were soon rescued by the Welfare Department.

"Coxey" often put out "set lines," a long fish line which is anchored in the stream and his many short lines, with baited hooks, attached to it. The purpose is to entice the fish to bite— and then get hooked. These lines had to be looked after at least once each day or night. According to one story about "Coxey," he and a companion were placing a "set line" one night. They had an oil lantern on the bow of the boat, and somehow, the set line became entangled and the lighted lantern was dropped into the water. The next night, when "Coxey" was looking after the line, he pulled it up—and lo and behold—up came the lantern. Even more remarkable, though, according to "Coxey" was that it was still lighted! "Coxey" was more amazed to find a big black bass clinging to the lantern—and, by its light, was reading the Fishing Laws to find when the season closed!

BONE MIZELL, FLORIDA COWPUNCHER

Bone Mizell was a Florida cowpuncher whose span of deeds covered about the same era as Buffalo Bill's. While the West was in transition from Frontier to more or less civilized communities and was gaining perspective on heroes responsible for that transition, the savannahs of South Florida were in the same process. Bone was a prominent character in the lore of pioneer Florida, although little information has been brought to light about him in accredited folk literature. The Seminoles had been subdued by 1837 (for all governmental intents and purposes) and there were no Indian-fighting stories about Bone, but he actually lived like an Indian in the swamp country and employed all the Red Man's legendary cunning to eke out his bachelor existence in Florida's wet wilderness. His reputation has endured in the Okechobee cattle country for many years as the popular genius of humor who brightened the leisure hours of the palmetto cowmen. It was Bone's "coming to town" that generally excited the masculine population to anticipate relief from their loneliness and boredom.

Bone (christened Morgan Bonaparte) Mizell stands as a central figure around which Florida cowboys have fashioned many of their best folk narratives. Actually, most of them are true; but Bone is becoming a legend now and it is evident that a few stories have adhered to him that didn't spring from his own experiences. I say evident because I know of two of the "Bone Mizell" stories which needed an ideal character for their successful narration and he appeared and sufficed as that figure.

Among the categories of folk heroes, Bone must stand as the fun-loving, humor-producing, jovial Irishman about whom the stories expanded as his reputation spread.

Bone Goes to the Circus

Bone Mizell rode into Arcadia one day and attended the circus that had lately pulled into town and encamped alongside the railroad track where it customarily set up for operations in those days. Bone became more entertaining to the audience than the actual performance, so the circus officials escorted Bone to the front door of the tent and fairly "tossed him out on his ear." This happened just as a freight train pulled into town. Bone looked around, picked up the biggest rope he could find and tied it onto the freight train. When the train left town it pulled the circus right out with it.

The next morning Bone met one of his friends on the street and told him how he had had nine-hundred and twenty-five dollars worth of fun the night before. He said they had thrown him into jail and fined him seventy-five dollars for the prank, but he figured it was worth just about an even thousand bucks to see that circus leave town the way it did.

Bone and the Holy People

Bone worked for a number of cattle bosses around Okechobee: Eli Morgan, the King Brothers, and the Parkers. Cow-hunting, marketing and branding occupied most of his time. With no family and no particular interest in respectable women, he generally took care of his share of whiskey on Saturday nights. One time the Holy Rollers were having a meeting and Bone, not bone-dry, stumbled onto them. He crawled in among them when they were down on their knees on the grass floor of the revival tent and ran his hand up under a woman's dress. A couple of nearby males noticed "the act," jumped on him and pummeled him "good and proper." Next day someone asked, "Bone, how do you like the holy people?" Bone replied, "God damn the holy people."

Bone Sells an Ox

Mr. Gene Brannon tells about Bone selling an ox to Zeb Parker:

Parker: Well, how much is he worth, Bone?
Bone: Oh, 'bout forty dollars.
Parker: Pretty much money ain't it?
Bone: Pretty much steer I got here.
Parker: O.K., take him on down and put him in my lot.
(Then he turned and started to walk off playing as if he'd forgotten about paying Bone, then he glanced back to see how Bone was taking it.)
Parker: Oh, was you waitin' to get paid?
Bone: Well, Zeb, that's the part of this here deal I was *particular* interested in.

Bone Buries a Friend

This is a story of Bone's last favor to one of his friends—a lad, a rich ne'er-do-well from the North, who occupies a nameless grave in the vast, flat cattle land of southern Florida.

The story begins with the companionship of Bone and the rich boy, who was broken in health and disillusioned after travelling the wide world round. He drifted into the palmetto country and somehow teamed up with Bone.

The lad finally died in the back country, and a lot of years rolled by before his wealthy family got the story and sent money to a certain county seat for the shipping of his remains. No official could recall where he had been buried. That is, no one but Bone. So Bone and a sidekick, Joe Daughery, went out to perform the chore and a body was shipped.

Some more years passed before Bone told the story. "Boys," said Bone in his revelation to his pals, "I got a confession to make to you all. I took money once under false pretenses. I never did send that rich boy's body north.

"I'm gonna tell you how it happened, and I believe that you'll decide that me and Joe didn't do so wrong in what we did. If we did, it's my fault, cause it was my idea. You see on the way out there to dig him up, I got to thinking of some of the things that kid had told me. He was fed up on everything and most of all on travelin'. He said he never wanted to see a railroad train again and never wanted to go back north.

"Then I got to thinking about old Bill Smith (that wasn't really his name, but the alteration is made out of deference to living family members). He was in a grave right near the rich lad's and that old cracker had hankered for a train ride all his life and never got enough money together to get out of his county.

"Well sir, it didn't seem right. It seemed even less right after a few drinks to sort of fortify us for the diggin' job. Here was a free train ride ahead, a funeral so damn fine this country had never seen and the likes of it—probably with four white horses pullin' the hearse.

"I talked Joe into it. It's my fault if any wrong has been done, but damned if old Bill Smith didn't get his train ride and the best buryin' a cracker ever had!"

Bone and the Public Doorknob

My last contact with an anonymous admirer of Bone Mizell was in Arcadia in 1959. He recalled for me a typical performance of this carefree, humor-bent character.

Bone was in jail for the following charge: "Drunk and disorderly and urinating on a public doorknob."

ETHNICS • OLD WORLD HEROES IN THE NEW WORLD

It is not unusual for ethnic origin to be an even stronger defining factor than either region or occupation. Many immigrants have arrived in the United States unable to speak English and unfamiliar with American ways. These people, "the uprooted," as one historian of immigration has called them, though they had to leave their old homes and often their trade behind, brought to America their tales, songs, and folk beliefs. Huddled together in Little Italies, Chinatowns, Yiddish ghettos, they sought the comfort of their own kind so that they could have the strength to make their way in an alien culture. While trying to adjust to the new ways, they held to the old, and with a tenacity equaled only by the most locally rooted of regional groups. In time, however, their children go to American schools, learn English as their first language, and come to remember less and less of their national background.

But for a generation or so, the old folks re-create the Old World within the New, and use the old lore as a means of stressing racial pride and evoking the satisfactions of nostalgia. Thus there is in America a large repository of folklore from other countries, most of it in the native languages of those who brought it here. Strictly defined, this is not American folklore at all but Italian, Syrian, Polish (or Portugese or Irish) lore that happens to have found its way here. Most of these tales, songs, proverbs, superstitions, and customs vanish as children and grandchildren of immigrants attend American schools and become acculturated. Some survive, flowing into the mainstream, contributing their wisdom and pleasures to America at large and finding their counterparts in the larger culture. In fact, one of the most reassuring events in the Americanizing experience is the moment when an ethnic realizes that a folk hero of his people like Zishe, the Yiddish strong man, or Stratouhotdas, the Greek trickster, is not that different from the Paul Bunyans, the Br'er Rabbits, and "Gassy" Thompsons of the other people who have come to these shores and intermingled.

Interesting, too, is the tendency to re-set Old World hero tales and songs in American locales where they are adapted and refurbished to fit the American environment. It is almost as if the people decided that they were going to emigrate and acculturate, and then their heroes and legendary figures followed after them. King Arthur turns up in Williamsport, Pennsylvania; the Wandering Jew wanders into Louisiana and Utah; a Finnish eyeturner works his magic in Northern Michigan; a Marshal of Napoleon lives incognito in North Carolina. And who is to say that such figures are less American than Kit Carson or Ben Franklin, than wieners or pizza?

The examples that follow under the headings "Ethnics" and "Old World Heroes" merely suggest the range of nationalities whose notable personages made their way to America. In other sections are to be found heroes of a dozen Indian tribes, of blacks, Chicanos, Puerto Ricans, French, Italians, Spanish, Germans, Dutch, Swedes, and other peoples. They are listed in the Index of Ethnic and Special Groups in the back. But the selections also suggest other things. They indicate that the prevailing culture, which is Anglo-Saxon, has its exotic strains. From the isles of Greece come anecdotes about a sharp operator, little changed by the distance they have traveled. They are told to the American-born children of people who heard them from their parents under different skies. From the East come versions of tales of poets and kings that Scheherazade recounted in Arabian Nights. On the other hand, some of the stories, like those about the blunders and blind luck of Pat Casey, have become as familiar to most Americans as wearing green on St. Patrick's Day. Pat Casey is a stereotype—not a novelty like Stratouhotdas, the street-smart Greek, or King Matt, the great Hungarian monarch. The Irish strain in American culture is so familiar that the Irish background of a number of folk figures in this collection, such as Ol Gallager, passes unremarked.

PETER FRANCISCO, REVOLUTIONARY WAR HERO

The basic facts of Francisco's life are simple and few. He was first seen in the early 1760's, as a child of three or four, on the wharf of City Point, Virginia, after he had been abandoned by an unidentifiable ship. Unable to speak English, the boy was taken to the Prince George poorhouse where he remained until removed to the home of Judge Anthony Winston, an uncle to Patrick Henry. There the unschooled boy remained, a worker on the Winston plantation, until the outbreak of the War of Independence when he was allowed to go off to war. Serving under a number of different commands in a series of separate enlistments, and always as a private soldier, he suffered several wounds while distinguishing himself in a number of engagements, the most notable being the Battle of Guilford Courthouse in 1781. After his third and final discharge he returned to Virginia where he became in the course of a long life a blacksmith, a tavernkeeper, and, in the last years of his life, sergeant-at-arms in the chambers of the General Assembly at Richmond. He married three times—to Susannah Anderson, Catherine Fauntleroy Brooke, and finally Mary Beverly West, nee Grymes, "each of whom," we are told, "belonged to representative Virginia families." At his death on 17 January 1831 the House of Delegates moved to pay him an official tribute. It reads: "Francisco was no common man—and he was happy that some record was to be left of his merits and his memory. In ancient times monuments were erected to men who performed worthy services; but in modern times their worth was inscribed on our records and by the aid of the press were sent far and wide." Out of respect the House then adjourned until the next day, having "determined to pay him the honors of a Public Funeral, and to bury him with the honors of war." His line of descendants has lasted to this day.

Francisco as Folk Hero

A list of some of the incidents and episodes told on Francisco, along with relevant Motif numbers from Stith Thompson's *Motif-Index of Folk-Literature* (1955–1958), will suggest the extent to which the "facts" of his life may be of folk provenience.

A strange child speaking an unidentifiable gibberish of foreign tongues and of unknown and unpromising origin (L111) is abandoned alone on a foreign coast (S144.1), and this future hero, found on a wharf, rather than on the shore (L111.2.2), is rescued by Judge Anthony Winston, not a King or a Prince to be sure, but something of an exalted person in a democracy (R131.11). Rapidly nearing full growth, he has, at an early age precocious energy and strength (F611.3.2). Enlisting in the army at the age of sixteen at the most, he becomes famous throughout the colonial forces for many remarkable feats of strength, skill and cunning (A526.7). When sent for horses behind enemy lines, he soon returns with eight (F615.2.3); faced at a crucial moment with the necessity to move a cannon weighing 1100 pounds across a battlefield, he carries it easily on his back (F631). Because his great size discourages his use of an ordinary sword, General Washington himself provides the young soldier with a custom-made giant sword (A523.1) that he alone is able to use effectively (D1654.4.1.1). And although it is never reported specifically that he cleaves both horse and rider in two (F628.2.10), he does manage on one occasion to split a man's head so that it falls evenly into two parts on his shoulders; while at the Battle of Guilford Courthouse he fights bravely against Cornwallis's superior troops, killing eleven men after he himself has been seriously wounded (F628.2). With the end of war the hero becomes a blacksmith (L113.6). Because of his continuing fame, however, he is periodically sought by other men, often coming from great distances, in search of a strong adversary (H1125). In one such encounter Francisco lifts and throws his opponent—and horse—over a wall, and in another instance hurls a workman onto a roof (F624.8 and

F636). On still other occasions, he lifts a dairy shed (F624.6) to enable some friends to crawl within, and he aids a teamster whose six horse team is hopelessly mired in mud by calmly lifting the team out (F624.3). And, in due course, the mystery of his origin evokes the theory that he has been abducted from his homeland and exposed in order to avoid a death decree (S329.1) in punishment for the political crimes of his father.

Yet it must not be ignored that these incidents and accounts, accreting as they do to traditional narrative motifs, are nevertheless founded upon a firm, albeit narrow, substratum of fact. The letters and journals of Francisco's contemporaries testify to the strength, size and affability of the young Francisco.

Francisco as Frontier Strong Man

The fame of Francisco's great strength spread far and wide through Virginia. Every man who could *"Whip his weight in wild cats,"* burned with the desire of reaping reknown by an encounter with Francisco. Among others, a bully from near the mountains, next to the land of *half horse and half alligator* men, determined on comparing his prowess with that of the reputed strongest man in the State. He deliberately commenced his journey with the intent of whipping Francisco, or being whipped himself. He arrived in the neighborhood of his intended antagonist, and meeting a man in a lane with a *stake and rider* fence on each side, he inquired of him if he knew Peter Francisco, and where he lived. The man answered that he was himself Peter Francisco. The business was made known, and Francisco, who was a very peaceable gentleman, remonstrated against such a foolish contest between two men; who had never injured each other. But in vain, the man would not be put off, and dismounting and tying his horse to the fence, told Francisco that he must either fight or run. Francisco, very coolly dismounting, replied that he had never been in the habit of *running*—if he must fight he could not help it. They met —Francisco seized his antagonist like he had been a child, and threw him entirely over the fence—when he got up, he very good naturedly asked him to be so good as to toss him over his horse also—he wished to be traveling.

Francisco in the Portuguese-language Press

The most passionately committed supporters of Peter Francisco . . . have been the American Portuguese. Since their discovery of Francisco in 1942 [through Thomas Malone's article in the *American Legion Magazine*] was brought to the attention of the editors of the *Diario de Noticias* [Portuguese-language daily, founded at New Bedford, Massachusetts, in 1919], there has been for most of them very little about Peter Francisco that smacks of the legendary. Their keen interest predicated on the conviction that he was born a native of Portugal, they are not concerned that the genuine evidence of the available documents, although it does not prove that he was not Portuguese, does actually demonstrate satisfactorily that it is now, and has been from the very beginning, virtually impossible to identify with any probability his original nationality. Consequently, to them Peter Francisco threatens to become a folk hero, not of the oral tradition, but of the punchpress of popular culture. Moreover, if heroes are created to fill the psychic needs of a nation, then for a minority group within such a nation, such as the Portuguese in the United States, the demonstration of a unique connection with any hero, or, for that matter, the demonstration of a relationship to any clearly definable aspect of the history of the nation in which they have chosen to live, is a means of direct and effective identification. Indicative of the prevailing ethnic climate in the case of Francisco is the public position of the *Diario* that "it is the moral duty of the 'luso-american' community to enhance the name of this great exponent of the virtues and qualities of our race."

THE WELSH WIZARD

Readers of *King Henry the Fourth*, Part I, will remember the Welshman Owen Glendower, who believed that he could "call spirits from the vasty deep." Such an one was Dr. Daniel Roberts, of "Welsh Medicamentum" fame, who was born in Wales, studied at Lampeter, emigrated from Llaniestyn, Caernarvonshire, and died in Steuben, New York, on September 13, 1820, at the age of forty-five. . . .

The Apple Thieves

The one [story] that made the deepest impression on our juvenile mind and rendered us truly thankful that no man in these parts possessed such wonderful powers in our day ran something like this: A number of truant boys, tempted by the fruit with which the doctor's apple trees were loaded, stealthily crept into his orchard and helped themselves. While returning to the road with their plunder, and just in the act of climbing the fence, they glanced toward the house to see if they had been detected and beheld the doctor looking at them from a window. Immediately all were transfixed and remained in that condition, each with a leg on either side of the fence, until the doctor came to them with a reprimand followed by words of good advice, after which he released them from the spell and bade them go.

Paying the Innkeeper

Another story related of the doctor is that, having occasion to visit a town in one of the counties north of us, he stopped for a night at a tavern where the accommodation afforded was decidedly bad and the price demanded in settlement excessively good. He paid without protest and, returning to the dining room then deserted, wrote with a piece of chalk a sentence upon the chimney above the mantel, and started on his journey, which was being made on foot. Presently, one of the maids entered the room, and seeing the chalked characters upon the chimney attempted to read them, when she immediately began involuntarily to dance. Her mistress soon appeared, and reading the sentence, likewise began to dance. At this stage the landlord, hearing the unusual racket and the wild ejaculations of the dancing pair, stepped into the room, and casting his eyes upon the mysterious marks, his heels also instantly began to clatter upon the bare sanded floor, in unison with those of his wife and servant. Being of a plethoric temperament, his breath soon showed signs of failing; so, while a little of it yet remained, he made use of it to call his stableman, whom he besought as he valued his legs not to read the sentence upon the wall but to go with all possible speed after the man who had lodged with them and beg of him to return. The stableman, mounting a horse, started in pursuit of the doctor, whom he soon overtook, and to whom he related how the devil had taken possession of his master's household, stating that he had been sent to beg him to come back and release them from the power of his Satanic Majesty. The doctor quietly told him to return and simply erase the characters chalked upon the wall and all would be well; but to tell his master never again to charge so exorbitant a price for such poor accommodation as he had furnished him.

Recovering Stolen Property

On one occasion an acquaintance called on him, reported the loss of a set of double harness that had been stolen from his barn, and asked him to aid in its recovery. After giving attention to the man's story, Dr. Roberts told him to return on a certain day and hour. Knowing fairly well who were the dissolute characters within a radius of several miles, the doctor notified each of these to be at his house at the hour of the appointment he had made for the man who had lost the harness. Upon their arrival they were all ushered into one room, when the doctor invited them to be seated, and explained his purpose in calling them there. "Mr. —— here" he said, "has lost a set of double harness, and one of you has stolen it. Now, when I count three, I want every one of you to stand up; and if the one who stole the harness stands up, he will immediately fall dead." When he counted "One, two, three," they all stood up but one.

Here is another instance of the doctor's shrewdness in detecting the wrongdoer and compelling the thief to restore to the rightful owner what he had purloined: On an occasion when several men were in a room together waiting to interview the doctor, one of their number approached him with the statement that his watch had been stolen since he came into the house. The doctor told him he hardly thought it possible that any of those present could be guilty of such an act, for he knew them all; but the man persisted in his claim, insisting that he had taken the watch out of his pocket after coming into the house to ascertain the hour. As it was late afternoon in the season of short days, the doctor, by failing to wait upon them and otherwise filling in the time, detained them there until dusk, when he ordered candles brought in.

Presently he called his son, William D., then a small lad, and instructed him to bring into the room a three-gallon iron pot that stood outside near the door, which Mrs. Roberts had used that day in steeping over a wood fire in the fireplace some herbs for the doctor's use in compounding his remedies. The pot was brought in and placed bottom upwards under the table. Then he quietly instructed the son to bring in a rooster from the barn, which he placed under the pot, all present marvelling greatly at the procedure. He then told them that a gentleman present had lost a watch since coming into the room, adding that he disliked to believe that any of their number could be guilty of so culpable an act as to steal it; but to satisfy the man who had lost the watch, as well as for his own satisfaction, he wished to determine whether it had been stolen in his house. He then put out the light of the candles, and requested them all to approach the table one by one, each to lay his right hand upon the upturned bottom of the pot, pressing firmly against it, stating that if any one of them were guilty of having stolen the watch, the rooster would immediately crow when that man put his hand upon the pot. So in the dusky room they drew near the table, and reaching under it, pressed each a hand upon the kettle; but the rooster failed to crow. The doctor then relighted the candles, and passing to each of the men in turn asked to be permitted to examine each man's hand—which he found covered with pot black; but finally he came to one upon whose hand there was no smut. To this one, looking him keenly in the eye, he held out his own hand, saying, "Give me the watch." The man immediately took it from his pocket and handed it to the doctor. The culprit had feigned to do as the others had done, but being fearful that the rooster might crow if he laid his hand upon the pot, had very carefully avoided touching it, to his undoing.

AN ABSENT-MINDED SCHOLAR

Francis Adrian Van der Kemp was one of those persons who epitomize a type of human personality to many of their fellows. To such persons are attached many of the current stories which seem to characterize them. The stories told of Van der Kemp are the group attached to the beloved and impractical, near-sighted and absent-minded scholar. These stories were current in New York at the end of the eighteenth and beginning of the nineteenth centuries.

Van der Kemp was a Dutch minister-scholar-revolutionist who left Holland as the consequence of his political activities. He settled in New York, first at Esopus, then at Kempwyck on the north shore of Oneida Lake, and finally in 1797, at Trenton, Oneida County. . . .

Two horse and wagon stories were used to illustrate his absent-mindedness. Once, when he was in Philadelphia, he hired a horse and carriage. Later as he drove about the streets, he stopped passers-by to enquire if they knew who owned his horse and rig. He had forgotten where he rented it. Another time he drove into a village and enquired where he was. On being told it was Trenton, he declared that that was impossible for he had just left Trenton. He had apparently either lost his way or forgotten turning to come back.

PAT CASEY WHO STRUCK IT RICH

Numerous instances might be cited where men who have arrived in the gold regions of Colorado without a dollar, have, in the course of three years, become possessed of small fortunes. The case of Mr. P. D. Casey is so familiar to all who are acquainted with the history of Colorado and can be so readily substantiated, that a statement in reference to it will undoubtedly prove interesting to the reader. Seven years ago, Mr. Casey landed at Castle Garden in New York City, from an emigrant ship from Ireland. Like the great majority of emigrants, he possessed little or no means, and was compelled at once to seek daily labor. For two or three years he gained only that comfortable livelihood which in America always rewards honest toil, and soon after the discovery of gold in Colorado, he repaired thither to better his condition. On his arrival in the gold regions *he had not a dollar in money*, and was in debt to parties with whom he journeyed across the plains. But he had energy and industry to aid him, and immediately went to work with a will. In less than three years he owned some of the most valuable mines in the country, and employed upwards of one hundred men to work them. His mill property, too, was very valuable, and he made money rapidly. Last August he came to New York, sold out his property in Colorado to New York capitalists, and realized some fifty thousand dollars, after paying liberal commissions to parties who had assisted him in his negotiations. Mr. Casey is now living in New York, drives one of the finest "turn-outs" in the city, and is conducting a successful business in stock and gold speculations.

Gold Is Where You Find It

Less dependable as fact but more important as lore are the following two episodes from the Casey legend. They were reported by Alice Polk Hill, in 1884.

Many amusing stories are told of that early gold excitement. It is related of a prospector from the Emerald Isle, whom we will designate as Pat, that while attending a funeral, he picked up some dirt that was thrown from the new grave, and just from force of habit examined it. He suddenly arose from his knees and commenced staking off a claim. The minister observed this, and concluded his prayer in this manner: "Stake me off a claim, Pat, this we ask for Christ's sake—Amen."

Pat afterward became one of the bonanza kings of the period; exchanged his suit labelled "superfine flour" for broadcloth, and went to New York to cut a swell. He stopped at the largest and most fashionable hotel, and was assigned a room on the fifth floor. When he left his room that evening for a saunter in the city, thinking the halls and stairways rather bewildering, *he blazed a way*, in order to be able to retrace his steps. It cost him $2,000 for repairs.

A Man of Affairs

Another Casey story, still circulated in the Gilpin County region, is the following:

Casey always carried, conspicuously displayed, a memorandum book, with a number of pencils. Notwithstanding the fact that he could neither read nor write, he made bold dashes at writing things in that memorandum book. Pat was singularly susceptible to flattery, extravagantly fond of telling how much business he had to do every day. It was his common boast that he "used up ten lead pencils a day and then didn't half do his business."

Satirical detractors even insisted that Casey's fine watch and chain were for show only—that he couldn't even tell time. Whenever anyone, to plague him, asked the time of day, he is reported to have been in the habit of displaying his watch, with the admonition, "See fer yerself; ye wouldn't believe me if I told ye."

ZISHE, THE YIDDISH SAMSON

Zishe Breitbart, the son of a blacksmith, was born in Lodz, Poland, in 1883. He died in Berlin in 1925 at the age of forty-two. Breitbart's fame is based upon both his physical strength and his unique personality. Newspaper accounts relate that Breitbart's feats included driving nails into boards with his hand, and lying barebacked upon a bed of nails while horses rode over him. The New York *Times* of August 27, 1923, reports: "Among other feats of strength he claims to be able to lift ten or twelve persons with his hands, twist bars of iron like scraps of paper, crack Brazil nuts between his fingers and haul a wagon with ten persons along the road by his teeth." The *Forverts*, a Yiddish language daily, of October 14, 1925, describes Breitbart as a talented showman and actor with a strong sense of theatrics. He would ride onstage in a chariot drawn by two white horses, dressed in a costume of a soldier of ancient times, with armor and a helmet. His assistants were also in costume.

Newspapers reports emphasize the contrast between Breitbart's physical strength and his gentle nature. He is described as generous, sensitive, and artistic. The *Forverts* writes: "He was built like a giant, with broad shoulders and tremendous muscles, yet he had a mild, almost childlike expression in his blue eyes" (October 14, 1925). A New York *Times* article telling of Breitbart's arrival in America notes that Breitbart "says that he is so sensitive that he would walk into the roadway to avoid treading upon a worm" (August 27, 1923). It continues: "He likes music and writes poems, but doesn't like prize fighting. He declined an offer received by telegram at the pier to go to Saratoga Springs and have a tryout with Jack Dempsey, the heavyweight champion. 'For me it is not,' the strong man of Poland said." A *Forverts* article tells of Breitbart's generosity, reporting that while Breitbart was in the United States he gave financial assistance and moral support to an injured strongwoman who also appeared at the Hippodrome.

Breitbart came to the United States in 1923 and performed in various cities for the Keith vaudeville theaters. He was the headliner at the Hippodrome in New York for a lengthy run, and performed in many other theaters as well. A Polish song about Breitbart tells of his travels to New York and Washington.

Breitbart's death at the age of forty-two apparently resulted from blood poisoning, the effects of an injury incurred during a performance in Radom, Poland, when he accidentally scratched or punctured his leg with a nail. (Various accounts specify "foot," "knee," or even "finger.")

One of the most interesting aspects of Breitbart's character, and of the impression he made on Jews throughout the world, was his sense of mission. He saw himself as a Jewish hero, a new Samson who would prove to the world that Jews were a strong, heroic people. Contemporary reports state the Breitbart had been the object of anti-Semitic harrassment and insults, and was particularly hurt by accusations that he was a fraud. Breitbart's autobiography, published in 1925, ends with the following passage:

> The greater my name grew, the more enemies I had. They were all not only my enemies, but the enemies of the Jewish people.
>
> I have, praise the Almighty, overcome them. All my enemies have had to admit, through clenched teeth, that I, Zishe, son of Yithak Tsvi Breitbart, the Jew from Lodz, am the strongest man in the world. The gentiles don't like the idea of a Jew taking the crown of strength from them, but there is nothing they can do about it.

Breitbart's story and personality made an extremely strong impression on people throughout the world, even those who never saw him perform. For instance, my father, Boris Blum, who as a child saw Breitbart ride through the streets of Vilna in costume, describes the scene vividly. People who have never seen Breitbart at all, and know of him only through reputation, describe him with the same immediacy.

The Song of Zishe

Below is a transcription of the song as sung to me by Yitskhak Milstein in Brooklyn, New York, on March 21, 1973. Mr. Milstein first heard the song in the 1920s in Shidlovtse (Szydlowiec), Poland, where he was born. The song was sung there by *hoyfzingers* (street singers), who also sold the text of the song along with pictures of Breitbart. The song was brought to America as part of the Jewish immigrant heritage; whether it was known in America in the 1920s as it was in Poland is something I have not yet explored. The tune is similar to tunes of other songs, including *Sorrento* and the Yiddish *Reyzele dem shoykhets*.

In a klayn-em en-gn shti-bl,   Nisht ba ra-khe ta-te-ma-me,   Hot der-tsoy-gn zikh a bu-kher,   Ir hot dus ge-hert mis-ta-me?   Zi-she hot men eym ge-ri-fn,   In ba-kant iz er ge-vo-rn,   A-les kref-ti-ker in shtar-ker,   Shoyn in za-ne kin-der-yu-rn.

1. In a klaynem engn shtibl
   Nisht ba rakhe tate-mame
   Hot dertsoygn zikh a bukher
   Ir hot dus gehert mistame.

2. Zishe hot men eym gerifn
   In bakant iz er gevorn
   Ales kreftiker in shtarker
   Shoyn in zane kinderyurn.

3. Nokh baysn gayn in khayder
   Hot er ale shoyn gehaysn
   Brengen zikh nor shtiker kaytn
   In geprivt hot er zay raysn.

4. Zane shreklikhe gevires
   Hobn dan bavindert ale.
   Nisht ayn mame hot ir tokhter
   Eym gevolt geybn a kale.

5. Zishe hot nor alts getsoygn
   Tsi ayn svive fin atletn
   In es hot gurnisht geholfn
   Khotsh zan mame hot gebeytn

6. Az er zol kan kemfer vern
   In kan tsirkn kaynmul shpiln.
   Nisht gekont hot ober Zishe
   Zan atletn-khayshik shtiln.

7. Dan farlozt er tate-mame
   In zan shtib fin kinderyurn.
   Tsi antviklen zane gevires
   Privt er in di velt tsi furn.

8. Es shpilt a mazl iber alem
   Yeyder iz eym interteynig.
   In me kroynt eym dort in osland
   Mit deym numen "Azn-keynig".

9. Iz zan numen bakant gevorn
    Imetim in ale krazn.
    Nor plitsling iz gesheyn an imglik
    Mit deym keynig fin deym azn.

10. S'iz geveyn a nakht a shayne
    Gedakhte shteyrn ofn himl.
    Dortn of di gas in Rudem
    Iz a rash in ayn getiml.

11. Es loyfn yinge, s'loyfn alte
    S'loyfn froen, s'loyfn kinder
    Val gedorfn hot dort Zishe
    Bavazn zane groyse vinder.

12. Veygn eym hot shoyn gevist yeyder
    Es hot gevist shoyn yeyder ayner
    Az dus iz der lodzher Zishe
    Vus brakht azn mit di tsayner.

13. Hel iz der tsirk balokhtn
    Hilkhik shpiln di trompaytn.
    Zishe shtayt in mitn stsene
    In er rast di grobe kaytn.

14. Dan nemt er a blakh in tshvekes
    In privt zay klapn pinkt vi nakhtn.
    Nor anshtut in di blakhn
    Treft er zikh in fis in rakhtn.

15. Zishe iz dan krank gevorn
    Nisht gekont shoyn er kaynem vayln.
    Tsirik kan osland upgefurn
    Zikh deym fis oshayln.

16. Es hot shoyn kayner nisht bavizn
    Eym tsi haltn ba deym leybn
    Khotsh er hot far di doktoyrim
    Zans a fis avekgegeybn.

17. Tragish iz der held Zishe
    Fin di velt avekgekimen.
    Es hot a shpitsik shtikl azn
    Eym zan leybn tsigenimen.

18. Ofn Berliner bays hakvures
    Iz a bergl dort faranen.
    Ver s'tit dort farbaygayn
    Miz zikh in deym troyer dermanen.

1. In a small narrow house
   With parents who were not rich
   There grew up a boy,
   You have probably heard this.

2. Zishe was his name
   And he achieved fame
   When he was still a child
   For his power and strength.

3. When he was still in school
   He would ask everyone
   To bring him lengths of chain
   That he would try to tear.

4. His awesome powers
   Filled everyone with wonder.
   More than one mother wished
   He would marry her daughter.

5. But Zishe always wanted
   To be among athletes
   And it was to no avail
   That his mother would plead

6. That Zishe not become a fighter
   Or a circus performer.
   But he could not still his wish
   To be an athlete any longer.

7. So he left his parents.
    And his childhood home.
    To develop his powers
    Over the world he roamed.

8. Fortune smiled upon him,
    All were under his command,
    He was crowned the "Iron King"
    In a foreign land.

9. His name achieved renown
    Everywhere, in all quarters.
    But misfortune suddenly occurred
    To the King of Iron.

10. It was a lovely night,
    Many stars filled the sky,
    And in the streets of Radom
    People noisily rushed by.

11. Young and old ran about.
    Women, children, ran too.
    For Zishe was coming
    His wonders to prove.

12. Everyone knew of him
    Everyone knew that this
    Was Zishe of Lodz,
    Who broke iron with his teeth.

13. The circus was lit brightly,
    Trumpets loudly played.
    Zishe stood in midstage
    And tore the thick chains.

14. Then he took a metal sheet
    To hammer as before.
    But he hit his right leg
    Instead of the board.

15. Zishe then grew ill,
    He could no longer perform.
    Back to foreign lands
    To heal his leg he roamed.

16. Now no one was able
    His life to save
    Although to the doctors
    He lost his leg.

17. The hero Zishe
    Left this world tragically.
    A pointed piece of iron
    Took his life away.

18. In the Berlin cemetery
    There is a little hill.
    Everyone who goes past
    Must remember this sad tale.

A POET TURNS THE TABLES ON THE KING OF BAGDAD

In the times of the Califate there lived in Bagdad a great poet, named Abu'n-Nuwâś. One cold and stormy evening, as a body of friends were sitting about the king discussing matters, the king, desiring to make a little merriment, said, "I will give thousands of pounds to him who will sit naked on the roof of the palace all night." Abu'n-Nuwâś said, "I'll do it," and straightway removed his clothes, and because he was poor and in need of the money, went up and sat on the roof all night. He suffered much. The wind the whole night long bit his flesh, but the remembrance of the promised gold encouraged him, so that he endured minute by minute. In the morning he was badly frozen and could not move. At last the king sent one of his body-guard to see what had happened to the poet. He brought Abu'n-Nuwâś down nearly dead, and they worked over him a long time before he opened his eyes. After he had clothed himself he waited impatiently for the reward, but the king, before giving him the gold, asked, "What did you see in the night, Abu'n-Nuwâś?" Abu'n-Nuwâś replied that he had seen nothing all night, and described to the king the bitter cold and the rain. He said, however, that in the early gray of the morning he had seen far, far away a tiny light, but that that was all he had seen. The king was angered and said, "Abu'n-Nuwâś, I shall not give you anything, for you have warmed yourself by that light." Abu'n-Nuwâś pleaded, but to no purpose, for the king wished to make fun of the poet. It was hard for Abu'n-Nuwâś, after suffering such pain, to be deprived of the reward, and he determined that some day he would get revenge, and even perchance the reward too.

A whole year passed, and the king had forgotten all about the affair. One day Abu'n-Nuwâś came, and invited the king to take dinner with him out in his country garden. The king accepted, for he thought it would be very pleasant to honor the poet, and also he was interested to hear his poetry. In the early morning of the appointed day the king and the queen, accompanied by their knights and pages, went to the garden of Abu'n-Nuwâś, expecting to be feasted on the most delicious food and the choicest wine. They sat down under the trees, and Abu'n-Nuwâś sang and played for them. There was an abundance of poetry and music there, but nothing to eat or drink. Yet no one ventured to mention refreshments, each thinking that the next moment they would be invited to the repast.

Nothing, however, was prepared. Again and again Abu'n-Nuwâś sang and played, and all his maidens and slaves, also, danced and sang. Of that the king had enough, for it was growing late in the afternoon, and he could endure his hunger no longer. Accordingly he called Abu'n-Nuwâś to him, and said, "O wicked one that brought us here, and filled us with music and poetry, but wished us to die of hunger!" Abu'n-Nuwâś bowed humbly, and replied, "Your Majesty, the food is not cooked yet, but is on the fire." After an hour the king asked the same question with more bitterness, and Abu'n-Nuwâś again replied, "Your Majesty, the food is still on the fire." Then the king, and all his retinue, was very angry, and was about to kill Abu'n-Nuwâś. But Abu'n-Nuwâś said, "Come, Most High King, and let me show thee that the pots are on the fire." He then led the way to another part of the garden, and there, indeed, were the pots hanging from the highest branches of a tree. On the ground beneath them there was a blazing fire, but no heat could reach the pots, only smoke. Then the king was very angry. "O wicked slave, most ignorant one," cried he, "do you suppose that the food will be cooked when the fire is so very far from it?" "Your Majesty," replied Abu'n-Nuwâś, "if pots cannot be boiled, nor even warmed by such a great fire as this, how could I, naked, on such a very cold night, be warmed by seeing a tiny light miles and miles away?" The king laughed, and laughed, and laughed. Then Abu'n-Nuwâś immediately ordered tables to be made ready, and a fine feast was spread, for everything had been prepared beforehand, and hidden away. They all ate and drank in merriment, and the king gave the thousands of pounds he had formerly promised to the poet, and made no more fun of him, for Abu'n-Nuwâs was too clever for the king.

STRATOUHOTDAS, BIGGEST THIEF THAT EVER LIVED

"I don't know whether this is American folklore, but certainly every American child of Greek parentage has heard stories of our 'Stratouhotdas' at one time or another; so one might consider this as American folklore. Stratouhotdas was a Turk by birth, and his name is very satirical indeed. Breaking his name into two parts, we find the first part 'Stratou,' the Greek word for 'street,' and 'hotdas,' the Turkish word for 'priest.' Putting his name back together, we have 'Stratouhotdas,' meaning 'priest of the streets.' This is actually the humor of it, for Stratouhotdas was far from being a holy person. On the contrary, he was probably the biggest thief that ever lived. The time at which he lived is not known, but his name has been carried down through many generations. . . ."

A Thief Outwits a Thief

When Stratouhotdas was still a schoolboy, his father was primarily to blame for his young and early thievery, for they worked together to better their family through unlawful means. He and his father, in some unknown way, had found out where the king of their land kept his treasure. 'Most any night they would steal into the palace and Stratouhotdas would lower his father into a deep well, which served as a vault. As time went by, the treasure was discovered to be gradually decreasing. The king became alarmed and called another thief whom he had in his prison. He called this thief to him for advice as to means for catching this unknown thief that was stealing his treasure. The king's thief advised that he take a big barrel of the stickiest tar that he could find and place it over the treasure, and when this new thief would lower himself into the well, he would get stuck in the tar and therefore be caught at daybreak. Now that night, as Stratouhotdas and his father were at the well of treasure, Stratouhotdas lowered his father into the well as usual and, lo and behold, he was caught and couldn't get out. When Stratouhotdas failed in his efforts to free his father, they decided that the father should be killed and that Stratouhotdas should cut off the father's head to prevent identification of the body. When Stratouhotdas reached home, his mother asked him where his father was; and, after some time of constant questioning, he finally broke the news. His mother cried bitterly for a long time.

The next day, when the king found the body without the head, he again called upon his robber. The robber told the king that this fellow was certainly a clever thief. He then advised the king to take and clean the body and hang it outside the palace gate. He was to set two disguised men to watch for any person who came by and showed any signs of sorrow, for this person would certainly be related to the headless thief. Then they could track down the other thieves in that family.

That afternoon as Stratouhotdas was returning from school he saw his father's body hanging there and quickly ran home. He asked his mother whether she wished to see his father's body or not, and of course she said that she did. Then he told her of the scheme the king had no doubt set up to catch them. He told his mother to take a basket full of glassware and set out for market, and, as she passed the palace gate and felt as though she wanted to cry, to trip herself and fall, breaking the glassware. Then she could cry out her heart. When she was caught by the men, she could answer that she was crying over the broken glassware. She did exactly as her son advised, and when the men caught her they took her before the king and he gave her some gold to pay for the accident she had suffered in breaking her glassware. She went home and told Stratouhotdas, and he was very much pleased.

After the body had hung there for several weeks, it was finally decided the plan for detection has failed, and again the thief was called for his services. This time he told the king to load a camel with gold and jewels and set it loose in the street with four men following it at an unsuspicious distance; and as this great thief would doubtless attempt to steal the camel, the king's men could follow him and catch him. The plan was in full swing when Stratouhotdas was on his way home from school. When he spotted the camel, he at once knew what the trick was; so he struck the camel with a stick and hung on to one side, and the animal went off at a tremendous speed. Therefore, in no time at all, he was out of sight of the king's men. Stratouhotdas took the camel and led it through his doorway into his home. In Greece, it seems that nearly all the houses are built next to each other, like the business districts of our towns; and, since the doors were big, Stratouhotdas had no trouble quickly disappearing with his camel into his home.

The four men went back to the king and reported their sad story. Once more the king called upon his robber. This time the robber advised that the king send out an old woman from house to house, begging for camel's meat, with the story that her little daughter was very ill and the only thing that could cure her would be camel's meat. When the woman finally came to Stratouhotdas' home, his mother answered the door and listened to the story of this elderly woman. His mother felt very sorry for her and gave her some meat under the condition that she would tell no one where she had gotten it. As the old woman was leaving the house, Stratouhotdas was just coming home from school and he temporarily hid in another doorway and watched this woman place a small chalk mark on the corner of the door. Stratouhotdas ran into the house and asked his mother what that woman had been there for. She finally told him, and he told her they would now be caught for sure. Nightfall soon came on, and Stratouhotdas not only removed the chalk mark but repainted every door in the nearby neighborhoods the same color. In the morning, when the elderly woman and the king's men came searching for the door, they were completely lost.

Stratouhotdas and the Blanket

It seems that Stratouhotdas was finally married; and one night as he and his wife were in bed, he heard two men fighting under his window. He told his wife he wanted to go down and find out why they were fighting. His wife said, "No, stay here and mind your own business." But Stratouhotdas finally got up, took a blanket off the bed for clothing, and went down. As the men saw him they got him in the argument, and both of them started to pull on his blanket. Finally the two men got the blanket away from him and ran down the street. When Stratouhotdas went back upstairs, his wife asked him what the men had been fighting about. He said, "My blanket."

Stratouhotdas and the Washtub

It was washday and Stratouhotdas' wife needed a washtub. When, at her request, Stratouhotdas went next door to borrow a tub, the neighbor gave him one of her largest. Stratouhotdas took it to his wife and then went down to the market to buy one, just like the neighbor's tub in design, but very much smaller. When his wife was finished with the neighbor's tub, Stratouhotdas returned both the large tub and the new little one. The lady asked him what the little one was for. "Well," he said, "when my wife was washing her clothes, this little one was born!" The woman laughed and thought Stratouhotdas to be a little crazy, but accepted both the tubs, and Stratouhotdas went home again. A couple of months later his wife wanted to borrow the large tub again, so Stratouhotdas again did the borrowing. This time months passed, and he did not return it. The woman next door finally went over and asked him what had happened to her tub. He said, "What tub?"—"Why," she said, "the one I let you borrow a few months ago."—"Oh, that one!" exclaimed Stratouhotdas. "That one died!"—"It died?" she said. "How could any washtub die?"—"Well," said Stratouhotdas, "anything that has the power to give birth certainly has the right to die." The lady went home without a word.

Stratouhotdas Plays the Violin

One night Stratouhotdas was sawing a lock on the front door of a house. It was quite obvious that he intended to break in and rob the house. A passing man asked him what he was doing. Stratouhotdas replied that he was playing a violin. The man said he couldn't hear a violin, or anything like one. Stratouhotdas told him if he couldn't hear anything now, he should go on his way and he certainly would hear plenty in the morning.

KING MATT'S RIDDLE

King Matt was a very famous king. He liked to go among his subjects incognito, to see how they were getting along. He often said that some of them were smarter than his ministers.

One day he came upon an old farmer, plowing his field with his oxen. He asked the farmer, "How far is far, old timer?"

The farmer answered, "Not very far now; only to the tip of my oxen's horns."

Then King Matt asked, "How many of the thirty-two do you have?"

The farmer answered, "Not so many, sir; only twelve."

King Matt said he had one more question to ask the old farmer. "Could you milk three billy goats?"

The farmer replied, "Yes, sir."

King Matt, at his next court meeting, mentioned this happening and admired the wisdom of the old farmer. He asked his ministers if they understood the riddle but no one answered. Three of his ministers were so curious that they went and talked to the farmer. Upon being asked the answer to the first part of the riddle the farmer said, "I will tell you if you will give me ten pieces of gold."

The ministers agreed.

"Well," said the farmer, "I used to be able to see as far as the horizon, but now I can see only as far as my oxen's horns."

Then they asked the meaning of the second part of the riddle.

"I will tell you for ten more pieces of gold," said the farmer.

The ministers agreed and the farmer said, "I used to have thirty-two teeth but now I have but twelve."

Now the ministers asked the farmer, "How would you milk three old billy goats? After all, they're not milkers."

The farmer said that he would tell the ministers for ten more pieces of gold. After the ministers had given the farmer the ten pieces of gold, he answered, "Milking three billy goats is very easy. I just got through milking three."

The three ministers hung their heads in embarrassment. They never did tell King Matt that they got the answers to the riddle.

KING ARTHUR'S GRAVE

There was this king who came to drink the water from the Great Spirits Spring, where vapor like steam rises from the water. This is called Great Spirits Breath. This King Arthur and his men all in armor came here and walked through the forest to this place. This spring is in Windfall Run about fifty feet from where Mudlick Creek joins Windfall Run. This King Arthur was wounded and he came here to drink these healing waters. He stayed twenty years drinking the water and then he died. His men cut down the living bed rock in the middle of Windfall Run to make him a grave. They made it three feet wide and nine feet long. In those days the juice of certain trees was used to soften the rock. When this juice was poured on the rock, the rock became soft as putty in a few minutes; then the rock was scooped out before it hardened. The grave was made ten feet deep and the king was put in it in a stone coffin. Then it was all covered over and the stones on top fitted with a keystone so that no one could loosen it. And on top they piled stones like a cairn.

It stayed like this for hundreds of years. In 1951 some boys took away the stones and got the keystone loose and they opened the grave. But it filled right up with water and a heavy steam came off the water. The grave was open like this until 1959 when one of these politicians, who was fishing down Windfall Run, stepped into it and his friends had to haul him out. He got after the Forestry Department and made them fill it up. It took twelve loads of gravel, twelve loads of oakum and twelve loads of sand. But that place never silts over because the spring comes out just above the coffin and keeps it from silting up.

THE WANDERING JEW IN LOUISIANA

To this day, "juif errant" remains a well-known expression in South Louisiana for a person who is never at home. This is attested to by Dr. Viron Barnhill for the district of Crowley and by Dr. John Guilbeau of Winthrop College for Lafourche. Dr. Guilbeau tells me he did not know the legend as a child, and thought of "juiferrant" as one word. But the most important persistence of the Wandering Jew legend in French Louisiana is the long narrative song collected in the thirties by Miss Irene Petitjean and in the late forties by Dr. Corinne Saucier. Dr. Saucier's collection contains two recordings, both from Avoyelles Parish, while Miss Petitjean's thesis offers us the words of an even fuller version from Rayne.

The words of this "complainte" are close to the best-known French and Canadian versions. If we add to this fact the great length of the Louisiana versions as compared with most songs collected . . . , we must conclude that this "complainte" entered French Louisiana in printed form, and probably circulated here in this way at first. Later diffusion became oral. Though there is at least one older popular song about the Wandering Jew in the repertory of French folksong, here we are dealing with a Louisiana survival of the most popular, the one which tells of the Jew's appearance at Brussels. This incident is alleged to have occurred in 1774. . . . Whatever the case, it was commonly believed by the Belgian and French populace, and inspired the anonymous *Complainte du Juif Errant*. This ballad was widely disseminated by the *imagistes* of Epinal and Troyes in France. These publishers of folk-broadsides catered to the semi-literate, offering for sale one-sheet colored illustrations, bearing a text which often includes the

words of a song, with the direction, "to be sung to the tune of
***." One French antiquarian of the nineteenth century states
that no hovel was too poor to possess a portrait of the Emperor
Napoleon and a copy of the *Wandering Jew*.

Le Juif Errant

1. Est-il rien sur la terre
   Qui soit plus surprenant
   Que la grande misère
   Du pauvre Juif errant?
   Que son sort malheureux
   Paraît triste, fâcheux!

   Is there a thing on earth
   More surprising
   Than the great misery
   Of the poor Wandering Jew?
   How his unfortunate lot
   Seems sorrowful and sad.

2. Un jour près de la ville
   De Bruquelembranbel
   Les bourgeois fort dociles
   L'accorsèrent en passant.
   Jamais ils n'avaient vu
   Un homme aussi barbu.

   One day near the town
   Of Bruquelembranbel
   The easy-going citizens
   Stopped him as he went by.
   They had never seen
   A man so bearded.

3. Son habit tout difforme
   Et très mal arrangé
   Leur fit croire que cet homme
   Etait fort étranger.
   Il portrait comme ouvrier
   D'vant lui un tablier

   His clothing out of shape
   And badly arranged
   Made them think this man
   Was very strange or foreign.
   Like a workman he wore
   Before him an apron.

4. On lui dit, "Bonjour, maître,
   De grâce, accordez-nous

   They said to him, "Good day, master,
   Please grant us

La satisfaction d'être	The satisfaction of spending
Un moment avec vous;	A moment with us;
Nous le refusez pas;	Do not refuse us;
Retardez un peu vos pas."	Slow down your steps a little."

5.
"Messieurs, je vous proteste	"Gentlemen, I protest to you
Que j'ai bien du malheur.	That I have much ill fortune
Jamais je ne m'arrête,	I never stop
Ni ici, ni allieurs.	Here or elsewhere.
Par beau ou mauvais temps	In fair or good weather
Je marche incessament."	I walk without cease."

6.
"Rentrez dans cette auberge,	"Come into this inn,
Vénérable vieillard	Venerable old man,
D'un pot de bière fraîche	Of a pot of cool beer
Vous prendrez votre part	You will take your share
Nous vous régalerons	We will give you a treat
Le mieux que nous pourrons."	The best way we can."

7.
"J'accepterai de boire	"I will agree to drink
Un coup-z-avecque vous	A glass with you
Mais je ne puis m'asseoir-e	But I cannot sit down
Car je dois rester debout.	For I must stand up.
Je suis trop tourmenté.	I am too badly tormented
Quand je suis arrêté."	When I keep still."

8.
"De savoir-e votre âge	"To know your age
Nous serions bien curieux;	We would be most curious;
De voir votre visage	To judge your face
Vous paraissez fort vieux;	You seem very old;
Vous avez bien cent ans,	You are at least a hundred,
Vous en montrez autant."	You appear that old."

9.
"La vieillesse me gêne,	"Old age troubles me,
J'ai bien dix-huit cent ans,	I am at least eighteen hundred,
Chose sûre et certaine.	A thing sure and certain,
Je passais encore douze ans;	I was already twelve;
J'avais dix ans passés	I was already more than ten
Quand Jésus-Christ fut né."	When Jesus Christ was born."

10.
"Etes pas vous cet homme	"Are you then the man
De qui en parle tant	Of whom people talk so much,
Que l'écriture nomme	Called in books
Isaac-e, Juif Errant?"	Isaac, the Wandering Jew?"
"Oui, c'est moi, mes enfants,	"Yes, my children, it is I
Qui est le Jui-ferrant.	Who am the Wandering Jew.

11.
"Héla', juste ciel! Que ma ronde	"Alas, just heaven, How my round

Est pénible pou' moi.
Je fais le tour du monde
Pou' la cinquième fois.
Chancien [sic] meurt à son tour
Et moi je vis toujours.

Is painful to me!
I am now going around the world
For the fifth time.
Every man dies in his turn,
And I live on forever.

12. "Je n'ai point de ressources
Ni en maison, ni en bien
J'ai cinq sous dans ma bourse,
Voilà tout mon soutien.
En tout et en tous lieux,
J'en ai toujours autant.

"I have no means,
Neither house nor wealth.
I have five sous in my purse,
That's all I have to support me.
All told, and in every place,
I have always as much.

13. "J'ai traversé les mer-e
Les rivières, les ruisseaux,
Les forêts, les déserts,
Les montagnes, les coteaux,
Les forêts, les jallons
Tous chemins me sont bons.

"I have crossed the seas,
Rivers, brooks,
Forests, wildernesses,
Mountains, ridges,
Forests, valleys.
Any road will do for me.

14. Je vis dedans l'Afrique
Ainsi que dans l'Asie
Des batailles, des choses
Qui coûtaient bien des vies.
Je leur [sic] ai traversé.
Sans y être blessé."

"I saw in Africa,
As well as India
Battles, things
Which cost many lives.
I passed through them
Without being hurt."

15. "Vous êtes donc coupable
De quelque grand péché
Que Dieu tout aimable
Vous ait tant affligé?"
"J'ai traité mon Sauveur
Avec trop de rigeur.

"You are then guilty
Of some great sin
That the all good God
Should thus have afflicted you?"
"I treated my Saviour
With too much severity.

16. "Sur le mont du Calvaire
Jésus portait sa croix.
Il me dit, débonnaire,
Passant devant chez moi,
'Veux-tu bien, mon ami,
Que je repose ici?'

"On Calvary's mount,
Jesus carried his cross.
He meekly said to me
When passing before my house,
'Will you allow me, friend,
To rest a while here?'

17. "Mon brutal et rebel-e
Lui répond sans raison,
Ote-toi, criminel-e
De devant de chez mon.
Avancez, marche donc
Car tu me fais affront."

"I, brute-like and rebellious
Answer him without cause,
Begone, criminal,
From before my house.
Keep moving, walk on,
For you are a nuisance to me."

18. Jésus, la bonté même,
Lui dit en soupirant,

Jesus, goodness itself,
Said to him, sighing,

"Tu marcheras toi-même	"You will walk yourself
Pendant plus de mille ans.	For more than a thousand years.
Les derniers jugements	The last judgments
Finiront tes tourments."	Will end your pains."

19. "De chez mon à l'heure-même,	"From my house at that moment
J'ai senti bien chagrin	I felt much sadness
Avec douleur extrême	Along with extreme pain.
Je m'ai mi-t'en chemin.	I started the road.
De ce jour-là je suis	From that day, I am
En marche nuit et jour.	Journeying day and night.

20. "Messieurs, le temps me presse	"Gentlemen, time hastens me on.
Adieu la compagnie.	Goodbye to all the company.
Grâce à vos politesses;	Because of your courtesies
Je vous en remercie.	I give you thanks.
Je suis en vérité	I am in truth
Confus de vos bontés."	Speechless at your goodness."

The Wandering Jew in the Utah Desert

There was surely a queer incident of that character down on the Muddy here. My brothers Adam and Billy was there—it was before I went down there. One day they was settin' around—kind of a windy day—and all at once they seen a man comin' along the desert. This desert was a plateau above the Muddy Valley, on the east of the Valley, and it was just only covered with evergreens, green bushes, so you could see all over. Well, this man, he come, and they was choppin' some wood there. He said, "How to do," and waited a few minutes and said, "I would like if you would let me have some dry bread and some patches to patch my clothes," and he says, "I am goin' to cross the desert here and I would like to have somet'ing of that kind." My brother Billy looked at him and said, "Do you know what kind of country you are goin' over? I don't see that you've got much preparation. I've been over that country lots of times, and you haven't hardly got anyt'ing to pack water wit'." He says, "Oh, yes, but I know how to get water." Then they says to him, "What do you want dry bread for? We'll give you some good bread to go over there." "No, I want dry bread, if you got it. Good bread sometimes spoils, but dry bread

won't spoil." They talked and finally he says, "I'll be goin' soon."
They says, "Well, what might your name be?" So he talked German to them: "Mann heisst mich den ewigen Juden"—Man calls
me the everlasting Jew. Well, they paid no attention to it, but
when he got away it come to them, "Well, that must be the
rovin' Jew." It was about as far as from here to the Temple (St.
George Temple, about eight blocks from Mr. Seegmiller's home),
to a drop off the valley. Everyt'ing was clear, and he couldn't
make that distance in the time since he left them. They run out
to look for him but they couldn't see him anywhere. I've often
wondered why they didn't follow his tracks.

MARSHAL NEY, NAPOLEONIC HERO IN AMERICA

The isolated and relatively poor farming districts of Rowan, Davie, Iredell, and Lincoln counties are the unlikely setting for a romantic and fascinating tale of a country schoolmaster named Peter Stuart Ney. Ney came to North Carolina in the early 1820s after a few years' sojourn in the Low Country of South Carolina. A man with bright red hair and several obvious scars evincing a fiery battling nature, Ney contented himself to work for a meager salary gathered as tuition from the families whose children he taught. He depended upon those same families to provide him room and board.

Yet it seemed to many that a man with such an imperious carriage and such personal dignity, a man so apparently self-possessed and so obviously cultivated, should be more ambitious than to work for $200 per year. Others who knew him felt that he was biding his time, that he had his eyes on other things, that teaching was simply a means of providing him a livelihood until he could accomplish another and grander design. His evident distraction and his propensity for writing to late hours at night in some secret journal kept alive rumors that he had much to reveal at some later date. And his voracious reading of newspapers, especially the news from Europe, suggested that he had an active interest in matters far beyond the confines of Piedmont North Carolina.

Indeed the man's behavior was strange. For instance, when news arrived that Napoleon had died, he fainted dead away in his classroom, dismissed classes when he was revived, and that night attempted suicide. In 1830, on learning that Louis Philippe, Duke of Orleans, had ascended to the throne of France and that the Bourbon line was therefore well intrenched, he flew into a rage and could not be consoled for days thereafter. When news arrived that Napoleon's son, L'Aiglon, had died in Vienna, Ney went into a deep depression which took months to dispel, months during which his friends feared he would try to kill himself, for he declared that he had nothing to live for anymore. . . .

Finally, those who lent Ney books knew him as a mischief-maker who defaced the pages of French histories with copious marginalia, declaring this or that false and this or that true, substituting his own versions of recent French history, and in one known instance, correcting the portrait engraving of a famous French marshal.

After his death in Rowan County on November 15, 1846, many of Ney's former students and their parents came forward with tales which seem too wild to be anything but legends. To at least one student in each of the schools in which he taught, Ney had declared that he was not Peter Stuart Ney, Scottish schoolteacher, but in fact was a French refugee, a loyal supporter of Napoleon Bonaparte, indeed was the chief lieutenant of Napoleon: Michel Ney, Marshal of France, Duke of Elchingen, Prince of the Moskowa. He revealed that contrary to common belief in France, he had not been executed before a firing squad in the Gardens of the Luxembourg on December 7, 1815, but had in fact staged the execution with the help of loyal soldiers—even with the help, some say, of a fellow Mason and his chief adversary, the Duke of Wellington!—and escaped with his life to America, where he hid himself to await Napoleon's next attempt on the throne of France. His distracted demeanor, so often observed, was attributed to his brooding long hours about the Bourbon kings, his hoping for the return of the Empire, and his dreaming of a reunion with his wife and sons in Paris. Most of these revelations came when he was delirious with fever or after long bouts of drinking.

There are strange congruences in Ney's confessed identity and in the person of Marshal Michel Ney. The men resembled each other in size and bearing. Both had bright red hair; indeed, Ney was known affectionately to his men as Red Peter Ney. Both had livid scar tissue on the left side of the face, extending from a deep depression in the skull above the ear to the lower jawbone. Both had gunshot wounds. And both had scars on the chest that were reputed to be those made by the steel-shod hooves of horses. Handwriting experts have attested that the penmanship of both men was that of one hand. Finally, Peter Stuart Ney's death was witnessed by at least three persons, all of whom reported that his last words were, "I will not die with a lie on my lips. I am Marshal Ney of France!"

AN OZARK FIDDLER PLAYS NAPOLEON'S BATTLE TUNES

[Uncle Absie Morrison] assumed—and maintained—the role of history teacher. He played for us many of the breakdowns and waltzes and song-tunes we had expected to find in the Ozarks. He also played many marches and tunes with an attached "This is what they played when . . ." The "when's" generally involved military events—marches, retreats, surrenders. Almost invariably these bits of speech and music occurred together.

Uncle Absie was descended from a long line of fiddlers, and many of those same musicians had been involved with one or another of our country's wars. That he should have been sensitive to fiddle tunes depicting historical events is thus not surprising. His great-grandfather, for instance, had fled to Virginia from the Highlands of Scotland because of a poaching infraction just before the Revolution; he joined the patriots, as did three or four brothers who came to America a year later. In 1812 he moved to East Tennessee. Absie's grandfather moved from Tennessee to southern Illinois about 1840, then in 1842 settled in Campbell Valley (later Landis), Searcy County, Arkansas. He was killed by Jayhawkers on his sixty-third birthday, 15 June 1863, because he refused to give up his money to them. Of his five sons, the two eldest joined the Confederate army, while the three youngest went into the Union army. Absie's father was eighteen when he joined the Union forces. He was with Sherman on the march to the sea. He kept his fiddle with him in camp.

Uncle Absie's comments follow the music.

Dry and Dusty

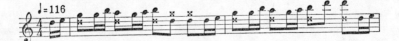

It's a better tune than "Bonaparte's Retreat," but it
ain't got the name. It's just Bonaparte's charge
piece. . . . It was played at the Battle of Waterloo when
he charged the British.

Well, it was a French music. . . . When he charged,
it's fast music, and of course the retreat's slow, you
know.

Bonaparte's Retreat

"Bonaparte's Retreat," now, comes right after ["Dry and Dusty"]. . . . That was played at the Battle of Waterloo. . . . Eighteen and fourteen.

Now that's bagpipe music on a fiddle. . . . That was when [Bonaparte] had to give back, had to give up the battle. And they started to retreat, and all his artillery and stuff just bogged down; they had to leave it, and his horses and everything. . . . That's in history.

Yeah, he had a tune he played when he charged the enemy. See, he charged the British and the Germans, you know, when he was annihilated. They just gobbled his army almost. When he started to retreat, it was so muddy and bad his artillery all bogged up on him; he just had to leave it. He just . . . captured it almost. Well, they did capture it. Put him in a dark dungeon long as he lived. . . . This is in what's called minor key now. . . . They didn't have fiddles in that march. Horns and bagpipes. . . . It's French music.

A FINNISH EYETURNER IN NORTHERN MICHIGAN

We have one instance of a New World eyeturner; an August Sundell [*sic*], who moved to Munising, Michigan, bought a house, and planted a garden which grew overnight. One night he left mysteriously, his garden with him, and only sand and weeds greeted his neighbors the following morning. "This man was an eyeturner," say the good folk of the Forest Lake and Munising region [in the Upper Peninsula]. "The garden never existed."

III. A PARADE
OF HEROES

A land rapidly expanding its frontiers, attracting immigrants from every quarter, and steadily becoming more literate inevitably generated a great quantity and variety of folkloristic and mass-media materials that evidence the emerging American character and experience. This material, as it relates to heroic figures, groups itself into categories less formal and more spontaneous than those in the preceding sections. These groupings—frontiersmen, Indians, badmen, sharp operators, dim wits, liars, storytellers, marvelous animals, and so on—seem to evolve naturally and organically. Taken together, they form a parade of American variety.

The heroes who march in this parade have a characteristic in common: they contain contradictions. This is largely because all American heroes trace some of their ancestry back to two contrasting European types that blended in this land: the backwoods Roarer, whose adventures are American adaptions of the astounding feats and mad escapades originally ascribed to the Russo-German Baron Münchausen; and the village Yankee, a character originating in the British comic figure Hodge, a sly Yorkshire countryman who was a rogue beneath his bland exterior. The Roarer is a product of the semibarbarism of the frontier that began just west of the settlements and preceded them toward the Pacific. He lives close to nature, where he learns that animal virtues best ensure survival. Courage, cunning, brawn, endurance; bragging, drinking, swearing, wenching: such are the terms associated with him as he struts and crows along the rivers and prairie trails. He wrestles grizzlies, fights and then befriends Indians, shoots with incredible accuracy, robs stagecoaches and gives his booty to improvident widows. Some of the tales about him are tall, designed to spoof city folks and take in greenhorns; some are sentimental; some are full of derring-do. All are told by a narrator who assumes a pose of seriousness. The Yankee, on the other hand, is characterized by hard work, common sense, thrift, steadiness, know-how, and handiness. He exists in a world where sales decide a man's worth and where bargaining is the means by which he demonstrates his salt. In many ways, the Yankee is not dissimilar to the tricksters of Indian and West African mythologies. Like Br'er Rabbit, he takes on those who appear to be his betters and whittles them down to size.

It was as the Yankee went West to try his luck on the frontier, as his old villages became cities, and as the Roarers settled down on farms and in towns or moved to the cities that the fusion of the two took place. This created stories of heroes who are typically American because they are at once Yorkshiremen and Münchausens, Yankees and Roarers. Thus Bone Mizell, a cowboy of the Florida savannas, shows his Roarer side when he evens the score with circus officials who had tossed him out, and his Yankee side in the give-and-take of a cattle trade; and "Big Shot" Bill Greenfield, an Adirondack farmer, tells roaring tales about tall turkeys and fast dogs and reveals his Yankee character in the way he pretends that playing checkers is the equivalent of doing the chores. Some of the fused material is generated as crassly as Annie Christmas, who was begotten on the streets of New Orleans; some of it is of ancient lineage, based on the most traditional motifs known to world folklore, like the anecdotes about Foolish John and the wash-pot or about "Oregon" Smith who wept a barrelful of tears. Nearly all of it is set in a turbulent environment where the force of the law is weak (in the West, in the bayous, in the shantytowns, on the street corners, and in the market places), where opportunity belongs to those who are able to grasp it.

FRONTIERSMEN AND PIONEERS •
INDIANS • BADMEN

In a seminal attempt to identify the forces that shaped the American character, the historian Frederick Jackson Turner pointed to the "existence of an area of free land, its continuous recession, and the advance of American settlement westward. . . ." For Turner the frontier with its open space was the most significant factor within the American experience. It shaped the institutions, the system of government, the tone of American life, and it imparted to Americans in general their characteristic qualities. These "striking characteristics," as Turner called them, include "that coarseness and strength combined with acuteness and acquisitiveness; that practical, inventive turn of mind, quick to find expedients; that masterful grasp of material things, lacking in the artistic but powerful to effect ends; that restless, nervous energy; that dominant individualism, working for good and for evil, and withal that buoyancy and exuberance which comes with freedom—these are traits of the frontier. . . ."

Coarseness and strength, of which Jim Bridger scalping a grizzly is an example, are traits of the Roarer, and Johnny Appleseed curing a bewitched cow shows Yankee acuteness and practicality. The rest of Turner's list applies to both Roarers and Yankees, and to that blend of Yankee and Roarer that developed as the Yankee moved from New England to meld with the Roarer on the frontier settlement line.

They are also the traits of the pioneers and badmen, for whom the frontier became a natural habitat. In the frontier space both found at once a freedom to the point of anarchy that exists beyond the reach of the law. For lore that depicts traits such as Turner saw is of necessity full of crosscurrents and contradictions. The pirate Jean Lafitte preys on shipping near New Orleans, yet fights gallantly to save the city from the British, and then flees west to resume his outlaw life and hide his treasure on the Texas coast. Desperadoes like Stagolee murder in cold blood but help women in distress. Legendary Indians, the original inhabitants of the frontier, are likewise replete with contradiction. Watkuese, who saved the explorers Lewis and Clark, or Deluvina, who befriended Billy the Kid, are remembered for their kindness; but Tecumseh and Black Hawk are remembered as dangerous foes. Like Tsali, the Cherokee who defied the troops sent to remove him from his homeland, they are remembered uneasily for their defiance and with sympathy for the maltreatment they received, and they are remembered in different ways by whites and by their own people. Like the frontier itself, the heroic figures of the frontier reflect human contradiction.

THE MAN WHO KILLED GENERAL BRADDOCK

The village of Ohiopyle, Fayette County, Pennsylvania, famous for the falls of the Youghiogheny River at the end of its main street, has a legend which may be lost to history if it is not recorded while some of its old residents are still living. It has been handed down from one generation to another ever since the French and Indian Wars. But the old folks have almost all passed away and only a few of us remember the story that was generally known twenty-five years ago. That an unrecorded story could have lived that long is almost unbelievable. . . .

It is the story of Thomas Fawcett, who lived in these mountains during the French and Indian Wars. Thomas and his unnamed brother were among the mountaineers who were mustered into service under General Edward Braddock to fight the French and Indians, in 1755.

The General undoubtedly was the most important man any of the mountaineers had ever seen and an imposing figure as the leader of the British colonial army. Nevertheless the mountaineers insisted on doing their own thinking and their own fighting. They knew their own country. Just as we modern inhabitants know it better than the people who come here from the cities. And it seems the woodsmen saw rash mistakes.

The details have been lost in the two hundred years that the story has been kept alive by word of mouth. We only know that Fawcett told his friends, later, that, in the thick of battle, the General tried to drive the woodsmen out into the open to fight the French Army. But the Indians were lurking in the shadows of the forest to pick them off and the woodsmen knew it would be folly to obey their leaders' orders. In a rage General Braddock beat Thomas Fawcett's brother across the back with his sword, trying to drive him into view of the enemy. Thomas Fawcett flamed with anger. He considered the General a mad man who would get them all killed if he had his way. From behind a tree he threw up his gun and shot the General off his horse.

History, of course, says that General Braddock fell in the battle. And history is correct. But history does not say who shot him. Only that he lost his life and his army was defeated. Fact, either way, will be proven. We only know that Thomas Fawcett retreated from what is now Route 40—where a monument stands over the remains of General Braddock—to the top of the mountain above the Youghiogheny River. This area was settled long before there was a village by the falls. Just when the first settlers hewed their farms out of the wilderness up there on top of the mountains would take considerable research. But it is known that there were farms there when the Revolutionary War broke out and that one of the pioneers was a man by the name of Mitchell, who joined the rebellion.

Thomas Fawcett hired out to this man as a farm hand and built himself a cabin nearby. It is said he built it without a door, going in and out the window, instead. He told only a few people that he had killed the General and was always wary, seeming to fear arrest. He apparently believed he could defend himself better with only one entrance to his cabin.

Thomas Fawcett died on the mountain-top farm above what is today the borough of Ohiopyle. His grave is marked with a rough stone but lies in land covered with underbrush on the upper side of a country dirt road.

THE COURTSHIP OF DANIEL BOONE

Jim Bryan was a good friend of Dan'l Boone's, and his cabin was in a clearing near the forks of the Yadkin. His daughter Rebecca wasn't more than fifteen, and she thought a right smart of Dan'l.

Late one morning Boone came out of the woods into the clearing and yelled Jim out of the cabin. Jim hadn't seen Dan'l for a long time, and was mighty glad to see him. After they had some dinner that Rebecca cooked herself, Dan'l said he might stay in that part of the country for a long time, but Jim didn't believe it.

Jim talked about how the mountain lions were getting so bad, and Dan'l said they ought to go hunting that night. Back then the men hunted mountain lions at night, and carried a big pan of wood coals to make their eyes show up in the dark. All the hunters had to do was shoot between the eyes.

Rebecca liked to hunt too, and after the men left that night, she followed them.

The men had already got six lions, and had started back to another place to hunt when Jim saw two eyes shining over to one side. He yelled, and Dan'l dropped to one knee and fired. There was a loud scream, and the men didn't know what to do. Then they heard some crying over where Dan'l had shot, and they went to investigate.

They found Rebecca behind a tree, and a dead kitten was on the ground beside her. She said she had been holding the cat in her arms and somebody had shot it. She went home crying, and Dan'l followed her to explain how he didn't know it was a cat.

Jim hadn't believed it possible, but Dan'l did stay in that country a long time—about two years, long enough to marry Rebecca.

The Last Days of Daniel Boone

Boon [sic], however, was not to end his days amid the advantages of social life. After his exemplary labours . . . he suddenly finds that he is possessed of nothing, that his eyes must be closed without a home, and that he must be an outcast in his grey years. His heart is torn, his feelings are lacerated by the chicanery of the law, which discovers that there is a defect in his title to the land of which he was the first settler, even in a state where no white man had put in the spade before him. . . .

He bade his friends and his family adieu for ever; he felt the tie which linked him to social life was broken. He took with him his rifle and a few necessaries, and crossing the Ohio, pursued his track till he was two or three hundred miles in advance of any white settlement. As the territory north of the Ohio was taken possession of, and peopling fast from the United States, he crossed the Mississippi, and plunged into the unknown and immense country on the banks of the Missouri, where the monstrous Mammoth is even now supposed to be in existence. On the shores of this mighty river he reared his rude log hut, to which he attached no idea of permanency, but held himself constantly ready to retire yet farther from civilized man, should he approach too near his desert solitude. With the exception of a son, who resided with his father, according to some accounts, but without any one, according to others, his dog and gun were his only companions. He planted the seeds of a few esculent vegetables round his fragile dwelling, but his principal food he obtained by hunting. He has been seen seated on a log at the entrance of his hut by an exploring traveller, or far more frequently by the straggling Indian. His rifle generally lay across his knees and his dog at his side, and he rarely went farther from home than the haunts of the deer and the wild turkey, which constituted his principal support. In his solitude he would sometimes speak of his past actions, and of his indefatigable labours, with a glow of delight on his countenance that indicated how dear they were to his heart, and would then become at once silent and dejected. He would survey his limbs, look at his shrivelled hands, complain of the dimness of his sight, and lifting the rifle to his shoulder take aim at a distant object, and say that it trembled before his vision, that his eyes were losing their power, rubbing them with his hands, and lamenting that his youth and manhood were gone, but hoping his legs would serve him to the last of life, to carry him to spots frequented by the game, that he might not starve.

Thus he passed through life till he was between eighty and ninety years of age, content in his wild solitude, and in his security from injustice and rapacity. About a twelvemonth ago, it was reported, he was found dead on his knees, with his rifle cocked and resting on the trunk of a fallen tree, as if he had just been going to take aim, most probably at a deer, when death suddenly terminated his earthly recollections of the ingratitude of his fellow-creatures, at a period when his faculties though he had attained such an age, were not greatly impaired.

JOHNNY APPLESEED AND THE BEWITCHED COW

According to Henry A. Pershing in his book "Johnny Appleseed and His Times," Johnny Appleseed was considered one of the "Witch Wizards" or a witch doctor. The following incident shows how this man who had much common sense for his time overruled his superstitious friends.

One day, when Johnny was sitting on a bench with a number of other men in front of the old United States Hotel [in Steubenville, Virginia], Squire Day who lived at Dry Fork on Cross Creek about fifteen miles west of town, came riding up to the tavern.

"Johnny," he called out, "I want you to get a horse and come with me. I've got a sick cow and I've done everything I can to cure her. I know she's bewitched and I've heard that you are quite a hex doctor."

Every man rose to his feet as Johnny started to get his pony, and crowded around the Squire to get all the particulars.

"Tell us about it, Squire," said the short man near him.

"Well, you see it's just this way," said the Squire, "I've got as healthy a cow as there is around Dry Fork, and a few days ago we tried our best to milk her and not a drop would she give down. I gave her a good thump on her side, but it wa'n't no use. Then she refused food and lay down and I can't make her stand up, so I says she's bewitched and I know who's done it. It was the work of Nancy Daugherty, and this ain't the first time she's done it either. I'll fix her, boys, and don't you forget it."

Just then Johnny came out astride of his pony. He

looked enough like a witch to be one, for he was bare-headed, barefooted, wore a sort of Mother Hubbard gown, while his long black hair hung down over his shoulders. His pants were short and ragged and, with his coffee sack for a shirt, he certainly looked odd.

"All right, Squire, where's your witch?" said Johnny as he turned to the men and winked one eye.

"Good luck to you, John!" cried the men and the two rode away. . . .

When they arrived at the stable where the sick cow lay under the witch's spell, Johnny was not surprised, for he knew animals, and he knew this one had not been well treated. She was poor and dirty, and looked at him as much as to say, "Now you're going to be kind to me, ain't you?"

"Well, old girl," said Johnny, "how are you feeling?" and he stroked her head and patted her.

The Squire was looking on, wondering what he would do next, when Johnny said to him, "Get me a handful of salt, Squire, and a bunch of clean hay. I'll soon fix her."

As soon as he got the hay, he sprinkled it with salt and waved it over the cow seven times, muttering some Indian words, which meant nothing, but he knew it would please the Squire. He then let the cow lick the salt from his hand which she greatly relished. She also greedily ate the salted hay and after a long drink of water, she at once rose to her feet and began munching the hay, and ate some bran which the Squire had brought. Then Johnny had a long talk with the cow, and petted her; he then told the Squire to get him a pail and soon filled it with milk from the distended udder, singing a crooning song as he milked.

"She's all right now, Squire, I broke the spell," said Johnny, laughing to himself.

One performance such as this would spread as rapidly as human tongue could pass it on, and he was very often called upon to use his wizard power.

HUGH GLASS FIGHTS A BEAR

Bears were almost as dangerous as Indians. The well-armed hunter who saw the bear first was safe; but a fighting grizzly, confronted unexpectedly, sometimes won. The most famous of Western bear stories is that of Hugh Glass, who killed his attacker but was so torn and bitten that he was unable to accompany his trapper band and was left behind to die. The two companions who were to wait until he should die and then bury him before rejoining the band, grew tired of waiting, deserted him after robbing his corpse-to-be, and told their companions that Glass was now under the ground. But he lived to appear like a ghost and to demand vengeance.

SCALPING GRIZZLIES

The story is told by Captain Randolph B. Marcy of a bear-fighting contest between Jim Bridger and Jim Baker. Upon meeting two young grizzlies Bridger "remarked to his friend that if they could 'pitch in and skulp the varmints with their knives,' it would be an exploit to boast of. They accordingly laid aside their rifles and 'went in.'" But the battle was fiercer than the trappers had counted on. Although victorious they resolved never to try the stunt again; as Bridger phrased it, he would "'never fight narry nother grizzly without a good shootin-iron in his paws.'"

KIT CARSON SHOOTS A BULLY

Living beyond the control of law courts, trappers settled their disputes in the primitive way. When inflamed by bad whisky, their normally unrestrained tempers often led to acts of violence long remembered and later narrated with appropriate additions. Reverend Samuel Parker, who stopped at the Green River rendezvous in 1835, described one such duel: "A hunter, who goes technically by the name of the great bully of the mountains, mounted his horse with a loaded rifle, and challenged any Frenchman, American, Spaniard, or Dutchman, to fight him in single combat. Kit Carson, an American, told him if he wished to die, he would accept the challenge. Shunar defied him." Both fired at close quarters. Carson's ball shattered the hand, wrist and arm of Shunar; then Carson went for another pistol with which to finish the job; but the now humbled bully begged for mercy. Probably Dr. Marcus Whitman, Parker's companion, dressed Shunar's wound, for at this same rendezvous he "extracted an iron arrow, three inches long, from the back of Captain Bridger, which he had received in a skirmish three years before, with the Blackfeet Indians." The manner in which this story of Carson's duel with Shunar has reappeared in many later versions, illustrates the easy transformation of fact into legend.

According to *Kit Carson's Own Story of His Life, as Dictated to Col. and Mrs. D. C. Peters about 1856–57*, edited by Blanche C. Grant (Taos, N. Mex., 1926), the French bully was Captain Drips, an employee of the American Fur Co., which was a bitter rival of Carson's own band, the Rocky Mountain Fur Company. Here Carson is reported as having told the bragging trapper that "If he made use of any more such expressions, I would rip his guts." The extended version by DeWitt Peters, *The Life and Ad-*

ventures of Kit Carson, the Nestor of the Rocky Mountains,
"from facts narrated by himself" (New York, 1858), describes
Carson's opponent as "Captain Shuman, a powerful Frenchman."
Peters sketched in the scene, elaborated on Carson's patience, and
gave a more romantic version of Carson's words to the bully.
Blanche C. Grant, in editing the manuscript which Carson dictated, comments as follows on DeWitt Peters' extended work,
"Carson never read the book as a whole but read enough so he is
said to have remarked that Peters 'laid it on a leetle too thick.'"
Charles Burdett in his *Life of Kit Carson* (New York, 1860), calls
the bully "Shuman" and adds a touch of romantic fiction by making the duel result from Carson's defense of a Blackfoot beauty to
whom "Shuman" was paying repugnant attention.

GRANDMA DOCTOR EMMA FRENCH

Flash floods are an all too common occurrence along the Little Colorado River in Navajo County, Arizona, but no flood in recent years has caused death and injury comparable to the one that roared into the Little Colorado from Cottonwood Wash in August of 1880, and incidentally introduced a most outstanding pioneer woman.

At that time the Atlantic and Pacific Railroad construction camp was located on the east bank of the river, across whose usually trickling stream workmen were in the process of building a bridge, which would extend the rails from Holbrook to the spot which was to become the town of Winslow.

When the great wall of muddy water rushed upon the workmen without warning, men and bridge materials were tossed about like straws. When the flood subsided men were found buried in the mud, their lives snuffed out in an instant, and others were found injured, many internally and others with broken limbs.

There was no doctor at the construction camp, and no quick means of alerting authorities at Holbrook, who knew nothing of the disaster. It was one of the workmen who came up with a solution.

"Send someone after Mrs. Emma French," he said. "She's as near to a doctor as you'll find around here."

His suggestion was immediately acted upon and in due time the messenger returned, accompanied by a short, stout, capable woman with a doctor's little black bag in her hand. There was no delay. She dismounted from the buckboard and went to work. Wounds were stitched, those suffering internal injuries were eased and with the help of the uninjured men broken bones were splinted.

What's more, this intrepid pioneer woman stayed in camp to treat the injured, and to allay the fever which struck some of them after the flood.

Mrs. French had endured many tragedies in her lifetime. She was an Englishwoman who had come to America as a girl of twenty, her passage paid by an emigration fund of the Church of Jesus Christ of Latter Day Saints. From the Atlantic seaport she had traveled westward with one of the "handcart" groups, walking the entire 1400 miles to Salt Lake City.

Two years later—in 1838—she became the sixteenth wife of John Doyle Lee and bore him several children before he was executed for his part in the Mountain Meadows massacre. After Lee's death she moved to Sunset City, at that time a Mormon settlement on the east side of the Little Colorado. There she met a Civil War veteran named Franklin French. He was a widower with two sons, Frederick and Charles. Emma soon married him and moved with him to Horsehead Crossing, near the present city of Holbrook. Raiding Apaches stole their stock and burned their house and all their possessions, necessitating a move.

When the rails reached the point now known as Winslow, French filed on a homestead, the first in that area, on the west bank of the Little Colorado, and he and Emma were joined by his two sons. The boys homesteaded next to their father.

Mrs. French continued treating everyone who called on her for help and soon became known to residents of the growing town as Doctor Grandma French [sic]. Many of the children born in Winslow during those early years were brought into the world by this kindly woman. The railroad authorities were glad to have her services and on many occasions provided a special engine and a caboose to take her to employees at isolated stations along the line from Gallup to Flagstaff.

Many flash floods have scourged the little towns along the Little Colorado since 1880, but none has ever brought to light a personality of such stature as Grandma Doctor Emma French.

WATKUESE SAVES LEWIS AND CLARK

"Lewis and Clark discovered our country," began a ninety-five-year-old Nez Percé, recalling some of the stories she had heard in her childhood. She is Lizzie Lowery, of the village of Kooskia, Idaho. She spoke her own language and was interpreted by Oliver Frank, a Nez Percé.

The people of my village ran away when they saw the white men. They were afraid of their beards. They had never seen people with hair on their faces. And they had never seen mules before. They thought the mules were some kind of overgrown rabbits.

Watkuese saved Lewis and Clark men from being killed. Watkuese means "escaped and return to her own country." The girl had been captured and taken away to some place in the East—somewhere on an island. Her baby was born there, a little boy. When he was six or seven months old, able to sit up and crawl around, she decided to come home to her people. She only knew that she should follow the sun. She tied her baby on her back and crossed the water on a drifting log. Then she walked toward the setting sun. For a long, long time she walked. She used elderberries for food. Old Grizzly Bear escorted her and protected her part of the way, and Chipmunk protected her part of the way. Some white men helped her, too.

Somewhere along the way, her baby died and she buried him. She continued to follow the sun, and so she came back home to her people. That is why she is called Watkuese.

She was in one of our villages when Lewis and Clark came from across the rising sun mountains. She heard the men talking about killing the white men, and she begged them not to, because white men had helped her. So our people made friends with Lewis and Clark and gave them food. They started trading what they had. They helped the white men across the river and escorted them part of their way.

BLACK HAWK REMEMBERED

The Sauks and Foxes were living together at the time, in the Rock River country. White people had been coming in for some time, and helping themselves to the land. Wherever they selected places to live, there they settled down and began to make homes for themselves. The people beheld these doings, and were not at all pleased. When they made protests, the reply they got was that the land was no longer theirs, that it was now the white man's.

About this time came officers of the government, and the chiefs and head men met them in council. The white men presented a paper. It said that an agreement had been made between officers of the government and head men of the Sauks and Foxes; that according to the agreement, the people had given up the possession of all the Rock River country, in return for which the government had paid money, sugar, coffee, pork, tobacco, salt, and whiskey; and at the bottom of the paper was signed the names of the men of both sides who made the agreement. The principal man on the side of the government was the head official at Shallow Water (St. Louis); and the principal man on the side of the Sauks and Foxes was Kwaskwamia. The agreement had been made in the winter-time.

The whole business came with great surprise upon the chiefs and councillors. The paper made clear one thing: it verified the ugly rumors that had gone from mouth to mouth about Kwaskwamia. It was known to all that he had gone to spend the winter near Shallow Water. His object was to be near a trading-post where he could dispose of his pelts as fast as he got them. But it was rumored that he spent much time at the post, and that he hunted little; that he hob-nobbed with the big official there, and that he had much money to spend; that he drank a great deal, and was often so drunk that he was absent from his camp for a long period at a time; and that all the while, even up to the time of his departure, he had plenty of food to eat.

Now, all this was very strange, and the people wondered how it had come to pass. Then, as now, they knew they kept tab on the wealth of one another, and it was easy to guess the limit of one's possessions. Moreover, it was particularly easy to guess how much a man like Kwaskwamia had. He was just a prominent man of a small group of people who happened to have their camps near by one another. This small band made up the party that went to camp near Shallow Water. It was men in this party who signed the paper with Kwaskwamia, and it was the people of this party who spread the gossip about Kwaskwamia and his doings at Shallow-Water post. Kwaskwamia and the men whose names were on the paper denied ever having touched the pen. They must have lied, or else they were drunk at the time and did not know they had touched the pen.

The chiefs and councillors tried to explain to the officers the position of Kwaskwamia,—that the man was not a chief; that he had no power to make a treaty with another nation; that his act was not known before or at the time he did it; that he was not made a delegate to make a treaty on behalf of his people; and that what he did, he did as an individual. They tried to explain to the officers that it was necessary, when a question came up about the cession of land, to let the whole nation know about it; and that when a cession was made, it was necessary first to get the consent of every chief and councillor.

It was of no use to talk about these things. The officers said that the agreement had been made, and that both parties would have to stand by it; that they had come, not to talk about the treaty, but to tell the people to move as soon as possible across to the west bank of the Mississippi.

Naturally the people were loath to leave their old homes; but some had made up their minds to make the best of a bad bargain, and go to the new country. Those most of this mind were the

Foxes. Pawiciga was chief of the Foxes then, and he led his people over across the river. With the Foxes went a band of Sauks.

Among the Sauks was a man who had been prominent in council; his name was Keokuk.

Most of the Sauks were not for going, especially men of the younger class. There was at this time among the Sauks a great warrior; he was of the Thunder Clan, and his name Big-Black-Bird-Hawk. The young men rallied about him, and talked to him about holding the old home, even if it meant war with the white man. He was not willing at first, because the number of his Sauk warriors was not big enough for a long, hard fight; and they had few guns and little ammunition, though they all had bows and arrows. He had fought with the English and with the Shawnee Tecumseh, and knew what it was to fight against the government.

In the midst of these events, he was visited by emissaries from other nations,—from the Potawatomies, Kickapoos, Winnebagoes, Omahas, and the Sioux,—all of them offering help to drive back the white man. A prophet among the Potawatomies told of a vision he had of the manitou, by which power came to him to foretell events. He said that the Big-Black-Bird-Hawk was the man to lead the nations and win back the old homes of the people; that when the fight began, speedily would rise the dead to life again, and the warriors would be without number; that back would come the buffalo and the game-folk that had disappeared; and that in a little while the white man would be driven to the eastern ocean and across to the farther shore from whence he came.

In the end the Big-Black-Bird-Hawk was prevailed upon to go to war. No sooner had he begun, when he discovered that he would have to do the fighting with only the warriors of his own nation and a few others that came from the Kickapoos and Foxes. The chief of the Potawatomies who had urged him so strongly to fight gave the alarm to the white people, and took sides with them as soon as the fighting began. Instead of the Sioux and Omahas coming to his help, they fought against him; and when the Winnebagoes saw how things were going, they joined also with the whites. Indeed, there was little fighting between the Sauks and the white men; most of the fighting was between the Sauks and the other nations. It was the Winnebagoes who made the Big-Black-Bird-Hawk captive. They turned him over to the white men, who carried him away to the east and kept him there a prisoner. After a time he was permitted to return to his people, whom he found living on the west bank of the Mississippi. A short while after he died. Some white men stole his skeleton, and placed it in a great building, where it was on view. The great building caught fire; and it was burned up with the bones of the warrior of the Thunder Clan.

THE LAST DAY OF TECUMSEH'S LIFE

Tecumseh was one of those young Indians who had to go through all the forms of those days, such as fasting, being deprived of a great many things in which other young people of his age took pleasure, in order to be better fitted for the great future that was before him. His parents knew that there was something in their son, and that by fasting they could find out if he was to be of any good to his people.

First they made him fast ten days. As he did not dream anything the first ten days, his parents gave him another ten days. Again he did not dream anything. Then another ten days had to be granted him and just a little food given him in the middle of the day. The last night of his thirty days of fasting he dreamt.

He dreamt that his body would be as iron during the battle in which he would lead. He was blessed with iron; which meant no bullets or anything could ever enter his body during his battles and although once in a great while he would lose a man they too would escape injury just by his being their leader. Tecumseh had to have a certain kind of a leather belt, taken from the hide of a buffalo and this he was to buckle around him to hold his garment, and he was to have a miniature canoe. With this he could always tell whether his battles were to be hard or mild for that day. This he told to his parents was his dream.

His father at once set to work to get him the needs of which he dreamed. From the day he set off for battle, before sunrise his little canoe would be in use telling him whether the battle fought that day would be severe or mild. He would go in the morning to a stream or lake by which they had rested during the night, and would put the little canoe into the water. It would set off and disappear from sight, but would sooner or later return to him. If its stay was long the battle of that day would be severe, and he would prepare for the hard fight which would be before him. If the little canoe hastened its return he knew the battle wouldn't be severe and by this blessing bestowed upon him many were the battles he won.

At last one morning his little canoe didn't return. He now knew his career was to end that day. Knowing that he was going to die he told his men that the blessing bestowed on him had ended. He bowed his head to meet his fate without murmuring.

When Tecumseh returned from any battle, he always unbuckled his belt, and the shot and shell which would have shattered his body would rattle to the ground. His men would stand amazed with wonder at the blessing that had been given him. Tecumseh would beseech in low tones that the blessing would be powerful for his men also.

Tecumseh at the Naval Academy

The War of the Rebellion sounded the death knell to wooden vessels of war. One by one they passed out of existence, supplanted by stauncher ships of more modern trend in design and utility. The old frigates had served their purpose. Not only had they proved their worth against the enemy, but it was upon their decks that our cherished naval tradition was born.

Just as nature has a curious way of taking its own course and finding means of preservation, so is there always a tangible something which links the present with the past and keeps tradition ever in the forefront of our thoughts and ideals. Thus, someone who loved the old frigates brought about the transfer to the Naval Academy of many old figureheads which had proudly graced the bows of the graceful wooden warriors. He linked the present with the past, and to countless young midshipmen provided the incentive for keeping fresh in their minds the thoughts of Service.

To the body of midshipmen, the figureheads, in general, represented glorious deeds on gallant ships. One figurehead, however, stood out above the others. It was the bust of the old Indian

Chief. Some knew it as Powhatan. Some gave it other names. But finally the nickname of Tecumseh was accepted by all. And as Tecumseh it is known today.

They called the figurehead the "God of 2.5" [the lowest passing grade], and as they marched to and from their recitations, they muttered a prayer for success. Eventually, Tecumseh became an important figure in the ritual of the student body. The statue became so great a symbol that every "Plebe" was required to show his humility to the great warrior and to the mythological power represented, by a reverent salute and a "by your leave" upon entering the august presence.

When, in 1906, it became necessary to move the carved figure to a new location, it was found to be in such a condition of decay that serious consideration was given to the thought of destroying it. The news spread and reached the ears of the Head of the Department of Seamanship, Lieutenant Commander A. W. Grant. The latter literally captured the old Indian Chief and removed him to the precincts of his department. There the statue was repaired. The decayed wood was replaced by concrete, putty, and paint, and Tecumseh, reinstalled on a new and firm foundation, again appeared to reinspire the midshipmen to nobler efforts.

Tecumseh in Bronze

On December 3, 1929, all available members of the Class of '91 assembled at the Naval Gun Factory to attend the ceremonies of casting in bronze the figure of Tecumseh. Rear Admiral Willard, Commandant and Superintendent, made the address of the occasion. Those members who were unable to be present will be interested in the following extracts from his speech:

"Fellow Members of the Class of 1891—U.S. Naval Academy:—

"We have met today to witness the act of casting in enduring bronze the sculptured figure of this man who

lived more than two hundred years ago, who may be
truly called a Great American, and who, through his
great virtues, so left the imprint of his character upon
the History of America that those who have followed
after him have been glad to do honor to his memory.

"After sufficient funds had been raised, we here at the
Gun Factory undertook to make the bronze TECUM-
SEH and I must say it was no easy task, for the wooden
image could not be damaged or destroyed in making the
mold. The Superintendent of the Naval Academy was
very clear about that!

"Throught the skill and cleverness of our Master Pattern Maker, Mr. W. Crawford, and our Master Molder,
Mr. J. E. Crown, and their able assistants, particularly
Messrs. A. A. Griest, F. A. Keaggy, patternmakers, and
Quarterman Molder Harry Hill and Messrs. H. King and
W. Hissey, Molders, we have finally made the precious
mold for our old Indian Chief and we will now pour
about thirty-five hundred pounds of bronze metal into
this mold and when the sand is cleared away I feel
confident that we will have a TECUMSEH who,
through his greater strength and resistance to the rav-
ages of the passing years, will exert even greater powers
than he did when he was made of wood.

"Next Spring when we return TECUMSEH to his sacred precincts at the Naval Academy, he will go with the
best wishes of the Naval Gun Factory where we have
faithfully and tenderly made him into bronze, and we
hope that he will shine in a new glory in keeping with
those high principles which he exemplified when this nation was in its infancy." . . .

Saturday, May 31, 1930, was designated as the day upon which
the statue would be presented to the Naval Academy. The
speaker, to whom was given the honor of making the speech of

presentation was, by unanimous choice, Vice Admiral Arthur L. Willard, U. S. Navy, Commander Scouting Fleet. [Extract from his speech follows:]

"In order that this bronze figure may lose none of the potent power with which the Midshipmen have endowed the historic wooden Indian Chief, we have been careful to transfer the 'wooden brains' and the 'heart' of the ancient wooden Indian into this new one of bronze.

"They were trepanned out of the wooden figure and together with the original arrows, tomahawk, and calumet —the pipe of peace—were placed inside the figure in a cast bronze box hermetically sealed after sterilization by heat and exhausting the air.

"In order that proper records for the future may be preserved, we have placed inside this bronze box a complete list of all members of the class of 1891 and a short resume of their history, photographs of the wooden and bronze busts, outline of the design of the U.S.S. DELAWARE, and other documents in connection with the HISTORY of this venerated character and his bust.

"It is well to touch upon the important points of this history.

"When the U. S. Ship of the Line 'Delaware' was being built at the Norfolk Navy Yard in 1817 to 1821, Commodore John Rodgers of the Navy Commissioners, asked of Senator V. Van Dyke, one of the senators from Delaware, for suggestions for a figurehead for the ship bearing the name of that State. On January 5, 1821 a letter signed by Senators Van Dyke and O. Horsey and Representatives Willard Hall and L. McLane of Delaware, stated that the Indian Chief Tamanend was the most distinguished chief of the Delaware Indians and his name was connected with the early history of our country, and suggested that his bust would be an appropriate figurehead for the Ship-of-the-Line, 'Delaware'.

"This suggestion was duly adopted and the figurehead representing Tamanend was carved and placed on the 'Delaware'. The records, so far examined, unfortunately do not disclose the name of the sculptor who carved this splendid figure. It seems probable however, that it was the work of William Rush, a sculptor of Philadelphia and famous at that time for his carvings in wood of similar character.

"It was, therefore, with a feeling of gratitude in our hearts to this great institution and those officers who guided our early footsteps here, and to all those who have maintained its high standards since the day of its establishment in 1845, that we of the class of '91 desired to place some memorial at this Academy which would be expressive of our appreciation of the rigid training we received here during the four years when we battled for a 'Two-Five' in order that we might win our commissions in the Navy. . . ."

TSALI AND THE CHEROKEE REMOVAL

The bare and undisputed plot of the Tsali tale is as follows: during the forced removal of the Cherokee Indians to the West by United States Army troops under command of Major Winfield Scott in 1838, a number of Cherokees escaped by fleeing into the mountains, particularly around the Little Tennessee River and its tributaries, where the "rhododendron hells" were so nearly impenetrable that pursuit would have been a nasty business. One family of escapees, Tsali (or "Charley") and his wife and children, killed United States soldiers in their flight. The Army made a deal (with precisely whom depends upon the version) that, if Tsali and his family were returned to Army custody for punishment, the rest of the escapees would be left at large until further notice. The deal was honored on both sides, and the surviving fugitives became the ancestors of the present Eastern Band of Cherokee Indians on the Qualla Reservation in North Carolina.

The Army Version

Fort Cass, Tennessee, Novr. 5, 1838

Lieut. Larned.
Sir:
Agreeable to your instructions dated Ft. Butler Sept. 17th, I repaired immediately to Oconeelufty, N. Carolina for the purpose of collecting all the Indians in that neighborhood belonging to the nation. . . . On our way down the Little Tennessee river, I heard of a party of Indians within a few miles of us, & thinking it my duty to collect them if possible, I proceeded in company with Mr. [William H.] Thomas & three men to their camp,

sending the other party on down the river in charge of a sergt. & eight men. I found but eight at their camp, but understanding that there were twenty belonging to the company, I concluded to stay with them until next morning, hoping they would all come in. I was, however, obliged to start with only twelve of the company. This day I expected to overtake the other command; but was forced to stop at Is. Welsh's. . . . On the evening of the 1st. I discovered an unwillingness among the Indians to travel, & in order to make greater speed, I put some of the children on horses, but it was with great difficulty that I could then get them along. I suspected all was not right; & frequently cautioned the men to be on their guard. Shortly after sunset I discovered a long dirk knife in the possession of one of the Indians, & ordered it to be immediately taken from him. He turned it over without any hesitation, & we had proceeded but a short distance before I spied an axe or [illegible word] which I also ordered to be taken from them, but, I am sorry to say, too late, for I had scarcely furnished the order, before I saw the axe buried in the forehead of one of my men. This being the signal for attack, the others fell immediately to work, & in less than one minute they killed two, wounded a third, & commenced searching them, & carrying off every article they could lay their hands on. I, fortunately, escaped unhurt, & owe my life in a measure to the spirit & activity of my horse.

(signed) A. J. Smith
2d. Lt. 1st. Dragoons.

A Journalist's Sketch

Another of the characters I intended to mention is named *Euchella*. He is a very worthy chief, and now in the afternoon of his days. He is quite celebrated among his people as a warrior, but is principally famous for important services rendered by him to the United States Government during the Cherokee troubles. He, and a band of one hundred followers, first attracted public attention by evading, for upwards of a whole year, the officers of Government who had been commanded to remove the party beyond the Mississippi. It having been ascertained, however, that Euchella could not easily be captured, and would never submit to leave his country, it was determined that an overture should be made, by which he and his brotherhood of warriors could be secured to assist the whites in their troublesome efforts to capture three Indians who had murdered a number of soldiers. The instrument employed to effect a reconciliation was the Indian trader, Mr. Thomas, who succeeded in appointing a meeting with Euchella on a remote mountain-top.

During this interview, Mr. Thomas remonstrated with Euchella, and told him that, if he would join the whites, he might remain in Carolina, and be at peace. 'I cannot be at peace,' replied the warrior, 'because it is now a whole year that your soldiers have hunted me like a wild deer. I have suffered from the white man more than I can bear. I had a wife and a little child—a brave, bright-eyed boy—and because I would not become your slave, they were left to starve upon the mountains. Yes; and I buried them with my own hand, at midnight. For a whole week at a time have I been without bread myself, and this in my own country too. I cannot bear to think upon my wrongs, and I scorn your proposition.' It so happened, however, that he partially relented, and having submitted the proposition to his warriors, whom he summoned to his side by a whoop, they agreed to accept it, and from that time Euchella became an ally of the army. It was by the efforts of Euchella and his band that the *murderers* already mentioned were arrested and punished. They had been condemned by a court martial, and sentenced to be shot, and the scorn of death manifested by one of them, named Charley, is worth recording. He had been given into the hands of Euchella, and when he was tied to the tree, by one arm, where he was to die, (to which confinement he submitted without a murmur,) he asked permission to make a few remarks, which was of course granted, and he spoke as follows: 'And is it by your hands, Euchella, that I am to die? We have been brothers together; but Euchella has promised to be the white man's friend, and he must do his duty, and poor Charley is to suffer because he loved his country. O, Euchella! if the Cherokee people now beyond the Mississippi carried my heart in their bosoms, they never would have left their beautiful native land—their own mountain land. I am not afraid to die; O, no, I want to die, for my heart is very heavy, heavier than lead. But, Euchella, there is one favor that I would ask at your hands. You know that I had a little boy, who was lost among the mountains. I want you to find that boy, if he is not dead, and tell him that the last words of his father were that he must *never* go beyond the Father of Waters, but die in the land of his birth. It is sweet to die in one's own country, and to be buried by the margin of one's native stream.' After the bandage had been placed over his eyes, a little delay occurred in the order of execution, when Charley gently raised the bandage, and saw a dozen of Euchella's warriors in the very act of firing; he then replaced the cloth, without manifesting the least anxiety or moving a muscle, and in a moment more the poor savage was weltering in his blood. And so did all three of the murderers perish.

A Cherokee Recollection

Charley, he got into trouble down to Bushnell, North Carolina, and he had four boys. You know, some people say he only had two, but they're wrong. And beside this was a boy named Lloyd, that makes five. Lloyd was somebody else, a boy who talked English. And the rest of the people being driven away was way down Chattanooga, resting. And Charley, he's one of the last to be rounded up. And Standing Wolfe—he's a great man too [ancestor of a large family now living on the Reservation]—is below where they had the trouble.

And Charley's wife had a baby two months old—that's what Washington [Tsali's son] said. And he said, "I can't tell you really what about it, I was too small," he said, "I'm too young."

He said, "My mother, she had a baby and she had to change his clothes or something. She sat down on a log. Then after a while a soldier got up. 'Hurry up!' and he was pushing her to get up and she won't move, and she just kept on cleaning it—her baby. Then the other one got up with a horse whip. He beat her up with a horse whip."

Then after a while they went and pick up both of them, her and the baby. Then they went and set them on the horse. As soon as the horse moved, then that lady, she's just trying to fall off and she got her foot hung in the stirrup. Then her baby dropped. It went that way, out yonder, and bust the head. And it died right then.

That's how come Charley got mad. He and his boys just used a stick and beat up, they killed two soldiers.

"Well," he said, "we're five, let's try to kill'em all."

They killed two and then the other one [escaped]; then he [Charley] just turned around and led the horses and went as fast as he can and he went to another place, where Standing Wolfe was. He told Standing Wolfe what happened.

Then Charley says he didn't know what they done with that baby, they pick it up, they just laid it down somewheres—they didn't bury it.

Then they all went together to the river. Washington said they had to go up to the bank in the bushes. It was at night, that happened. Then they sat down way out somewhere, and you can't hear nothing, it's just so quiet. They sat there long time.

Then Charley said, "Let's pray." They went to pray.

After they got through praying . . . "Let me look round so we could cross somewhere." And he got out and went to the creek and after a while he came back.

He said, "I guess we could, I guess I find it."

Then they all started. Washington said, 'The mommy and daddy they lead me. I was too small yet.' He said, 'It wasn't deep, just a trace where we crossed. Then we went up on the hill.' He didn't know all about it much. He said he was just kinda scared.

And they find a great big drought—dry place—he said, they all lay down right there.

Next morning early they started again. He said he didn't know how far they gone. About noon, he said, they saw somebody farming way out there, somewhere. He saw hops [?], and he didn't know where it was. His daddy sent that other boy, the one who could talk English.

"Go, you go over there to that house and ask him if they have some bread." They was hungry. They never had a bite, two days.

Then he went out there, then after a while he came back. He had some bread and meat. Then that man, the one that lived there, he followed that boy and then he come behind. He come right there. And he was kind, that man. (He was White man.)

He said, "I know what's happened and I want you to stay, about three, four days, and rest. There's another dry place. It's a little ways right there above where you're at." And he showed them a great big rock overhang, where they could stay. He said, "You just stay right there and rest. I'm going to feed you long as you're here. If you stay about four days it be all right."

Washington said they did stay about two nights and two days. He said he brings the bread and milk and meat, sometimes beans. He fed them.

Then they took a notion that they just leave and they left then. Washington said that they went over to the Tennessee side. They crossed somewhere, he didn't know where, he was too young.

Then the Army made out that the Indians had to go look for their own people—Cherokee Indian! They had to kill them their self too—not White man, not Government. And they did find them over in Tennessee somewhere.

When Charley and his boys got caught and they got ready to be killed, they were just tied up on the tree, and they kill them— Charley and the three older boys. Washington didn't say they use a gun. He just said, "They dressed me up just like they did the other ones." He said they put on a coat—black; then they tied up their heads—black. And he was all ready to be killed too.

"Then after a while," he said, "two men come, they got me to leave me run. Way out yonder, talking . . . they was talking. Then they just unbuttoned my coat, then they took off my coat and they took my cap off and they gave me my mother's things, they give them back."

They spared his mother too.

And this man Washington, every time when he talk about his mother and daddy, tears run down his eyes. And I just sat there watching. I just heard it when he was telling my mother and step-father.

DELUVINA, FRIEND OF BILLY THE KID

Deluvina was an Indian girl adopted by Lucien Maxwell in the late 1840's. I figure that she was about the same age as Pete Maxwell (borned in 1848). When Lucien sold his interest in the Maxwell Land Grant (in 1870), he bought the improvements of old Fort Sumner and moved his livestock and family from the Rayado Ranch to Fort Sumner. Deluvina grew up as a slave or peon in the Maxwell family at Rayado and Fort Sumner. When the four big cattle companies bought Fort Sumner from the widow after Maxwell's death in 1875, Doña Luz Maxwell moved a mile and a quarter to a place just off the Fort Sumner Navajo Indian Reservation, and established a new home, which is still standing today.

When the four Companies took charge of the Fort, there was a dozen or two families living in the soldiers' barracks and other buildings. The managers let them stay, as we needed help, and many of them filed on vacant lands for the cattle companies.

At this time Deluvina did not move with the Maxwells, but remained at the Fort and lived by herself. She was a natural-borned nurse. She helped with the sick, and did washing and ironing for the men. And at times, when transient cattle herds were moving north, if one of the men took the fever or had an accident, they never did stop the herd—just brought him over to one of the old Barracks buildings, unloaded him and his bed, and sent for Deluvina to take care of him. I saw this happen with a boy that got his leg broken. She took charge, swept and cleaned the room, cooked the meals, and took care of the boy until his leg healed. She had the Indian custom of gathering herbs for her "remedios." I have often seen her walking across the prairie far from the settlement, stooping every little while to gather some little weed or wild flower to use in her homemade medicines.

Deluvina was short and very stout and not at all attractive. She would get drunk sometimes, but was very temperate on tobacco. She worked for me once when my wife needed help. She would prepare a meal and, while we were eating, she would sit and roll a small cigarette and smoke it. She would smoke only three a day.

I believe that she was a Navajo or a Ute. I know that she had a terrible hatred for the Comanche Indians. When the younger cowboys wanted to tease her, they would yell, "Heap Comanche!" When she heard this, she would run into the house, get her big butcher knife, and try to catch the boys and cut them up. She never could catch them; she was too short and stout to run very fast; but we all used to enjoy seeing her run after the fleeing boys, waving the big knife and shouting curses.

Deluvina first became acquainted with Billy the Kid when he and his outlaw friends were arrested and brought to Fort Sumner in 1880. Billy and his four companions were handcuffed and placed on the bare floor of a little adobe hut in the town. It was a bitter cold day, and Billy had no coat. Chilled from twenty-four hours of exposure, he sat, pale and shaking and looking very young and pitiful. The kind-hearted Indian woman pushed her way through the crowd of curious spectators around the door, pulled off her black shawl, and wrapped it around Billy's thin shoulders. After that, she and Billy became good friends. Some people have tried to say that she was Billy's sweetheart, but she was always more like a mother to him. It was to her that he gave the tintype picture of himself, said to be the only authentic likeness of the famous outlaw.

Several months later, when Billy was shot by Sheriff Pat Garrett in Pete Maxwell's darkened bedroom, Deluvina was the only one who dared to go into the room to see if he (Billy) might be still alive. While the men hesitated, arguing that The Kid might still be alive and just pretending to be hurt in order to kill anyone who tried to investigate, the Indian woman lit a candle and went boldly into the room. When she found that her friend was indeed dead she burst out crying, smoothing his hair and saying, "Mi pobre Beely! Mi querido Beely!"

For many years she visited Billy's grave regularly. She very probably was the one who put the first marker: a cross made of two
pickets from the parade ground fence on which were written
Billy's name and the date, with the added sentiment: "Duerme
bien, Querido." (Sleep well, Beloved.) Once I saw her leaving the
graveyard in a big sandstorm. I shall never forget her face all
covered with dust in which were little tracks where the tears had
run down.

Badmen

JEAN LAFITTE'S TREASURE

In the Abbeville country, Louisiana, there is a legend, handed down from the last century, to the effect that Lafitte and his pirate crew, having run a schooner up into White Lake (Louisiana coast) through a bayou which has long since been filled and grown over with marsh grass, at some spot along the shore built a brick vault in which they stored a vast amount of their ill-gotten treasure.

About the year 1908 a man named C—— claimed to have stumbled upon the vault while hunting alligators. He further claimed to have torn away, though with much difficulty, portions of the brick work, revealing untold wealth in gold coin, the hidden treasure of Lafitte.

Numbers of persons to whom this story was told became interested in making a search for the treasure. Owing to the swampy condition of the country and the inaccessibility of the spot where the vault was located, C—— advised the digging of a small canal as the best means of reaching it. This idea was adopted, money was advanced for the purpose, some five or six thousand dollars, and the digging of the canal was begun. After weeks of toil, of chopping through dense canebrakes, and of floundering through the swamp mud, the party reached a lone cypress tree that was supposed to stand sentinel over the crypt. The treasure could not be found.

Disappointed in their quest and disgusted at their own credulity, the treasure seekers caused the arrest of C—— on the charge of having taken their money under false pretenses; C—— claimed as the reason for their failure that he had lost his bearings. Who knows?

Lafitte's Lieutenants

John Smith and W. C. Callihan of the old town of Liverpool, Brazoria County [Texas], are [in 1924] each eighty-four years old; each is sound in mind and body; and each has spent practically his entire life in the vicinity of Liverpool. These men speak familiarly of Warren D. C. Hall, of Lamar, and of Lafitte's lieutenants. The legendary material here given is based on their separate statements. However, the stories told by them coincide to a remarkable degree. Liverpool is situated on Chocolate Bayou, and is so near Galveston Island that the early history of the two places is closely related. Consequently Smith and Callihan are familiar with the lore bearing on Lafitte's life. What they have to say is not based so much on legends in general circulation as on the stories told them by Lafitte's associates. One of these followers of Lafitte was Jim Campbell, who, after the departure of his chief from Galveston Island in 1821, settled on what became known as Campbell's Bayou. The other was an odd character called Captain Snyder.

No story of Lafitte proceeds very far without referring in some way to buried treasure. The lives led by the two strange characters just mentioned caused many to believe that they had stored away some of their chief's wealth. According to Smith and Callihan, these ex-associates of Lafitte never lacked money, although they were engaged in no profitable business. Long after the death of Jim Campbell, it was generally believed that his widow knew where money was buried but was unwilling to reveal the place.

Captain Snyder was likewise known to have plenty of money. He was engaged in carrying some kind of trade from the Brazos to Liverpool, for which he used a one-eyed mule, but he got little income from this occupation. His actions at times, too, were rather strange. Smith was often on the boat with him, and when they would approach Galveston Island, Snyder would frequently get off and go ashore. There he would go to a clump of bushes, and apparently try to get his bearings for some point.

Some of the buried treasure stories, however, are based on more direct information. In the fifties, according to the authorities already quoted, there appeared at the mouth of Chocolate Bayou a small vessel, which remained in that vicinity for several days. During the daytime it would go to the opposite side of the bay, and at night it would return to the near shore. This odd procedure aroused a little curiosity, but would doubtless have been soon forgotten had not an important discovery followed. A few days after the vessel had gone, Smith and Callihan paid a visit to the mouth of the Bayou and, to their surprise, found that excavations had been made. Beginning at the shore, a long trench had been opened, and at the end of this a large hole had been dug. Apparently, a chest of some kind had been taken out, for the imprint of the box—even to the handles—was plainly visible. As further evidence, there was lying to one side a broken earthen jar that had been sealed with sealing wax, and upon its fragments were imprints of coins. . . .

Captain Snyder, who has already been mentioned, was a strange character. Those who knew him declare that he slept with one eye open, and that often he would cry out in his sleep, "Boys, the Spaniards are coming." He told many Lafitte stories. He had seen service with his chief on voyages against the Spanish. According to his description, these encounters with the Spaniards were bloody affairs. Blood ran off the decks like water, and when the fight was over, the enemy dead were thrown into the sea. One of the most remarkable incidents related by Snyder, however, pertained to the storm of 1819. Lafitte, with his four ships, was in the bay when the hurricane arose. The storm became so intense that he decided to go with his vessels to the high seas and take his chances there. He headed toward the channel, but, as the wind was blowing from the east, he was unable to get out that way. He therefore came back and drove his vessels straight across the island in six or seven feet of water.

The Iron Box

There are stories [current in Beeville, Texas] of buried treasure left by the pirate and buccaneer Jean Lafitte. A certain Steve Pipkins was instructed by a "spirit" to go to a tree on the San Antonio River, and from it to step twenty-five feet south, one foot east, and one foot north, and then to dig down three feet. "Then," said the spirit, "you will find a square iron box left by Jean Lafitte." The man did not believe in spirits or buried treasure, and refused to go; but his wife urged and insisted until he had to for the sake of peace. When he arrived at the place, he found—no, not the box, but the hole from which it had just been removed, and around which the dirt was still fresh.

MUSTANG GRAY, HORSE THIEF AND HORSEMAN

... Mustang Gray, Pat Quinn, and another "Mustanger" named Andy Walker were in Corpus Christi, when some Mexicans came in with a *caballada* from the Rio Grande. They camped near a mud flat, about where Portland is now. Gray and his companions wanted the horses—and, of course, considered them legitimate prey. They rode to the mud flat, dismounted, pulled off all their clothes, wallowed in the mud, tied *cabestros* (hair ropes) around their foreheads, all to give themselves the appearance of wild Indians, and charged into camp. The Mexicans stampeded in one direction and their horses in another, all except one *viejo* too old to run, who stood his ground and picked up an *escopeta* (blunderbuss). Mustang Gray was in the lead, the loose end of the *cabestro* around his forehead dragging the ground. At the edge of the camp Andy Walker's horse stepped on the rope, jerking Mustang from his mount just as the old Mexican fired. His gun did no damage. Mustang finished him while the other two men scurried after the runaway horses.

How Mustang Gray Won His Name

As long as the *mesteños*, or mustang horses, that used to roam all over the Southwest, but nowhere else in such numbers as between the Nueces and the Rio Grande, are remembered, the story of how Mabry Gray won his name will, I think, be told. The story has been printed more than once. I have heard several men, all scant of detail, tell it.

Soon after coming to Texas, young Gray with some other men went far out from the settlements to hunt buffaloes. In a chase

after a bunch of them that scattered and ran Gray became separated from his companions. His horse fell, throwing him to the
ground. Gray was uninjured, but when he jumped to his feet he
saw the horse, excited by the chase and frightened by the
buffaloes, racing rapidly out of sight. For hours Gray wandered
about afoot, hoping to catch sight of one of the other hunters.
Darkness found him still alone and afoot in the vast solitude.

After a restless night of thirst and anxiety he arose with the
dawn to try to retrace his steps. Before long he spied a wounded
buffalo in a small thicket. He still had his gun and ammunition,
and he quickly killed the animal. Then, having cut off a portion
of meat, he turned to look for water. A clump of green guided
him to a pond. There he drank, made a fire, cooked the meat, and
after he had eaten it, felt fortified. He had wandered about the
preceding day so much that he was completely lost; but now he
could calmly plan. Around the pond he saw horse tracks—
mustangs. He must capture one and ride it to the settlements.
But he had no rope or saddle. He could do without the saddle.

About this time he saw a band of mustangs galloping towards
the pond. He climbed a tree and watched them pass beneath, paw
about, drink, and leave. His plans were made. Of course he carried
the customary Bowie knife of the frontier. He returned to the
carcass of the buffalo he had killed, skinned it, brought the hide
back to the pond, and spent the remainder of the day carving it
into a strong reata. All animals have regular hours for watering,
and when, next morning, the time approached for the mustangs
to come again, Gray tied one end of his reata to a strong limb of
the tree over the trail, with the other end of it in hand climbed
up, and, loop open, took a position that would give him a clear
space in which to swing and cast it. He knew that he would have
but one cast, or throw, at the mustangs. He must not miss. He did
not miss.

The animal he had selected was a stout stallion. It ran on the
rope, threw itself, and still the reata held. It reared, kicked,
plunged, but all to no purpose. It was held fast. For a long time
Gray worked with the stallion, somewhat accustoming him to the

sight and smell and feel of a man. He had made a hackamore (halter) and reins out of some of the buffalo hide, and this he finally adjusted on the mustang's head. Then he managed to get astride. The stallion tore away, but he did not run far until he hit the end of the rope, which was still fastened to the tree, jerking himself down and throwing his rider. After this Gray petted the animal and worked with him some more. At last he felt confident of being able to keep his seat and direct the course of the mustang.

Now he fastened his gun to his own back, untied the reata from the tree, again mounted, headed the mustang towards the settlements, and let him go. The prairie was open without bush or bluff. The wild horse ran for many miles until he was completely exhausted. That night Gray staked him out. A wild horse learns very readily to fear a rope; the stallion grazed. The quickest way in the world to tame a wild horse is to ride him off his range into solitude, where he soon comes to depend upon as well as fear his master. On the second morning Gray had little trouble in mounting the mustang and controlling him.

Thus riding bareback, he traveled for several days. Then, quite by accident, he came to the camp of his companion hunters, who had given him up for lost. They at once dubbed him Mustang Gray, and by that name he went until he died.

There are various tales illustrative of how well-trained Mustang's horses were. After the capture of Monterrey [in 1846], as Pat Quinn used to tell the story, General Worth, acting under orders from Taylor, ordered the city cleared of soldiers—particularly of Texans. When the order was announced, Mustang Gray and other rangers were on the plaza mounted. The plaza was spread with tables used for serving *tamales, enchiladas,* and other food upon. Turning to one of the riders named Thompson, Mustang shouted, "Will your horse take that row of tables?" "Yes." Both rangers started leaping their horses from one table to another. Thompson's crashed through a table, but Mustang rode clear across the plaza—and then, obedient to military orders, out of town.

The Curse on Goliad

After the Texas Revolution the outlaws were worse around Goliad and Victoria than anywhere else. One day while a good old Mexican priest was saying mass in the mission church of La Bahia, a band of these terrible men from Goliad, across the San Antonio River, entered, and with sombreros on their heads, pistols in their belts, spurs on their heels, and quirts in their hands, strode down the aisle towards the padre, cursing and threatening as they came. Mustang Gray was at their head. The padre paused in his prayers, and, turning to them, requested them to leave the house of God in peace. Perhaps it was the reserve and dignity of the old padre that halted the bandits. Anyhow, they left.

An hour later, all worshipers having withdrawn, the padre closed the church door and set out walking for his home in Goliad. He had not gone far when Mustang Gray and some other bandits stepped out of the brush in which they had been awaiting him and seized him roughly. "Now you are in our house," they taunted, "and must do as we say." They roped him and bound his hands and made him dance to what they called "pistol music." The padre was still dancing to this music and some of the bandits had begun to enliven his jumps with sharp blows of their quirts, when a party of responsible citizens came along. These men quickly overpowered the bandits and freed the priest.

"Now, Father," they said, "these vile wretches are in your power. They deserve to swing from the stoutest live oak tree in Goliad County, and we will do with them whatever you say. You name the punishment and we'll give it."

"Then release them," simply replied the old padre. "Let their consciences be both their accusers and their punishers."

The padre paused, swept his arms toward Goliad, and concluded, "From this day forth may God's curse be upon that town."

And, to conclude with the words of the old Mexican woman of La Bahia, "that is why Goliad, since the time of the padre and Mustang Gray, never has amounted to anything and never will amount to anything."

The Song of Mustang Gray

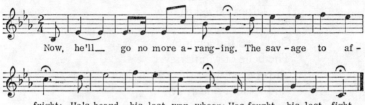

Now, he'll__ go no more a-rang-ing. The sav-age to affright; He's heard his last war whoop; Has fought his last fight.

There was a noble ranger,
They called him Mustang Gray;
He left his home when but a youth,
Went ranging far away.

    But he'll go no more a-ranging
    The savage to affright;
    He's heard his last war-whoop
    And fought his last fight.

He ne'er would sleep within a tent,
No comforts would he know;
But like a brave old Tex-i-an
A-ranging he would go.

When Texas was invaded
By a mighty tyrant foe,
He mounted his noble warhorse
And a-ranging he did go.

Once he was taken prisoner,
Bound in chains upon the way;

He wore the yoke of bondage
Through the streets of Monterrey.

A señorita loved him
And followed by his side;
She opened the gates and gave to him
Her father's steed to ride.

God bless the señorita,
The belle of Monterrey;
She opened wide the prison door
And let him ride away.

And when this veteran's life was spent,
It was his last command,
To bury him on Texas soil
On the banks of the Rio Grande.

And there the lonely traveler,
When passing by his grave,
Will shed a farewell tear
O'er the bravest of the brave.

Now he'll go no more a-ranging,
The savage to affright;
He's heard his last war-whoop
And fought his last fight.

JAMES COPELAND OF THE MURRELL GANG

In the early eighteen hundreds a trading route was opened from Georgia through Alabama across to Natchez, Mississippi. On this route traveled traders, settlers, land speculators and often adventurers.

In the location now known as Walker Springs, Alabama, a man by the name of William Walker opened an inn for travelers on this old route.

Mr. Walker had a lovely young daughter named Elizabeth, and on the particular date that our story begins, Elizabeth and a group of neighborhood girls were together at the inn. As young girls will, they were gaily talking about their future husbands and upon an impulse decided to go look in the well where traditions said the face of their lover would appear. Elizabeth was the first to look in the well, and upon peering into it, she gasped and fainted. When she revived, she told the other girls that she had very clearly seen the face of a man in the well. Of course this was not believed by the other girls, and for a while the incident was forgotten.

Time went on, and one day a handsome young stranger on a sleek, dark horse came riding down the trail and stopped at the Walker Inn. Elizabeth gave one look at him and ran into the kitchen. She was very excited and upset, and told her mother that this was the man whose face was reflected in the well.

The stranger gave his name as James Collins and said that he was a land speculator and trader. Mr. Collins rode away but returned about two weeks later. He asked Elizabeth to marry him. She became his bride and left to make her home with him on the Natchez Trace. Here not far from Natchez James built them a comfortable home.

Time went on, and twin boys were born to James and Elizabeth.

One day during one of James's frequent absences Elizabeth was seated on the front porch watching her babies play. Suddenly she looked up to see herself surrounded by a group of men on horseback. One of them spoke, "Mrs. Copeland, is your husband at home?"

Stunned, Elizabeth replied, "My husband's name is not Copeland. It is Collins."

The man laughed. "Well, Mrs. Collins, is your husband at home?"

Elizabeth told him no, and said he was on a trading expedition and would not be back for another day or so.

One of the men said to her, "Mrs. Collins, I can tell that you are a nice person and a lady, and for your own good you should know this. Your husband's name is not Collins; it is Copeland, and he is a member of the Murrell clan. We know about where he is, and soon will catch up with him."

Now the Murrell clan at that time was notorious in Alabama. It was composed of men of all kinds and from all stations of life. The clan worked along the trade route robbing travellers, stealing horses, cows and slaves and not holding the slightest value to a human life.

Of course, Elizabeth was completely shocked to hear this, and upon the armed man's advice and help, she and the babies returned to her father and the Walker Inn.

Time went on, and Elizabeth heard no word from James. Then one night while she was sitting up with a sick neighbor and an old negro mammy was keeping the sleeping children, a loud knock was heard at the door of Elizabeth's home. The old negress went to answer the knock and found, standing in the doorway James Copeland.

He spoke quickly, "Where is my wife?"

The old mammy was afraid, but replied, "She ain't here, and you better go on, cause us knows 'bout you and us knows you is a bad man."

James did not pay her the slightest attention, but demanded to see his babies, pushed the old woman aside, and walked in. The twins were asleep in a trundle bed. James stood looking at them for a long time and tears rolled down his cheeks.

Finally he spoke, "Tell my wife that I have deceived her and been unjust to her. Everything they have said about me is true, for I am a Copeland and a member of the Murrell clan. I am afraid that she will never see me again, because the law is after me and I can't escape. I can't even sleep at night for the image of a man on a white horse is constantly chasing me, and I always have to move on. Tell Elizabeth that I love her and the babies."

And with that he was gone.

Time went on, and no more was heard from the handsome Copeland, until one day an old wagoner stopped at the inn for a night's lodging. Elizabeth was serving the tables, and as she worked in and out of the kitchen she happened to catch a familiar name from the wagoner. She listened more closely and heard thus:

"Heard the Murrell clan had a bad day not long ago. Nearly all the Copelands were killed. There was one of them, though, young Jim Copeland, that could have gotten away if the sheriff hadn't overtaken him. Sheriff had just gotten a new horse from Tennessee, a beautiful light gray stallion; ran like lightning. They've got Copeland in a Mississippi jail, and he's to hang soon."

After a family conference Mr. Walker sent Elizabeth's two brothers to the jail to talk to Copeland. Here he fully admitted his guilt. His last word to Elizabeth was an entreaty to bring his boys up as good honest men.

THE GOLD CAP OF JOAQUIN MURIETA

My cousin Josefa used to tell me stories about Joaquin Murieta, the bandit. He was a good man once, with a wife and son and a ranch down south. He came to California to dig for gold. While he was mining along the San Joaquin, some Americans tied him up and mistreated his wife. About the same time, he heard that Americans had killed his father and brother, and driven his mother out of their ranch home down south. He went home to see his mother, and found out it was all true. Then Joaquin Murieta took his horse and saddle from the ranch and told his mother that he was going to be a bandit. He came to Bakersfield, and after that he started robbing alone. He never killed anyone— just robbed them. He never carried a gun when he robbed people. My cousin Josefa told me that until all these things happened to him, Joaquin Murieta was a good man.

I don't know where he met Maria Anna Lorca—perhaps it was at Hanford, perhaps in Lemoore. This woman always traveled with him. My cousin Josefa knew Maria Anna Lorca. That was a long time after Joaquin Murieta was killed, when Maria Anna was an old woman. Once I saw Maria Anna Lorca too. Josefa and I had driven a wagon down the valley to pick berries. After we had filled our buckets, I said, "Let's go home." We started back, then Josefa said, "Wait a while, I want to see Maria Anna Lorca." We came back by Kingsburg. We stopped our team at the pump by the house. Maria Anna was pumping, while a man was sitting on the porch smoking.

Josefa called to her: "Hello, Maria Anna Lorca." No answer. Josefa called again to her. I think Maria Anna was hard of hearing.

Finally Maria Anna replied, "I haven't seen you for a long time. Do come down from the wagon."

Josefa told her we couldn't stay. Maria Anna said, "No, stay a little while, I want to talk to you." She was a tall, thin woman. When she talked, it looked as if she had no teeth. "You know, Josefa, I am awfully hard up for money."

"How can you be hard up?" Josie asked her. "You have money in Devil Mountain. Why don't you get it?"

"We tried to get it," said Maria Anna, "because I know there is a lot of money there. But I can't get it."

"Why not?"

"Everytime I go to the mountain I see the Devil right where the money is. Everything is shining, but I see the Devil right there."

"Why don't you pray when you go in there?" Josie asked.

"I do pray, but Joaquin Murieta stands there in front of the gold. I told him I needed the money. He said to me, 'No, you can't have it. You are living with another man. The Devil will take you if you touch the money.' I went up to Devil Mountain with this man. We were both scared, so we left the place without taking out any money."

"If you can't get that money," said Josie, "why don't you sell your hat? It is surely worth over two thousand dollars."

"No, I don't want to sell it. Joaquin Murieta had it made for me. It is my keepsake."

"When you die, somebody else will have it," said Josefa.

"When I die, I shall never know it. I am lonesome for Joaquin all the time."

Then I told my cousin Josefa it was time to go. Both Josie and Maria Anna asked me to get down from the wagon, but I couldn't since I was holding my baby. Maria Anna tried to talk to me in Spanish. I said I didn't understand Spanish. She couldn't understand English much. "Is Josefa your cousin?" she asked me.

"Yes, she is my cousin," I replied.

"Ah, Josefa, you never told me you had a relation. Now I see your cousin." Then Maria Anna added, "Josefa, you won't see me any more. Perhaps I shall die pretty soon."

Josefa looked at the hat Maria Anna wore. She took it off. "I'll bet this wore your hair off," she said to Maria Anna.

Maria Anna didn't have any hair on her head. She said to Josie, "Show it to your cousin. Let her hold it."

I took the hat. It was heavy, like lead. The cap was thick on top, but thin on the sides. There were eagles all over the cap, and the top was pointed. The cap was made of gold. It was shiny inside. I asked if the sweat wouldn't turn it black.

Josie said, "She cleans it all the time." Then she turned to Maria Anna and said, "Wearing that cap took your hair off."

"Yes, I know it. I wear the cap all the time," Maria Anna replied. "People try to buy it from me, but I don't want to sell it." Then she said to Josie, "You wake me up when you come down here. I am so lonesome for Joaquin Murieta, I am barely living. Once when I was praying, Joaquin Murieta came, stood here, and asked what I was doing. 'Nothing,' I told him. I felt so good when I saw him."

"You're crazy," said Josie. "You know he died a long time ago."

"I don't care, I want to see him again. I wish I could die. I want to run around with him again." Then Maria Anna shook hands with Josie, and kissed her. "Goodbye, Josefa, you won't see me any more. Where are you living now?"

"I am with my cousin at Lemon Cove," said Josie.

Maria Anna said, "I used to know that country well. Joaquin Murieta and I used to travel around there." Then she added, "I might die sometime. Maybe something will kill me."

Josie said, "You can't die. You're half-devil anyway."

Maria Anna laughed, showing her toothless gums. She said, "I feel good when I talk to Joaquin Murieta."

"You're crazy, you are going to die," Josie told her.

That's the last and only time I ever saw Maria Anna Lorca. About a year later, in the springtime, she was run over by a train. A Spanish fellow came from Hanford and told Josie about it. He said, "I have bad news for you. Maria Anna was killed."

"How?"

"The train ran over her, the other side of Traver. You know how she was—couldn't hear anything, just kept walking along the track. She didn't hear anything."

"How about her hat?"

"I guess the undertaker took that," said the Spanish fellow.

That's what I remember about Maria Anna Lorca and the gold cap Joaquin Murieta gave to her.

MY KIN KNEW JESSE JAMES

I'm former Della May Crouch, married now to Joe Lundman. An' as my own personal knowing other than my grandparents, has told me that they knew Jesse an' Frank James personally. They have ate a many a meal in their home in Missouri, an' they knew 'em personally. They seem to think they were wonderful people and all of this, and my folks told me that they knew 'em from the time they were small, the James boys, until they were growed up an' before they were killed off, we moved from Missouri to Wyoming. An' all of this added up to great friends among my folks an' the James boys. They tried to do what was right, seemed like to my folks, but, of course, to others it didn't. An' they knew when they ran 'em off the clift in the river, they remembered that. They remembered when the bank was robbed an' when many a train was robbed, many a people was killed. Which, of course, my folks didn't approve of, but they have passed on an' gone now. My father is buried in Kalispell, Montana, an' my mother is buried in Missouri. An' what they have told me is all I know. But they like 'em; they seemed to think they were good. An' they never done nothin' to my folks, to any of 'em, an' I had lots of folks in Missouri, I still have some there. They seemed to be real great people. They liked 'em real well around the community where my folks lived, an' they were, I guess, treacherous, an' as far as I know Frank James is somewhere in Montana, yet. And they came to my folks's house, they ate there, they slept there, they left, they never bothered nothing. An' Granmaw said a many an' a many a time, when they were sick, they would bring medicine an' bring doctors an' stuff to help 'em out what they could, an' even stay an' take care of the stock when my Granddad was sick an' couldn't work. They would take care of our stock that they had outdoors an' in

the sheds an' stuff. An' Granmaw really liked the James boys an'
she said that they were great toward helping the poor. Now she
didn't know any further than that fer, you know, fer her actual
knowing, an' my Uncle Jim, one of my oldest uncles, he eventually got old enough, and my father, John Crouch, to know the
James boys personally. And they were good to them, too.

[Question: Della, what got them started being outlaws? Do you
know?]

They shot Jesse and Frank's mother is what the folks said.

[Q: Who shot their mother?]

That I don't know. That name I don't know. Granmaw said
that when the railroad was goin' through they tried to buy, or
take right a' way, or buy, from Frank and Jesse's mother which
she didn't want to let go, see. An' she was pretty well I guess, an
invalid now the way Granmaw talked to me. An' Frank was the
only one there, he was kind small. An' she told him "No," said,
"that's all they had, her and the two boys." An' she didn't want to
let it go so, therefore, he walked up and slapped Jesse's mother,
an' Frank's mother. An' Frank went in the house an' got a gun
and shot him. Now that's what she told me, see, I'm just goin' by
hearsay, 'course I wasn't even here yet. And she said that's what
really started it. An' naturally then the law came after Frank. An'
Jesse an' Frank just went from there. Now Granmaw is buried up
here at Gillette. Just north a' here. That's what actually turned
'em inta outlaws, is because that man walked up and slapped
their mother. She was sittin' out on the porch in a rockin' chair
peelin' potatoes when it happened, for supper. An' Granmaw said
that that's what Frank an' Jesse told them. An' because she
wouldn't give up their place, see, this guy finally got mad an' just
walked up an' slapped her.

[Q: You said something about Frank James was still up in
Montana?]

As far as I know he's still in Montana and getting very old.

[Q: Well, where did you hear this, how do you know this?]

Well, now I saw it in the paper but it's been several years ago
that he was still there.

[Q: Tell them about when Jesse died, what he said.]

Well, all I know about that, honey, is what I seen in the paper. An' everybody should know that because that, I think, was in every paper in the United States. It was somewhere in Nebraska, an' he evidently knew he was goin' to die an' he called all these people in, ya know, an' told 'em where they could find him. Now I don't know how true this is, as I say it's just all of this is just what I've got from other people cause I didn't never know either one of 'em. I don't know it all to be the actual truth. He called for someone an' told 'em where to find some money they'd taken from a bank, an' what tree to find it under.

[Q: Do you know if anybody ever looked?]

I don't have no idea. Now when that was in the paper I do believe I was working at some livestock company. But it was in the, was it the Cheyenne paper or the Denver paper? I don't remember which paper it was in, but it was in the paper. Or maybe it was before then, I can't remember, it's been so long ago. 'Course I never paid much attention to it, ya know, only I just noticed it. I don't remember even who brought it to my attention it bein' in the paper. But it *was* in the paper. What I got of that, you know, I told you that I read it in the paper.

[Q: That's something, so after that guy shot his mother, they just up and left?]

Well, the law got after 'em an' they started fightin' back, see. No, he didn't shoot his mother, he just slapped her.

Jesse James Robs a Bank

Jesse robbed the First National Bank of Huntsville, Alabama, where he had heard that a large sum of money from the sale of cotton had been deposited. He came alone to the town to see how the bank operated. He got a room in a hotel next to the bank and discovered that it was left unprotected at closing time. He robbed the bank and escaped by riding his horse off a cliff into the river. The horse was killed but Jesse borrowed another from some relatives who lived nearby and escaped.

Generous Jesse James

On a mild summer day Mr. James was riding his dashing black horse down a lonely country road and he heard the cries of an old woman from a country shack. He discovered that her landlord was putting her out of the house because the mortgage could not be paid. Very modestly and shyly he handed her the required amount and rode on down the road. He stopped his tired horse by a thicket and rested in the dark shadows.

In the meantime, the humble creature met the landlord much to his surprise, with the cash for his mortgage. He started down the road. Very soon he, too, came to the thick bushes by the side of the road. Quite suddenly, Jesse James came out with a black mask on, poked his ugly gun in the ribs of Mr. Landlord and demanded his money.

By lending his money for an hour or two he gave happiness and security to a wretched soul without causing any loss to himself.

EL TEJANO

El Tejano, or the Texan, used to rob banks, the rich, and stagecoaches. But they said the money he took to Texas and gave it to the poor there. When he was in a great hurry to escape from the many bands that were without cease after him, he would bury the money or put it in a cave. They never could catch him though he was always spied on. They couldn't get him because the shoes of his horse were on backwards so that he always appeared to be going in a different direction than that in which he actually was.

He had a Mexican who did the errands for him when he was away from town. The Mexican it was who betrayed him. El Tejano would whistle and the Mexican would whistle back if all was clear. One time he whistled and the Mexican whistled back that all was well. The posse was waiting, in hiding, and when El Tejano rode in, shot him down.

The Law put his body in state at the courthouse for all the world to see. There was a great scandal after his death since all longed to see who was El Tejano. He had worn a black mask. One of those who filed past to see him was Aunt Rimbaud. She recognized El Tejano as the one who in his youth had worked in a blacksmith's shop and done errands for her.

All or Nothing

A father and his son were near Cerro del Gato when the son said, "Papa, I know where there is a cave in these mountains, and I am sure there is treasure hidden inside of it. I am going over there to get the treasure!" His papa replied, "Son, you had better not go unless you have the nerve and the courage to face up to the Tejano. Be sure you can answer his spirit when he talks to you."

The boy said that he had the courage, and that he was going over to get the treasure. He took two gunny sacks with him into the cave, and he found lots of money and gold and silver. He filled one sack, then he started to fill the other. All of a sudden, the air became chilly and the man heard a voice, "All or nothing, you take all of it or none!" The young man could not face up to the ghost; he shivered and couldn't talk; then he fainted.

The father waited a long time for his son to return, then he climbed up into the cave where he found the boy. The boy woke up, looked around and said to his father, "Where is the treasure? When I came in, I already had one sack filled and had started to fill the other one when I heard the spirit say, 'You take all of it or nothing.' Then I passed out." The father said, "Son, there is no money here; there's nothing."

The Tejano rode a beautiful black horse with all the trappings. He robbed the stage at various places. One of his favorite places was La Posta de la Canoa, which is about thirty-five miles south of Tucson near the Santa Cruz River. Another favorite place was the pass as Picacho Peak. People used to go there to search for treasure. No one lived there and they couldn't see the ghost, but someone kept shooting at them from the mountain top.

He hid the treasures all over this part of the country because he robbed so much he couldn't carry it all with him. All of these treasures will have to be found before the spirit of El Tejano can have peace, and that is why he says, "You take all of it or nothing."

AN OBITUARY FOR BILLY THE KID

Billy Bonny, alias Antrim, alias Billy the Kid, the twenty-one year old desperado, who is known to have killed sixteen men, and who boasted that he killed a man for every year of his life, will no more take deliberate aim at his fellow man and kill him, just to keep in practice. He is dead; and he died so suddenly that he did not have time to be interviewed by a preacher or to sing hymns or to pray before that vital spark had flown, so we cannot say positively that he has clum the shining ladder and entered the pearly gates.

The bullet that struck him left a pistol in the hands of Pat Garrett, at Fort Sumner, last Saturday morning, about half-past 12 a.m. in the room of Pete Maxwell. Governor [Lew] Wallace will now breathe easier, as well as many others whom he had threatened to shoot on sight.

No sooner had the floor caught his descending form which had a pistol in one hand and a knife in the other, than there was a strong odor of brimstone in the air, and a dark figure with wings of a dragon, claws like a tiger, eyes like balls of fire, and horns like a bison, hovered over the corpse for a moment, and with a fiendish laugh, said, "Ha, ha! This is my meat!" and then sailed off through the window. He did not leave his card, but he is a gentleman well known to us by reputation, and thereby hangs a "tail."

Billy the Kid and the Biscuits

"Some of our big writers that had to borrow their information claim that after the Kid had killed the two deputies, he came out on the balcony and asked the crowd that had assembled to throw him up a file.

"The fact is that no crowd assembled. The hitch rack was full of mounts in front of the big store and if there were any people in town, they did not show up in the street. The only person that the Kid contacted was Old Man Goss. He was the jail cook and handy man. Old Goss had no fear. The Kid was very active; he hobbled down the stair steps and out to the cook shack and said, 'Dad, I have a delicate job for you. While I squat down and place these leg irons across a stove wood log, I want you to cut them in two. Be careful with that axe.'

"The Kid had a forty-five in hand as a persuader.

"Dad was asked afterward why he did not hit the Kid in the head with the axe. 'Well,' he said, 'the Kid would of got me. He would of been a fraction of a second faster.

"'And furthermore—I like the Kid. He was always bragging on my sourdough biscuits.'"

STAGOLEE

I got up one mornin' jes' 'bout four o'clock;
Stagolee an' big bully done have one finish' fight:
What 'bout? All 'bout dat raw-hide Stetson hat.

Stagolee shot Bully; Bully fell down on de flo',
Bully cry out: "Dat fohty-fo' hurts me so."
Stagolee done killed dat Bully now.

Sent for de wagon, wagon didn't come,
Loaded down wid pistols an' all dat gatlin' gun,
Stagolee done kill dat Bully now.

Some giv' a nickel, some giv' a dime,
I didn't give a red copper cent, 'cause he's no friend o' mine,
Stagolee done kill dat Bully now.

Carried po' Bully to cemetary, people standin' 'round,
When preacher say Amen, lay po' body down,
Stagolee done kill dat Bully now.

Fohty dollah coffin, eighty dollah hack,
Carried po' man to cemetary but failed to bring him back,
Ev'y body been dodgin' Stagolee.

Stagolee Blues

1. I was standin' on the corner
   When I heard my bulldog bark;
   He was barkin' at the two mens
   Who gamblin' in the dark.

2. It was Stagolee and Billy,
   Two men who gamble' late;
   Stagolee throwed seven,
   Billy swore that he throwed eight.

3. Stagolee told Billy,
   "I can't let you go with that;
   You have win my money
   And my brand-new Stutson [Stetson] hat."

4. Stagolee went home,
   And got his forty-four,
   Says, "I'm goin' to the bar room,
   To pay the debt I owe."

5. Stagolee went to the bar room,
   Stood four feet from the door,
   Didn't nobody know when he
   Pulled his forty-four.

6. Stagolee found Billy,
   "Oh please don't take my life!"
   I got three little children,
   And a very sick little wife."

7. Stagolee shot Billy,
   Oh he shot that boy so fas'
   That the bullet come through him,
   And broke my window glass.

8. Some folks don't believe,
   Oh Lord that Billy dead
   You don't believe he gone,
   Just look what a hole in his head.

Stagolee and the Widow

Stag and his partner came to a Negro woman's house, get them some food. And so she didn't know who they was or anything like that, but she said, "Well, I'll fix you something to eat." So she fixed it and while they [were] sitting there eating, said, she got to talking about, well, she said, she had mighty, I'll call it, a mighty problem before her.

They said, asked her, says, "What is that?"

"Well," she says, "I'm buying this little place. I'm buying it. I been paying on it, trying to get it paid for." Say, "Well, I don't get no money, I don't make no money, and now the man's fixing to close me out." Says, "Today is my last day." Say, "If he give me time to get up the money and I have to get it up, I could. I can't, I can't raise the money, so he gonna close me out today."

Say, "Well, okay." Says, "We'll just take care of that for you. You're so good about feeding us, we'll just take care of that for you. Get your, get your papers and let's see." She got her papers and they looked at 'em, says, "Yeah, uh-huh." Think it were five hundred dollars or maybe a little better, something like that. But, anyway, they just told her, "Here. Take your papers and this money and just go on over there." Says, "You say that's the house up yonder? You just go on over there, take your papers, and pay him off. And you'll have your place." And she didn't know that, what they did. Said, they watched her as she goes in to settle the debt and she coming back, they say, "Well, let's [see] your papers. Uh-huh. Yeah. You got your clear." Oh, she was so happy, and thanked them. "Oh, you welcome."

And they, say, they went right on, kinda turned, whipped around, came back there and taken that money right back. And so, I say, I don't care how bad a man he was, he did some good things. That's right. That's right.

SHARP OPERATORS · QUICK WITS ·
DIM WITS

In a new country, new opportunities and new modes of behavior
are likely to be the order of the day, especially if the restraining
hand of the law is but lightly felt. Physical prowess is pre-eminent,
and during the first phase of settlement mountain men like Hugh
Glass, who survived incredible hardships through brute strength,
or the guide and scout Kit Carson, celebrated for his woodcraft,
loom as heroic figures, along with bandits like Joaquin Murieta,
who took what he wanted, or gunmen like Billy the Kid, who
killed whenever he chose. But the frontier environment produced
contradiction and paradox. The physically weak might show remarkable strengths. Frederick Jackson Turner observed that
among the "striking characteristics" of Americans, which originated in the frontier experience, was the robust strength of a
Hugh Glass, but he also noted an inventive turn of mind, a knack
of finding the expedient, and an acquisitiveness. Physical skills and
prowess were prized, but the sharp operator and the quick-witted
might also survive and even turn a profit. Johnson J. Hooper's
fictional frontier rascal, Simon Suggs, had as his credo: "It's good
to be shifty in a new country." American lore has a place for
Yankee tricks and trickster opportunism. The used-car salesman is
an American archetype. We have even been known to vote such
types into the highest offices of the land.

Yankee-born Jemima Wilkinson, a back-country religious
leader, is recalled in the lore of New England less for her own
piety than for her ability to line her pockets with the coins of the
pious and for the shifty ways she used to avoid proving her claims
as a miracle worker. "Gassy" Thompson was famous among hard-
rock miners of the West for the way he flimflammed mineowners
in the days of the bonanza. The success of their maneuvers

depended upon their brashness, their amorality, and mostly their ability to spot weaknesses in people stronger or better positioned than themselves.

A quick retort is as highly prized in folklore as a sharp operation. Contrary to the usual case, the Arkansas Traveler, city slicker though he is, gets the best of the squatter when he supplies the missing part of the fiddle tune, as the squatter graciously acknowledges. Ol Gallagher, the West Virginia bumpkin, unexpectedly proves to have the gift of tongues when his college friends expected him to be tongue-tied. Both are remembered for their quick wits in folk tradition and in local histories.

If American tradition extols the sharp operator and the quick-witted, it also has a place for the simpleton. Jean Sotte, or Foolish John, is a fool on a heroic scale, and we can laugh at the magnitude of his stupidity. He is so hapless and such an easy mark that he does not trouble us. But American folklore often treats its fools sympathetically. Local characters like Nick the Fiddler and "Boots" Van Steenburgh evoke pathos, perhaps because they remind us of our own weakness.

JEMIMA WILKINSON,
"PUBLICK UNIVERSAL FRIEND"

The historical facts about Jemima Wilkinson are interesting enough. She was born into a large Quaker family in Cumberland, Rhode Island, in 1752, and grew up on the farm there. Left motherless in her early teens, she had little formal education but read the classics of Quaker theology and history and studied the Bible so thoroughly that scriptural phrases became integral parts of her ordinary speech. She could quote from memory long passages of the Bible almost verbatim. In 1776, troubled by religious conflicts, Jemima Wilkinson became ill. During the course of her sickness, she experienced a vision that convinced her that she had died, gone to heaven, and had been sent back to preach to a dying and sinful world. She rose from her sick bed declaring that Jemima Wilkinson was dead and that she was the "Publick Universal Friend" whose mission was to work for the salvation of sinners. For the next forty-three years until her death, this resolute woman never faltered in her role of a reborn spirit called to preach to an unregenerate world.

Walking on the Water

The legend that is most commonly associated with Jemima Wilkinson in every region in which she is remembered is about walking on the water. In the tradition of the true folk tale, it is always told in relation to a specific location, which varies, of course, with the story teller. Sneech Pond and other bodies of water in Cumberland and Smithfield, Worden Pond in South Kingstown, Yawgoog Pond in Exeter, the Taunton River near Swansea, the Housatonic River near New Milford, the Schuykill River near Philadelphia and various sites on Seneca and Keuka Lakes are all credited with being the exact spot. The story has several varieties although not as many as locations. In the most common version, Jemima Wilkinson agrees to satisfy skeptics of her divine power by agreeing to walk on the water like Christ. A crowd gathered at the appointed place and Jemima appeared in her usual robes and began to preach a stirring sermon on faith, punctuated by the question, "Do ye have faith?" Finally, at the end of her long exhortation, she looked straight at the assembled group and asked, "Do ye have faith? Do ye believe that I can do this thing?" "We believe," chorused the crowd. "It is good," declared the prophetess, "if ye have faith ye need no other evidence," as she departed with a flourish.

Raising the Dead

Another legend associated with Jemima Wilkinson also involves miraculous powers—this time ability to raise the dead. It is possible that she may have prayed for a miracle by the coffin of Susannah Potter, the lovely, twenty-two-year old daughter of Judge William Potter who died on May 19, 1780. The nineteenth of May, 1780, was the celebrated "Dark Day" in New England when some strange, natural phenomena blotted out the sun for about four hours at midday. The unusual circumstances may have encouraged the Universal Friend to hope for a dispensation of the laws of nature. The story most commonly recounted, however, is a typical folktale exaggeration that bears no resemblance to the historical Jemima Wilkinson. Again, according to the story, the event is staged to impress critics. One of the faithful is persuaded to feign death, wrapped in a winding cloth, and placed in a coffin. In the crowd attracted by the announcement that the Universal Friend would raise this person from the dead is an army officer who interrupts to ask if he may plunge his sword through the corpse before the resurrection to prove that it is really dead. As he unsheathed his sword, the "corpse" sprang from the coffin and dashed away trailing his winding sheet after him. An early version of this story was recorded by the Marquis de Barbé-Marbois about

1782, but was told as pertaining to Mother Ann Lee, of the Shakers.

Ministering to a Lamb

Undoubtedly, some of the stories about Jemima Wilkinson were too ribald to be written down and have been lost in time. One such, recorded only recently, is still told by old-timers in Kingston, Rhode Island. A true folktale, it is phrased in several different ways but describes Mrs. William Potter's reaction upon apprehending the Judge in Jemima Wilkinson's private quarters. She was, according to the story, singularly unmoved by Jemima's explanation that she was simply ministering to one of her lambs. "Minister to your lambs all you want," Mrs. Potter is supposed to have retorted, "but in the future please leave my old ram alone."

"GASSY" THOMPSON AND HIS MINING SWINDLES

Still to be found in the oral tradition of Rocky Mountain mining regions and in the yellowing pages of ghost-town newspapers
are many tales or yarns about various amusing and memorable
mining figures. Some of these narratives and descriptions are
worthy of further preservation and analysis. They not only belong
to informal cultural history, but also portray recurring types of
human nature, shaped by period and by place.

Outstanding among local characters in the early boom days of
Colorado was "Gassy" Thompson of Georgetown and Empire.
The following stories about his doings came to me from various
sources and, often, in several different versions. Although some of
them are still in oral circulation, others had to be dug out of the
old files of Clear Creek County and Denver newspapers.

"Gassy" Digs a Snow Tunnel

Perhaps the most famous of "Gassy" Thompson's mining swindles was that of the snow tunnel. I heard it first from the lips of
Jim Garrett, who has lived in Silver Plume, Colorado, practically
all of his more than three score and ten years. Mrs. Jennings,
postmistress in Silver Plume for many decades and a resident
there for fifty-nine years, referred me to him when I asked for
local tales. Later I found the following version in the Georgetown
Courier for February 18, 1886, nineteen years after the events
recorded. It differs only in minor details from the story told by
Jim Garrett in 1945.

George, better known as "Gassy" Thompson, an incident in whose life was published in the *Tribune-
Republican* last week, was one of the pioneers of this

country. His doings and sayings were much of the Munchausen style, and his speculations in mining will long be remembered by some of his victims. His snow tunnel was probably his coolest piece of rascality.

In the winter of 1867, "Gassy" obtained a contract from the St. Lawrence Company who were operating in the vicinity of Montezuma, to run a cross-cut 100 feet into Decatur mountain about one mile and a half from the top of the range and about 300 feet from the base. "Gassy" worked in through the snow for about 86 feet; he then penetrated the mountain for about 14 feet, utilized the rock and dirt to fill in behind the side lagging and daubing the sides up with mud, so as to make it appear that the entire tunnel had been run in the ground. "Gassy" was a fine timberman, and the job he did in that line in this tunnel could not be excelled in the West. So well was everything done that one would naturally think that all was straight and honorable, yet had a practical miner visited it he would have readily detected the fraud. Twenty dollars a foot we believe, was the price paid for the work, and the winter months furnished an excellent opportunity to hoodwink the unsuspecting. The agent for this company at that time was Watson B. Rockwell, of Central, who went over and measured this famous snow tunnel, pronounced everything all right, and paid "Gassy" $2,000 for his work. With the advent of spring the snow vanished like dew on a summer morn, leaving the vast skeleton of a gigantic fraud as a memento of the oily-tongued "Gassy." Some of the timbers stand today as monuments to tenderfoot credulity.

According to Jim Garrett the tunnel was built through the snow around Kelso Mountain. Mrs. Mamie Sturm of Glenn Arbor Inn, near Empire, tells the story a bit differently. She contends that "Gassy," who was prospecting in the Peru District, where the mountains form a horseshoe-shaped valley, causing the snow to drift in very deep and to lie there all winter long, took the tunnel contract from an Eastern company. He cut the timbers and brought them to the site. There he erected them in the form of a tunnel leading a few feet into the side of the mountain. After the first big snow had covered it, he sent for the company's agent to come and measure the tunnel. "Gassy" furnished a tapeline, with several feet cut out of the middle, and accompanied the agent through the dark tunnel until they reached the end where they could feel the rock breastwork. The tapeline registered the required one hundred feet, and "Gassy" was paid off.

How "Gassy" Unwatered a Mine

Jim Garrett, of Silver Plume, assured me that he had grown up hearing about "Gassy" Thompson's swindles, including the following one explaining how "Gassy" unwatered a mine at Central City. Although Gassy himself was smart, Mr. Garrett recalled that the popular characterization in the Clear Creek region for a "dumb" person was "He has no more sense than 'Gassy' Thompson's jackass."

One time "Gassy" took a contract to unwater a mine shaft at Central City, not far from Black Hawk. Having a distaste for manual labor, he decided to secure help. Accordingly he caught a stray dog, cut its throat, and daubed some of its blood on an old coat and hat lying nearby and, also, around the mine opening. Then he tied a heavy rock around the dog's neck and dropped it down the shaft. It splashed when it struck the water and sank to the bottom.

By scattering hints of possible foul play in the region of the mine that he had contracted to unwater, "Gassy" stimulated curiosity and suspicion among the loafers in the saloons which he visited in Central. Finally a group of citizens set out to investigate. They found the bloody coat and hat and the signs of a body having been dragged to the edge of the mine shaft. When this evidence was presented to the sheriff, he aroused the county commissioner, who secured a number of mine pumps and with the aid of much volunteer help soon unwatered the mine, only to find the corpse of a mangy cur.

In the meantime "Gassy" had slipped out of town. Later on he returned to collect his bill from the mining company in accordance with their contract, for the quick and efficient unwatering of their shaft.

An Easy Way to Sink a Shaft

At one time "Gassy" and a partner obtained a contract to sink a shaft on Gunnel mountain, near Central, 100 feet at $30 a foot. "Gassy's" policy was to make all he could with as little work as possible, so after the shaft was down 80 feet the rock taken out was utilized in building up the shaft on top, and the fine dirt was thrown into the crevices. Suffice it to say that everything was put in such nice shape that no one but a miner would detect the fraud. The agent, who was a tenderfoot, when he came to measure the work, was highly elated over the appearance of things, and "Gassy" and his partner pocketed the price of a 100-foot shaft.

"Gassy" a Game Sport

Mrs. Mamie Sturm also told me the following story about "Gassy," who was well known to her parents, the pioneering Lindstroms of Empire.

When "Gassy" had money he was fond of gambling, and patronized the same gambling house night after night, although he usually lost. One evening he did not show up, and the proprietor was greatly disappointed. Not only did he miss the humorous antics of "Gassy," but the profits were decidedly off. The next morning, however, he noticed some shattered glass on the floor and a good sized rock with a letter wrapped around it which had been thrown through the transom. Opening the envelope he found a note which said, "Here is your money. I was too damn busy to come in last night. Gassy." Enclosed was Gassy's average loss, in gold pieces.

HOW TO CARRY A WATCH

In Calhoun, Greene, and Jersey counties [Illinois] there is currently a whole cycle of tales in circulation about "ol' Dan'l" [Stamps]. . . . A few aged descendants of the pioneer families still living in this remote section remember that their parents spoke of "Uncle Dan'l" in those early years in none too kindly a tone. A Rip Van Winkle in his habits, he was, like his Yorker prototype, looked at askance by his more industrious neighbors. "He never worked a day in his life that I can remember, but he had done everything anyone else had—and twice as good, at least twice as good." By the time he came back to Otterville for his last few years—he died in nearby Jerseyville in 1950—he had become something of a legend. "He musta been two hundred years old. Year, that's right, 'cause he worked twenty years in Arkansas, twenty years in Nebraska, twenty years in Iowa, thirty in Missouri, and I knew him all my life." Actually, Dan'l was only eighty-four when he died. . . .

"Dan'l always wore a vest, and he carried a watch in every pocket—the best watches in the county. I remember the last trade he made, 'cause it was with John Patton. He sold John a watch for a dollar, and it wasn't fifteen minutes 'fore John was back with a dead watch. Dan'l look at him and said, 'Damn it, John, you just don't know how to carry a watch!' "

KEEPING AN ODD BARGAIN

Once there was a man who was always thinking of a way to live without work. He put an advertisement in the paper for someone to watch his sheep, and a youth, seeing the advertisement, came to see about the job. The owner had already made up the contract, stating that the person who took the job was to watch a thousand sheep and a dog. The employee was to have one loaf of bread a day and a quart of wine for his meals. On this he was to feed the dog and himself. If he could do this for a year without getting angry, he could have the sheep for his own use. However, he was to receive no pay during this time, and neither he nor his employer was to become angry. According to the contract, the first one who lost his temper would have his nose cut off.

After reading the contract, the youth told the owner that he would let him know. He then went home to tell his mother and brothers about the job. His mother said she could not see how he could do this. He told her he would take more bread from home, and, if he could only manage for a year, they would have plenty of sheep. His brothers agreed that he could probably do this, so the boy went back and signed the contract.

The next day he took the sheep and the dog out into the fields and watched them. When a week or two had gone by, the owner tried to feed the dog, but it would not eat. This pleased the owner, since he wanted the contract to continue longer. If the dog ever ate, the employee lost his job. About a week later, the boy lost all patience and went to see his employer. As he gave the sheep and dog back, the owner cut off his nose and sent him home.

The boy went home crying, without a nose. His mother asked him what had happened, when she saw his mouth and face covered with blood. After he told his story, everyone became very angry and one of his other brothers said that he was going to work for the man in order to get even with him.

The second brother went as the first had done, and signed the contract. About two months later he came home without a nose, as his brother had.

The third brother, John, said he would go and fight it out. Although he was the youngest, he was determined to win out. He was not going to lose patience or give up. He went to the employer, asked to see the contract, signed it, went back home to his mother, and told her he had accepted the job.

The next day he went out to watch the sheep and the dog, but before he left home, he asked one of his brothers to meet him at a certain spot that night, as he had a plan. When night came, he killed one of the sheep and gave it to his brother to take home. He killed another sheep for himself, roasted it, and gave part of it to the dog to eat. Later that night he took the dog to the employer, who tried to feed it, but it did not want anything to eat. The employer was very pleased to see that the boy and dog were getting along on one loaf of bread a day.

The next morning the youth went back to the fields to take care of the sheep. Again his brother was waiting for him, and again John killed a sheep and gave it to his brother to take home. Also, he prepared another for himself and the dog. He told himself that before the year was up he would have all the sheep. He was determined too, to get his employer's nose before he got his.

After taking care of the sheep that day, John went to the butcher and asked if he would like to buy a sheep. In fact he went to more than one butcher. He made plans for them to meet him the next day at a certain place where he would have his sheep for them to see. They asked him how much he wanted for his animals, and he told them he was selling them for half price. He took the money, and the butchers left. He then killed another sheep and made a roast for himself and the dog.

That night he was to take the sheep to his employer for him to see. His boss noticed that he was about a hundred sheep short and asked where the missing ones were. John said that he had called and called, but some of them did not want to come. He asked the owner if he were mad, but he said he wasn't.

The next day John went to the fields and made arrangements for selling more of the sheep. This time he sold about four hundred, and as usual, he killed one for himself and the dog. When he returned to the employer that night with the sheep, he was asked where the others were. John gave the same answer he had given before—that the sheep had not come when he called. He asked the man if this made him angry, and the answer was again "No." John tried his best to make him angry, but could not seem to do so.

The owner told John to bring the sheep to him the next day, that they must all dance for him, and that John was to play the flute while they danced. John said, "How can I do that?" The man told him if he did not make the sheep dance, he was going to cut off his nose.

When the butchers arrived the next day to buy more sheep, John told them about his problem. They all said that they would help. They took a sharp knife and cut off one leg from each sheep. Since the dog was to dance also, John put him up against a tree and cut off one of his legs too. When the animals tried to walk, they all limped and this made them look as if they were dancing.

When the employer saw this, he said, "This fool has ruined all of my sheep. What am I to do now?"

John asked him if he were angry. However, the man was not going to give up either. He said that it really didn't matter, but told John that he could not watch the sheep any more. He then bought pigs for the boy to take care of. He tried his best to make John angry, but could not succeed. He gave him about seven hundred pigs to watch.

This made John quite unhappy, but he decided that he would call the butchers and see if he could sell them as he had the sheep. It wasn't long before he had sold about two hundred pigs.

When he was to present the pigs to the owner, he was short, but gave the man the same old answer: "They wouldn't come when I called."

The employer then said he must bring the pigs to him the next day, and that all the pigs must laugh. John told him that he could not make the pigs laugh, but the man said this was in the contract. John had not saved the contract, and therefore he could say nothing, but he did not know how to make the pigs laugh.

While John was going to work the next day, he was looking very sad, and walked with his head down. An old man, who had always known John to be smiling, asked him what was wrong. He said if John would tell him his troubles, maybe he could help him. The boy told him that his boss insisted that he make the pigs laugh. The old man told him to get one of the pigs and he would show him how he could make it laugh. He took a knife from his pocket and cut the pig's upper lip. This made it look as if it were laughing. It sounded as if it were laughing too, although it was really yelling from pain.

John did this to all the pigs that he had left. When he was on his way to the owner's place, all the people he passed looked at the pigs, and thought they were really laughing. When the man saw this, he called John a fool, but again he said that he was not angry with him. He asked John where the other pigs were.

John told him that a good many of them were stuck in the mud. He had sold most of the pigs to the butchers, but had kept about twenty tails and twice as many ears. He stuck the two ears and the tail in the mud, here and there, to make the place look as if a number of pigs needed rescuing. He then called the owner to help him get the pigs out of the mud.

When they arrived at the place, he told the boss to take hold of the pig's ears, and he would get him by the tail and pull him out. When the boss pulled and only an ear came up, John told him he had pulled too hard. John gave him a shovel and told him to dig for the pig, but the boss could not find any pig. He then became very angry and began to yell. John cut off his nose and went home to his brothers with the nose of his employer and the remaining pigs and sheep.

THE ARKANSAS TRAVELER

Sometime about the year 1850 the American musical myth known as "The Arkansas Traveler" came into vogue among fiddlers. It is a quick reel tune, with a backwoods story talked to it while played, that caught the ear at "side shows" and circuses, and sounded over the trodden turf of fair grounds. Bands and foreign-bred musicians were above noticing it, but the people loved it and kept time to it, while tramps and sailors carried it across seas to vie merrily in Irish cabins with "The Wind that Shakes the Barley" and "The Soldier's Joy." With or without the dialogue, the music was good for the humor, and it would have shown to the musical antiquary, if he had noticed it, the boundary line between the notes of nature and the notes of art as clearly as "Strasburg" or "Prince Eugene" or "The Boyne Water" or "Dixie."

It lost nothing where showmen caught it from Western adventurers in the days before the Union Pacific Railroad, and gained vogue in the hands of negro minstrels, who, if they touched up the dialogue, never gave the flavor of cities and theaters to the outdoor tune. When the itinerant doctor made a stage of his wagon-top of a Saturday night, it helped the sale of quack medicines on the village square, and there was a tapping of feet in the crowd under the torches when a blackened orchestra set the tune going from fiddle to fiddle.

I learned of the myth nearly thirty years ago from Major G. D. Mercer, who had brought it from the Southwest in the pioneer days and played the tune on the violin as it should be played to the dialogue.

First there comes a slow, monotonous sawing of the notes, which prepares one, as the curtain rises, for a scene in the backwoods of Arkansas.

The sun is setting over the plains. A belated horseman in coonskin cap, and well belted with pistol and bowie-knife, rides up to a squatter cabin to ask a night's lodging. By the door of a rotting shanty sits a ragged man astride of a barrel, slowly scraping out the notes you hear. There are children in the background, and a slatternly woman stands on the threshold. The man on the barrel plays away, paying no attention to the visitor, and the dialogue begins.

"Hello, stranger!" says the horseman.

"Hello yourself!"

"Can you give me a night's lodging?"

"No room, stranger."

The playing goes on.

"Can't you make room?"

"No, sir; it might rain."

"What if it does rain?"

"There's only one dry spot in this house, and me and Sal sleeps on that."

The playing continues for some time. Then the horseman asks:

"Which is the way to the Red River Crossing?"

The fiddler gives no answer, and the question is repeated.

"I've lived hyar twenty years, and never knowed it to have a crossin'."

The stranger then begins to tease, the tune still playing.

"Why don't you put a roof on the house?"

"What?"

"Why don't you put a roof on the house?"

"When it's dry I don't want a roof; when it's wet I can't."

The tune goes on.

"What are you playing that tune over so often for?"

"Only heard it yisterday. 'Fraid I'll forget it."

"Why don't you play the second part of it?"

"I've knowed that tune ten years, and it ain't got no second part."

The crisis of the story has come.

"Give me the fiddle," says the stranger.

The man hands it to him, and a few moments of tuning are needed as a prelude to what follows, which has been immortalized in the popular print [by Currier & Ives] known as "The Turn of the Tune."

When the stranger strikes up, turning away into the unknown second part with the hell-tingling skill of a true jig-player, the whole scene is set in motion. The squatter leaps up, throws out his arms, and begins a dance; the dog wags his tail; the children cut capers, and the "old woman" comes out, twisting her hard face into a smile.

"Walk in, stranger," rings the squatter's voice. "Tie up your horse 'side of ol' Ball. Give him ten ears of corn. Pull out the demijohn and drink it all. Stay as long as you please. If it rains, sleep on the dry spot." . . .

The turn of the tune.

The Lock Boat after the Scow

There may be many other stories and fiddle tunes with which it ["The Arkansas Traveler"] might be compared, though I have heard only one, called "The Lock Boat after the Scow" (with music as follows) . . . :

As a canal-boat approaches a lock after dark, the boatman's tune, played slowly on the fiddle, sounds above the noise of the sluice and the tinkle of mule-bells. When the mules have passed, the boat comes into place as the barefooted lock-boy skips over the gliding rope. Then the tune stops for the following dialogue between boatman and boy.

"Got the gate shut behind there?"

"Yes."

"How many laps did you take?"

"Three."

"Are the mules on the tow-path?"

"Yes."

"Are you ready?"

"All ready."

"Let her come."

Then comes the quick turn of the tune to the rush of the water, while the boat settles quickly down into the lock. When she rests on the low level the notes cease for more questions and answers.

"Is the gate open ahead?"

"Yes."

"Is the rope clear of the bridge?"

"All clear."

"Mules on the tow-path?"
"Yes."
"Out of the way, then. Gee-e-ed up!"
And the boat glides away, as she came, to the swinging music.

OL GALLAGHER, HOMESPUN ORATOR

Oliver Gallagher (originally spelled Galliher, but changed to Gallagher and pronounced "Gallihue" by local residents) was born near Mobley in Wetzel County. At an early age he showed an inclination toward "books" and did well in school, so well in fact that around the turn of the century he enrolled at the old Fairmont State Normal School. Here the Wetzel County lad, clad in the homespun clothing and high boots, became the object of much teasing, some ridicule, and the object of practical jokes by his "citified" fellow students.

On one occasion "Ol" as he was always called was persuaded to attend a performance at the Opera House in Fairmont. Unknowingly he was to be the victim of a practical joke. The young men secured a ticket for him and at the precise moment they had planned, they entered the theatre. Ol was ushered in by his fellow students who tipped the regular usher to step back and let them handle things. A singer was just finishing a number and the boys fell in behind Ol until he was forced to walk down the aisle to the front, looking for a seat in the crowded theatre. The audience applauded the performer; then stopped suddenly and stared at the strange sight. A tall, awkward youth, dressed in a homemade coat and breeches, wearing the high boots so common in his native hills was surely no part of the program. This was opera—high class.

Someone giggled; then the audience roared at the spectacle of the boy standing bewildered in front of the orchestra.

Undaunted, Ol rose to the occasion. He mounted the stage and took command. He looked straight at the audience, lifted his hand for silence, then began what was to be an eloquent address. . . .

"You may ask, where do I hail from?" began Ol. "Not from the rock-bound coasts of New England, nor the pine clad forests of Maine. Not from the sunny shores of Florida, not even from the Old Dominion, mother of us all," he continued, "but from Wetzel County, land of the brave and the free. Wetzel County, whose sons are brave and whose daughters are fairer than Athena or Persephone. Whose sons bore arms to protect the liberty we all value so dearly and who will fight to the last breath to preserve it."

For half an hour Ol waxed eloquently, tempering his speech with quotations from the poets, homespun humor, and closing with the oft-repeated phrase, "Wetzel County, a land with oil enough to lubricate the world, with gas enough to ignite it, and last but not least, with brains enough to rule it." The entire speech was recorded in shorthand by an army colonel who happened to be in the audience.

No sooner had the boy launched his delivery than he captivated his audience. Laughter gave way to chuckles, and then complete silence as the audience listened intently, the boy's clothes forgotten. When he finished, members of the spellbound audience arose and offered him their hands.

Ol Gallagher on the Other Side of the Question

His eloquence and ability as a speaker became known throughout the area and he was often sought after to make speeches at local gatherings. He was always present at "literary," as the old time debates were called, and if he chose, he could take either side of a question and soon dispose of an opponent.

The story is told that he was asked to deliver a political address at an ox roast being held by members of the opposite political faith, when the regular speaker failed to show up. Since he was on the "other side of the fence" as he expressed it, he agreed to accept a five dollar fee. He proceeded to outline the party's platform in his best manner of delivery.

Smiling broadly, the well-pleased chairman withdrew a five dollar bill from his pocket and slipped it to Ol. Ol held up the bill for the audience to see. He folded it carefully as he spoke, then deftly creased it between his fingers. As he dropped it into his pocket, he concluded his speech with, "I don't believe there is one man among us here today who is big enough fool to fall for such a platform as I have just outlined." With that, Ol stepped from the rostrum, mounted his horse, and rode away from an audience in mirth and a chagrined chairman.

IS UNCLE BILLY DEAD?

There's a family by the name of Miller. They're a rather distinct set of people, they talk differently, got plenty of sense and all like that, good citizens, most of them, but they talk differently from other people, they say "dis" and "dat" instead of this and that. They really know better but the whole family does that. Well, in 1922 I was in Circuit Court, Judge Roberts was judge, and I was defending Scott Miller for having moonshine liquor in his possession. And we got off into the witness room, and he kinda grinned and said, "Did I ever tell you about Uncle Bill a dying?" I said "No." "Well, me and the boy were riding up the creek and we come to the ranch and I says to the boy, 'Let's go up and see if Uncle Bill's dead.' We rode up to the fence and Aunt Mance came out and I said to Aunt Mance, 'Is Uncle Bill dead?' Says, 'Yes, didn't ya know the damned ole thing went out and worked all one morning and come in and eat him a big hearty dinner and laid right down and died and left me with all that wheat and corn to hoe?'"

JONES TRACY AND THE GAME WARDEN

Jones had just poached a moose and he came out to the road to flag down the first person he saw to help him drag it out to the road. He'd give some meat for the help, of course. Well, he flagged down this fellow he didn't know and asked his help. The man said, "Do you know who I am?"

"No," said Jones.

"I'm the new warden."

"Well," said Jones. "Do you know who I am?"

"No," said the warden.

"I'm the biggest liar in the State of Maine," said Jones.

Jones Tracy Washes His Hands

It was about the first winter I was out of high school. We were chopping wood, came out at noon. Of course I always went along and washed my hands. So I washed my hands. He says [Jones], "What are you doing that for?"

I says, "Why, I don't like pitch on my food when I'm eating."

He said, "Oh you don't want to let that worry you." Said, "When I was a young fellow I was working in the woods." Said, "The next spring when I washed my hands I found a pair of gloves I didn't even know I had."

He could think of such things so quickly, just when I washed my hands.

A MIND LIKE A COMPUTER

Back in the 1930's, the late beloved Professor William L. Kennon had acquired among Ole Miss students the nickname of "Wild Bill Kennon" because his courses in astronomy dealt with such tremendous numbers of lightyears and distances. So, when he told a small group of us graduate students a story about how he found a lost wagon wheel, I assumed that it was one of his astronomical exaggerations; but now, in this age of computers, his story seems prophetic and folkloristic.

According to Dr. Kennon, during the summer before he entered Johns Hopkins, he earned his tuition and fees by driving a wagon and team of mules for a farmer who sold blocks of white-oak timber to some kind of mill. Just before dark on Dr. Kennon's last Saturday before entering upon his freshman year, he felt a bump and discovered that the right back wheel of his wagon had come off and had gone crashing down a steep hill covered with weeds, brush, and vines. He heard the wheel stop in the sandy creek bottom below the hill; but failing to find the wheel in the dark bottom, he resolved to find it in the morning, dragged the wagon home, and took his wages—less the price of the wheel but with the understanding that he could get the cost of the wheel when he found it. However, because a rainstorm that Saturday night covered the whole creek bed with a deep layer of sand, he could not find the wheel the next Sunday morning.

During his freshman year, Bill Kennon took a heavy load of courses, receiving help and guidance from some of the finest teachers in the world, studied algebra, trigonometry, calculus, physics, and other subjects, and returned to his home for the summer vacation. Still thinking of that lost wheel, he decided to apply his college training to the problem. With pencil, paper, trigonometric tables, level, steel tape, shovel, and ax, he went to the top of the hill where the wheel came off. He began his calculations by taking into consideration the circumference and weight of the wheel, the incline of the hill, the angle between the wheel and the road at the point where the wheel left the road, the probable velocity of the wind on that fateful night, the probable resistance of the brush on the hillside, and the probable braking effect of the sand in the creek bed. From all of these values, amounts, and factors, he calculated the acceleration and speed of the wheel down the hill, the distance it traveled, and the exact spot where it came to rest in the sand before the rainstorm covered it with sand.

When he probed for the wheel with a long stake, it hit nothing but sand. Then he drove the stake four feet into the sand at the exact spot where his calculations told him the wheel should be; but again he hit nothing. Fully confident of his calculations, he began digging around the stake. After digging down three feet, four and one quarter inches, he hit the wheel. The stake had gone through the hub of the wheel!

"BOOTS" VAN STEENBURGH AND JENNY LIND

When ["Boots" Van Steenburgh] was young it was said that he was perfectly normal mentally. He was tall and good looking and fairly well-to-do, judging by the rural standards of the times. "Boots" would probably have lived out his days in comfort with a wife selected from among the neighbor girls if it had not been for the advent of the Swedish Nightingale. That was in 1853, over a century ago. And Castle Garden, the famous old theater at the tip of Manhattan beyond Battery Park, was crowded to capacity as long as that golden voice was lifted.

"Boots" heard of her beauty, of her magnetic personality, and above all, of her wondrous voice. The farm boy, who loved music, vowed that he would go to the big city and hear the golden bird that was imprisoned in the Swedish girl's white throat. . . . New York was not the vast place it is today, but it was no country town. It was one of the biggest cities in the world. Poor "Boots" must have been confused and amazed by the sights and sounds of the teeming metropolis. Yet somehow he found his way to Castle Garden where Jenny Lind sang each night to thousands of people.

He listened to the voice which had cast its spell over millions, and the infatuated lad vowed he would see the singer and talk to her. He made his way past the hangers-on at the back door of the theater. They snickered audibly at the awkwardness of the gawky country boy, painfully shy, dressed up in his Sunday best to come to the Big Town. However, "Boots" cared nothing for them, did not see them, did not hear them. One burning desire filled his heart—to see Jenny Lind face to face, to touch her hand. Then he would be satisfied, and not till then. After that, he would go back home and spend all the rest of his days toiling in the fields. But, ah, his nights would be free to dream of Jenny.

Poor Boots! He never did get past the guards that surrounded the great singer. They would not let him in. In fact, he was thrown out bodily by the stalwart police who were set to keep out just such intruders as he. For several days he lingered around the stage door, but when he finally realized that his utmost efforts were in vain, he gave up in despair and returned to Saugerties.

After his return, folks began to notice that Boots was getting "queer." He talked wildly and incoherently at times. He paid no attention to his personal appearance. For several years he grew gradually worse. . . .

As the years went swiftly onward, Boots grew more unkempt and ragged (if that were possible). His long white hair and beard floated over his shoulders and chest, and the rags of his nondescript garments waved in the wind as he roamed the woods and fields or plodded along the highways. Often he talked to himself and gestured with his dirty, claw-like hands. But he was harmless. Nobody feared the poor old creature. Everybody was kindly and tolerant toward Boots.

One evening in the early spring when Boots was near the end of his earthly pilgrimage, a boy of twelve or thereabouts, who had been sent by his mother on an errand, went whistling toward Boots's little cabin. When near the shack, the lad stopped his whistling and crept softly to the window to peep in upon the old man. The boy meant to give the lonely old hermit a friendly hail and "pass the time of day," for Boots had endeared himself to all the children of the community.

In spite of his good intentions, when he reached the window, the youth could not see inside, for the dust, smoke, and filth of a generation had collected upon the small panes.

"Boots must have company," mused Jack, for the sound of voices was clearly audible. The rumbling tones of Boots's harsh old voice fell upon the boy's ears, and then, suddenly, in the pause that followed, that of another voice.

Slowly the hair began to rise on Jack's startled young head, his hands clenched, and his eyes bulged in horror. The unearthly sweetness of the second voice held him spellbound. Then softly upon the evening air floated the aria of one of the great operas (had Jack only known it), the aria of a great opera sung in an unknown tongue, sung in a woman's voice so sweet that the evening thrush stopped to listen.

When the voice finally sank into silence, Jack stood transfixed for one moment of breathless horror. Indelibly was stamped upon his soul the conviction that the tones he had just heard were not those of any human voice.

HARD ON THE HORSES

He [Jones Tracy] was coming up from Northeast Harbor. One of the Richardsons over to Hall's Quarry was coming up with a bag of grain on his back. So grandfather [i.e., Jones Tracy] stopped and asked him to get in and ride. Had brought one of the pungs, single sled. This old fellow got in and grandfather waited a few minutes and the old fellow still kept the bag of grain on his back and, so he said, . . . "You don't have to carry that, keep that bag of grain on your back. Why don't you put it on the sled?" and he said, "Oh well," he says, "I don't want the horse to have all that load to, to haul." Yes, it was a truth, the old fellow really said it. It wasn't a story. This is true.

FOOLISH JOHN

The character Foolish John is very old in world folklore, and he seems to have taken particularly firm root in Louisiana. He represents a combination of the country bumpkin and village idiot, doing things *à tort et à travers*. He is good natured but feebleminded. "Putting out the light" to him means "throwing it out the window." Sometimes he may show an inarticulate wisdom by some round-about process, but such occasions are rare. He never gets on in life like the clever individual who understands nuances of meaning which govern his behavior. He always interprets words and situations in their perversely literal sense. The verbs "to milk" and "to shoot" are the same word in Louisiana French, *tirer*. Thus when his mother tells him to go milk the cow, he goes to shoot her. He is an unwitting sadist. He burns his grandmother to death to keep her warm, and thinks she is smiling with contentment when her teeth show after she is roasted to a crisp. He is kind to inanimate objects. He will bundle up a tree to keep it warm, grease a cracked up and drying mud-hole to relieve its chapped condition and will give money and clothes to a lifeless statue because it does not contradict him as other people do.

Foolish John and the Errands

Once there was a woman who had a boy whom she named Foolish John. He was very foolish, backward and stupid.

One day his mother called him, "Foolish John, come here. Go buy me some cotton cloth and thread at the store." He came, she gave him the money and he left to go buy the cloth and thread.

On his return, he saw a little gum tree shaking in the wind. It was cold that day. Eh! the wind was blowing at the tree. It was cold. Foolish John looked and stopped to notice the little gum tree. "Poor little gum tree!" he exclaimed, "I'm sure you are cold. Wait I'll fix you so you won't be cold!"

He took the cloth, wrapping all the little tree with it. He then took the thread, winding it all around so the cloth would not untwist or unwrap.

Then he left for home. When he reached the house, his mother asked, "Where is my cotton cloth?"

"Well, mama," explained he, "I met a poor little gum tree. Indeed it made me feel sorry. It trembled, had a chill and was cold."

"Oh my! Foolish John, a tree does not get cold! My! you're a big boob! You should have brought my cotton and thread to make your shirts."

"Well," said he, "I bundled up the little gum tree with it. It was chilly."

The next day she sent him to the store to buy some lard. On his way back he passed alongside a little pond that had dried up. It was very flat, and where the water had withdrawn it was all cracked up.

Now Foolish John saw this, took the lard and began to grease the cracks by smearing the lard over them with a little stick. "Poor little pond!" said he, "I'm sure this poor little pond is aching. It is chapped up. Let me grease it well." He greased the little pond well, filling all the cracks with the lard.

He returned home. "Where is my lard?" requested his mother.

"Why," explained he, "I met a little pond, mama. It was all chapped, and I greased it with the lard. I am sure it ached."

"Ah, but you're a big boob!" she cried. "You should have brought my lard to cook supper for you!"

Well, the next day it was something else. "You will go buy me some needles," said she. "I want number seven."

"All right," he replied.

Foolish John left and got the needles when he reached the store. On his return he passed alongside a ditch where there were frogs croaking, "Eight, eight, eight, eight!"

"You're a liar; it's not eight!" shouted Foolish John. "I tell you it's seven!"

"Eight, eight, eight, eight!" croaked the frogs.

"You lie, it's seven! Here, count! Look and you will see for yourself," he said, throwing the needles into the ditch.

The frogs did not return the needles. He stayed standing, waiting. Finally he returned home. "Where are my needles?" asked his mother.

"Well," explained he, "a frog persisted in telling me the needles were size eight. I threw them into the ditch for her to see for herself. The nasty thing never returned them to me!"

"Why, you are a boob!" she screamed. "Frogs croak at night. It's night time now. You should have brought me my needles to do some sewing."

So never, never was the mother able to get any good results out of Foolish John or get him to do anything straight. He was a real foolish John for good.

Now she told Foolish John, "You will go milk the cow this evening."

The mother went into the kitchen to get the milk pail ready. She washed it to give it to Foolish John to milk the cow.

Suddenly she heard the shot of a gun outside—bang! She looked outside, saw the cow limp about, fall over and kick around. "Foolish John!" she yelled. Meanwhile Foolish John had the gun in his hands. "Why, you shot the cow!"

"Why surely, you told me to shoot her for supper. So I shot her."

"Oh my! you've killed the cow! We'll have no more milk now. How will we do now without milk? Ah! it is a misfortune indeed to have around the place someone so stupid!"

[In the Louisiana French, *milk* and *shoot* are the same word *tirer*, the expression that Foolish John used.]

Foolish John and the Washpot

Foolish John gave his mother lots of trouble. She sent him to fetch a washpot. He went and was returning with it. He reached a fork in the road. Foolish John says to the pot:

"You see these two roads? Well, both lead to the house." He put the pot on one and he took the other. Foolish John said to the pot, "You have three feet; myself, I have two. "We'll see who gets there first."

When Foolish John reached his mother's place, she asked him where the pot was. He said he had placed it on one road and, himself, he had taken the other, that it had three feet and he thought it could run faster than he. She beat him and sent him back to get the pot. The pot was no longer there. His mama said the neighbor's pot had to be paid for. It cost seven dollars. She gave Foolish John the money, and he left with it.

Along the road he heard springfrogs singing in the pond. The frogs sang, "Little eight, little eight, little eight."

Foolish John says, "You lied! I only have seven!"

The frogs still sang, "Little eight, little eight, little eight." Foolish John asked them to stop it, but they continued. He threw his money into the pond, telling them to count and see if there were not eight dollars.

He returned, and his mama asked him if he had given the money to the neighbor. He said that he had given it to the springfrogs. She beat him again.

One day she sent him to get flour at the neighbor's house. As he was returning with his flour, he came upon an anthill. He said to himself that these poor ants were hungry. So he gave them the flour.

When he reached his mother's, she asked him where the flour was. He said that the poor ants were so hungry, he had given it to them. She beat him.

Next time she sent him to get lard. While returning with the lard, he saw that the ground was cracked up. He put all the lard into the cracks. When he got home, his mama asked him where was the lard. He said he had greased the ground that was chapped, adding it was all cracked up. His mama beat him again.

His mother had a goose that was hatching eggs. Every time Foolish John went by where the goose was, she would cry out and try to peck him. He took a stick and killed her. He was sorry to see the eggs lost; and for fear of his mama, he got the notion of hatching them himself. Now there was some tar in a barrel; so he tarred himself. Then there were feathers in a box. He got in and rubbed them all over himself. The feathers stuck. He went to sit on the eggs.

His mama saw him. She came with a whip, whipped him, and he fled into the pond, swimming like a goose. Foolish John got another whipping. He ran off, going wild in the woods.

JEAN SOTTE GETS DRUNK

One day the old woman said to Jean Sotte, "My son, I am old and stiff, but you are young and active and can go on my errands; so go into the storeroom and bring me a bottle of wine you will find there." Jean Sotte went to the storeroom, and, having found the bottle, he thought he would take out the cork and make sure it was wine; and when he had smelled it, he thought he would taste it to be sure it was all right; but the wine was so good and old, he soon felt very merry, and continued to drink until the bottle was quite empty. Now, in a corner of the room an old duck had made her nest in some straw; and when Jean Sotte began capering around, she cried out, "Quack, quack!" and flapped her wings, which so frightened him that he caught her by the neck, and wrung her head off, and seated himself on her eggs. The old woman, having waited some time for Jean Sotte's return, determined to see what was keeping him. What was her surprise, on hobbling to the storeroom, to find her old duck dead and Jean Sotte sitting on her nest. "Silly boy!" she said, "why have you killed my duck, why are you sitting on the nest, and where is the bottle of wine you were to bring me?"—"Mother," said Jean Sotte, rolling his head and looking very sleepy, "I drank the wine; and when the old duck saw me, she cried out, and I knew she would tell you, so I killed her to keep her from telling; and, now she is dead, you will never know!"

GRANDPA WEEMISH AND HIS PUMPKIN ROCK

Old Enoch Weemish, a later early settler in East Tennessee, had only a narrow valley but lots of steep hillsides that raised fair corn and excellent pumpkins. When first frost was on his crop of huge pumpkins, Enoch would lead a mule up the steep hill. There he put a pumpkin in one end of a gunny sack and a nice smooth rock in the other. Then he put the sack across the mule's back and led him to the barn. Back and forth went the pumpkin rock, as it was called, until the harvest was finished.

When Old Enoch passed away, Enoch, Jr. harvested the same way, until he himself was gathered home. Enoch III kept up the pumpkin rock tradition, but his son Buck went to settlement school for six weeks and got a new idea. Buck took sack and rock up the hill, then he rolled the rock down the hill and put a similar-sized pumpkin in each end of the sack. This cut transportation in half.

But Buck's pa made him take the rock and pumpkins back to the field and complete the harvest in the old way. Said he, "What was good enough for Pa and Grandpa should be good enough for you. So no more edgecation! It makes you work your fool head off. Us Weemishes are just naturally smart."

BIG MEN PUT DOWN

There are few things Americans enjoy more than seeing somebody bigger and stronger and brighter and more respectable cut down to size. It is consistent with a tradition of egalitarianism. By implication, jokes we tell about our Presidents make this point. From George Washington to Jimmy Carter, American Presidents have been the butt of anecdotes that prove they are made of common clay like the rest of us, and while the Washington of legend still seems distant and austere, the cherry tree story so intimately associated with him has come to serve the uses of parody. Washington may not have been able to tell a lie, but politicians who followed after him easily mastered the trick. And a part of us is not displeased, for it shows that, like us, they are mostly no better than they should be. It is a fact that the same jokes have been told about President Lincoln and President Kennedy, and that certain stories and parodies emerge at four-year intervals as if they were a regular feature of the presidential election process.

The distrust of their pragmatic political heroes Americans reveal in their folklore has a counterpart in jokes and anecdotes about impractical geniuses and renowned medicine men who purvey cure-alls. For every Welsh physician famed for his "medicamentum," there is the remedy of a Lydia Pinkham made ridiculous by exaggerated praise. The absent-minded professor is not an American invention but he has certainly flourished in this country. Americans show a certain uneasy respect for their Einsteins and Norbert Wieners, but since they are not quite sure what these geniuses are up to, they tell stories about their ineptitude in everyday matters. Curiously, these stories are often relished by other scholars, who seem to share the common desire to see their betters exhibit human frailty. Though intellectuals themselves, they covertly share the popular anti-intellectual, anti-authoritarian streak. If so, it is a healthy sign that they are not taking themselves too seriously.

Like the floating presidential jokes that attach themselves to the current office holder, there are absent-minded professor jokes that come down through the years. For instance, the celebrated Dutch scholar Francis van der Kemp, who lived in New York in the early nineteenth century, had as much trouble remembering where he was and where he had been as Norbert Wiener.

As the mass media become an increasingly potent force in the generation of popular heroes, public reaction is more immediate and intense. Celebrities who have been oversold, particularly entertainers and politicians whose existence depends heavily on promotion, become vulnerable to negative response. Again we see the democratic leveling tendency, but here it is combined with a distaste for having been taken in. *Bunk* is an old American word, originally meaning political claptrap, and it is rather admired as long as it is seen for what it is and is not dished out in excessive helpings. When this happens, Americans may respond quickly and cruelly, as the jokes, puns, and parodies that circulate among the people demonstrate.

GEORGE WASHINGTON IN TEXAS

The Washingtons lived in a modest cottage on the north bank of the Rio Grande. In the front yard was Mr. Washington's favorite huisache tree. Little George found one Christmas morning that Santa Claus had left him a brand new machete. Naturally George was very proud of it and could hardly keep from trying it out on nearly everything to see how well it would cut.

It seems that a few mornings later Mr. Washington awoke and looked out into the front yard and saw his favorite huisache tree cut down. He yelled to his son, "George, come here at once!"

Little George came in with a sort of sheepish expression on his face, "Yes sir, what do you want?"

"George, I want you to tell me the truth. Did you or did you not cut down my favorite huisache tree?"

George looked him right in the eye, "Sir, I cannot tell a lie. I cut your favorite huisache tree down with my own little machete."

"Well, George, I must say that I am really disappointed in you; and there's only one course left open to me now. I can see that, if you cannot tell a lie, you'll never make a good Texan. I'll have to take you back to Virginia."

George Washington and the Outhouse

It seems that a family of father, mother, and young son lived on a farm in a rural community in Texas, not far from the Neches River. Now the boy was what you would probably call a problem child; he was a kind of a little devil, always doing things that caused trouble.

This caused the father and mother to worry, but they had another problem, too. She was always complaining about the run-down condition of their privy. One day, rather than listen to her complaints, the father took the privy down and transported it farther away from the house on to the bank of the Neches and hoisted it up on four stilts, so that the back end stuck out of the water.

Now what happened was that the parents decided one day to punish the boy for playing hookey from school and made him scrub the kitchen floor and carry in all the wood for the day. To get even, he decided to run away from home, and just for extra measure he took his axe and chopped the stilts holding up the privy, so that it crashed into the river and floated downstream.

Later on, when he decided to come home, he met his mother in the doorway. She told him the best thing for him to do would be to go into the bedroom where the old man was and own up to everything he'd done. But she warned him,

"Yore paw's plenty sore about something, and you'd better be keerful."

"But, maw, whut's he sore about?"

"I don't know, but you'd better shore watch out."

With this in mind the boy cautiously approached the old man, "Paw, I come back. I'm sorry I run away. And it was me who cut down the privy. I done it with my own axe. I'll behave now if you promise me you won't lick me."

The father glared at his offspring, "I've a mind to give you a larrupin."

"But, paw, remember George Washington told *his* paw he cut down the cherry tree and *he* never got no lickin."

"I know. But this here's a powful sight different. When George cut down the cherry tree, *his* paw warn't UP IN THE TREE!"

JIMMY CARTER AND THE BAMBOO TREE

One day Jimmy Carter's dad took a walk out in his beautiful orchard and discovered that his favorite bamboo tree had been cut down.

It just so happened that Jimmy had gotten an ax on the day before.

Well, Jimmy's dad asked Jimmy, "Jimmy, did you chop down my bamboo tree?"

And Jimmy replied, "Daddy, I cannot tell a lie. Maybe I did, and maybe I didn't."

A JOHN BROWN BALLAD

I

There was a man come from the west
An' settled in our taown
The fust three letters of his name
Was Ol' Ossawatomie Braown

  Ol' Ossawatomie Braown
  Ol' Ossawatomie Braown
The fust three letters of his name
Was Ol' Ossawatomie Braown

II

The sodgers from the mounting top
The arsenal did surraound
An' when they come to the back house door
They faound Ossawatomie Braown
  Ol' Ossawatomie Braown—etc.

III

Then ol' Judge Wise stood up in court
An' ca'mly looked araound
Sezzee where is that son of a ———
They call Ossawatomie Braown
   Ol' Ossawatomie Braown—etc.

IV

Ol' John Braown then stood in court
An' he ca'mly looked around
Sezee Judge Wise you kiss my ———
Fer I'm Ossawatomie Braown
   Ol' Ossawatomie Braown—etc.

Old Ass Waterbee Brown

I

There was a man came from the West
And settled in our town,
The first three letters of his name
Was Old Ass Waterbee Brown.

chorus
   Old Ass Waterbee Brown
   Old Ass Waterbee Brown
   The first three letters of his name
   Was Old Ass Waterbee Brown.

II

The soldiers from the mountain top
The arsenal did surround,
And when they came to the back house door
They bagged Ass Waterbee Brown.

REPUBLICANS TAUNT CLEVELAND

Ma, Ma, where's my Pa?
Gone to the White House, ha-ha-ha.

MCKINLEY AND BRYAN

McKinley drinks soda water,
Bryan drinks rum.
McKinley is a gentleman;
Bryan is a bum.

GOLDWATER AND JOHNSON

Political jokes circulate in great abundance during election time. After the election, they seem to vanish. Their temporary abundance and relatively quick disappearance (to be resurrected in altered form in four years) suggests their very immediate use in expressing hopes and fears of the immediate situation.

In the campaign between Senator Barry Goldwater and President Lyndon Johnson, there was a difference between the jokes which made it easy to recognize a Goldwater joke and a Johnson joke. Jokes told about Goldwater usually dealt with his political views. These jokes concentrated on such matters as Goldwater's opinions on nuclear weapons, integration and the Supreme Court. Johnson jokes were more personal. The population in general accepted the Civil Rights Bill, the Anti-poverty proposal and the administration's foreign policy. Hence, the joke makers concentrated on Johnson in a more personal way. Johnson was attacked, not so much as a political figure, but as an individual. . . .

Some jokes made light of Goldwater's inability to cope with a nuclear disaster; and at the same time criticized his reactionary attitudes. An example is the following:

> At a recent press conference a reporter asked Senator Goldwater, "What would you do, Mr. Goldwater, in the event of a nuclear attack?" Goldwater promptly responded, "I'd have the wagons form a large circle. . . ."

Goldwater desired less involvement with foreign countries. It was his political attitude toward isolationism and his reverence for the past that this joke criticized:

> Two men sat discussing the merits of Senator Gold-
> water: "You know," said the first, "that Goldwater is a
> pretty good fellow."
>
> "Yes," answered the other, "Goldwater is a great
> American—from the tip of his head to the soles of his
> high buttoned shoes!"

Goldwater, throughout the campaign, concentrated on the morality of the United States. Morality, Goldwater professed, needed
boosting by a Republican because of its decline during a Democratic presidency. Exemplifying the Goldwaterite's concern over
the President's own loose morals is this joke:

> Mrs. Goldwater spoke to Mrs. Johnson over the
> phone: "I just slept with the next president of the
> United States, Mrs. Johnson."
>
> "That's just like Lyndon," came the reply, "he'd do
> anything for a vote."

This same anecdote, with slight variation, was told about both
Nixon and Kennedy during the 1960 campaign. Richard M. Dorson, in *American Folklore*, states that the story can be traced as
far back as 1860, when Abraham Lincoln told it in a local election
in Illinois.

NIXON AND FORD

Nixon was walking around Washington, going to all the monuments to see if he could find a way out of his problems, so he went up to the statue of Washington and said, "What should I do?" And Washington said, "Always tell the truth." And he said, "That's a good idea." Then he went to the statue of Jefferson and said, "What should I do?" And Jefferson said, "Make a declaration." And he thought, "That's good." So then he went to the statue of Lincoln and said, "What should I do?" And Lincoln said, "Go to the theater."

"Gerald Ford wanted to donate his papers to the National Archives, but they wouldn't take them. They don't take coloring books." The coloring-books joke has also been told about such varied political figures as George Wallace, Orval Faubus, and former Governor Don Samuelson of Idaho.

THE PRESIDENTIAL PSALM

The parody of the Twenty-third Psalm as a political lampoon is indeed an old one. Ray B. Browne collected a version of it from the 1930s:

> Hoover is my shepherd and I am in want. He maketh me to lie down on park benches. He leadeth me beside free soup houses. He restoreth doubt in the Republican Party. He leadeth us in paths of destruction for his party's sake. Yea through the valley of the shadow of Starvation I fear evil, for they are against me. Thou preparest a reduction in salaries before me in the presence of mine enemies. Thou anointest my income with taxes, my expenses over my income. Surely unemployment and poverty will follow me all the days of the Republican Administration, and I will dwell in rented houses forever.

Variants of it have appeared frequently since then. Michael J. Preston recalls a similar psalm in circulation during the 1956 election, beginning, "Ike is my shepherd; I shall not want. He maketh me lie down on park benches; he leadeth me beside stilled factories." The following updated version was circulated in Williamsport, Pennsylvania, in November and December of 1970, a gubernatorial election year in the state:

Nixon Psalm and Joke

Nixon is my shepherd, I am in want,
He maketh me lie down on park benches,
He leadeth me beside still factories,

He guideth me in the path of unemployment,
For the sake of his party.
Yea, though I walk in the path of the soup kitchen, I am hungry—
He anointeth my income with taxes,
So my expenses runneth over my income,
Surely poverty and hard living will follow me,
All the days of the Republican Administration,
And I shall live in a rented house forever.

5000 years ago, Moses said,
"Pick up your shovels, mount your camel or your ass,
And I will lead you to the promised land."

5000 years later, Roosevelt said,
"Lay down your shovel, light up a Camel,
Sit on your ass,
This is the promised land."

Now Boys, be careful—.
Today, Nixon will take your shovel,
Sell your camel, kick your ass,
And tell you there is no promised land.

THE PRESIDENT'S STATUE

This is the story of "The President's Statue." The satire usually takes the form of a letter appealing for funds to construct a statue of the then current President and generally resembles the following example collected by Alan Dundes in 1962:

Dear Friend:
We have the distinguished honor of being members of the committee to raise fifty million dollars to be used for placing a statue of John F. Kennedy in the Hall of Fame, Washington, D.C.

This committee was in quite a quandary about selecting the proper location for the statue. It was thought not wise to place it beside that of George Washington, who never told a lie, nor beside that of Franklin D. Roosevelt, who never told the truth, since John F. Kennedy can never tell the difference.

After careful consideration, we think it should be placed beside the statue of Christopher Columbus, the greatest New Dealer of them all, in that he started out not knowing where he was going, and in arriving, did not know where he was, and in returning, did not know where he had been, and managed to do it all on borrowed money.

The inscription on the statue will read:

"I pledge allegiance to John F. Kennedy and to the national debt for which he stands, one man, expendable, with graft and corruption for all."

Five thousand years ago, Moses said to the children of Israel, "Pick up your shovel, mount your camels and asses,

and I will lead you to the Promised Land." Nearly five
thousand years later Roosevelt said, "Lay down your
shovels, light up a Camel, sit on your ass; this is the
Promised Land." Now Kennedy is attempting to steal
your shovel, raise the price of Camels, kick your ass, and
tell you there ain't no Promised Land.

If you are one of those few with money left after paying taxes, we will expect a generous contribution from
you for this very worthwhile project.

Sincerely,
The Committee

LYDIA PINKHAM RHYMES

There's a baby in every bottle.

Elsie W. had no children,
There was nothing in her blouse.
Now she's taken the Vegetable Compound
And they milk her with the cows.

We sing, we sing of Lydia Pinkham
And her love of the human race.
You take the Vegetable Compound
For the pimples on your face.

One old woman found she couldn't pee.
They gave her the Vegetable Compound.
Now they pipe her to the sea.

It sells for a dollar a bottle,
Which is cheap enough you see,
And if it doesn't cure you
She'll sell you six for three.

GUS BAILEY AND THE BOSS'S DAUGHTER

Gus Bailey was a strongman and the hero of Township Seven,
but everything he tried didn't turn out right. Once when he was

working a camp where wages were low and conditions miserable, he decided to take things into his own hands. Hearing the boss was coming for a visit, Gus prepared himself a speech on conditions in the camp and stationed himself on the road leading from town. When he heard sleigh-bells approaching, he ripped off all his clothes except his cap and snowshoes and began chopping down a nearby tree, as if this were just another ordinary day. It was well below zero, and when the sleigh turned the bend the driver pulled the horses up in amazement at the sight of a logger working in his birthday suit in such weather. Gus dropped his axe, turned toward the sleigh, and began to give his speech on the kind of company that would let its loggers work without clothes in winter. He sort of bowed before starting, and when he looked up he was facing not the boss but the prettiest girl he had seen in a long time, the boss's daughter. For once, Gus didn't know what to do. He just sort of blushed all over and left the scene so fast the girl thought he had vanished into thin air. All that she could see was some melted snow where he'd been blushing.

SICK JOKES ON THE DEATH OF KENNEDY

A people's tragedy and trauma will often find expression in the folklore of that people. Immediately following such events, for instance, country music writers record local or national catastrophes in songs, some of which go into oral tradition. There is, for example, the oft-collected song, "Charles Guiteau" concerned with the fate of the murderer of President Garfield. . . .

It should, therefore, come as no surprise to learn that the tragic events of late November, 1963, have served as the impetus for a series of jokes and joking questions which are essentially a continuation of the sick joke cycle. These jokes should not be construed as demonstrating any lack of affection for President Kennedy, but rather should be seen as a release mechanism. The people's feeling of utter helplessness was perhaps in some sense alleviated by their ability to joke about the assassination. If one jokes about a subject, one has a feeling of control over that subject. Moreover, one must remember that is is only the most serious matters which are joked about. One such serious matter is the expression of sentiment after the death of a loved one. Humor based upon this topic appears to function as a counter-sentimental agent and thus serves as a defense against grief (much as superstitions warn against excessive weeping for the recently deceased). The following texts may be considered representative:

Did you hear what John-John got for Christmas? A jack-in-the-box.

Did you hear President Johnson's favorite song? "I Love a Parade."

What did Johnson say to Mrs. Kennedy? "I guess Jack needed that trip to Dallas like a hole in the head."

With Gestures

"Bang, bang, you're president!" (This was accompanied by a hand gesture in which the hand is made to look like a pistol. The index finger, representing the barrel, is pointed at the addressee, and moved slightly twice to represent the recoil of the two shots.)

"What did Johnson do right before the shot that killed Kennedy was fired?"
"I don't know. What?"
The person who asks the question puts his hands over his ears.

CRUEL JOKES ON FAMOUS PEOPLE

"Don't worry, Mrs. Arnold, Benedict is probably hanging around the East somewhere."
"Happy Father's Day, Mr. Lindbergh."
"Mrs. Dean, has Jimmy got his car fixed yet?"
"Did your husband get his polio shots yet, Mrs. Roosevelt?"
"Does your husband like his new plane, Liz?"
"Other than that, Mrs. Lincoln, how did you like the play?"
"How did your husband like the theatre, Mrs. Lincoln?"
"Mrs. Custer, would you like to contribute to Indian relief?"
"Hi, Anastasia, how's the family?"
"Helen Keller says—'Uh! Uh! Uh!'"

"I Don't Care . . ."

"I don't care what you are President of, that's my golf ball."
"I don't care if your name is Napoleon. Get your hand out of my blouse."
"I don't care if your name is Santa Claus. Get you hand out of my stocking."

NORBERT WIENER, THE GREAT MATHEMATICIAN

Norbert Wiener, the great mathematician who taught at MIT for over forty years and who was perhaps best known among the general public for his coining of the word cybernetics, became the subject of dozens of professor tales, jokes, and representatives and attributive anecdotes. Some of the Wiener stories had to do with Wiener's real idiosyncracies, but many of them were universal donor types such as often attach themselves to the best-known theoretician on a campus (I remember several of them told about Einstein at Princeton in the late 1950s, for example). Conditions at MIT in the 1950s and 1960s were perhaps more supportive of this sort of narrative than they were at most urban universities: almost everyone there (with the exception of a few wild English majors) was in a technical field, and so at one time or another had to deal with some aspect of Wiener's work. Unlike many students of the physical sciences, Wiener was interested in the relationship between his science and the human condition, so he was of considerably more interest to students and even faculty than the run-of-the-mill genius. At MIT, everyone knew of Norbert Wiener.

In the stories he comes out as absent-minded, nearly blind, brilliant, elliptical, savagely moral, egotistical, and insecure. These characteristics are not, of course, mutually exclusive: the egotism and the insecurity are flip sides of the same coin; the absent-mindedness and the blindness are variants of a similar projective condition. One curious characteristic of the absent-minded professor (not just Wiener) is that he is often presented as someone who in certain areas is capable of prodigious feats of mind and memory.

Wiener and the Little Girl

I heard my first Wiener story at a Society of Fellows dinner shortly after I moved to Cambridge in 1963. Several of the Junior Fellows in the Society at that time had done their graduate work at MIT, and one told me a story that went something like this:

Wiener and his family bought a new house. They had been living in the old place for years and years and they needed a place with more room for the growing family, so they moved out of their house in Concord or Waltham to a new house not far away. Wiener was notoriously absent-minded, so his wife gave him a slip of paper with the new address. She even put it in his coat pocket. She knew he'd come home and forget they had moved, and then when he found out they had moved he wouldn't remember where they had moved to.

Wiener takes the train into Cambridge and spends the day at MIT, comes home on the train and, just as his wife expected, he goes straight to the old house. He is very upset because no one is there. He looks inside and the furniture is all gone. He remembers that he moved and that his wife wrote out the new address for him.

He begins to look through his pockets, then remembers that the new address is in his raincoat, which he left at his office.

A little girl goes by on a bicycle and Wiener is sure she lives in the neighborhood, so he stops her and says, "Little girl, little girl: I'm Professor Wiener. I used to live here. But we moved today and I don't know where the new house is. Do you know where my family moved?"

She says, "Mommy thought you'd forget, Daddy."

Then I Had Lunch

The first one that comes to mind is perhaps very typical of the Wiener that was always seen by people walking in the halls at

MIT rather than the people who actually had contact with him personally.

He'd be walking along with these fantastic bifocals so that his head was at such an angle that he looked more as though he was looking at the ceiling than where he was going on ahead. And even with those tremendous glasses on, he'd still be tapping the walls with one hand to make sure that he didn't take the wrong turning. He must have been pretty close to being legally blind.

And one of the classic stories is this. Wiener is walking along and he's in the halls and he's accosted by one of his pupils about some matter or other and they finish their business and Wiener says, "Oh, by the way, ah, which way was I going when you stopped me?"

And the student says, "You were going that way, sir?"

He says, "Oh, fine. Then I had lunch."

The Calculus Class

There's the one where he walks into a freshman calculus class.

Almost all the rooms at Tech have a front door and a back door, they're on the side wall. So he comes scooting in, starts writing very hairy differential equations on the board and, finally, one of the freshmen—they've been snowed by normal calculus anyway, so that it takes them a while to recognize the difference—realizes that this is not what they were supposed to be snowed by today. So he raises his hand and, finally, Wiener notices him and he says, "Yes?"

"Ah, excuse me, sir, but, uhm, I think you're in the wrong classroom. This is freshman calculus."

And Wiener says, "Oh." And walks out the door.

Five minutes later, the freshmen are still waiting for their instructor to come in, and who comes in the back door and starts writing differential equations on the back board?

Wiener.

The Right Answer

Wiener had this nasty habit, besides wandering into the wrong classroom and scrawling these silly equations on the board, of solving them in his head, which is, you know, not only difficult, but noninformative for students.

So Wiener finally did this once too often with one of his classes and one of the fellows got quite pissed off on that. So after class he comes up to Wiener and he said, "Ah, Dr. Wiener, on problem 27, I found your solution very interesting, of course, but I did it in a different way." So he writes the equation out on the board and—just as Wiener did—he stood there for about a minute and then wrote out the answer with none of the intermediate steps, which should take up about a whole board.

And Wiener sort of looked at it for about five minutes and scratched his head and he said, "Well, your answer is right, but your method is wrong."

Where Is the Car?

The other standard one about him was that he had gone to New Haven to give a lecture or something and he came back and greeted his wife and his wife said, "Where's the car?" And he realized that he had taken the train back, having left the car in a parking lot in New Haven.

There's a very famous story about his actually forgetting his car, and I sort of remember it was Providence, Rhode Island, and he arrived back in Boston on the train and they had to send back to Providence to pick up the car.

Folk societies have their keepers of the culture, men and women who know literally hundreds of songs, tales, superstitions, proverbs, and riddles, and who hand them down from generation to generation as the folk heritage of their group. These people are performers, gathering listeners about them after work in the evenings, on social occasions, or whenever suitable opportunities arise. Often they vie with one another, contesting to see who can last the longer or show the greater artistry. Sometimes they represent their group against the challenge of a culture-keeper from a nearby community or a rival occupation. Money, local pride, and the reputation of the performer ride on the outcome. Contests of this sort have been known to last all night.

Most storytellers and singers are not creators. They merely relate widely known tales, like the one about the famous hunter who shoots a deer with a peach pit and the next year shoots a deer with a peach tree growing out of its back, or about the simpleton who gets stuck in the mud and goes to get a shovel to dig himself out; or they sing old songs about mighty men like Robin Hood and John Henry or play fiddle tunes that memorialize the battles of Napoleon. Their performances remain fluid, each one a unique re-creation, modulated to suit the audience of the particular occasion. Often they localize or embellish their materials considerably. "Oregon" Smith and John Snyder do this with their yarns, and so does Aunt Molly Jackson with a Robin Hood ballad she learned from a printed source late in her career, but most of them do not make things up out of whole cloth. Only a few seem capable of this, of seeing themselves in the role of originator rather than repository and performer. These few fabricate some of their lies, like John Snyder, or compose their own songs, like William Pleasant Ewell or William Henry Scott, and thus help to revitalize their folk communities. But given the processes of folklore, their original compositions will likely pass into the anonymity of oral tradition, their names eventually dissociated from them. Other performers will supplant them, and most of them will be forgotten even when their words endure.

There are exceptions. The reputation of a rare storyteller or song maker does sometimes survive. Just a few, like Hunter Ellis and Jones Tracy, will be remembered locally, more for the stamp of personality on their stories than for the stories themselves. A superlative performer—"Leadbelly," or Huddie Ledbetter, the singer and guitar player discovered by John Lomax in a Louisiana prison, is a classic instance—may gain national audiences and the attention of the mass media. Aunt Molly, seeking support for striking coal miners in Kentucky, also managed this. These exceptional culture-keepers might well be thought of as artistic prowess heroes, paralleling at the folk level the professional careers of Enrico Caruso, Elvis Presley, Will Rogers, and Stephen Foster. Of all American folk performers and composers, Larry Gorman is perhaps the most remarkable, for his talents are held in such esteem by lumbermen that today, sixty years after his death, it is not unusual for a folk singer to attribute to him the authorship of a song he never wrote, the phrase "a Larry Gorman song" still adding luster to the performance.

JIM BRIDGER'S BIG YARNS

Champion of all tellers of Western tall tales, according to Lieutenant J. W. Gunnison, Captain W. J. Raynolds, and others who employed him as a guide, after the fur period was about over, was Jim Bridger. As early as 1844 he had brought back to St. Louis stories of the wonders of the Yellowstone region, but the newspapers were afraid to print such big yarns. Little wonder, then, that Bridger decided no longer to be restrained to the truth that no one would believe. Among the charming lies attributed to Bridger in later years are tales of an accurate echo that could be used as an alarm clock if one would just call out "Get up! Get up!" when he went to bed; of the mountain of glass, or Obsidian Cliff, with the heap of bones at its base—mute reminder of the animals and birds who had tried to pass through without noticing that there was a mountain in the way; of the petrified valley where he rode over a chasm without falling, for even gravitation was under the spell; of Scott's Bluffs, standing nearly four hundred feet high in the place where there was only a deep valley when he first came West; of his ability to tell the elevation of any place by boring down until he struck salt water and then measuring the distance to sea level; and of the great snow in the Salt Lake Valley that killed the vast herds of buffalo, which he pickled in the Great Salt Lake, thus preserving them for himself and the Utes for many years.

HUNTER JOHN ELLIS

John Ellis was born in Smithfield, Me., in 1784, resided for a time in Mercer and came to Guilford in August, 1844, and from that time until his death in 1867, spent most of his time as hunter and guide in the forests about Moosehead Lake.

He was a hunter before coming to Guilford, even in his youth.

As a boy he had a cat which he had trained to accompany him in his quest for squirrels and other small game, and who was as sagacious and helpful as a dog. The delight he took with this intelligent companion in these early days may have been largely influential in making him a lover of life in the woods.

Yet he was no hermit. He enjoyed his fellows, was a genuine wit, and his return from the woods was an occasion for rejoicing in the village; while the circle in the loafing places had to be enlarged when Hunter Ellis returned, that all might listen to his stories and adventures.

Could these stories but be collected, they would make a valuable asset to the literature of the county; and yet they would lack the inimitable setting of his magnetic telling.

Hunter Ellis Bides His Time

In trapping, hunting and fishing his skill was unsurpassed. Spare of figure, lithe as an Indian, no white man was his equal in his chosen craft.

From his trips he ever returned laden with furs, often most valuable; frequently with four or five hundred muskrat skins and in the earlier days with wolfskins. Frequently he was alone for weeks and perhaps months, seeing no white face. As a guide, his services were eagerly sought by sportsmen who rarely failed to render him due courtesy.

However on one occasion, one of a party of New York men failed to show him the respect to which Hunter was accustomed. Ellis bided his time. One day "New York" complained that his watch, an elegant gold one, had stopped. Hunter said he was used to watches and could take it apart all right and see what ailed it. He did so and told the sportsman it was but a bit of dirt which had got in and he had removed it. "Well put it together now." "O!" says old Hunter, "I can't put watches together; I can only take them apart."

The Big Trout and the Little Hole

Around the fireside at the Kineo House a party of sportsmen were recounting the wonders which they had at various times accomplished in the way of trout-catching. Hunter John listened for a while in silence. At length with a contemptuous whiff from the pipe which he was smoking, he broke in: "Call that fishing do you boys? Let me tell you: I get trout on this lake anywhere, day or night any time or any season of the year. Let me tell you: I was crossing the North Bend last winter; ice three feet thick; I happened to have with me a one-inch auger which I was going to use for some purpose or other. The thought struck me: wonder if trout could be found here this time of year! No sooner said than done. I had a bit of twine and a pointed nail in my pocket. I just took the auger, bored a hole in the ice, and in less than five minutes had a sixteen-pound laker on the ice before me. What do you think of that?" The crowd was dumb with astonishment, while the hunter smoked his pipe in triumph. Presently one of the number, turning suddenly, exclaimed: "Uncle John, how came that sixteen-pound trout through that one-inch auger hole?" "Goodness gracious!" exclaimed the old man, starting to his feet and clapping his hands together, "I never thought of that." Laughter went round at once, but no more big fish stories were told that night."

"OREGON" SMITH OF INDIANA

[Abraham "Oregon" Smith] was supposed to have lived in Bloomington [Indiana] from sometime in the 1800s up to 1904. At one time he lived at Ninth and Morton streets. . . . he would disappear from Bloomington at various times and when he returned, would tell tales of Oregon—thus giving rise to his sobriquet.

In addition to his notoriety as a story teller he had another reason for local fame. "It was he who first made and introduced 'sassafras oil' to Bloomington. It was used in the making of liniment which at the time he lived was a panacea for practically everything wrong with humanity. The old grannies and midwives all knew their 'yarbs' and liniments. He cut blocks of green sassafras wood and put them under an overturned kettle. Around the kettle he built a hot fire and let it burn down to coals. The blocks of wood were sitting on a stone block that had a groove hewn in it. The oil would be cooked out of them and 'Oregon' caught it as it came trickling down the groove in the stone."

Buffalo-milk Butter

One time when I was out in Oregon walkin' along the foot of a hill, I come to a little cold stream. About half way across I started noticing little bits of yaller stuff floating on the top of the water and a bit further on down I saw a small pool of pale yaller churning around slowly. Well now, that interested me considerable. I looked at it and then, thinks I, it won't hurt none to taste the stuff. Well, I did and, do you know, it tasted just like butter—unsalted butter. Such a curious thing kinda got my dander up, and I decided to investigate. I looked around and didn't see nothin', so

I started to climb up the side of the hill that the stream was flowing down. I clumb and I clumb till finally I come up over a little rise, and there was a herd of buffalo cows a-standin' in a wide spot in the stream to keep cool. . . . They was packed so clost together and a-stompin' so hard that the milk was squirtin' outa their bags and a-flowin' into the water. There was so much of it a-runnin' over the rocks that it churned itself on the way down and the cold water made it gather at the bottom of the hill. Yes sir, there was a mighty practical way to get good clean butter going to waste right there in the wilds of Oregon.

The Peach Tree Deer

One day while out walking, I saw a deer standing looking at me from the edge of a clearing. I happened to have my gun with me; and when I put my hands in me pocket for a bullet, there warn't none. All I could find was a peach seed—small one at that. Well, I pulled up and shot at that deer, but it wheeled and ran away. About a year later I was on my way back to the states and thought I'd pass through that same clearing in hopes of finding my deer again. I was just about through the opening, and I saw the nicest peach tree just loaded with peaches. Well, now, I climbed up in the tree and started eating as all I had in me pack was cold corn bread and salt pork. Right in the middle of a bite I'll be gum if that peach tree didn't get up and run off in the forest with me. I looked down and there was the peach tree growing out of the head of the deer I had shot a year ago.

"Oregon" Sheds a Barrel of Tears

"Oregon" joined church, and after he'd been in church a while, the congregation knew his weakness for stretchin' the truth so they thought they would remonstrate with him. So several of the men went to him, talked to him, and one of 'em says, " 'Oregon' we've taken into consideration you're a good man, but you tell some awful hard stories to swallow; and since you're Christian, don't you think you had better stick closer to the truth?" Seems "Oregon" looked kinda sad and he says, "Yes, you know I've grieved an awful lot about that failin' of mine, and I guess I've shed 'most a barrel of tears over it." About that time, one of the men spoke up and says, " 'Oregon,' is that true you've shed a *barrel* of tears?" "Oregon" looked kinda sad and he says, "Well, no, I guess I'm wrong. I haven't shed a barrel of tears—I've shed *barrels*."

LEN HENRY, IDAHO SQUAWMAN

Len Henry was the last survivor of the pioneer squawmen on the Nez Perce reservation at Lapwai, Idaho. He had moved there with his Indian wife about 1889 while the government land was being allotted, and he died on March 14, 1946, near the site of his original cabin. A photograph of Len Henry taken two months before his death showed him as a tall, erect old man with long light hair and mustache, wearing baggy trousers, a vest, and a floppy hat, standing with one hand on his hip and his eyes looking directly into the camera lens with a serious air. He had just told the photographer that he was going on 105 years old, but it seems clear that he was following the habit of a lifetime and stretching the truth—this time by about eleven years. It is said that people had commented *then*, "That's the last lie that old Len Henry will ever tell."

Sweetwater, Idaho, an unincorporated village, today consists of a grain elevator and a grocery store bracketing the highway, and a cluster of houses off the east side of it. Bert Ankney, age 70, has lived there all his life, and heard Len Henry tell stories as far back as he can remember. Mr. and Mrs. Ankney commented:

> Whenever you met that man he was telling stories. The man could set for hours at a time and tell one after another, and it was so odd that anyone could think up stories constantly like that. . . . He always had something, no matter what you brought up. . . . He could tell one, and later on he'd tell the same story exactly the same way.

The store at Sweetwater was opened in 1929 by Phil Crawford, now retired at 81 and living in Clarkston, [Washington,] who

said Len Henry could tell stories "anytime, anyplace, anywhere."
He said Len liked to come to the store where he could gather a
knot of five or six men around him, sit cross-legged on the floor,
and cut loose with the tall tales. Phil thought that Len had said
he helped with the camp outfit for Alice Fletcher when she came
out from Washington, D.C., for the land allotment, but nothing
in the records shows this. In 1944 Dick Alfrey acquired the Sweetwater store, and he observed Len Henry getting up from his cross-
legged position without touching his hands to the floor until two
weeks before he died. He said that as many as fifteen or twenty
men would cluster around when he started talking—either before
the stove inside, or at a bench in front on sunny days, and "people
got a kick out of his stories and would try to start him off telling
them." Len chewed tobacco and spit towards the stove when he
talked, and Alfrey remembered that when he got through he always had to mop up after him.

The single best informant interviewed to date was Mylie Lawyer of Lapwai, daughter of the prominent Nez Perce Indian, Corbett Lawyer. Miss Lawyer's sister collected from her for my
folklore class, and later I visited her to record this description of
the unique circumstances in which she heard Len Henry narrate:

> I graduated high school in 1929, and two or three years
> prior to that time I had to write English themes every
> school day for the English teacher. And I run out of ma-
> terial, so that's how I began to go up there to get the
> Len Henry stories. We'd go up there in a mixed group,
> and sometimes there'd be more white kids than there
> would be Indians. But they'd be just whoever I hap-
> pened to be with. We'd go up there and listen to his sto-
> ries. We always sat out on the porch, and he knew I was
> taking these for class. . . .

Some Len Henry Stretchers

There was one about the echo, you know, was frozen. He was
going along in a canyon and he camped overnight, and he knew

that there was an echo there. And he hollered, "How are you?" And no answer, 'cause it was real cold. So he banked up his fire and he lay down and he went to sleep. Then he got up the next morning and he listened, and no echo. So he left. And he said in the summertime he'd come back to the same place and he fixed his campfire, and just as he started to eat his supper somebody said, "I'm fine." [Laughter]

And then there was another echo story. He said one time he was going down into this deep, deep canyon. And it had cliffs on each side, and he was travelin' a long, long ways, and he knew he had to get up early in the morning. So he fixed his fire again, and he lay down and then he thought, "Well, how am I goin' to get up early in the morning?" So he got up by the fire and he stood there, and he said "Wake me up at sunrise!" And he said it three times before he laid down. He had a good night's sleep, and pretty soon somebody said, "Wake up! Wake up! Wake up!" so he got up and he said the sun was juuust coming up over that cliff.

On one occasion the Indians were chasing Len on horseback and were getting so close he was sure to be overtaken. Right in the midst of the danger he came to a big washout in the trail. There wasn't time to turn back: the banks were too steep to go either up or down, and it seemed they were doomed. But being Len Henry, he at once saw a way out. There was a ledge of rock immediately above the wash over the trail, so he threw his lasso rope over the crag, backed his horse a few steps, half-hitched the rope over the saddle horn, got his knife in readiness, then threw the spurs to his horse. The rope held and swung the horse to the other side. Len cut the rope and the horse landed on his feet on the other side safely. He stated he left the rope hanging so those following could see what he had done and could also get across.

One day he was goin' someplace a-horseback, and he come to a crik. Crik wasn't so awful wide, but it was deep, and he was afraid to swim it, 'cause he'd get so wet, see; so he got back and took a run and jumped his horse across. Wasn't too wide. Just before he got there he looked over on the ground—there was a great big rattlesnake a-layin' there, see? So he just turned around and went back.

I don't remember very many of Len Henry's stories, but will write the ones I know. . . . He said he was camping on top of the Swallow's Nest. (This is a steep cliff overlooking the Snake River near Clarkston, Washington.) He said there was a level place up there for a camp. One day he was riding a bucking horse. It started to buck toward the cliff, he figured he would go over with the horse and be killed, so he reached down and unfastened the cinch and rolled off with the saddle, just as the horse went over, leaving him and saddle on top of the cliff. He didn't like to see the horse fall all the way down and suffer, so he pulled his six-shooter and shot him seven times before he hit the ground. He must have loaded pretty fast to shoot him seven times.

Well, Len came into Heckner and Carlson's store in Lapwai and said, "I want two 30-30 shells." Old Heckner, was kinda slow on the think, said he should buy a *box* of 'em. Then old Len says, "I only need two; your damned game laws only allow me one deer and one elk."

JOHN SNYDER OF SLIPPERY ROCK

Every district at some time has some unusual character, story teller or the like; of these John Snyder, who lived a mile or so from the Old Stone House [near Slippery Rock Creek, Butler County, Western Pennsylvania], was locally famous. The stories are old today that he told a century ago, and probably were old before his time. . . .

He did not like the quality of steel in the scythes for mowing grass, so he gathered up enough razor blades and got a scythe made from them. He could mow all summer with it, then set it on the ground, edge up, drop a hair on it, and it would cut the hair right in two.

He was a very strong man when young. He was down at Pittsburgh and the hunting season was coming on, he thought he would buy some shot. He wanted enough of it to last him through the season, so he bought a bed-tick full. He carried it on his shoulder up Liberty Avenue, sinking to his knees in the cobblestone pavement at every step for two blocks. Then he carried it up three flights of stairs to the third story where he was staying, and thoughtlessly dropped it off his shoulder. It broke right through the floors right down to the cellar.

He shot a deer on the other side of Slippery Rock Creek. He puzzled for a few minutes, but could see no way to get the deer but to swim the creek. He was wearing boots, but did not take his clothes off, as he was a good swimmer. He was having a bad time of it before he reached the other bank; thought he wasn't going to make it. But a limb, fortunately, stuck out over the water so that he could get hold of it, and so he managed to get up on the bank. Then he pulled off his boots to get the water out of them and found out why he had so much trouble swimming. His boots and his pants were full of fish. When he got the fish shaken out and gathered up, he had a string of them reaching from his shoulder to his heels. No wonder he came near to drowning.

He went out in the morning to hitch up his team, intending to plow that day, but going out to the corn-crib he saw a snake. He thought that a sort of bad omen, so he did not plow that day, but went to Butler in the wagon. When he came back in the evening he drove into the barnyard, and there was the tail of that same snake just going by.

He had a fine yoke of young oxen. He took them out in the morning before breakfast to open up a ten-acre field. He plowed the first three rounds next the fence, then went in to breakfast. When he came back after breakfast, the oxen had the whole ten acres plowed.

JONES TRACY OF MOUNT DESERT ISLAND

In his mature years Jones became quite well known for his ability to entertain with stories. Ira Bunker and Frank Thompson were well known too, but they do not seem to have been remembered the way Jones has. What seems to have made the difference in Jones' favor was mentioned briefly in the last chapter: after 1918 he ran a dance hall. The hall was connected to the house and people from all over Mount Desert Island congregated there weekly for the dances. Since Jones was sixty-two by 1918 and a cripple from arthritis, he didn't dance, but he did provide an attraction to the dances by his very presence. According to Grace Reed who was often present (she was Caleb Tracy's wife), Jones stayed in the kitchen of the house in his rocking chair by the stove telling stories by the hour to anyone who would listen, and he never lacked an audience. Tired dancers, wall flowers, and connoisseurs of the storytelling art flocked downstairs from the second floor dance hall to the kitchen to hear old Mr. Tracy perform. Every week he had new stories and he never grew tired of telling them. A few years of this and Jones had been heard by many interested people, many of whom never forgot the old man's wit and the stories he told. His reputation spread so that he could not stop telling stories even if he had wanted to, particularly at the dances. Whenever he went to Lawrie Holmes' store in Somesville, or showed up at the post office, there was always someone who wanted a story. Lawrie Holmes Jr. recalled that when Jones came into his father's store, everyone who had nothing to do came over to get the old man going and find out his latest story. Jones had a reputation to uphold, and he always satisfied his listeners. Frank Thompson and the others, however, though they may have been equally good as entertainers, were not as much in demand. They told stories less in public, had a smaller audience than Jones, and consequently their stories were not remembered by as many people.

When we come to a consideration of Jones' style, we find that it was by no means totally unique, but it was distinctly memorable. Both Clark Manring and Ralph Tracy recalled that Jones' tales were so vivid they never left their minds. John Carroll, Jones' son-in-law, made a point of mentioning the detail Jones would include in his tales. John and Charles Carroll had a conversation on this topic which gives the best description of Jones' style I have found:

> *Charles:* Well, when he started [a story] he had [described] the day and the time and the moon and the stars and the sun. And I never heard anyone else tell it that way.
> *John:* [He'd say] Just what kind of day it was. Now if he started out on a hunting trip there'd be a frost on the grass and he always started out before daylight. When the sun came up, why there was the bushes all white with frost.
> *Charles:* He'd be in a green grove for a while and then he'd be on a hardwood ridge. And you's right along side of him all the time. And then you'd wind up, *out of this world!*

A Heavy Fog in Maine

Once in a while we have a heavy fog in our neighborhood and you have to work quite fast to keep warm. These Maine fogs kind of, kind of cut through you, especially in the late fall of the year when the temperature starts to drop. So, one of these boys, and I don't remember who it was. It could have been Jones Tracy. I think it was possible that he was the hero. Well, he had a time limit on this shingling job or he wouldn't have, he wouldn't have shingled on that foggy day I'm sure. Well, he, he was trying to hurry to get the job done, and he got shingling away and he said the nails went in awfully easy along the last of it . . . but still he was hurrying up and finally he begun to get hungry, thought it must be dinner time. He hadn't looked at his watch and he did look at it and yes it was way past dinner time so he started to slide down off the roof towards the staging and he landed ten feet off one end of that building. He'd shingled out ten feet beyond the end of the roof. Fog was so thick, held that, held those shingles right up. I suppose also the fog was so thick that it kept him from falling down real fast.

The Snakes That Ate Themselves

Oh yes, the time he saw two snakes fighting over the toad in there. Each snake wanted to eat that toad, or frog, whichever it was. He said he stood and watched them and they kept circling each other and the frog was in the middle. And by and by one snake grabbed the other feller right by the tail, and the other feller reached right around and grabbed *him* by the tail. And he said they started swallering. He said, "I commenced to blink my eyes and watch them. One would swallow and the other would swallow," he said, "and pretty soon there wasn't no snakes there; they'd swallowed each other!" And one fellow said, "Could that be so?"

Keeping Dry

Then he went to Ellsworth with his horse and wagon, you know, and a thunder shower came up. He kept ahead of it all the way with his horse, and the only part of the wagon got wet was the back part of the wagon.

Saving the Powder

You knew about him going across the Sound, picking up firewood and finding the keg of powder? Black Powder? Well, he got his firewood loaded in his boat, and this keg of powder and he had this bucksaw. And Jones said, "Like a cussed fool," he said, "when I got about half way across the Sound," he said, "I stopped rowing and thought I'd light up my pipe." And he says, "When I did," he says, "That keg of powder got afire." He says, "I took my bucksaw quicker'n hell and sawed that keg in two and saved half of that powder!"

JONES TRACY GOES HUNTING

The Bunghole Story

This happened over here on Sargent's mountain. The most of his deer stories were on Sargent's mountain. Well, he, what made them interesting, he'd tell about what time he started, generally started before daylight early in the morning. This morning he got up early and milked his cows and fed his stock and it was the first, there wasn't any storms, but he said the trees was covered with frost. You've seen these mornings with the bushes all white with frost. When the sun comes up it soon melts it and runs off. And he said it was dark when he left. The old Tracy house up there and he went right down across the road you know over on Sargent's mountain. That was his hunting ground and he got up the mountain and of course he went slow after he got down on his hunting ground. And he was looking and peeking and creeping along through the woods and he said it was, he judged it was about eleven o'clock before he got up there, then settled down the mountain and looking and creeping as easy as he could; and he sighted this buck deer not far from him and he up with his gun and took good aim and he said he had plenty of time. Took good aim with his rifle and fired. And he hit him in the, on the side of the head. Knocked one horn off, and I think it hit him on the, it almost hit his brain, but not quite, and . . . it numbed him. He fell down when it knocked his horn off. He dropped right in his tracks just the same as you'd hit him with a hammer. And Jones he said he started along there and when he got up to him he said he stood his gun up side of a tree there and went along and pulled his knife out to bleed him you know. And just as he reached out to bleed him, to jiggle him, the deer opened his eyes and looked up at him and turned over and got up on his feet. And he said, "I made a grab for him like that," he says, "my big finger went

through his bunghole and," he says, "I hooked him and of course
he was towing me. It wasn't so hard for me as it was for the deer."
And he said he run along there. He described the road down to
the south there for quite a while right along the side of the mountain and then he turned over on the other side of the mountain
and then he turned over on the other side. "Well," he said, "it
was about eleven o'clock when I fired that shot and before I
gained on him enough to give him a slat, slat him off his feet
down . . . it was about two hours and fifteen minutes." Just as
tight as he could run before he could slat him off his feet and
stick his knife in his neck.

Speeding Up a Slow Bullet

Jones had an old 50-95 gun which shot pretty slow. He used to
carry a wooden paddle along with him when he went hunting on
foggy days. When he saw a deer he'd up and shoot at it and then
chase the bullet along with the paddle and pat it, correcting its
speed and course so that it would hit the deer accurately. That
was some slow gun.

A Bear Turned Inside Out

Of course, . . . there's another one Grandfather, I have heard
him tell it, but he told it more for a joke than anything. It wasn't
one of his regular stories, but, that was a bear in that time and as
far as I know he never saw but two bear in the woods in his whole
life. He said, . . . this bear was coming right at him, opened his
mouth, and he said he reached right down, reached right out
through, took him by the tail and pulled him right 'round inside
out so he was headed the other way. And instead of a black bear
it was a white bear.

Double-jumping a Brook

Well, he was fishing, he was fishing, and . . . he hadn't got to
the brook; it was a mile or two further to go through to this

brook. It was a brook they had caught a lot of fish in and some big ones and he was on his way and he . . . didn't have any shooting irons with him. All he had was his fishing rod and bait. And he come across this bear and a cub, the cub was near the bear, and when a bear has cubs she's pretty, she'll fight to the last minute. And so he started to run. He wasn't going to put up any fight to that bear. He started to run in the direction of the brook. And the bear followed him. And glory he said he thought the bear was gaining on him. And he was a running as hard as he could run, and when he come to this brook the bear wasn't far behind. And he jumped. 'Twas a wide brook; he guessed it about twelve or fifteen feet wide, and the water was deep and he jumped just as tight as he could jump to the other side. And he saw he wasn't going to make it and in the air there he jumped again and made the other side and got away from the bear.

Lifelike Decoys

Jones had another one about wooden tolers, making tolers, decoys. This is just a, there's no story to it but he was making himself some wooden decoys and whittled them out and painted them up and they looked pretty natural. And he put them behind the stove and let them dry over night. Came down in the morning and thought he'd take them out and try them. He went to take them out from behind the stove and the cat had eaten the heads off of all of them.

Song Makers

LARRY GORMAN,
"THE MAN WHO MAKES THE SONGS"

Lawrence Gorman, "The Man Who Makes the Songs," was born in Trout River, Lot Thirteen, on the west end of Prince Edward Island in 1846. As a young man he worked on his father's farm, in the many shipyards along the Bideford and Trout Rivers, as a fisherman, and as a hand in the lobster factories along the shore from Cape Wolfe to Miminigash. Up to about 1885 (age forty), he spent many of his winters in the lumberwoods and his springs on the river drives, mostly along the Miramichi River in New Brunswick. Then he would usually return to "The Island" in the summer. About 1885 he moved permanently to Ellsworth, Maine, bought a house there, was twice married, and worked in the woods and on the drives along the Union River. In the early 1900s he moved to South Brewer, Maine, just across the Penobscot from the great lumber port of Bangor. Here he worked mostly as a yard hand for the Eastern Corporation, a paper mill. He died in Brewer in 1917 and now lies buried in Mount Pleasant Cemetery in Bangor.

All through his seventy years, wherever he went he left behind him a trail of stories, songs, and consternation. Let us sample a few of his songs. . . . From Ellsworth, Maine, comes "Billy Watts":

> For forty-odd years I've been known in this place,
> And the name that I go by is "Old Dirty Face."
> I never once washed it but once in my life,
> And that was the first time I went courting my wife,
> Derry down, down, oh, down, derry down.
>
> When I get to Ellsworth I must have a wash,
> My face it is covered with gurry and moss;

I'll bottle the water to poison the botts—
Now what do you think of your friend Mr. Watts?

Gorman is reputed to have had a nasty gift for spontaneous rhyming. A man he was working for asked him to say grace in the company dining hall. Larry looked down at his plate and said,

> "O Lord above, look down on us,
> And see how we are forgotten,
> And send us meat that is fit to eat,
> Because by Christ, this is rotten!"

[Larry Gorman] is important because he was so well known. His neighbors and companions may not always have liked him, but they remembered his songs and sang them. He made songs that caught on and went into oral tradition, albeit a limited tradition. There are several explanations for this fame. For one thing, the songs he wrote were so personal, bearing so clearly his individual stamp, that they stayed associated with his name. He did not follow the more traditional patterns like the "come-all-ye," which would tend to obscure the author behind standard devices and morality. Interestingly enough, many people remember him but have forgoten his songs. On the other hand, Joe Scott, who wrote "come-all-ye's" is almost forgotten but the ballads he wrote are still being sung. For another thing, the very personal, satirical, invective quality of Gorman's verse attracted attention to the man. Larry was apt to song anyone around at the slightest pretext, and, as I have said, his songs were apt to catch on. He was a man to watch out for; one could laugh at him or beat him up, but either way, Larry Gorman attracted as much attention to himself as to his songs.

A *Larry Gorman Cante Fable*

[The] following is a very clear example of a *cante fable:* Larry was fishing one season off Lot Seven shore on [Prince Edward

Island] with a fellow by the name of Matt, who had a wife who was terribly religious. One day when they pulled in the nets they found a small anchor in it, which just happened to be one Matt had lost some time before. When he told his wife about it, she was simply transported with joy. Later that day, someone asked Larry what luck he and Matt had had, and he replied,

> " 'Tis to the Virgin we must pray
> And every day must thank her;
> Matt went out to fish today
> And caught his little anchor."

Here the story *requires* the verse to complete it and would be pointless without it. The verse here would be meaningless without the story leading up to it.

Larry Gorman and "Old Henry"

In 1892, James E. Henry bought a large tract of land in Lincoln, New Hampshire, set up a sawmill and several woods camps, and went into business making a fortune as fast as he possibly could—and as boldly. . . . Once, before he came to Lincoln, when he was still operating up in Zealand Valley, he had hired Larry Gorman and Larry had given him considerable sass. But he had asked for it.

Anyone could have predicted how Gorman would have served Henry, for "Ave" Henry was the type of the tight-fisted, hard-driving lumberman. It is said that he charged his men for every bit of equipment they used. One time a man sluiced a horse, for which Henry charged him sixty dollars. Since the man had only about twenty dollars coming to him, his brother asked Henry if he was going to keep back *his* pay too. Henry walked up to the brother and grabbed his gold watch: "Yes," he said, "and this too." He had the legendary boss's contempt for the humanity of his men. The story goes that a man died in camp, and, since they did not know where he belonged, they decided to bury him right there.

They sent a man out to dig the grave, but later in the morning the man returned, saying that the soil was just too hard and rocky to dig a grave in. "Oh hell," said Henry, "don't bother with all that. Just sharpen him and drive him in!" A similar story tells of another man who died. "George," he said to his son, "was he a good man?" He was told that the man was one of the best. "Then take him out and bury him next to old Ranger," he said, "because he was one of our best horses."

Henry had an excellent "chance" there in Lincoln Valley. There was very little pine left, but straight and clear spruce was plentiful. "I never cut so many one-to-a-thousand trees in my life," said Peter Jamieson of East Bathurst, New Brunswick (who, following the example of his older brother John, had gone out to work for Henry about 1900) but added that the work was all up and down hill, hard on the legs for anyone used as he was to the flat land along the Bay Chaleur. Henry didn't have to drive his logs at all, because he had his own sawmill right near where the cutting was going on, while over in Zealand Valley he had his own log railroad seven miles long. The whole operation was a family affair, too, for his three sons worked right there with him: John took charge in the office, George was walking boss and took charge in the woods, and Charlie ran the sawmill. "All I care about a dollar is to see it tick," said old Henry. And he saw plenty of them tick.

Before we come to Larry Gorman's song on the Henrys, let's take a brief look at the credit side of their ledger, something it is easy enough to ignore. John Jamieson claimed that Henry and Co. always used him well, and his brother Peter said it was the best outfit he ever worked for—strict but good. They both claimed that this strictness was excusable: the general quality of men that were coming to work for Henry was not high, and he had been losing so much money on stolen equipment that he had to charge the men for it to stop the pilfering. However, if a man turned in the broken ax-handle he would get a new one without any trouble at all. Further, Henry and Co. was not alone in this practice; many men who worked on the Penobscot have told me that they too were charged "for all things broke or lost." But Larry Gorman was not a Penobscot man; he came to New Hampshire from Union River, and there it was not customary to charge for lost or broken tools. . . .

Here is Larry's song on the Henrys, as it was sung for me in 1957 by eighty-five-year-old John A. Jamieson of East Bathurst, New Brunswick:

The Good Old State of Maine

Rubato (♩ = 60)

Dorian

Oh bush-men all, an ear I call, a tale I will re-late, My ex-per-ience in the lum-ber-woods all in this Gran-ite State; Its snow-clad hills, its wind-ing rills, its moun-tains, rocks and plains, You'll find it ver-y dif-f'rent, boys, from the good old State of Maine.

1. Oh bushmen all, an ear I call, a tale I will relate,
   My experience in the lumberwoods all in this Granite State;
   Its snowclad hills, its winding rills, its mountains, rocks and
      plains,
   You'll find it very different, boys, from the good old State of
      Maine.

2. The difference in the wages, boys, is scarcely worth a dime,
   For every day you do not work you are forced to lose your
     time;
   To pay your passage to and fro you'll find but little gain,
   You would do as well to stay at home in the good old State
     of Maine.

3. For here in Zealand Valley you'll find seven feet of snow,
   And work when the thermometer goes thirty-five below;
   It averages three storms a week of snow or sleet or rain,
   You seldom find such weather in the good old State of
     Maine.

4. They reckon things so neat and fine 'tis hard to save a
     stamp,
   For every month they do take stock of things around the
     camp;
   Stoves, pots, kettles, knives, and forks, a spokeshave or a
     plane,
   Of those they take but small account in the good old State
     of Maine.

5. Then every night with pen and ink they figure up the cost,
   The crew are held responsible for all things broke or lost;
   An axe, a handle, or a spade, a bunk-hook or a chain—
   The crew are never charged with tools in the good old State
     of Maine.

6. Those rules and regulations as I've mentioned here before,
   They're in typewritten copies posted up on every door;
   To lose your time and pay your board or work in snow or
     rain,
   They would call us fools to stand such rules in the good old
     State of Maine.

7. The boss he will address you in a loud commanding voice,
   Saying, "You know the regulations boys; therefore you have
     your choice."

We know *he* did not make them, and of him we don't com-
plain,
For a better boss I never knew in the good old State of
Maine.

8. If you don't like their style, my boys, you can go down the
line,
But if you leave them in the lurch they'll figure with you
fine;
They'll cut down your wages, charge you carfare on their
train,
We never heard of such a thing in the good old State of
Maine.

9. The aliens and foreigners they flock in by the score,
The diversity of languages would equal Babbler's tower;
Italians, Russians, Poles, and Finns, a Dutchman or a Dane,
We never had such drones as those in that good old State of
Maine.

10. And for those sub-contractors now I have got a word to say,
If you work for a jobber there you are apt to lose your pay;
For there is no lien law in this state, the logs you can't re-
tain,
While the lumber is holding for your pay in the good old
State of Maine.

11. Now for the grub, I'll give it a rub, for that it does deserve,
The cooks become so lazy they will allow the men to starve;
For it's bread and beans, then beans and bread, then bread
and beans again,
Of grub we would sometimes have a change in the good old
State of Maine.

12. Our meat and fish are poorly cooked, the bread is sour and
old,
The beans are dry and musty and doughnuts hard and old;
To undertake to chew one, that would give your jaws a pain,

They are not the kind we used to find in the good old State
of Maine.

13. So now my song is concluded and my story is to an end,
If I have made a statement wrong, I am willing to amend;
I like the foreman and the crew, of them I can't complain,
For a better crew I never knew in the good old State of
Maine.

14. So here is adieu to camp and crew, to Henery and Sons,
Their names are great throughout this state, they are one of
her largest guns;
I wish them all prosperity e'er I return again,
For I'll mend my ways and spend my days in the gold old
State of Maine.

A BALLAD COMPOSER OF THE NINETIES

I remember my childhood experience of skipping to the pasture for the cows to the tune of "Ti, Ti, Ti, Tum Yo . . . but he comes around a courtin' Dutch." I recall pausing for a moment to watch Aunt Dutch as she busily applied the grubbin' hoe to the honeysuckle vines around her garden fence. I remember bringing the cows from the pasture to the slow tempo of "It's Hard Times Pore Boys." William Pleasant Ewell and his songs lived in the minds of many people when I was a child; and they still do.

Even though his name was William Pleasant Ewell, he was known to the public as Sol Ewell; and when people hear his real name, they are apt to exclaim, "Why, I thought all the time that his name was just Sol."

Even though the men and children enjoyed Sol's visits, he was not a welcomed guest by the women folks. They considered him trifling, and it is not uncommon to hear expressions similar to the following: "That old pup—I reckon I do remember him. He warn't no count a-tall, but I reckon he was powerful smart in his books. I've cooked a many and a many a meal for him." "Yes, he used to stay at our house. It seems to me he was just sort of a rovin' tramp . . . larnin' as he went, and forever making up songs on people."

Even though the women folks sometimes resented Sol's presence, they never fail to relate how he could sit in a straight chair, tilt it backwards, balance himself by placing his feet on the front rounds and read a newspaper for an hour at a time in that position. "Yes, and here is something else he could do: He could take an old-fashioned school bell, one with a handle, and throw it around and around his head without ringing it. I never could understand how that clapper stayed still."

Even though people remember Sol as the man who knew all the answers to all the questions, he is best remembered for the songs he composed. Although approximately sixty years have elapsed and his songs were never printed, you only have to hum a bit of "It's Hard Times Pore Boys" to hear those who knew Sol say, "Why, we used to play and sing that at 'Play Parties' when I first started a courtin'."

The following incident furnished just the right kind of material for Sol to compose a song:

A fellow by the name of Hobson moved into the quiet little village of Big Spring. Now, the people of the village took a liking to Mr. Hobson, and all went well for awhile. Then suddenly, the men began to notice that corn was being taken from their cribs, the women talked of missing an old Dominick rooster, and sometimes there was no meat for breakfast for the last side had been stolen. Since Hobson was the only new-comer in the village, naturally all eyes were turned on him. The people decided that they wouldn't tolerate a thief in their neighborhood; so they devised a plan to catch Hobson. It was decided that the plan should be carried out by Christopher Robinson.

Robinson soon became a confident of Hobson; and they agreed in conjunction with Adam Garner, a Negro, to make a raid on someone's smokehouse. Now, there was Aunt Liz Earp who lived all alone over the hill; and she had killed two pigs for her meat and lard. Since Aunt Liz didn't have a shotgun, her smokehouse could easily be raided.

After the three had consulted the almanac and found out just when the dark of the moon would occur, Robinson went across the hill to tell Aunt Liz of their plans. As Robinson expected, he found Aunt Liz spinning cotton for roping to make plow lines. Robinson, knowing "the tricks of the trade," purchased a couple of ropes and then told her of their plans. She readily agreed to write her name on some pieces of paper and slip a piece under each meat skin so that the meat could be identified easily.

So on a dark night of the moon, the meat was taken without

any difficulty and hid in Hobson's wagon under a load of broom corn. The next day the party started to Nashville with the load of broom corn and the stolen meat.

In the meantime, "Dinks" Alexander, a citizen of Big Spring and well-known for his extreme honesty, heard of the trip to Nashville. "Dinks" decided since he hadn't been to Nashville in several years he would join the party.

Robinson had also notified Rice Jacobs, an officer, when to make the arrest. Just as the party was passing through Gum, the officer overtook them and searched the wagon; and sure enough, the meat was found beneath the broom corn.

All four of the men, including "Dinks," were arrested and carried to the jail in Murfreesboro. Poor "Dinks" was so humiliated that he cried when they arrested him. Of course, "Dinks" and Robinson were released; but Hobson and the Negro were sent to the penitentiary.

It wasn't long after the crime had been committed that Sol told the story in the following song:

It's Hard Times Pore Boys

Three old coons a prowlin' did go
'Twas Chris-ti, Hob, and an Old Neg-ro.
It's hard times pore boys; it's hard times pore boys.

The evening they started, Hob said with a wink
"We'll make a big rise for our children I think."
It's hard times pore boys; it's hard times pore boys.

They traveled the hills that led to the East
On old Miss Earp's bacon expecting to feast.
It's hard times pore boys; it's hard times pore boys.

The old Lady Earp expecting their sins
Slipped her name beneath the meat skins.
It's hard times pore boys; it's hard times pore boys.

They loaded the wagon and to Nashville did start;
Rice Jacobs overtook them and halted the old cyart.
It's hard times pore boys; it's hard times pore boys.

They searched the wagon; and as sure as you're born,
They found the bacon beneath the broom corn.
It's hard times pore boys; it's hard times pore boys.

They presented the warrants to those standing by
When "Dinks" Alexander, he began to cry.
It's hard times pore boys; it's hard times pore boys.

They took them to town; and "Dinks" he gave bail,
But Hob and the Neg-ro both went to jail.
It's hard times pore boys; it's hard times pore boys.

Hob said to the jailer, "Please lend me your knife
For I believe that these bed bugs are taking my life."
It's hard times pore boys; it's hard times pore boys.

My wife and my children are without any meat or meal;
I wish I was out, so I could help the boy steal.
It's hard times pore boys; it's hard times pore boys.

The old brick store that stood at Big Spring
Got burned the same night, the pore old thing.
It's hard times pore boys; it's hard times pore boys.

We wonder who burned it, but nobody knows.
Someone could have burned it for a suit of old clothes.
It's hard times pore boys; it's hard times pore boys.

AN ANGRY OZARK SINGER

[William Henry Scott's] son Charlie wrote in a biographical sketch in 1958, "My father . . . was born May 15, 1868, at Louisburg [Missouri,] in Dallas [county]. And as a boy in school he was quick to learn but disagreeable and hard to get along with and loved to fight."

Between the years 1905 and 1910 at the midpoint of his life, William Henry reached the height of his disagreeableness. His love for fighting with his fists was almost gone. His disagreeableness took on a new dimension: protest. Five children and a wife to feed, clothe, and shelter, coupled with an almost changeless environment, made the new dimension inevitable.

Having homesteaded near Brice (now Bennett Spring, Missouri) in 1896 and having proved up his claim by 1904, William Henry found his hilly, timber covered, and rocky land inadequate to support his family by farming. He turned as did many Ozarkians to making railroad ties. In this economic venture he discovered a societal barrier he could not hurdle. Some tie buyers culled perfectly good ties that he and others had hacked and hewed. Culling them after they had been hauled by wagon to Lebanon, banked on the Niangua River, or floated down the Niangua to near Corkery, deepened further the bitterness of the tie makers, particularly William Henry Scott. The poor tie maker was at the mercy of the buyer.

How could a man provide for his family when it took two days to hew a wagon load of twenty ties and most of another day to haul them, only to see sixteen or seventeen of them sold at the top price of about twenty-five cents each?

From the depth of his being William Henry protested the practice of the buyer who culled ties indiscriminately. His spirit cried out and a song was born:

The Tie Maker

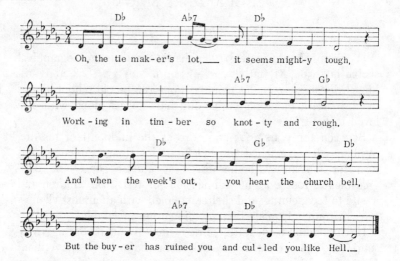

Oh, the tie mak-er's lot,___ it seems might-y tough,

Work-ing in tim-ber so knot-ty and rough.

And when the week's out, you hear the church bell,

But the buy-er has ruined you and cul-led you like Hell.___

Oh, the tie maker's lot, it seems mighty tough,
Working in timber so knotty and rough.
And when the week's out, you hear the church bell,
But the buyer has ruined you and culled you like Hell.

You work in the timber, you work mighty hard,
You hope that misfortune has played her last card.
You are ragged and tired, more than tongue can tell;
But the buyer comes along and he culls you like Hell.

When he goes to the store, things are very high;
But he cannot make ties unless he does buy.
He starves half the time and thinks he does well,
If the buyer would only quit culling like Hell.

The buyers it seems haven't got any heart,
They only buy half and cull the other part.

They tell you they lose and how the price fell,
And wind up by laughing and culling like Hell.

Then you get the ax where the chicken did,
And wish your grandfather had died when a kid.
You hope that the buyer would fall in a well,
Especially the one that culled you like Hell.

The buyer drives around with a fine team and rig,
And wears a white collar and acts mighty big.
You are only a slave and not treated so well,
You are owing him some, so he culls you like Hell.

Sometimes he comes 'round in an automobile,
The tie makers gave him, or so I do feel.
So high is the gasoline, and oil he will tell,
To be on the safe side, he will cull you like Hell.

And it soon makes you think that religion's a sham,
Especially got up, poor folks to flim flam.
You think there's no God, or He'd ring the death knell
Of the pot bellied buyer, who culled you like Hell.

While William Henry Scott does not mention any buyer by
name, the tie makers knew he was singling out one buyer—Fred
Johnson. Mr. Johnson owned a general store in Corkery. Thus the
last line of stanza six, "You are owing him some, so he culls you
like Hell." He also owned one of the first cars in Dallas County—
mentioned in stanza seven. Yet the clincher—the give-away for
the tie makers—came in the last line of the song: "Of the pot
bellied buyer. . . ."

Hominy Hoe Cake and an Old 'Possum's Head

Prior to his family responsibilities, William Henry lived in How-
ell County, Missouri, steamboated up and down the Mississippi
River, and worked in the cotton fields of Arkansas and Louisiana.
In the former state he created his earliest known song.

Picking cotton was interrupted one day while William Henry sang a traditional song for the Arkansas boys called, "Bill Stafford in Arkansas." For seven long stanzas the cotton pickers listened. They heard their state and its people ridiculed. They enjoyed the song, especially the respite from toil that it afforded them. Yet they pretended to take offense at it, and they threatened to wallow William Henry in the dust. If he came to the cotton field the next day and failed to sing a song giving Missouri the dickens, look out!

Rather than have his mouth filled with dirt, William Henry gave the Arkansas boys an earful of a song the next morning. During the night he reportedly composed and committed to memory the song "Hominy Hoe Cake and an Old 'Possum's Head."

Come all you good people, I pray you draw near;
A comical story you shortly shall hear.

A comical story to you I'll unfold,
I came to Missouri at thirty years old.
Sing down, down, down—down, derry, down.

(Refrain repeated after each stanza.)

I called at a tavern to stay all night,
My supper and breakfast I thought would be right.
The table was set and the knick knacks spread,
'Twas hominy hoe cake and an old 'possum's head.

Now when these good people had scarcely fed,
On hominy hoe cake and the old 'possum's head;
The straw it was scattered and the sheepskins spread,
And now said the old man, 'Let's all go to bed.'

I laid down there I thought for ease,
But I scarcely could sleep for the bedbugs and fleas.
The bedbugs would bite, the fleas they would crawl,
'Twas enough to torment any human at all.

I kicked them and scratched them and cuffed them all night,
But I scarcely could scratch them as fast as they'd bite.
And the worst night's lodging that ever I saw,
Was lying on a pallet of sheepskin and straw.

Adieu to Missouri, I'll bid you farewell,
Go back to Arkansas where I used to dwell;
Where the girls were crying and tearing their hair,
For the loss of a true lover when I left there.

The Battle of Kudd

A happening in the late fall of 1910 caused William Henry to create an ironic ballad. A Pie Supper was held three miles west of Bennett Spring at the Kudd School. Prior to this William Henry had taught at this school one or more terms. His children attended Kudd School at the time of the Pie Supper. His son Charlie said this is what took place:

And there were a few drunk men in the crowd that night and one got a pie and threw it down on the floor and 'stomped' it and another drunk man 'batted' him a lick with his fist between the eyes and knocked him down, and my father, W. H. Scott, and Grover McVey, being school directors, tried to keep order. And a drunk man slashed a knife at Grover's throat and missed him, and soon all was peaceful again.

In the excitement several young ladies stood on top of the old-fashioned long benches, and while they wore long dresses, their stockings showed and most of them wore black stockings (mentioned in the song).

No one was seriously hurt, but my father pictured it as a very, very great battle and composed this song accordingly.

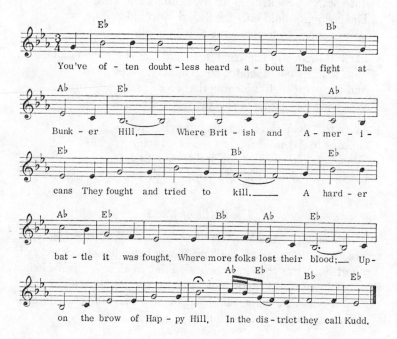

You've of-ten doubt-less heard a-bout The fight at Bunk-er Hill,___ Where Brit-ish and A-mer-i-cans They fought and tried to kill.___ A hard-er bat-tle it was fought, Where more folks lost their blood;___ Up-on the brow of Hap-py Hill, In the dis-trict they call Kudd.

You've often doubtless heard about
The fight at Bunker Hill,
Where British and Americans
They fought and tried to kill.
A harder battle it was fought.
Where more folks lost their blood;
Upon the brow of Happy Hill,
In the district they call Kudd.

Within the depths of a brush pile
Three regiments did die;
Drownded by the scalding tears,
Scared females they did cry.
Upon the tops of benches high
Black stockings were the rage,
As friend and foe they hurried up
The enemy to engage.

Still in my dreams I seem to hear
The strokes and yells of pain;
Still in my dreams I climb that tree,
Of rough Black Oak again.
Still in my dreams I hear the screams
Of startled feminine,
As the battle it surged back and forth,
'Till the dead they checked the line.

Within the top of a tall tree,
A jumper long did fly;
The owner he went on through it,
And on up to the sky.
Ten thousand men did perish there—
Their souls have gone to God,
Their bodies laid beneath the turf,
And covered up with sod.

And children passing by the road,
Gaze on the monuments,

They hurry on and do not stop,
With startled innocence.
The pale moon she averts her head,
The wind sweeps shuddering by,
As on the field of battle dead,
The slaughtered heroes lie.

And grief is floating 'round in chunks—
We're buried deep in gloom;
To think about the perished ones,
Now sleeping in the tomb.
For war is Hell, I'd have you know
That war is mighty grim;
'I hope 'twill never come again'
Is the prayer of 'Truthful Jim.'

In genuine folk fashion William Henry reports what happened at the Pie Supper. His message of ridicule with its coat of irony and its vest of humor never mentions the culprits who fought. Perhaps humor was the best way he could absolve himself of the part he played in the whole affair.

As told by a person present at the Pie Supper that evening, the fight between William Newton Franklin and Rhoder Smith, "Didn't amount to much." It probably would not have started if William Henry hadn't sold the young men hard cider. It was further charged that he got fifty cents a quart for the cider.

AUNT MOLLY JACKSON ARRIVES IN NEW YORK

Mrs. Molly Jackson, wife of a soft-coal miner, a woman known in southeastern Kentucky in the fold between Pine mountain and the Cumberlands as "Aunt Molly" Jackson, midwife and general nurse, arrived in New York yesterday "to be on hand in case" Theodore Dreiser, John Dos Passos and the several others should need her help in the effort they are making to have conditions improved in the Harlan and Bell section from which she comes.

Aunt Molly left the mountains on Sunday evening. She came all the way by bus and had not slept since Saturday, but she made no complaint. "I had a right nice trip, I reckon," she said to Mr. Dos Passos. "No bad luck nor nothing like that on the way."

She said the men and women in the mountains "were powerful thankful" to Mr. Dreiser and his party "for the foreign help" they had given them. "Some of the other folks in Kentucky have talked about it, but what we say is that if they hadn't come from New York when they did, the Lord only knows what would have happened to us. They came to us and found us in the midst of the worst destitution on earth." Aunt Molly said she was going to speak at the meeting in the Star Casino, 107th Street and Park Avenue, at 2:30 o'clock next Sunday. She would sing the song which "Judge Jones said he was going to get me for. I sang it at the meeting in Harlan County."

. . . Aunt Molly said, "I missed it [the indictment] in Bell County, where I live, but they got me over in Harlan." She said all she did was "just to open my mouth and sing." She wrote the song herself. One morning she was "feeling blue" so she began to sing. She called "the piece" the "Kentucky Miners' Hungry Blues." "I don't like it so well," she said, "but I reckon it is that way because I was feeling so down and out that morning."

Aunt Molly was "born and raised in the mountains—a real mountaineer." "The land was rich and good in those days," she said. "Now the land is wore out. There is nothing but the mines." Her father was a Baptist preacher. On week days he worked in the mines and on Sunday he "conducted the meeting." Her first husband also made a living in the mines. He died several years ago. "After he died," she said, "my two children—they died. Then I married a widow man and I raised his four children from the time they were wee mites. Now they are grown."

Her husband is descended from Andrew Jackson's family. "All the Jacksons in that part of Tennessee and Kentucky," she declared, "belong to the same generation. We are of the same descent." Her father belonged to the Garland family. Aunt Molly said "I am almost ashamed to tell you how old I am—I look so old. I was forty-six years old the 30th day of last month. I know I look tough but I am not tough. Wait until I get a little sleep." . . .

Her manner was gentle. She rose when Mr. Dos Passos entered. Shaking his hand, she said, "Howdy, I'm proud to see you again, sir." She is staying with Mrs. Adelaide Walker at Park Avenue and Ninety-sixth Street. She calls Mrs. Walker "Miss Adelaide" in old-fashioned Southern style. It is no startling thing to Aunt Molly that she is visiting on Park Avenue.

She told of children starving. Times had been hard since "the work got so bad about nineteen months ago."

The houses were built thirty-nine years ago, she said. "Nobody with a heart would put a milk cow in such a place to live. Law me alive, it's an awful state we're living in. There are cracks in the floor, holes in the roof with the rain leaking down. My sister has twelve children. She has herself, her husband and her young ones —all in a three-room house. For a long time all we had to eat was what I call bulldog gravy—lard, salt and flour—bread and pumpkins. The farmers send us pumpkins by the load. They are good people—the farmers, but they haven't much either."

Aunt Molly was met at the bus station by Mr. Dos Passos and Mr. and Mrs. Walker. Messages were sent to her from Sherwood

Anderson, Mr. Dreiser, Waldo Frank, Lewis Mumford, Lester
Cohen, Melvin P. Levy and others.

The following is Aunt Molly's song:

Kentucky Miners' Hungry Blues

I am sad and wearied, I have got the hungry
      ragged blues,
Not a penny in my pocket to buy one thing
      I need to use.
I was up this morning with the worst blues
      I ever had in my life,
Not a bit to cook for breakfast, or for a
      coal miner's wife.

When my husband works in the coal mines, he
      loads a car on every trip.
When he goes to the office that evenin' and
      gits denied of scrip
Just because it took all he had made that
      day to pay his mine expense.
Just because it took all he had made that
      day to pay his mine expense.
A man that will just work for coal, light
      and carbide, he got a speck of sense.

The poor women in this coal camp are a
      sitt' with bowed down heads,
Ragged and barefooted and their children
      a-cryin' for bread.
No food, no clothes for our children.
      I am sure this ain't no lie.
If we caint get no more for our labor, we
      will starve to death and die.

Please don't go under those mountains, with
      the slate hanging over your head,

Please don't go under those mountains with
    the slate hanging over your head,
And work for just coal, light and carbide
    and your children a crying out for
    bread.
I pray you take my counsel, please take a
    friend's advice.
Don't load no more, don't put out no more
    till you can get a living price.

This minin' town I live in is a sad and a
    lonely place,
This minin' town I live in is a sad and a
    lonely place,
Where pity and starvation is pictured in
    every face.
Everybody hungry and ragged, no slippers
    on their feet,
Everybody hungry and ragged, no slippers
    on their feet,
All a-going 'round from place to place a
    bummin' a bite to eat.
Listen my friends and comrades, please take
    a friend's advice,
Don't load no more of this dirty coal until
    you get a livin' price.

Mrs. Jackson has helped at the births of more than 600 babies
in the mountains of Kentucky. She is tall and thin. She had on a
cotton print dress yesterday and wore gold earrings. She crossed
her hands on her lap when she spoke. She is pleasant and friendly,
and still knows how to laugh.

Aunt Molly Remembers Robin Hood

Whether Aunt Molly is deliberately trying to deceive, or
whether she has convinced herself that these ballads were learned

in her childhood is a matter hard to decide, since even her prodigious memory is exceeded by her imagination. To confirm my suspicion that the Sargent and Kittredge one-volume compilation of Child ballads was the source of Aunt Molly's knowledge of the Robin Hood pieces, I wrote to Mary Elizabeth Barnicle, one of the early collectors of Aunt Molly's songs. "Yes," Miss Barnicle replied, she had lent Aunt Molly a copy of the book in the early thirties. "I was scraping the bottom of the barrel so far as her memory of British ballads went and lent her the book in the hope that she might find something that would revive further memories. In a few days she came padding back to tell me that she now remembered some RH ballads. She sang them, more or less verbatim, as she found them in the Child book."

Aunt Molly will be furious if she hears this. She insists that she learned these as a four-year-old from her great-grandmother, Nancy Robinson, who was then ninety-two. She maintains also that it was a tradition in her family that many of the Robin Hood ballads were written by her paternal ancestors, the Garlands, before they came to America in the eighteenth century. She says that she remembers her great-grandmother often humorously referring to her great-grandfather, William Garland, as a "Northumberlander," and there is only one other English shire to be preferred to Northumberland if we wish to accept Aunt Molly's story concerning the provenance of her ballads. Finally, Little John himself was a Garland!

Little John Garland and Robin Hood

1. Of Little John and bold Robin Hood
   A story to you I will tell;
   Which being rightly understood,
   I am sure will please you well.

2. When Robin Hood was about twenty years
      old
   He met with Little John;

They had a fight, and Robin Hood
Was tumbled in the pond.

3.   Now Little John was large and strong
He was seven foot tall;
And always when he struck a man,
He always had to fall.

4.   Now I will tell you how they first met
If you will listen awhile,
For this is one joke among all the rest
I am sure it will make you smile.

5.   Now Robin Hood said to his jolly bowmen,
"I want you to stay in this grove,
And carefully listen to hear me call
While through the forest I rove.

6.   "We have had no sport for fourteen long
days,
So out looking for excitement I go;
And should I get beat till I cannot retreat,
My horn for you loudly I will blow."

7.   Then Robin Hood shook hands with his
merry men all
And bid them at present goodbye;
Then by the side of a brook a journey he
took
And a tall stranger he happened to spy.

8.   They happened to meet on a long narrow
bridge
And neither of them would give way;
Said bold Robin Hood as proudly he stood,
"I will show you the Nottingham's play."

9.   Then from his quiver an arrow he drew,
A broad arrow with a long goose wing;

Then Little John replied, "I will sure tan
    your hide
If you offer to touch your bowstring."

10.   Said brave Robin Hood, "You say that you
    would,
But if I ever bend my bow,
I will shoot a dart right through your proud
    heart,
Before you could strike me one blow."

11.   "You talk like a coward," said Little John
    Garland,
"With a bow and a sword as you stand;
You could shoot at my chest, but sir, I pro-
    test,
I don't even have a staff in my hand."

12.   "I am not a coward," said bold Robin Hood,
"And the name of a coward I scorn;
And to prove you do lie, my bow and
    sword I'll lay by,
And the truth of your manhood I shall try."

13.   Then Robin stepped over to a thicket of
    trees
And chose him a staff of red oak;
And over to Little John Garland he stepped
And these are the words that he spoke:

14.   "You see my staff is large and tough;
Now here on this bridge we will play;
And if you knock me in, we will say you
    have won—
Now, stranger, what do you say?"

15.   "With all of my heart," Little John replied,
"I am too proud to give in

As long as I'm able to handle my staff,
And believe me, I'm sure I will win."

16. So they started the fight, and they struck
      left and right;
    Robin Hood made his oak staff ring.
    Then Little John said, "You must be re-
      paid;
    I shall give you the very same thing."

17. Then Little John gave Robin a lick on the
      head
    That started his blood to flow.
    "Fight on, stranger," said bold Robin Hood,
    "You are a brave good fighter, I know."

18. Then thick and fast Little John mended
      his licks
    And faster his anger did grow;
    Then with a scornful look he tumbled
      Robin in the brook
    About fifty feet below.

19. "Tell me, brave fellow, where are you
      now?"
    Little John with laughter cried.
    "I am under the bridge," said bold Robin
      Hood,
    "And drifting around with the tide.

20. "I must acknowledge you are a strong brave
      man;
    With you I would like to be friends."
    Then to the bank of the brook Robin did
      wade
    And with Little John Robin shook hands.

21. Then Robin Hood put his horn to his
      mouth
    And with it he blew a loud blast;

Then came his bowmen in green, most
    brave to be seen,
And they said, "We heard you at last."

22. "What can we do, good master, for you?"
One of his bowmen cried.
"You are wet to the skin; where have you
    been?"
Then Robin Hood replied,
"This good man that you see has been fight-
    ing with me,
And he tumbled me into the tide."

23. "He shall not go scot-free," the bowmen
    said.
"Do not touch him," Robin replied;
"For I do declare he is as stout as a bear
And we need such good men on our side.

24.* "I am your true friend," said bold Robin
    Hood,
"So please don't be afraid;
You are a brave man as I understand
And I'm proud of the part you have played.

25. "These men are my bowmen that come at
    my call,
I have three score and nine;
And if you'll agree to stay here with me,
I will make you a bowman of mine.

26. "Now what do you say? You have nothing
    to fear,
I will teach you to hunt deer and bear;
I will always see, if you stay here with me,
You always will have equal share.

27. "I will give you my hand, you will be my
    top man,
And always my friend, I declare;

My offer is good," said bold Robin Hood,
"Now Little John, what do you say?"
"Since you put it that way, with you I will
    stay,
And we will live from the fat of the land.

28.* "They call me Little John, but as you can
    see,
I am not little at all;
You will find lots of men much smaller
    than me—
You see, I am seven foot tall."

29. Then Robin and Little John walked hand
    in hand
And to Robin's wardrobe they did go;
Then Robin Hood dressed Little John in
    the best
From his head to the tip of his toe.

30. Then in his hand Robin Hood put a fine
    bow;
"As an archer you'll be one of the best;
We will take from the rich and give to the
    poor,
You'll never need for gold and silver any
    more.

31.* "We will take gold from the priests and
    bishops and monks
While they slumber and snore;
As long as bishops and monks has gold in
    their trunks
And we are able to open the door.
We will live good ourselves with good food
    on our shelves,
And give lots to the needy and poor.

32. "We will live here and eat deer and bear
         meat
     Like squires and lords or renown,
     And as long as our life shall endure I am
         sure
     With plenty we shall always be found."

33. With music and dancing they finished the
         day
     And Little John uniting, did celebrate;
     And Robin rejoiced at the top of his voice
     Because he had found a true mate.

34.* Little John and Robin Hood remained true
         friends
     Until brave Robin Hood's death;
     And on Little John's chest, as I have heard
         it said,
     Is where bold Robin Hood drew his last
         breath.

35.* And again I have heard that old folks of England said,
     And after brave Robin was dead,
     That Little John Garland helped place the stone
     At bold Robin Hood's head.

ELVIS PRESLEY: A KING DIES BUT A LEGEND LIVES

He was a Hillbilly Cat who became the King.

While Elvis Presley, undoubtedly among the most influential performers in the history of pop music, did not exactly invent rock 'n' roll, he certainly was the force that gave this music its direction. He was the one who shaped it into the palatable form that made him an international superstar and altered the course of music for years to come.

Presley took the raw bones of two totally contrasting musical idioms, black R&B (rhythm and blues) and music that exploded out of Memphis in 1954—termed Rockabilly—provided a younger generation with its very own music for the first time. Until Elvis Presley came along, teen-agers of the world had to settle for the mainstream pop that was geared generally toward an older audience.

Presley created music to rebel by, to rattle the sensitivities of the Establishment: hard-nosed, throbbing, audacious, pulsating, with an abundance of sexual overtones.

And if the music alone did not shake up the genteel masses, the gyrating Presley image did. It was something the older folks wanted relegated to a burlesque house, not displayed on a concert stage. Such was the controversy that cameramen were ordered to focus only above the waist when Presley first performed on "The Ed Sullivan Show," in 1956.

The uproar ended, of course. Such things usually do. And, in time, Elvis Presley became a mellower and accepted member of the show-business scene.

In recent years, critics said that Presley had lost the old motivation, that he was merely going through the motions to enhance a bank account that had become extraordinary.

Elvis Aron Presley started out little more than "white trash" in Mississippi.

But when he died yesterday [August 16, 1977] at the age of 42, Presley was among the wealthiest entertainers in America, residing in a Memphis mansion called Graceland, purchased only a few years after his smashing success in the mid-1950s.

Some Myths and Facts

Last night [August 16, 1977], on radio stations across the country, "Houn' Dog," "Heartbreak Hotel," "Blue Suede Shoes," "Love Me Tender" and all the other Presley hits were being played again and again—a tribute to the King.

Presley also made movies—about 25 of them between 1956 and 1969. The plots were minimal, mostly giving Presley a chance to sing his songs and woo pretty women.

When his film career ended in 1969, there were those who said Presley was finished. But he bounced back, starting with a lavish comeback concert in Las Vegas that year. The crowds thronged to see him.

Presley's fans would not let his career die.

The Elvis Presley story was a publicist's dream and, as such, quickly became something of a myth: A young truck driver, the son of a poor Mississippi farmer, buys himself a cheap guitar and sings his way to fame and fortune after being accidentally discovered while making a record as a birthday present for his mother.

But like all myths, there is some grounding in fact. Presley, born in Tupelo, Miss., on Jan. 8, 1935, did drive a truck while waiting for his musical break.

And it was after he had paid $4 to cut a record for his mother that Sam Phillips, head of Sun Studios in Memphis, signed him up.

Phillips had heard something in Presley that sounded like success, but he was not sure quite what.

In an effort to come up with a successful product, he teamed Presley with guitarist Scotty Moore and bass player Bill Black. And history, as they say in the fan magazines, was made.

Moore would later recall that the three men, who had played around with both country material and rhythm & blues, were sitting around the studio one day when Presley began pounding savagely on his acoustic guitar and singing an old blues tune called "That's All Right, Mama."

Moore and Black began playing behind him, and as the three of them worked out a hard-driving sound, Sam Phillips hollered out, "What the devil are you doing?"

"We don't know," he was told.

"Well, find out real quick and don't lose it," Phillips said.

They found out and held onto it. Presley became a local star and then, after a P. T. Barnum-like-hustler named Col. Tom Parker took over his management, signed with RCA Records and made "Heartbreak Hotel."

Oozing sexuality and redneck chic, he became a superstar.

The Shrine

Memphis, Tenn. —Inside, a white cross of flowers and a scarlet crown. Outside, thousands of pilgrims. Only three days after Elvis Presley's death, his tomb has become a shrine.

Some of Presley's fans waited all night outside the gate of Forest Hill Cemetery. Two hundred were there when the gates opened yesterday morning. By early afternoon, according to the cemetery superintendent's estimate, tens of thousands had passed through, and there was no letup.

The mausoleum housing Presley's remains, along with those of 300 others, was closed for the entire day to allow the singer's family to visit in private.

But the fans could pass by the columned building and receive a flower from the 3,116 displays that hid the lawn under a bright canvass of color. By noon, the flowers were gone—many destined to be pressed between the covers of books. Some lucky fans got a ribbon. . . .

Many of the women, and some of the men, wept as they stood

before the mausoleum. A few knelt. Most photographed the building.

The Sale

Bear, Del. —The first of what will be millions of Elvis Presley iron-on transfers slipped off the flat-bed presses here yesterday [August 25, 1977].

Every third iron-on bore the slogan, "Elvis—The Legend Lives On."

The words are more than an epitaph. They are a promise, say the people who operate a small factory here, in the cornfields along U. S. Route 40, about 12 miles southwest of Wilmington.

The company, Factors Etc. Inc., has purchased "forever" the rights to merchandise Elvis souvenirs. . . .

"This is going to be a long-term thing. Anybody that can sell 20 million records in death will go on "forever" [Lee Geissler, a company official, stated].

A Song Is Over

What Presley brought to his young fans was a sneering pout, long sideburns, a gyrating pelvis and an animal vitality that appealed to them largely because it was anathema to their elders.

America has an insatiable appetite for both celebrities and rebels. And not since another rebel without a cause, James Dean, went east of Eden have the plebs had such a rogue-hero to mourn.

Now those blue suede shoes stand empty, and Elvis's fans have checked into Heartbreak Hotel. The earthy king of rockabilly is dead, and salt for them has lost its saltiness.

It was, of course, a necessary part of his legend that the 42-year-old Presley should die young. Strictly in terms of artistic symmetry, death should have come sooner. For American pop heroes, be they Marilyn Monroe or Jackson Pollock, Janis Joplin or Ernest Hemingway, die when they have nothing more to say.

Presley, who peaked when he was 28, had nothing more to say. . . .

A fat, aging idol, his hair tinted, his teeth capped and his colon tied in knots, can hardly implore his fans to love him tender.

Like Hemingway in his last years, Presley had become a grotesque of himself, a broken icon surrounded by bodyguards and sycophants, that once-narrow waist swollen by countless peanut butter and banana sandwiches washed down with an endless stream of Cokes. . . .

In a sense, those who came to grieve were mourning the passing of their own youth. . . . For them as for him, the song is over, although the melody lingers on.

A combination of contraries, the factual and the fantastic, is one of the oddities of American folk and popular heroes. For example, the life of Davy Crockett can be firmly documented. In itself—his frontier exploits, his career in Congress, his death at the Alamo— there is ample substance to make him a popular hero. But Crockett encouraged comic exaggerations and downright fabrications about himself in the almanacs, newspapers, and theaters of his day in order to serve the cause of partisan politics and to make some fast dollars. At the same time, the facts and mass-media promotion stimulated his emergence as a figure in oral tradition, a folk hero. When he trades off the same coonskin for repeated rounds of whiskey, he shows his kinship with the mythic trickster and the sharp-operating Yankee trader. When he thaws out the frozen sun, he reminds us of the demigod Prometheus who brought fire to man. But there is still another dimension to the Crockett legend. At a certain point the songs and tales take on a wildly extravagant, frenzied quality. Davy's ride on the wild stallion is extravagant beyond credence, and his fight with Pompey Smash is so fantastically impossible that we are not expected to believe it. It is this delight in the incredible excess of both behavior and language that marks the fantastic streak in the American hero.

A major source of the fantastic vein may well be, in Frederick Jackson Turner's phrase, the "buoyancy and exuberance which comes with freedom" produced by the frontier experience, but Turner failed to see in this exuberance its potential for earthy poetry, almost rhapsodic, which is one of its main characteristics. Sam Patch, a daredevil who did in fact overleap waterfalls, left behind a legend of crackbrained words and deeds. And local eccentrics like Joe Root and Huckleberry Charlie are remembered for their wild and whirling words. In a song like "Old Joe Clark" and in the sketch of Love Mad Lopez, we get pure fantastic nonsense at a poetic level.

The menagerie of fabulous animals, the giant bears that defy hunting and the hypersensitive horses that save their riders also extend fact into fantasy. The grizzly inspired awe because, in fact, it was a beast of heroic proportions, and it was as a result of this natural fact that it became a legendary and literally totemic object. But the American folk have a way of undercutting revered figures of any species. The story of Old Satan, the super-mule, is a comic antidote to tales of super-bears. Where but in American folklore would you find a *mule* as a totemic figure?

DAVY CROCKETT, FANTASY AND HORSE SENSE

The image the name of Crockett conjures up today is, it appears, anything but that of a person tied up with a virtue so unimaginative as horse sense. The Tennessean, as he is now recalled, is a backwoods demigod, a fabulous hunter and fighter wafted to immortality in the rifle smoke of the Alamo. And the frontier yarnspinners created an even more fantastic figure than people now recall. In the 1830's and 1840's, a series of almanac stories, some of them written by Crockett's one-time neighbors, set forth details of a biography which claimed that even when he was born, Davy was the biggest infant that ever was and a little the smartest that ever will be; that, watered with buffalo milk and weaned on whiskey, he grew so fast that soon his Aunt Keziah was saying it was as good as a meal's vittles to look at him. The biography went on to tell about his boyhood. The family used his infant teeth to build the parlor fireplace. At eight, he weighed two hundred pounds and fourteen ounces, with his shoes off, his feet clean and his stomach empty. At twelve, he escaped from an Indian by riding on the back of a wolf which went like a streak of lightning towed by steamboats.

That was just the start of his amazing life story. According to the almanacs, by the time he was full grown Crockett had got such a name, among the animals themselves, that some would die when he just grinned at them, and others, looking down from a tree and seeing him reach for his gun, would holler, "Is that you, Davy?" Then when he'd say, "Yes," they'd sing out, "All right, don't shoot! I'm a-comin' down." In the almanacs of a century ago, there were many details just as amazing as these. According to the almanacs, for instance, instead of getting killed at the

Alamo Davy actually gave Santa Anna an awful licking. Then, riding his tame bear, Death Hug, from place to place in Mexico, he wrought havoc among the enemy armies. At last accounts he was still alive and kicking.

Such a preposterous biography would seem to be very remote from common sense. It seems, one would say, to be a creation of the West which passed hours by campfires genially manhandling facts until those facts vanished in woodsmoke from the workaday world and, greatly changed, turned up in fantastic fairylands inhabited by the Big Bear of Arkansaw and other creatures as imaginary. If the tall tales of wilderness yarnspinners gave the only clue to the character of Crockett, one might decide that he had nothing to do with homespun philosophy.

But there was a quirk of Crockett's character, in real life, which made frontier folk elect him and re-elect him to the state legislature and to the United States House of Representatives. That he was poor, that he was uneducated, made no difference to them: they thought he could get along because they guessed he had good horse sense. This fact suggests the paradox of Crockett's renown. He won fame and office because he had horse sense; he remained famous because of the nonsense associated with his memory. . . .

What myth-makers did, then, was make Davy's boasts come true—put him in an imaginary world consistent with the kind of beasts and people his tall talk described. Temporary things such as changing political alignments vanished, but the one abiding element—strangeness—remained. As early as 1832, the legend-makers had begun to develop this abiding version of their hero: the apotheosis was suggested in a news story, widely reprinted, which read:

APPOINTMENT BY THE PRESIDENT. David Crockett, of Tennessee, to stand on the Allegheny Mountains and catch the Comet, on its approach to the earth, and wring off its tail, to keep it from burning up the world!

Davy Crockett Rides a Wild Stallion

Here and there a historian has suggested that Crockett's fame, both in his own lifetime and after his death, was created by Whig politicians, and that these evoked the legendary Crockett. But the politicians who possessed this singular imaginative power have not been identified. And the historians cannot have scanned the almanacs. Few traces of a political bias appear in these small paperbound volumes.

Is it true that some of the stories seem to have been made to order in printers' offices. Many are as crude as woodcuts by an unpracticed hand. Some may have had their origin in earlier printed material about Crockett. In one story he

> sighted a stallion on the prairie, wild as the whirlwind, and tall and strong. Crockett came within a hundred yards of him, and the stallion threw back his ears, spread his jaws, and came snorting at him. As the horse reared to plunge Crockett seized his mane and mounted him as easy as a cow bird sits on the back of a brindle bull. The stallion made off like lightning and a big thunderstorm came up. Lightning struck all round but it flashed to either side of the horse as he ran and never struck him. The stallion was off to the West and Crockett thought he was going to be flung against the Rocky Mountains. He ran for three days and three nights until he came to the Mad River. There the stallion ran under a tree, trying to brush Crockett off his back, but Crockett pulled his mane and he leapt over the tree and the boiling river besides. Then he stopped quiet and Crockett got off.

This story may have been evolved from that of C
riences with the little mustang as related in
Exploits and Adventures in Texas. But surel
other, more primitive elements went into the

It should be allied with contemporary tales of the white steed of the prairies and with certain Indian legends. Even so, it springs clear of obvious origins and is complete in itself. However it began, somewhere along the way it received a fresh infusion of creative energy.

The sources of this energy are not far to seek. When all alliances have been noted, the legendary tales about Crockett seem to have a firm basis in popular story-telling. Their humor is of an order that was rising like a tide toward the middle of the nineteenth century. Crockett himself had given this movement a strong momentum. By his character, his repartee, his stories, his exploits, he had captivated the popular imagination, and his name kept this imagination afire. These stories constitute one of the earliest and perhaps the largest of our cycles of myth, and they are part of a lineage which endures to this day in Kentucky and Tennessee, and in the Ozark Mountains.

Pompey Smash: Davy Crockett on the Minstrel Stage

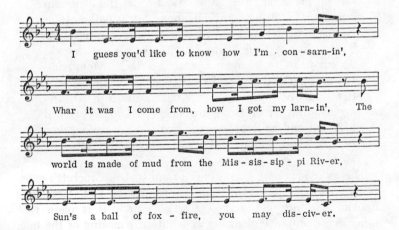

I guess you'd like to know how I'm con-sarn-in', Whar it was I come from, how I got my larn-in', The world is made of mud from the Mis-sis-sip-pi Riv-er, Sun's a ball of fox-fire, you may dis-civ-er.

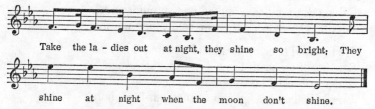

Take the la-dies out at night, they shine so bright; They shine at night when the moon don't shine.

I guess you'd like to know how I'm consarnin',
Whar it was I come from, how I got my larnin',
The world is made of mud from the Mississippi River,
Sun's a ball of foxfire, you may disciver.

Take the ladies out at night, they shine so bright;
They shine at night when the moon don't shine.
And so one day as I was goin' a-spoonin'
I met Colonel Davy, and he was goin' a-coonin'.

Says I, "Where's your gun?" "I ain't got none."
"How you goin' to kill a coon when you haven't got a gun?"
Says he, "Pompcalf, just follow after Davy,
And he'll soon show you how to grin a coon crazy."

I followed on a piece and thar sot a squirrel,
A-settin' on a log and a-eatin' sheep sorrel.
When Davy that did see, he looked around at me,
Saying, "All I want now is a brace agin your knee."

And thar I braced a great big sinner.
He grinned six times hard enough to git his dinner!
The critter on the log didn't seem to mind him—
Jest kep a-settin' thar and wouldn't look behind him.

Then it was he said, "The critter must be dead.
See the bark a flyin' all around the critter's head?"
I walked right up the truth to disciver.
Drot! It was a pine knot so hard it made me shiver.

Says he, "Pompcalf, don't you begin to laugh—
I'll pin back my ears, and I'll bite you half in half!"

I flung down my gun and all my ammunition.
Says I, "Davy Crockett, I can cool your ambition!"

He threwed back his head and he blowed like a steamer.
Says he, "Pompcalf, I'm a Tennessee screamer!"
Then we locked horns and we wallered in the thorns.
I never had such a fight since the hour I was born.

We fought a day and a night and then agreed to drop it.
I was purty badly whipped—and so was Davy Crockett.
I looked all around and found my head a-missin'—
He'd bit off my head and I had swallered his'n.

THE FANTASTIC SAM PATCH

TO THE LADIES AND GENTLEMEN OF WESTERN NEW-YORK AND OF UPPER CANADA.

All I have to say is, that I arrived at the Falls too late, but to give you a specimen of my Jumping Qualities, on the 6th inst.; but on Wednesday, I thought I would venture a small Leap, which I accordingly made, of Eighty Feet, merely to convince those that remained to see me, with what safety and ease I could descend, and that I was the TRUE SAM PATCH, and to show that Some Things could be Done as well as Others; which was denied before I made the Jump.

Having been thus disappointed, the owners of Goat Island have generously granted me the use of it for nothing; so that I may have a chance, from an equally generous public, to obtain some remuneration for my long journey hither, as well as affording me an opportunity of supporting the reputation I have gained, by Aero-Nautical Feats, never before attempted, either in the Old or New World.

I shall, Ladies and Gentlemen, on Saturday next, Oct. 17th, precisely at 3 o'clock, P.M. LEAP at the FALLS of NIAGARA, from a height of 120 to 130 feet, (being 40 to 50 feet higher than I leapt before,) into the eddy below. On my way down from Buffalo, on the morning of that day, in the Steam-Boat NIAGARA, I shall, for the amusement of the Ladies, doff my coat and Spring from the Mast head into the Niagara River.

SAM PATCH,

Buffalo, Oct. 12, 1829 Of Passaic Falls, New-Jersey.

So boasted Patch, jauntily, in posters plastered a month before the leap that terminated his mortal life and ensured him a legendary existence tenacious as any in American annals. Few persons in the United States of the 1830's and 40's could have avoided all the poems, ballads, rhymes, anecdotes, allusions, reminiscences, tall tales, and theatrical farces that celebrated the braggadocian jumper of history, fantasy, and hoax. A century later the myth is dead as the man, and like Mose, Fink, and Crockett, Patch must be reintroduced to his present legatees.

The biographical data about Samuel Patch prior to his first jumping exploit in 1827 are extremely slight. Almost all accounts assign his birthplace to Pawtucket, Rhode Island, about 1807, but a niece, Miss Emily Jones, disputes this statement, saying he was born to Greenleaf Patch, a farmer, in South Reading, Massachusetts, before 1807. After his father's death his mother moved to Pawtucket. As a boy Sam worked in the famous cotton mill founded by Samuel Slater, located just above the Pawtucket Falls, on the east bank of the river. For the long-working mill hands, particularly for the boys, swimming in the river or jumping into its considerable depth from the top rail of the bridge afforded rare sport. This height not satisfying the hardier spirits, these took to venturing from the peaked roof of the Yellow Mill, a paper mill at the east end of the bridge, nearly a hundred feet above the pool, and even to making running jumps from the flat roof of the six-story stone mill adjacent to but farther removed from the deep water. Young Patch with other daring jumpers appreciated the plaudits of onlooking townsmen.

According to Miss Jones, Sam on reaching manhood went into partnership with a Scot named Kennedy in cotton manufacturing in nearby Central Falls. When Kennedy skipped off with the firm's funds, Patch sold out and betook himself to the Hamilton cotton mills in Paterson, New Jersey, for a fresh start. In the meantime he may have deserted his trade for a brief career as a sailor. At Paterson the scenic Passaic Falls provided Sam with a test for his jumping ability, and on the occasion of the placing of the first bridge across the chasm by Timothy B. Crane, on September 30, 1827, he entertained the spectators with a seventy-foot jump from the highest cliff. Although town constables were on hand to prevent him from executing his vaunt, he suddenly appeared by a whitened pine at the edge of the precipice at a moment of high excitement among the crowd; one of the rolling pins had slid from the guide ropes and plummeted into the chasm as the bridge teetered precariously halfway across. Performing his jump, he swam to the wooden pin, took its trailing rope in his mouth, and brought it ashore, whereupon it was returned to position on the guide ropes and the bridge successfully pulled across the gap. A less dramatic version has Sam jumping after the bridge was placed and making a short preliminary speech (as later was his wont): Mr.Crane had done a great thing and he meant to do another.

Buoyed up by the notoriety garnered in the Passaic jump, the mule spinner took to electrifying crowds throughout New York State with other astonishing leaps for the remaining two years of his life. He seems to have repeated the first performance on July 26, 1828, this time jumping from the bridge itself. A fortnight later, on August 11, he made a still more daring ninety-foot descent at Hoboken from a platform erected on the masthead of a sloop moored offshore. Some five hundred to six hundred spectators watched from the green before Van Buskirk's Hotel, while many more observed from surrounding boats. From the fall he suffered a slight bruise over one eye.

Nothing less than Niagara's falls now challenged Patch and afforded him his crowning conquest. Apparently plans to blast off a portion of Table Rock, treacherously overhanging the chasm from the Canadian bank, suggested to Buffalo citizens a way to secure an additional attraction for October 6, 1829, namely, to invite the Jersey jumper to perform, or at second best, to send the shallow-draught schooner "Superior" careening over the Falls. (Two years earlier the unseaworthy brig "Michigan" had floated down the rapids with an animal crew of bears, foxes, geese, and a buffalo, and an effigy of Andy Jackson, before fascinated thousands.) Patch accepted, but as the handbill first quoted indicates, he missed the festival day, and the throngs saw a ship fall and smash, rather than a man leap and live. On the seventh Sam did demonstrate his powers to a limited audience with a preliminary plunge of some seventy feet from the lower end of Goat Island. Robbed of his rightful turnout, however, Patch publicized a second and greater leap for October 17 of approximately 120 feet. For these exhibitions, the wooded islet splitting the cataract in an uneven half between the American and the Horseshoe Falls provided a logical springboard. Observers congregated on the island and lined the American and Canadian shores. For this second leap, the platform on Goat Island stood about two thirds the elevation of the 160-foot-high neighboring banks, a fearful height when scanned from the depths below.

On this rainy Saturday Sam boldly climbed the perpendicular ladder to the scaffold, despite tearful farewells and protestations from persons at the foot. Before ascending, he shed his shoes and coat and tied a handkerchief about his neck. Atop the ladder, built from four trees spliced together and fastened by ropes running back upon Goat Island, he mounted the narrow, reeling platform, barely large enough for a man to sit upon, and for ten minutes displayed his poise and tested the stand, while the spectators repeatedly cheered. At length he rose upright, took the handkerchief from his neck and tied it about his waist, waved his hand, kissed the American flag which flew over his head, and stepped off steadfastly into the swirling flood. A general cry of "He's dead, he's lost!" swept through the crowd, according to one account; a second reports a benumbed silence broken only by joyous congratulations when Sam's head burst out of the waters. While handkerchiefs waved and huzzas roared, the Jumping Hero swam briskly to the shore, to inform his first onrushing admirer, "There's no mistake in Sam Patch!" Unanimously the surrounding group exclaimed, "This is the real Sam Patch!" Commented the *Buffalo Republican:* "The jump of Patch is the greatest feat of the kind ever effected by man. He may now challenge the universe for a competitor."

Flushed with the publicity of press notices and the public

excitement, Sam turned to Rochester and the Genesee Falls for a new conquest. A. J. Langworthy recalled that a "tramp" came into the foundry near the precipice on November 1, and stated his desire to jump the falls, whereupon the owner lent him his boat to sound the depth of the water; Joseph Cochrane later testified that Patch gave him, a youngster, his watch and clothing, made a practice plunge, and then called back the frightened boy who was running away. A group of local sportsmen, accustomed to patronizing boxers, gymnasts, wrestlers, and such, lodged him at the "Rochester Recess" and supplied his wants—one of which was alleged to be spirituous. An advertisement in the *Rochester Daily Advertiser* for October 29 arrested the local citizenry by announcing: "Another Leap! Sam Patch against the World! . . . He puts off the jump till after election, out of regard to all parties. Let every man do his duty at the Polls, and Sam will afterwards do his at the Falls!"

Somewhere Patch had picked up a pet bear, which he led by a chain to the principal cascade of the falls on November 6 and with a sudden jerk sent whirling into the air from the jutting rock. Bruin emerged from the foaming waters with a half-drowned aspect and swam to the bank. Then Sam, arrayed in pantaloons, shirt, and slippers, with a colored kerchief tied about his head, bowed to his five thousand admiring beholders, reknotted the handkerchief about his waist, balanced himself, and shot down the cataract. Reappearing some rods downstream he contemptuously spurned a little boat waiting to receive him and made the shore under his own power.

By now the newspapers of the nation were playing up Sam enthusiastically as good copy, and his sponsors determined to provide a still greater, climactic feat, by erecting a twenty-five foot scaffold on the rock's brow to extend the jump to a new distance —125 feet. In the posters Sam announced, with unwitting irony, "HIGHER YET! SAM'S LAST JUMP. SOME THINGS CAN BE DONE AS WELL AS OTHERS. THERE IS NO MISTAKE IN SAM PATCH." Monroe and Ontario counties poured out for the November 13 leap; schooners and coaches ran excursions; betting ran high in the local bars as to the outcome; nearby roofs and windows and both banks swarmed with the curious. But when Sam walked out on the grassy, tree-covered rock that divided the greater and lesser branches of the cataract, at two P.M. (bruin was to jump at three), and climbed up to the platform, various spectators thought he staggered and lacked his usual aplomb. Some assert that the jumper was reeling drunk; others stoutly deny that he took more than a glass of brandy to counteract the chilly day. Sam made a brief speech: Napoleon was a great man and conquered nations, Wellington was a greater and conquered Napoleon, but neither could jump the Genesee Falls— that was left for him to do. So saying, he jumped. But this time the descent lacked its usual arrowy precision. One third of the way down his body began to droop, his arms parted from his sides, he lost command of his body and struck the water obliquely with arms and legs extended, not to reappear before the horror-stricken assemblage. Dragging for the body proved unsuccessful, perhaps because of pinioning branches on the river bed. Nor was it found until the following March 17 at the mouth of the Genesee near Lake Ontario, the black kerchief still tied about the waist—found by a farmer breaking the ice to water his horses. An autopsy revealed a ruptured blood vessel and the dislocation of both shoulders. The body was buried in a nameless grave and lay long forgotten in the Charlotte cemetery, until finally identified by a board head-marker reading, "Here lies Sam Patch; such is Fame."

An Elegy to Sam Patch

Good people, all, attention give,
And list with mournful brow,
If you have any tears to shed,
Prepare to shed them now.
Sam Patch is dead, that famous man;
We'll ne'er see him more.
He used to wear an old felt hat
With rim torn all before.

His jacket was of iron grey,
His heart was full of glee
They say he's killed by jumping off
The falls of Genesee.
Full six score feet they say he jumped
And struck upon his side.
He sunk beneath the roaring flood
And thus Sam Patch he died.

Sam Patch's Epitaph

Poor Samuel Patch—a man once world renounded
Much loved the water, and by it was drownded.
He sought for fame, and as he reached to pluck it,
He lost his ballast, and then kicked the bucket.

Sam Patch's Last Leap

Sam Patch was a great diver, and the last dive he took was off
the Falls of Niagara, and he was never heerd of agin till t'other
day, when Captain Enoch Wentworth, of the Susy Ann, whaler,
saw him in the South Sea. "Why," says Captain Enoch to him,
"Why, Sam," says he, "how *on airth* did you get here? I thought
you was drowned at the Canadian lines." "Why," says Sam, "I
didn't get *on earth* here at all, but I came slap *through* it. In that
are Niagara dive I went so everlasting deep, I thought it was just
as short to come up t'other side, so out I came in these parts. If I
don't take the shine off the sea serpent when I get back to Boston, then my name's not Sam Patch."

Sam Patch Lives

Many refused to believe that Sam had really died. Knowing his
propensity for stunts, one faction accepted the surmise that Sam
had previously discovered an eddy that ran under a shelving rock,
where he had hidden a suit of dry clothes, a bottle of Santa Cruz,

and something to eat. Following his jump he swam to the spot, remained there till dark, and then traveled eastward incognito. A man in Albany had seen and talked with him; another in Rochester bet one hundred dollars that Sam would reappear in that city before the first of January; a notice posted prominently in Rochester stated that Patch would recount his adventures at Acker's Eagle Tavern the forenoon of December 3; reports spread that he had been sighted at Pittsford, Canandaigua, and other places on his way to New Jersey. Capitalizing on these stories, an elaborate explanation of the mystery, purportedly by the person most concerned, shortly burst into print in the *New York Post*, November 30, 1829.

SAM PATCH ALIVE!
Albany, Nov. 19, 1829

Mr.——: "Some things can be done as well as others." "There's no mistake in Sam Patch." You have no doubt seen the villanous [*sic*] account of my death published in the Rochester and Albany newspapers, by which they have attempted to prove my last motto a lie, and otherwise do me great damage; for now they have once killed me, they are determined I shall remain under water, notwithstanding the best of all evidences to the contrary. But some things, you see, can be done as well as others; and I am resolved to let the world know that I am still alive and kicking. It was a capital hoax though, wasn't it? You must know though that I performed my last jump by proxy. It was a pleasant thing too, I can assure you, to be myself a spectator of my own doings. I thought how it would be, for when they made up the effigy, there was a stone too much on the right side. They said "the less weight will not sink it." "Well," said I, "do as you like, but it will be a bad jump." Sure enough it was a rascally jump; and when I saw my man of straw and paint grow dizzy before it had half reached the bottom I had a mind to leap down and stop him. But however, before I had time to prepare, splash it went into the water; and the weight of sand and stones, which as I told you made a part of the stuffing, dragged it to the bottom. I was a bit afraid that the mock man would rise; but when the mob began to say, "Sam's dead"—"he's made his last jump"—"poor fellow!" given to gravity as I am, it was more than I could well do to contain myself, it was such a capital joke.

There was everybody there to witness the feat, and they lingered a long while, hoping to see my body rise; but it was all in vain; the sand and stones had fixed the business. The printers immediately got the story, and in a few hours I read my own death, done up in all the mournfulness of an elegy. I was half sorry I wasn't dead, there was so many long faces about it. And so I thought it best to remain incog (as they have it) a few days, until the mourning was over, and then show myself. And so I did: but when I thought proper to appear in public, they all declared that there was "some mistake," and that I was not Sam Patch. At first I thought they were only joking; but faith, they kept it up, and the printers wouldn't contradict the report of my death, because they said it was "too good a joke to be made known." Thinks I, this is "burying alive," and not to be borne by the illustrious Sam Patch. So I came down to Albany, and tried them there; but they said I was an imposter, and wouldn't do me even the favor of barely saying I was not dead. Wishing to get out of my watery tomb as soon as possible, I have sent this to you; and if you will say I am yet alive, when I come to Boston you shall see me jump for nothing.

The real, no mistake

SAM PATCH, of New Jersey.

Even after the finding of the body the jumper continued to be seen, for there were those who at twilight perceived Sam sporting at the Falls, and repeating his fearful feat to a concourse of sea gulls and fishes.

OLD JOE CLARKE

Old Joe Clarke he killed a man,
    And buried him in the sand;
He took his bloody handkerchief
    And wiped his bloody hand.

Yo ho ho for old Joe Clarke,
    Joe Clarke has come to town.
He's boarding at the Big Hotel [jail]
    And courting the Widow Brown.

I never did like old Joe Clarke,
    I'll tell you the reason why;
He rode all over my garden patch,
    And trompled down all my rye.

I hauled me up a load of brush,
    To fence the garden round;
Old Joe Clarke's hogs got into it,
    And rooted up all the ground.

I planted my corn in the month of May;
    By June it was knee high.
I counted on a crop, till one fine day
    Joe Clarke came a-riding by.

He turned his cows into my corn,
    That they might eat their fill;
For all I know, them . . . . cows
    Are in there eatin' still.

Sheriff Brown were a mighty fine man,
    He never told a story.

He always wore his long black coat
    To carry his soul to glory.

But Betsy Brown I can't abide,
    I'll tell you the reason why;
She'll . . . . a corn bread crust
    And call it custard pie.

Sheriff Brown went out one day,
    To ride the country round.
He came on murdering old Joe Clarke,
    A-sleeping on the ground.

The Sheriff laid down his forty-four,
    Likewise his ammunition.
Says he to murdering old Joe Clarke,
    "I'll quell your damned ambition!"

They clinched, and first the Sheriff squoze.
    Joe found his breath were gone.
Said he: "I never were squoze so hard,
    Since the day and the hour I were born!"

They fought a while and then they agreed
    To leave each other be.
Says Joe: "I am too strong for you,
    And you're too strong for me.

"Let's go to town," said Joe to Brown:
    "To fight I have no mind."
The Sheriff said: "I'll ride in front,
    And you shall ride behind."

Joe rode behind the Sheriff
    A mile and a half or more.
Then he drawed a great long bowie knife
    And he stabbed him to the core.

Old Joe Clarke killed Sheriff Brown,
    And buried him in the sand.

He took his bloody handkerchief
    And wiped his bloody hand.

Betsy Brown went out one day
    To walk around the town
She came upon the Sheriff's corpse
    A-lying on the ground.

The wind had blowed the sand away,
    From his crown down to his chin.
The beetles were a-crawling out,
    And the worms were a-crawling in.

When Betsy seen that black, black face—
    'Twere black as a face can be—
A-laying there in the bloody sand
    Under a black-jack tree,

"My Gawd!" says she, "I know I shall
    Look like that when I'm dead!"
The Preacher said: "You certainly will!"
    She taken to her bed.

Yo ho ho for old Joe Clarke!
    Joe Clarke has come to town;
He's boarding at the Big Hotel
    And courting the Widow Brown.

Now the Widow Brown is a . . . . fool.
    As widows often be;
So she slipped him the key to the jail
    For the sake of his company.

"Now I am out of that . . . . jail,
    As free as a man can be.
I'll leave the town to Betsy Brown,
    For the jail's no place for me.

"When next you see Miz Betsy Brown,
    Won't you please to tell her

No more to make her mind to me,
   But to look for another feller!"

So it's "Fare ye well to old Joe Clarke,"
   And it's "Fare ye well to town;"
And it's "Fare ye well to the Big Hotel,"
   And "Good-bye Betsy Brown!"

Ole Joe Clark, a Variant

Chorus

Ole Joe Clark 'e killed a man
En buried 'im in the san';
Said ef 'e had another chance,
He'd kill another man.

Good-by, ole Joe Clark!
Good-by, I'm gone!
Good-by, ole Joe Clark!
Good-by, Betty Brown!

Ol' Joe Clark, Play-party Song

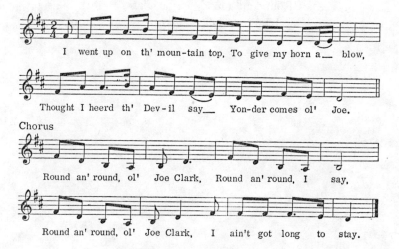

I went up on th' moun-tain top, To give my horn a— blow,

Thought I heerd th' Dev-il say— Yon-der comes ol' Joe.

Chorus

Round an' round, ol' Joe Clark, Round an' round, I say,

Round an' round, ol' Joe Clark, I ain't got long to stay.

I went up on th' mountain top,
To give my horn a blow,
Thought I heerd th' Devil say
Yonder comes ol' Joe.

I went up on th' mountain top
A-huntin' sugar cane,
Stuck my foot in a holler log
An' out jumped Liza Jane.

I went down t' ol' Joe Clark's,
Went right in th' door,
He slep' on th' ol' feather bed,
An' I slep' on th' floor.

I tuck her down t' ol' Joe Clark's,
Didn't know whar 't put her,

She hung her hat on th' table leg
    An' stuck her foot in th' butter.

Chorus:
Round an' round, ol' Joe Clark,
    Round an' round, I say,
Round an' round, ol' Joe Clark,
    I ain't got long to stay.

THE PIGS OF THE LOVE MAD LOPEZ

Now another piece of folk lore that has been forgotten are the tales about the Great Don Jose Lopez—The Love Mad Lopez who was the first man to grow the crying frijole in California. It was none other than he who trained the singing coyote. Most of his life was spent in riding around California Arizona & New Mexico on his flying palm tree hunting the sangua lima. What a sangua lima is nobody seems to know, but anyway the great Love Mad Lopez when he would have a yearning to go on an errand of love he would call together the Order of Caballeros of the Love Mad Lopez jump on his flying palm tree, & away he would ride ever ready to succor some poor lady in distress.

It was the great Lopez who first caused San Francisco Bay to form. He chased the evil spirit from Mt Diablo & finally run him to earth. The earth then became sick & sunk out of sight & the evil being was drownded. This spirit was making the cattle sick & had been causing much sorrow among the californians. Unlike Paul Bunyan the Great Lopez did not spend his time cutting down the trees & denuding the forests; making way for future erosion. He was the one who first planted the Redwoods, he made the painted desert red, cut the grand canyon, not Paul Bunyan, kindled Mt. Lassen made Mt. Shasta, in fact erected most of California. He was greater than Paul Bunyan. For he was Bunyan, Barron Mauchesun & Don Quijote all rolled into one.

Anyway one story that stands out in my memory & it has appeared under many forms is the yarn about the first hog Ranch in California.

Once upon a time a Spanish Ship brought a boar and some sows to California. Well the Love Mad Lopez thought it would be a good idea to raise pigs to supply food for his Caballeros. So he bought the pigs & started raising them. They grew fat and healthy and multiplied exceedingly. Even the poor buzzards were out of luck for they ate up all the carcases left them nothing. These pigs were quite wild & just couldn't even seem to get enough to eat. One old sow wandered off the home range into the mission garden ate up everything eatable & what she didn't eat she rooted up. Now this made the Padres very angry at the great Lopez for letting one of his swine steal from the Holy Church. So they sent one of their employees an Indian fellow to shoot the pig dead which he promptly did.

Now this was against the whole idea & principles of the Order for the Caballeros did not believe in killing, being motivated only by love. They used the pigs only for food, but they didn't eat the pig flesh they only drunk the milk.

Apparently these Caballeros of the Order of Don Jose Lopez— the Love Mad Lopez—were the first to milk pigs, drink pigs' milk & make pig cheese.

When Don Jose found that one of his pigs were dead he was heartbroken he called the Caballeros together & they laid plans on how to teach the padres a lesson. Anyway late one night they crept up to the mission & stole the bell and carted it back to Ranch. You may guess there was a great hubbub at the mission in the morning when the indian whose duty it was to ring the bell found that it had been purloined away.

Well anyway the Caballeros took the Bell back to the ranch and would ring it at milking time every day. The pigs soon got used to its clang & they would stampede into the Caballeria [stable] to be milked at the very first bong. It mattered not how far an old sow had wandered when that bell sounded they would come rushing in squeeling like locomotives.

This bell became very handy for whenever a caballero wanted a little pig milk all he had to do was ring the Bell & he would be immediately surrounded by a horde of squeeling milk factories. Well this went on for a number of years and the whole ranch was over run by wild pigs gray old tuskers gay young squeelers & just plain pigs, fat sows, thin sows & pleasingly plump sows. It soon became painfully apparent to the great Lopez and his Love Mad Caballeros that they would be forced to part with some of these beloved pigs. It was very sad indeed all the noble Caballero wept bitter tears Anyway come spring round up the great Lopez got the whole Order together & they started to drive the pigs to town with the aid of the singing coyote Anyway when they got to town & were passing the mission, the bell—a new one having been since acquired—started to ring calling the indians to mass Well the pigs came charging and stampedeing into the sacred edifice squeeling & oinking so that the devout thought they were being attacked by the devil and they ran to the priest for protection. The Padres were very much enraged & ordered the Pigs slaughtered immediately for this sacrelidge against the Holy Church. Now there was a yankee ship waiting to take on some pig meat & when the captain heard the great commotion on shore mingled with shots & so forth. He became very much alarmed thinking it was a revolution & fearing for the safety of his vessel, he ordered all sails set & the anchor weighed immediately. As the ship was drawing away from the coast a bell was sounded aboard here & the pigs hearing it rushed down into the Blue pacific & headed for China. Anyway when last seen they were approaching Hawaian Islands. This disheartened the Great Love Mad Lopez so much that he rode back to his ranch dug up the roots of the flying palm tree climbed aboard & flew away to return no more.

ENTER JOE ROOT AND THE JEEBIES

On Presqu' Isle Peninsula the afternoon sun was declining toward the coolness of evening. The shadows of the big oaks lengthened toward the east as we trudged into the grove, walking on a hushed path of pine needles and last year's oak leaves. Just as the heavy picnic baskets were placed strategically about, ready for a sudden assault, the bushes parted and without a sound Joe Root stepped into our group. His entrance was always dramatic. He was an undersized man, in tattered clothes and medieval hat, quietly soft spoken, with a smile that all children love and their elders envy. His exit was equally dramatic—he simply vanished without a sound, usually after accepting all the food he could carry. And between entrance and exit, Joe, the born clown, entertained his audience.

"What's the weather going to do, Joe?"

"Oh, they tell me nice day tomorrow, and thunderstorm next day."

"Who told you, Joe?"

"Why, the Jeebies, of course. I call 'em up."

"You telephoned them?"

"Sure thing. Always tell me true."

"Well, call them up now and tell me what they say."

Then Joe, with his soft, shuffling gait, would sidle to the end of a log, put his hat against it, and after a few grunts and chuckles and whistles would ask loudly, "What's the weather coming up?" The reply would be a long series of mysterious sounds, bird chirps and dog laps, and then Joe would replace his hat on his head and announce in his funny little voice, half squeak and half lisp, "Yep! That's right! Hot tomorrow and rain next day." And it always turned out to be an accurate forecast.

"Joe, have you had your dinner?"

"Yes sir, indeed," he answered with a longing look at our baskets. "Had a good dinner."

"What did you have, Joe?"

"Fried mosquitoes today, but I eat only the white meat. I save the dark meat for breakfast." . . .

Joe's appearance was not prepossessing. His felt hat had made acquaintance with so many winters and summers that it would be called that only because it rested on the proper portion on his anatomy, and it remained there mainly by capillary action. His long hair was a sandy gray, covering his neck and his coat collar. His beard—he said he shaved every Christmas—was scraggly and of the same indeterminate color; his moustache protruded sideways about as far as his buck teeth protruded forward. His coat covered but did not conceal a high cut vest, which in turn covered and almost concealed the apparent lack of shirt. His shoes were serviceable, or had been, even though they did not match. But his sartorial pride was, or were, his trousers; he always wore four or five pairs, and in his pride he arranged them carefully so that the holes of one were covered by the next pair; it usually required at least four pairs to attain complete coverage. . . .

Perhaps Joe could have been a successful businessman. It was at a bar on lower State Street that first he disclosed his plans for what might have become a profitable enterprise, had he been able to secure capital. Certainly he had vision. Long before the days of airplanes, his ever-active mind grappled with the problem of speed of transportation, and having observed the flight of ducks all his life, he realized that travel by air was faster than any other medium. In this he admittedly was far ahead of his times. His well-matured plans were simple: a balloon farm on his beloved Peninsula! To travel anywhere, even as far as Buffalo, the passenger simply stepped into one of Joe's balloons, and—whoof!—the wind blew him there instantly. Cheapest possible voyage. No fuss, no dirt, no clanking engine. In answer to a criticism that perhaps the wind might blow in the wrong direction, he replied that his Jeebies always told him true, invariably.

HUCKLEBERRY CHARLIE AND HIS SPIEL

The *Watertown* (New York) *Standard* of January 14, 1921, had this to say when Charles R. Sherman died:

"Huckleberry Charlie Sherman's days of spellbinding are over. Watertown will miss a familiar figure. The champion huckleberry picker of the United States has passed away.

"The age of Charlie was 78, but everytime he came into Watertown he announced a birthday anniversary. On the strength of that he garnered many gifts from the merchants, as he made his pilgrimage about Public Square. His early life was passed in Watertown, and he was connected with some of the best known families of this city. As long as the present generation and the generation preceding can remember, Charlie lived in Pine Plains, emerging during the huckleberry season to dispose of the noted Pine Plains product.

"His presence here always meant innumerable speeches, in which he recited that he was born in Watertown, lived at Pine Plains and was the champion huckleberry picker. He always said the Plains was good only to 'raise hell and huckleberries.'

"At each store he would be given an unsalable article of dress. At the end of the tour he would be decked out in the colors of the rainbow. Joseph's coat of many colors was tame beside Huckleberry's duck trousers, checked pongee coat, brilliant red necktie and a college boy's panama. Added to this Charlie was certain to have a stogie poised at the Joe Cannon angle.

"At county fairs he was always a visitor—his entrance was gratuitous for he was one of the midway attractions. Lucky was the vendor in front of whose stand Sherman took his position. The crowd followed him and listened avidly to the time-worn theme.

Charlie talked so fast that it required three renditions of the speech to comprehend the ideas and sequence. If one remained any length of time, he would hear the third rendition."

The following sayings of Huckleberry Charlie were gathered together by the late Harold B. Johnson, former editor of the *Watertown Daily Times*, as Huckleberry's *spiel*:

"These huckleberries were picked on Pine Plains, two-and-a-half miles this side of Great Bend. They're free from sticks, stones, stems, and bruises. Some are black and some are blue. Come up, kind people, and purchase a few, for this is my last time through. Get yer huckleberries!"

"The stars are high and the sky is low. If the wind changes, it'll rain afore mornin'. I do my business on a capital called wind and keep my head partly out of warm water. I don't bore with any large augur, but I have as many shavings as the rest of 'em by night."

"If they ever get me to the 'Burg, I'll show 'em some new loony stuff they never heard of!" (In Ogdensburg there is an insane asylum.)

"I was never sick but once in my life. That time I had the measles. Aunt Lucy gave me a decoction of sheeptick tea. Less'n three days I was around on my dewclaws again."

Man: "How're yer huckleberries, Charlie?"
Charlie: "Talk about them when they're ripe, tell yer mother."
Man: "Nice night, Charlie."
Charlie: "Yeah, rather nice up overhead, but there ain't very many travelin' that way."

"I've been to Barnum's. I've seen the elephant shake his trunk an—

"I went down to New Orleans
          An' jumped on to the landin';
I struck against a cotton bale
          An' there I sot a-standin';

"For Maria plays the concertin',
          An' Julia plays the flute;
An' all around the room was heard
          Such a peccable, peccable toot."

Way, way down in Chaumont
Where the big potatoes grow,
Where they catch the ciscoes, big an' small,
An' they eat them guts an' all—
In Chaumont;
Where they chaw terbacker thin
An' it trickles down their chin,
Then they lap it up again,
In Chaumont.

"Wished I lived where it was six months night and six months day. Like to get there about sundown where you could get a good night's sleep. Be hell to get there sunup, wouldn't it? Be a long time afore dinner." [End of *spiel*]

At one time his wife, Dell, requested that he be confined to an institution. Dell said that in addition to Huckleberry's eccentricities he was becoming irritable and dangerous. The doctors said that there was no question of Huckleberry's insanity; but because of the question of which town would defray the costs of his treatment, he was allowed to return to his home in Great Bend.

THE GREATEST OF THE GRIZZLIES

Through the interpreter I said to Yellow Brow: "I have heard of man heroes, heroes of your own people. I have heard many bear stories and of brave men fighting hand-to-hand with fierce bears. Perhaps you know of some bear that was greater than all other bears, a bear with power above all other bear-power."

Yellow Brow was silent a little while after the interpreter had translated my words. He sat facing the Big Horn Mountains, and something as far off as those mountains, as intangible as the air shrouding them yet as physical as the mountains themselves, seemed to be gathering in Yellow Brow's mind.

He said: "Yes, I know a story of a bear who was braver than all other bears, just as a hero among men is braver than all other men. I will tell you." . . .

I was about four years old at the time this happened. My father saw it all. We were making camp on Plum Creek, which flows into the Missouri River, northeast of what is now Lewistown. Across the creek and down it some distance from us a hunter named Bear's Heel, who had ridden ahead early that morning, was coming to the camp site with a young deer across his horse.

He was riding at the edge of brush when he heard a kind of grunting sound—hughh-hughh-hughh-hughh, like that—coming from the hidden ground. He had never heard anything like this in his life. He stopped to listen. The sound came repeated like a song Indians sing around a drum—hughh-hughh-hughh-hughh-hughh-hughh. Bear's Heel sat there on his horse. The horse was trembling. The sounds went on. Bear's Heel dropped the deer carcass from his horse. Then he rode into the bushes towards the sounds. The bushes were buffalo berries.

Before long Bear's Heel came to the edge of an opening, and in the middle of it he saw an enormous grizzly standing up like a man and looking at the place where the Crow Indians were beginning to make camp. The bear put his left hand, open, out in front of him, thus, towards the camp, and then brought it back, cupped, to his chest. This is the sign which means, "I have your heart. You cannot conquer me." Then the bear made the same sign with his right hand, holding it out open against the people a long time and then bringing it tight against his heart.

Then this bear moved his right hand across his brow and moved a finger down from each eye across each cheek, as if he were painting the bear sign on his own face. He did not seem to have any paint in his hand, but after he made the lines the paint showed plainly—war paint. All this time Bear's Heel was watching him. The bear's whole attention was on the camp. He seemed to be challenging.

Bear's Heel had not ridden out of the bushes, but had kept partly hidden. Now he backed his horse quietly until he could turn without being seen. He rode to the deer carcass, loaded it on again, and made straight for the camp. Some of the women were still unloading their travois. The chiefs were sitting in a circle. Highest among them was Chief Two Bellies.

"My younger brother," Bear's Heel said to him, "I have seen something strange and ominous." Then he described the rhythms made by the bear in grunting, the sign he had made of taking away the hearts of the warriors, the way he had painted himself for war.

"Camp is not yet made," Bear's Heel said. "There is no time to investigate. I have seen too much already. Let us move up the creek and put distance between us and this wise, ferocious animal. He has very plainly said that he does not want us in his hunting grounds here."

Chief Two Bellies agreed. He at once gave orders to repack and move farther up the creek. "Everybody go," he said, "and let no young man give way to his curiosity."

Now, in any big camp there were always young men who did not obey orders. Some of these had heard the account given by Bear's Heel and his description of the place in which the grizzly was threatening. For them the orders by Two Bellies were an invitation to investigate. From the confusion of camp about a dozen galloped to the bear's ground. The bear had not changed his mind. He was ready. He charged out to meet them. He began to prove that he meant what he had said.

The warriors were not slow in answering his challenge. Some were armed with guns, some with bows and arrows. They aimed well. Every time a bullet hit the grizzly he would fall, but then would immediately rise. Not an arrow could penetrate his hide, though men who could put an arrow through a buffalo were shooting at this bear.

From so many enemies the bear now retreated into timber and underbrush. A big pine log lay out over the ground which he occupied. A brave who had a two-barreled horse-pistol and a knife stepped out on this log, hunting for a shot.

Just at this time Chief Two Bellies rode up. "Leave," he cried. "You have knocked the grizzly down as many times as I have fingers. You have seen that you can't kill him. If you don't get out, he will kill more than one."

Before a move could be made, the bear rose up charging the young man on the log. The young man seemed to be overcome with fear. His straight-seeing was gone. As he stepped back, he lost his footing. The bear caught him around the body with his right arm and began running on three legs, carrying the man with head and feet dangling, back into his lair beyond the log.

By now many warriors had come to the battle ground. Some stood on a bluff overlooking it. Of all who saw not one made a sound. The whole conduct of the bear seemed beyond the laws of nature.

Chief Two Bellies up on the cliff said: "I told you not to come here. Now one of you has been taken by the grizzly. You invited a fight. You have it. Go in and rescue your friend."

A warrior named Poor Assinaboine stripped. He was armed with a breech-loading gun and had his knife in his teeth. "I challenge another to go with me," he cried.

Black Head stripped, put his knife in his teeth, and held his gun in readiness.

The two men moved from two directions towards the bear's lair. As they got nearer they could hear the young man moaning, "Oh, how it hurts! Oh, how it hurts!" They disappeared in the thick growth. There was not a move among the spectators. They heard one shot and then another shot. Soon the two reappeared carrying their comrade, one by the head and the other by the legs. One eye was hanging down by its cord. The bone above it and the cheek bone below it was crushed in. One arm was literally torn out of its socket. A hole in the side exposed the man's vitals. He writhed for a little while and then was dead.

The rescuers reported that their shots had knocked the bear down but not killed him.

Chief Two Bellies said: "Now, you warriors who know better than to obey orders, listen! One of you is already dead. There is only one bear. There are many of you. Go in and get him."

"That is what we came for," yelled a brave. One of them started to sing a strong-heart song—but it did not sound strong. There was some delay while three young braves who had bear ears in camp raced to get them. Each tied a bear ear over his own ear. That is strong medicine. Other braves painted the bear sign on themselves.

Two Bellies also took off his robe and sat ready on his war horse, the Strawberry Roan. "When I give the word, charge," he said.

He yelled and led the way. All gave the warwhoop. The bear rushed out, headed towards another thicket. Two Bellies managed his horse as if he were shooting buffaloes and knocked the bear down with a ball of lead. Two other warriors emptied their guns into the bear's body.

But the grizzly got up and chased one man on horseback. He was lucky to be riding a fast animal. He ran a long way out on the prairie, the bear at his heels. Finally the bear stopped, sat down, and then in a slow shuffle made towards a thicket. By now other warriors had caught up, and they went to shooting. But the grizzly no longer fell at the impact of a bullet. He merely flinched. He walked into the bushes, looking back at his enemies.

Chief Two Bellies said: "Men on fastest horses follow me. Guns and arrows have proved worthless. Leave them here. Now we use knives. When I spear the bear down, let each man knife him right and left."

Two Bellies in the lead, the warriors charged with knives. At the same time the bear plunged out of his cover, headed for an open flat. The chief could not knock him down. Finally he halted, as did the other warriors. The bear sat on his haunches in full view, facing his enemies.

Two Bellies said: "If now we attack with nothing but knives, some man will be killed. Apparently nothing can kill him. We have conquered the Sioux, the Blackfeet and other tribes. We are masters of our land, but this grizzly remains our conqueror. Leave him. Let us move our camp before he kills women and children."

After that the Crows gave this place of Greatest of all Grizzlies plenty of room. Years later two Gros Ventre hunters went into it and never returned. The Crows had no doubt that the grizzly killed them. There is no more to tell.

SLUE-FOOT, THE INDESTRUCTIBLE BEAR

John Tallhorse was an ageless old Indian of nearly pure blood. His ancestors were among the first human beings ever to set foot in the hills of West Virginia. John's skin was a deep red and was wrinkled from years of age and weather. His old frame was very strong and his gray hair still revealed traces of its original black. He possessed many of his ancestors' habits and characteristics. John always wore moccasins on his agile feet and he hunted with his self-made bow and arrow. He was exceptionally quiet and spoke only when the occasion for speech was necessary. Although John never meddled in other people's affairs, he was very helpful if someone needed him. He provided a living for himself and enjoyed a quiet existence of solitude in a hermit-like environment. John lived in a small shack deep in the mountains. He owned a small farm and raised a few crops on his tiny plot of land. However, John was most widely known for his skillful trapping abilities. He maintained his livelihood through his trapping. Besides the majority of his income resulting from trapping, many of the garments he wore were made from his pelts.

A true American Indian, John was familiar with all of the forest animals and their habits. However, John Tallhorse respected one single animal more than any other in the entire forest—a huge, old bear called Slue-foot. The giant bear had inhabited the mountains for as long as John could remember. He had been given the name old Slue-foot by the hunters who pursued him. The great bear, when he was quite young, had been shot in one of his hind feet. Being nearly severed by the deadly bullet, his foot was mangled and had healed crookedly. Therefore, he was characterized by the odd track which he left and was easily distinguished by all hunters. For years hundreds of different hunters had stalked the mountains on the trail of old Slue-foot. But not one hunter had managed to even wound the elusive bear since his first injury. Bands of men had been known to trail the bear for as long as a week, only to have him vanish at any particular time. To stalk and kill old Slue-foot was the challenge for all hunters who had ever heard tales about the massive beast. Few men were fortunate to boast of even having an opportunity for a distant shot at the bear. However, John Tallhorse had been in bow and arrow range of the beast numerous times. But John respected old Slue-foot and the bear seemed to respect and trust John. After all, John only killed an animal when he needed the meat, so he naturally had no desire to slay the bear. In addition, old Slue-foot had never been harmful or aggressive toward anyone. Still each hunter wanted only to have the huge bear's head mounted on his den wall. To John, old Slue-foot dominated the mountains. He was the leader of all of the other animals. When John spoke of Slue-foot, there was a proud gleam in his dark eyes. He always said, "Old Slue-foot is indestructible. He is the mighty one of the forest!"

The knowledge was widespread that old John Tallhorse was familiar with every inch of ground in that particular mountain region. Since he was directly in the center of Slue-foot's habitat, he was the target of many inquiring hunters.

Early one morning John was busy in his small garden when four men approached him. Only one glance at the men was required to determine their destination—they were planning to go after old Slue-foot. John laughed to himself at the culminating eagerness which gripped the men. The men were dressed in complete hunting attire and were armed like fortresses. They also were reinforced by five, savage-looking, hunting dogs. The hunters asked John many questions concerning the habits of old Slue-foot, mountain terrain, and the climatic conditions. Naturally, John did not betray his mighty friend. He talked to the men, but he cleverly supplied them with very little information. When the four hunters felt that they had quizzed the old Indian sufficiently, they were confidently prepared to begin on their exciting hunt. However, John warned the men that old Slue-foot was very sly and dangerous. He also made his proud statement, "Old Slue-foot is indestructible. He is the mighty one of the forest!" The men, led by the five large hounds, began their stalking trudge into the mountains.

John went about his daily routine of life in his normal manner. Three days after the visit of the desperate hunters, John was checking some of his traps which were placed in a mountain stream. Suddenly his acute hearing detected some noises which were foreign to the quiet forest. He listened intently for several minutes. He then recognized the sounds and immediately set out in their direction. What he heard was the savage growling and barking of a full scale battle to the finish. Then several shots were fired. John ascended a small hill of which the noises and shots had come from the opposite side. At that moment, one of the hunters crossed the summit of the hill from the opposite side and was running toward John. He shouted, "We got him! We got him! We killed your mighty bear!" The hunter was hurrying off the hill to his car. There he was seeking ropes that would be used to help the men move the bear out of the woods. The hunter yelled as he went by John, "I guess your mighty bear wasn't so indestructible after all! Yes, you're going to remember this hunt for many moons, my Indian friend!" Old John hastened his pace and continued toward the top of the hill.

When he reached the peak of the mount where he could view the small valley on the opposite side, he stood, puzzled, for a long while. He quickly sighted the scene of the terrible battle. The ground and small bushes in the area were coated with fresh blood. Three of the vicious, killer dogs were lying motionless, their bodies mangled. The remaining two dogs were moaning and whining from pain. The dogs, in attempting to slaughter old Slue-foot, must have encountered a greater resistive force than the cruel hunters had suspected. However, John could not understand the situation. Not only had the hunters vanished, but also had old Slue-foot, who was supposedly dead! John wonderingly searched the area, but he could find no sign of either the bear or the men. He knew that the three hunters could not possibly have moved the body of the massive bear within the short length of time it required for him to mount the hill. John walked about the area for a while longer, but being able to conclude nothing concerning the situation, finally returned to checking his traps.

Time passed and John preceded along his journey down the path of life. Several days following the mysterious incident, he was setting some new traps in a stream which ran through the mountains near his home. He was bending down near a large, sycamore tree placing a trap in a hidden position. Suddenly he saw the bushes move and heard a low growl. He looked up and there was old Slue-foot, standing on his hind legs, on the opposite bank of the stream. John Tallhorse thought of the missing hunters who were never found, smiled, and spoke aloud, "Old Slue-foot is indestructible. He is the mighty one of the forest!"

GRAY BESS, THE HORSE THAT
TRAILED COMANCHES

One fall afternoon in the last century, Will Hampton and some of his neighbors who lived near Pearl (Coryell County) were out in Mr. Hampton's pasture looking at some stock. There was a briskness in the air, and Gray Bess was taking her ease, lamely, among some riding horses and colts.

One of the stockmen turned to Hampton and said, "Will, what are you going to do with Gray Bess? Might as well put her to sleep with a .45, she'll freeze to death some morning this winter."

Mr. Hampton, almost as near the end of his westering as Bess, looked them all in the eye and said, "I'll take care of Bess this winter, and every other winter as long as she lives. See my house down there in the ranch cup? Bess and me come to this valley together, and she picked it out. I let her have her head and she stood stock still at that bend in the creek and that's where I cut my roof rafters."

"I'll say one thing for old Bess, she can stay on the trail of a bunch of Comanches better'n any horse I ever heard of—or used to could."

"She still can," said Hampton, "better'n any hound dog in the whole wide West."

As they were riding in about dusk some of the men thought they saw furtive forms stealing along the forest edge. They pulled up and watched.

"Comanches, by God!"

"A dozen of them!"

The first thing to do was to see to the security of their houses, for the red men might be planning an attack against the settlers' homes. Each man rode to his own place to post outlooks and ready their guns. Then they gathered again at Hampton's, where the Indians had been seen last. They kept up the watch all night but heard no sound, no shot, no signal.

In the gray of the morning, however, a savage lot of yelling and whooping broke loose from up toward the high pasture. The men grabbed their guns, mounted, and made off. They got to the upper pasture just in time to see the tail end of the Comanche band disappearing in the trees and heading toward the mountains. They had driven off all of Hampton's horses, including old Bess.

Hampton and his men followed hot on the trail. It was easy tracking such a large party, but not easy to come up to the thieving red men in spite of the handicap they had with Gray Bess. Hampton's party caught sight of the band on the mountainside two or three times, but they were not closing fast enough. Old Bess must have been taking a terrible punishment; they found blood on the gravel in several places.

"I'll follow them to Devil's Den," said Hampton, "and if they kill Bess in this drive I'll follow them to the Devil himself."

They pressed on and about midmorning came to where the trail forked. There was Bess tied to a tree, her feet bleeding and her limbs trembling.

"Now if old Bess can travel, she'll show us the way sure."

One trail led south to the canyon, the other west to the higher plateau.

"Cut that grass rope," ordered Hampton. "She'll show us which trail they took, though the signs around here point to the canyon. Could be a trick."

As soon as Bess was free she headed for the south trail to the canyon. Then she did a puzzling thing. She put out her forefeet and stopped short, wheeled, and galloped up to Hampton and laid her head on his shoulder. Then she turned and took the west trail up the mountain, making what time she could. She whinnied low from time to time but kept on the up trail.

Thus she led them on for miles, and when she could go no farther, she stopped and faced her master and his men. She stumbled up to Hampton, laid her head over his shoulder for a great spell of hard breathing, and then dropped dead as a stone at his feet.

Hampton couldn't talk, but the look in his eyes said enough. After a respectful silence, one man said, "Gray Bess has led us up the wrong trail. If they was any Indians on this plateau we could see them."

"It's deeper than that," Hampton said. "Bess knows Indians. Why did she start toward the canyon first?"

Worn out and dejected, they backtrailed down the mountain and came again to where the trail forked. They stopped to look around. The canyon rim was not a quarter-mile away. They had not explored that trail very far till they all realized what a great debt they owed to old Gray Bess. The gun prints in the dirt and the many moccasin tracks and animal leavings showed plainly that the Comanches had laid an ambush for their small party. The raiding Indians had joined with a larger band in the canyon to wipe the settlers out. Realizing this, Gray Bess had led them away from the ambush and had saved their lives.

MURDEROUS MARY, CIRCUS ELEPHANT

Incredible as it seems, late Wednesday afternoon, September 13, 1916, Mary, a circus elephant, was hanged in Erwin, Tennessee.

The day before, in Kingsport, Tennessee, after the daylight performance, Mary had killed Walter "Red" Eldridge, who reportedly had joined the "Sparks World-Famous Shows" only two days earlier in his home town of St. Paul, Virginia, because he wanted to be an animal trainer.

According to some reports Eldridge was not Mary's first victim. One Erwin resident (Bud Jones) who witnessed the hanging states: "She'd killed one man up in Virginie and killed a man in Kingsport." Another witness of the hanging (James Treadway) says: "She killed—one at Kingsport, one at Bristol, and one over there [Erwin]. But I didn't see that there at Erwin." Others (Mont Lilly and W. H. Coleman) think she killed two before the one at Kingsport. The number expands in various oral accounts, such as the following (by Kary Gouge): "He took spells that he'd kill 'em, you know, and that's made about six or seven that he'd killed."

In one published account, carried ten days after the event in a Chicago newspaper and illustrated by a 7×10 sensational drawing, Mary was reported to have killed seven other men (*The Saturday Blade*, 23 Sept. 1916, p. 1); and the *Johnson City Comet* [Tennessee] stated the day following the hanging: "It is said that Mary had killed 18 men" (p. 1). The Ripley's "Believe It or Not" cartoon of August 29, 1938, numbers the victims as three. On the other hand, another article in the *Johnson City Comet* (14 Sept. 1916, p. 1) quotes Mr. Heron, the press agent for the Sparks Shows, as saying: "'I have been with the shows for three years and have never known the elephant to lose her temper before.'" The *Nashville Banner* (13 Sept. 1916, p. 9) reported similarly: "'Murderous Mary,' as she was termed by spectators, has been . . . performing . . . for fifteen years, and this is the first time anyone has come to harm.'"

Mary was billed as "THE LARGEST, LIVING, LAND ANIMAL ON EARTH. 3 INCHES TALLER THAN JUMBO AND WEIGHING OVER 5 TONS." The *Johnson City Staff* (13 Sept. 1916, p. 3; 14 Sept. 1916, p. 6) reported her to be one of a trained quintette, 30 years old (interestingly only half her life expectancy in captivity), and estimated her loss to the show at $20,000; another newspaper valued her at $8,000 (*The Saturday Blade*, 23 Sept. 1916, p. 1).

Her attack on Walter Eldridge was flamboyantly reported by the *Johnson City Staff* as follows: "Suddenly [Mary] collided its trunk vice-like about his [Eldridge's] body, lifted him ten feet in the air, then dashed him with fury to the ground. Before Eldridge had a chance to reach his feet, the elephant had him pinioned to the ground, and with the full force of her biestly [sic] fury is said to have sunk her giant tusks entirely through his body. The animal then trampled the dying form of Eldridge as if seeking a murderous triumph, then with a sudden . . . swing of her massive foot hurled his body into the crowd" (13 Sept. 1916, p. 3).

Twenty years later Mary's attack is reported quite differently: "The elephant's keeper, while in the act of feeding her, walked unsuspectingly between her and the tent wall. For no reason that could be ascertained, Mary became angry and, with a vicious swish of her trunk, landed a fatal blow on his head" (*Johnson City Press-Chronicle*, 16 Aug. 1936, p. 1). (Reasons for Mary's attack, however, are in circulation. David Hatcher told me that it was commonly said when he was growing up in Erwin that the person Mary killed had once given her a chew of tobacco to eat instead of peanuts and that Mary, keeping the incident in mind over a period of years, took her revenge when she recognized her offender during a parade. Eugene Harris says that another local

explanation for Mary's violent behavior is that she had two ab-
scessed teeth, and the pain incurred from Eldridge's striking her
with a stick drove her into a fury.)

W. H. Coleman of Kingsport, who witnessed the event as a
youth of 19, described to me Mary's attack on "Red" Eldridge as
follows:

> There was a big ditch at that time, run up through Cen-
> ter Street, . . . [an] open ditch that had been put there
> for the purpose of draining all of Kingsport. . . . And
> they'd sent these boys to ride the elephants. . . . There
> was, oh, I don't know now, seven or eight elephants . . .
> and they went down to water them and on the way back
> each boy had a little stick-like, that was a spear or hook
> in the end of it. . . . And this big old elephant reach
> over to get her a watermelon rind, about a half a water-
> melon somebody eat and just laid it down there; 'n he
> did, the boy give him a jerk. He pulled him away from
> 'em, and he just blowed real big; and when he did, he
> took him right around the waist . . . and throwed him
> against the side of the drink stand and he just knocked
> the whole side out of it. I guess it killed him, but when
> he hit the ground the elephant just walked over and set
> his foot on his head . . . and blood and brains and stuff
> just squirted all over the street. [Later Mr. Coleman
> specifically says Mary did not gore Eldridge.]

According to Mr. Coleman, Hench Cox who was 65 or 70,
came out of the blacksmith shop close by when he heard the elephant "blow" and shot it five times with a 32-20 pistol; the elephant "just doubled up and just groaned and carried on, you
never heard the like; he just stooped down and shook all over."
Then, as Mr. Coleman relates: "The crowd kept hollerin' and
sayin', 'Let's kill the elephant, let's kill him,' an' he [the "management" or "owner"] said, 'People, I'd be perfectly willin' to kill

him, but there's no way to kill him. There ain't enough gun enough in this country that he could be killed; there's no way to kill him.' "

Nevertheless, Mary was quickly brought under control and even performed in the evening show—according to the newspaper, "without having exhibited the slightest indication of 'bad temper' " (*Johnson City Staff*, 13 Sept. 1916, p. 3). Nothing was apparently done by the circus officials at that time to exterminate the elephant; furthermore, Mr. Coleman thinks that they did not plan then to execute Mary and would not have executed her solely for the killing of Eldridge. He bases his opinion on a conversation, held some six or seven years after the hanging, with one of the operators of the Sparks side shows. The showman told Mr. Coleman that Mary "wouldn't never been destroyed if he [Mary] hadn't of come in an ace of destroying the owner. . . . He . . . come so near of gettin' him that he said, 'That'll be the last of you,' and just took and had him killed." In reality, Mr. Coleman thinks, Mary was executed because she was old, mean, and dangerous to handle, not because she had taken a human life. And not, one might add, because of the analysis, seemingly serious, offered by one newspaper: "It is stated that when an elephant kills one or more people that they are liable to do the same thing again and at a time that they [sic] keepers are least expecting it" (*Johnson City Staff*, 14 Sept. 1916, p. 6).

It is difficult to establish definitely, however, the authority responsible for sentencing Mary to death. The *Johnson City Staff*, the day after the execution reports: "Not wishing to take any more risks as to the loss of life, the Sparks Circus management had Mary . . . hung and killed" (p. 6). The 1916 December issue of *Popular Mechanics* states that Mary "was condemned to death by the state authorities and executed" ("Vicious Elephant Hanged for Killing Man," p. 803). Some of the residents of Erwin also place the decision on the state of Tennessee; as one (Mont Lilly) says: "The state of Tennessee preferred charges against [Mary]. . . . They charged her with first degree murder"—or as implied by another (Bud Jones): "They couldn't take her out

of Tennessee, you see, and they had to do somethin' with her."
Erwinians certainly do not hold their city responsible, as is made
perfectly clear by one lady (Mrs. E. H. Griffith): "It was decreed
that she [Mary] must be killed in the interest of public safety by
whom I do not know, certainly not by anyone here" (from a
typed manuscript of an answer to Bert Vincent, furnished by P. O.
Likens, Clinchfield Railroad).

At any rate on Wednesday, September 13, the day following
Eldridge's death, the Sparks Circus moved from Kingsport to
Erwin, taking Mary with it.

In Erwin, it had rained; and Mary, along with the other elephants helped push the wagons out of the mud; James Treadway
described the scene to me as follows: "They come in there and
they 'as a wet spell, rained awful for several days. . . . They
shipped them [the animals] in there by train at that time—they
wasn't any trucks then—and the railroad just set 'em on the sidin'
there and rolled them wagons off . . . they was mired down, and
they couldn't pull 'em with horses. And this feller took this elephant down there and she just pushed 'em out with her head."

Later that day, following the afternoon show, Mary was taken
down to the shop yards of the CC&O Railways. Mont Lilly, at
that time a 16-year-old relief man on the derrick car crew, gave me
the following details of the hanging (he was present that day but
not on duty):

> They brought those elephants down there, they had four
> or five of them together. And they had this here Mary
> . . . she was bringin' up the rear. It was just like they
> was havin' a parade, holdin' one another's tail. . . .
> These other ones come up . . . and they stopped. Well,
> she just cut loose right there . . . and the show men,
> they went and put a chain, a small chain around her
> foot, and chained her to the rail. Then they backed the
> wrecker up to her and throwed the big ⅞" chain around
> her neck and hoisted her, and she got up about, oh, I'll
> say, five or six feet off the ground and the chain around

her neck broke. See, they had to pull this chain loose; it broke the smaller chain, and that weakened the other chain. And so, when they got her up about five or six feet from the ground, why it broke.

Bud Jones, the fireman on the 100-ton derrick car that was used to hang Mary, gave me the following details:

They had eight 'r ten other elephants. They brung 'em all down there and she seemed to know they 'as somethin' wrong someway, you know, and she'd walk off around to one side, you know, and wouldn't stay hardly with the others a-tall. And finally got her up close enough to throw a chain around her neck. And we picked her up about, well, I'd say about three foot off the ground, and then the chain broke. And it kind o' addled her when it fell you know. And we quick 'n' got another chain and put it around her neck then and hooked it before she could get up.

James Treadway told me that Mary "kicked with both feet, one at a time, and that broke the chain." When the chain broke, he says, "she sat down just like a big rabbit . . . she haunkered down, and a fellow ran up her back and throwed the cable 'round her neck and hooked it." According to Mr. Lilly, it was not two minutes before the circus people had the second chain around Mary's neck and Sam Harvey, the regular fireman acting as engineer that day, had her hoisted once again: "She kicked a little bit and that was about all; see, that thing choked her to death right quick." . . .

After Mary's execution and after the pronouncement of her death, supposedly by local physician R. E. Stack, her five-ton corpse had to be disposed of. P. H. Flanary relates, "We . . . buried him with a steam shovel. I dug the grave after we hung the elephant . . . and also covered him with a steam shovel." According to Bud Jones she was held swinging about ten minutes before the derrick dropped her in the hole, some four or five hundred feet away from where she was hanged. The site itself, however, is a disputable subject, but according to Mr. Treadway it was "south of the roundhouse, below the tracks where the river [Nolichucky] comes up so far there." The reported length of time Mary was held aloft (before her shame was decently covered) also varies considerably—from a short period of 5, 10, 20 or 30 minutes to a long period of several hours. After Mary was dropped into her grave, her tusks reportedly were sawed off—according to some (e.g., M. D. Clark) before she was buried, according to others (e.g., James Treadway): "They dug down that night and cut her tushes off." With one of the tusks, says Mr. Lilly, "one fellow . . . made a set of dice." . . .

From another point of view the hanging of Mary was a serious matter. Mrs. B. O. Bailey says that the people were quiet: "They's just standing around, just like anybody else, you know, a-watching'. . . . They just wanted to get rid of that elephant that was killing everybody. . . . Nobody was sorry for it, for it was a-killin' too many people." Bud Jones says that everyone was "very serious," about the hanging; "they was all mighty quiet," but, he says, "the people, most of them, thought she ought to be killed." Mr. Lilly states: "Well, the general attitude was they just wanted to see the elephant hung. . . . They, of course, a lot of 'em, thought too that the elephant ought to be killed . . . they ought to destroy her, you know, for killin' so many people." Similarly, Mr. Monk recalls, "There wasn't much sympathy for old Mary. . . . Most people thought that the elephant ought to be hung—at least I did." Mrs. Griffith goes even further in saying, "We did not sit in judgment on her fate and I don't believe any of those who witnessed the event felt it was inhumane under the circumstances. She paid for her crimes as anyone else would."

OLD SATAN, THE MIRACULOUS MULE

Old Satan was the blackest, ugliest, most ornery, and least desirable mule in Carolina. He fought off work and when put into the barn, he kicked everything to pieces. He would chase dogs and scare women and children.

One day the farmer who owned Old Satan saw a remarkable thing happen. The mule was in the yard kicking things around as usual when suddenly he discovered a half of a barrel of soft soap that the women had made and hidden under a few boards near the kitchen. Old Satan knocked the boards off and drank the soft soap to the last drop before the farmer could even stop him.

The soft soap worked a miracle in Old Satan. He now became mild, good-natured, gentle, and quite agreeable to work. He played with the children. The farmer rode him to town, and the women hooked him to the buckboard and drove to church on Sundays. Old Satan was soft-soaped for life.

The tough old mule became a great benefaction to the town where soap was scarce. One Sunday morning, one of the hired hands could not shave because he lacked soap. Then he remembered that after each rain Old Satan broke out in a thick lather. The mule lathered so easily that people used to say, "The soft soap is coming out of him." So this hired hand took a cup of warm water, poured it over Satan, worked up a thick lather, and shaved with it. And then on Mondays, the women stood Old Satan over a washtub, poured water over him, and did their washing in the soapy water.

When at last Old Satan became very old, the farmer sold him to a barber. With the mule as a source of supply, the barber never had to buy any more shaving soap. Old Satan set the style for the shaving brush tails that mules wear today.

THE LEADER OF THE PACK

On one of the highest peaks in this section of the country, near Mannington, West Virginia, and known far and near as Red Tank Hill, a group of dog lovers gathered one night to indulge in their favorite sport, fox hunting.

To those of you who have never been on one of these hunts, I must say you have missed a lot of downright good enjoyment, and a chance to learn a lot about mother nature. The song of the night birds, the chirping of the cricket and the katydid, the old owls hoot, and an occasional peep from a tree frog tend to make a continuous but most enjoyable kind of music. The fresh, sweet scent of fallen leaves, mingled with the smoke from the camp fire, are indeed a most desirable part of the hunt.

It was on just such a memorable occasion that the story of Old Drum originated.

Yarn telling, pipe smoking, tobacco chewing, and friendly banter were always exciting parts of the evening's entertainment, as was the age-old question as to whose dog was the best runner or trailer in the pack. Old Drum, whose canine qualities were known far and wide, was generally accepted by everyone to be the best of them all. Numerous stories had been told of his great achievements, many of which were actually true.

On this particular night, after everyone had talked and listened the usual amount, a peaceful quiet settled down on the gathering, and was broken only by the snapping of the fire, and the sighing of the wind in the tall trees. This same wind carried faintly to their ears the sound of barking dogs, and it was silently agreed, by nodding of heads, that Old Reynard had been routed, and the chase was on. This silence was a kind of soothing something that everyone expected and everyone enjoyed.

The baying of the hounds was getting louder when someone unable to keep quiet any longer voiced his opinion, and perhaps the opinion of all those present, that Old Drum, as usual, was leading the chase.

By ones and twos the hunters would slip away from the fire and listen carefully, turning first one ear and then the other toward the sound.

After careful deliberation a voice from the darkness said, "That's my dog coming up there now, getting a little closer to the front all the time, just as liable to beat Old Drum tonight as not." Some way he didn't sound very eager, just a little hopeful, yet kinda fearful, that perhaps some day some dog would beat Old Drum.

"Sure," they would brag, "my dog's gonna do it some day." But still they just couldn't hide that feeling of pride as they would say, "Yep, that Old Drum is still head man."

So on went the chase, mile after mile. Time slipped by. Tension grew. Everyone was getting excited; arguments arose; bets were made. The pace was faster. Positions of certain dogs were disputed, but about that head dog, everyone was certain that Old Drum was still leading the chase.

So time passed by. The fire burned low. The light grew dimmer, and the air just a little colder, when a rustle in the leaves that sounded like an avalanche, caused them all to turn and look.

And to their amazement, there lay Old Drum, stretching and yawning, and edging just a little closer to the fire.

HEIGH-HO SILVER

Heigh-ho Silver everywhere
Tonto's lost his underwear.
Tonto says "Me no care,
Lone Ranger buy me brand new pair."

HI-O SILVER, JUMP-ROPE RHYME

Hi-O Silver,
I've got a date.
Meet me at the corner
At half-past eight.
I can do the rumba,
I can do the splits,
I can wear skirts
Above my hips.
Hi-O Silver,
I have no date.
Don't meet me at the corner
At half-past eight.
I can't do the rumba,
I can't do the splits,
I can't wear skirts
Above my hips.

For most Americans the printed page and the moving picture are far more important ways of transmitting ideas, inspiration, and entertainment than oral tradition, the method of folklore. This means that we must look to the media of mass communications as the main source of the popular heroes of today and tomorrow. Their gestation period, compared with that of the folk hero, is very short. Indeed, it seems often to occur overnight. The media make it possible for us to watch the process whereby a popular hero is born and grows up. Furthermore, we may sometimes see a popular hero, who is produced by a kind of artificial insemination, achieve the legitimacy of a genuine folk hero. The material on Paul Bunyan collected here provides a case study of this process.

Because the popular hero is artifically generated, the purpose for which he is designed is often obvious. It may be clearly commercial: to sell lumber, like the Paul Bunyan tales, or to sell a new liqueur, like the Renegade advertisement. It may be promotional, in a Chamber of Commerce sense, to instill local pride and to attract attention to a locality. It may be a creative whimsy like the Annie Christmas hoax, the brain child of roguish newspapermen who wanted to sell a feature story and to see how much hokum the readers would tolerate. In most cases, something is being offered for sale, and a Marxist critic might well ask what else is to be expected in a capitalist society. But this isn't the full story.

Once Paul Bunyan was established as a popular hero, he inspired imitation. Pecos Bill, the cowboy; Joe Magarac, the Hungarian steelworker; and Febold Feboldson, the prairie strong man, are among his robust progeny. And fabrications though they are, invented by clever writers, usually for some identifiable purpose, and transmitted by the mass media to a literate audience, they still have a significant relationship with genuine folklore. In the first place, they conform to the same patterns as the culture heroes, tricksters, prowess heroes, and ethical heroes of traditional lore. In the second place, whatever their initial purpose, once they have arrived they give coherence to various groups such as people of the same occupation (Bunyan) or locality (Feboldson) or ethnic background (Magarac), while at the same time they help to unite these groups with the nation as a whole. Finally, they are a measure of the fertility, adaptability, and creative imagination resident in American culture today. The way we learn about our heroes is the biggest thing that has changed. The heroes themselves and their essential functions haven't changed very much.

So phony, perhaps calculated, somewhat mercenary and controlled at first, it is heroic material like the titanic doings of Paul Bunyan and his kin that Americans in the twentieth century have come to recognize most readily. Popular heroes created by the media have settled into the national consciousness as surely as the folk legends and songs and sayings about John Henry and Jesse James. In time other heroes will join the parade: Superman, maybe, taking his place beside Paul Bunyan, Muhammad Ali beside John L. Sullivan, Snoopy tagging along behind the Lone Ranger's silver steed.

THE BIRTH OF PAUL BUNYAN

Mr. Carleton C. Ames of River Falls State College, Minnesota, writing on "Paul Bunyan—Myth or Hoax?" . . . does not accept the tales of Paul Bunyan as indigenous folklore, i.e., as yarns actually spun by the shanty boys of logger camps in Wisconsin, Minnesota, and Michigan. His father, he says, was raised in an atmosphere of logging camps and his grandfather spent most of his active life in the logging industry. They had never heard of Paul Bunyan nor did those old-timers with whom Mr. Ames had informal conversations, men from camps representing Minnesota, Wisconsin, Maine, also some from Canada, including Scandinavians. Not one had ever heard Paul Bunyan mentioned. . . .

The real impetus given the Paul Bunyan legends seems to have been commercial. They first gained currency in the publications of the Red River Lumber Company of Minnesota, which started giving Paul Bunyan stories in 1914. At that date Paul was unknown to the general public and to the distributors and sawmill people. Whether Paul was an earlier or a new creation . . . it seems certain that America in general would not have heard of him but for W. B. Laughead, who may be termed the real promoter of the yarns and who was no doubt the creator of many of them. . . .

Since this article was written I have heard from Mr. W. B. Laughead, who now represents the California Plant of the Red River Company at Westwood, Lassen County, in that State. His tall tales seem to have been the first to appear in print. I have a copy of the first booklet of the Company on Paul Bunyan, issued in 1914. . . . The part of Mr. Laughead's letter responding to my inquiries concerning Paul Bunyan is of especial interest to folklorists:

Where and how Paul Bunyan started no one seems to know, although there is evidence that he was known in Eastern States, where logging was at its height before the Great Lakes period of the industry. The material in the 1922 Red River book *Paul Bunyan and His Big Blue Ox* was gathered from many sources. It started with what I remembered from Minnesota logging camps (1900–1908). I then picked up odds and ends from letters we received from columns that ran in various newspapers, in the Seattle *Star* by Lee J. Smits, the Portland *Oregonian* by DeWitt L. Hardy, and others. Correspondence to the *American Lumberman* also provided clues. Most of this had appeared between the publication of our first booklet in 1914 and the trade journal advertisements we ran in 1914–1916, and the compilation of *Paul Bunyan and His Big Blue Ox*, 1922.

At original sources (conversation of loggers and other workers) I never heard the narrative form. Even the extemporaneous additions came as offhand mention of events and Paul's inventions, as if referring to well-known facts. My own "invention" included names of characters, "Babe," "Brimstone Bill," "Johnny Inslinger," "Sourdough Sam," etc. . . . My writing has been almost entirely advertisements.

On the whole, the testimony of Mr. Laughead tends to strengthen the assumption that the floating of Paul Bunyan stories was commercial. . . .

Paul Bunyan in 1910: First Time in Print

On June 24, 1910, in the Illustrated Supplementary Section of the Detroit News Tribune appeared an unsigned story called The Round River Drive. Looking into the authorship of the tale I was informed by Ford M. Pettit, Director of Reference Work on the staff of the Detroit News, that The Deacon Seat Tales in which the story appeared were written by James MacGillivray. Subsequent correspondence with Mr. MacGillivray at Oscoda, Michigan, confirmed Mr. Pettit's statement. Consequently to Mr. Mac-Gillivray belongs the distinction of being the first known writer to record any of the exploits of Paul and his hardy crew. . . .

The portion of the News Tribune item which told the story of the Round River Drive reads as follows:

She broke up early that spring. The river was runnin' high, and black from the color of the snow, of course, and all hands went on the drive. Bunyan was sure that we would hit either the 'Sable' or Muskegon, and he cared not a dam which, fer logs was much the same allwheres.

We run that drive for four weeks makin' about a mile a day with the rear, when we struck a camp what had been a lumberin' big and had gone ahead with its drive, what must have been almost as large as Bunyan's from the signs on the banks. They'd been cuttin' on a hill forty too, which was peculiar, for we didn't know there could be two such places.

We drove along for another month and hits another hill forty, deserted like the last one, and Paul begins to swear, for he sees the price of logs fallin' with all this lumberin' on the one street.

Well, we sacked and bulled them logs for five weeks more, and blamed if we didn't strike another hill forty. Then Bunyan gets wild. "Boys," he says, "if we strike any more of them d—n camps, logs won't be worth 30 cents a thousand, and I won't be able to pay you off—perhaps some of you want to bunch her? Let's camp and talk it over," he says.

So we hits for the deserted shacks, and turnin' the pyramid corner, we was leadin' butts right into—our schoolma'am. And there at her feet was those two coons what had been blown up months ago, and at their feet was the hams! Then we knowed it was Round river, and we'd druv it three times.

Did we ever locate it again? Well, some!

Tom Mellin and I runs a line west, out of Graylin' some years afterwards when logs gets high, thinkin' to take them out with a dray-haul and we finds the old camp on section 37. But the stream had gone dry, and a fire had run through that country makin' an awful slashin' and those Round river logs was charcoal.

Paul Bunyan in 1910: *The Oral Tradition*

We spent the summer of 1910 working in the camp of the Palmer Lumber Company at Palmer Junction, Oregon, some fifty miles north of LaGrande. During all this time Tabor kept a careful diary, so that when we began to hear tales told, he made notes on them. Among other things we heard stories about Paul Bunyan told by a lumberjack named Duffy. Recently I asked Tabor whether he had read any of the books about Paul Bunyan and it appeared that he had not, but had his entire impressions from the accounts heard thirty-five years ago. Fortunately, he has been able to find his old diary. For the rest, I let him speak through his diary and accompanying letter.

From Edward O. Tabor's Notebook

Paul Bunyan digging Puget Sound—first logger in the West. His big blue ox—fed bales of hay—men could drown in its tracks—winter of the blue snow—windmills pump water 3 hours before breakfast for the crew—3 men to oil it—3 windmills run hot boxes twice a week.

Big camp—waiters on roller skates in the diningroom —potato peels carried out by cartloads and fed to the blue ox—prune seeds shoveled out of the kitchen window. A garden rake was the curry comb for the blue ox. You had to climb a Sycamore to get the hayseed out of his left ear. Paul's son and his 48" cylinder threshing machine in Dakota and their eighty-five 3-horse teams to carry away the grain, looked like the tail end of the Ringling Brothers Circus—3 men riding on horseback telling the farmers "next." Took two men to blow the whistle because there was so big a crowd for dinner.

Old man Bunyan is now running the Jerusalem Short Line hauling holy water from the Dead Sea to the River Jordan.

Dear Stith:

The above sketchy notes are copied almost word for word from a Notebook which I have kept and which happens to have 3 pages given to our lumber camp experiences in Oregon in 1910. I wish I could remember the stories which I told your mother and your brother, Bill, about Paul Bunyan. At that time, we remembered the story distinctly and I can remember how your mother and brother enjoyed the tales fresh from the woods. The notes in my book recall some of the themes vividly, even now. I wish we had Duffy and Duffy's language and brogue to give the story the proper flavor. No university man could do that. Victrola recordings might. Duffy should be found, if he still lives, to preserve a body of great themes. . . .

I remember one theme not mentioned above, namely, that when Paul decided to either move camp or haul big timber (trees 300 feet long), he would hitch the blue ox's tugs, which were elastic, to the camp or timber and then would get Babe (the blue ox) to take three or four steps forward, each step being about 20 rods, and he would stand still, with his breast and yoke forward, his feet planted in the ground, and he would wait a second or two until the elasticity in the tugs pulled the camp or the timber up to him, and then he would repeat this performance until the camp was moved. Duffy had better language than I have. The Puget Sound theme was very dramatic as I remember it. Paul had cleaned up all the lumber in the middle West and when he came to the Pacific coast he found the trees so big and the work to be done so large and the facilities so small, that he decided to dig Puget Sound in order to have room enough to float his logs. He hitched Babe to this giant scoop or shovel, and in a day or two, he dug out Puget Sound and had enough water for the logs and the mill.

Many of the lakes in Minnesota and in Washington were made by the hoof prints of Babe.

Our gang also made a great deal of the winter of the blue snow. I also seem to remember that he had Big Swede as a helper, but details slip me. . . .

Sincerely yours,
Edward O. Tabor

Told at the Paul Bunyan Winter Carnival

An old timer, who likes to spin yarns of the great Paul Bunyan, sat in the back of a Bemidji [Minnesota] store.

A severe cold wave, driving down from the Arctic, had dropped the temperature to 30 degrees below zero.

"Bathin' weather," the old timer sneered.

He cocked his feet on the stove rail and inquired: "Ever hear about Paul Bunyan and the Year of the Two Winters?"

And then, over the crackle of the fire, he told of a winter so cold the snow turned blue.

The tale is only one of many that compose the legend of the mythical Paul Bunyan.

Bunyan yarns now are being spun by the hundreds because this week Bemidji will celebrate its annual Paul Bunyan winter carnival. Every man in town must grow a beard for the carnival, at which the winter sports enthusiasts will seek to rival the feats of the mythical Bunyan.

According to old timers:

Bunyan built Lake Huron as a corral for milk whales when he learned whales were mammals.

He started the Mississippi river by emptying a pan of dishwater.

He built a fire under a lake in which he dumped a carload of peas and a herd of oxen, and made pea soup for his logging crew.

(He brought a paddle wheel steamer from New Orleans to cruise around the lake and stir the soup.)

He brought the Swedes to Minnesota after selling the state to the king of Sweden.

And went through the longest, coldest winter ever heard of.

It was so cold the snow turned blue, and it grew progressively colder until next fall, when winter set in again.

Loggers in Paul Bunyan's day grew beards to protect their faces, and the beards grew to tremendous lengths.

"Some of the boys had the ends of 'em knitted into sox," the old timer said.

A low lying cloud bank was swiftly converted into a mountain of solid ice. That was the first of the glaciers.

The mercury in Bunyan's thermometer dropped so low it was three years climbing back to zero. Snow fell so heavily Paul had to dig down to find the forests, loggers were lowered on ropes to fell the trees.

"It was so cold," the old timer said, "the wind froze up in sheets."

Bunyan then had it sawed and stored in chunks for summer.

Paul Bunyan in the Oil Fields

With the development of the oil industry in the second half of the nineteenth century, it was quite natural that the heroic Paul Bunyan should be adopted into a trade which called for just as much strength as logging and even more courage, determination, and resource. Beginning in West Virginia, Paul became the embodiment of superhuman ability as an oil man, and he was known wherever there were American oil-workers.

My introduction to this legendary figure came during the summer of 1920 spent in the Hewitt field, near Ardmore, Oklahoma. I was learning the game as a "boll-weevil" and so was the victim of many "sells," such as being sent for a left-handed monkey-wrench or the pipe-stretchers. The old-timers particularly enjoyed making casual references to miraculous time and labor saving practices that the powerful and ingenious Paul Bunyan used on his rig. There was nothing, however, like a cycle of stories; there were no extended tales. . . .

. . . I went out to the camps, but I found no considerable body of narrative. Either I failed to discover an old-time tale-teller with the genuine creative fancy, or I lacked the key to unlock their word-hoards. My efforts resulted in a heterogeneous mass of incidents that spoke of Paul Bunyan more often as a rig-builder and driller, but also as a pipeliner, a tank-builder, and even as a constructor of telegraph lines.

These fragmentary incidents, I became convinced, were the shreds of a widespread and varied legend of Paul Bunyan as an oil field hero; yet the legend, new as it was in a comparatively new industry, seemed to be succumbing to the machinery of modern life so fatal to all folk creation. I have tried to give this disjected material a semblance of coherence.

Paul Bunyan appears in the oil-fields as a jack of all trades who nevertheless is proficient in each far beyond the best of his rivals. He is regarded by the different groups of workers as having had a large part in developing the tools and methods of their trade. His own huge strength and uncanny skill, however, enable him often to discard the slow and cumbersome conventional practices. For instance, as a rig-builder, as the oil-field carpenter is called, he demonstrated clearly that he was supreme. He could sight so accurately that no plumb line was necessary. The arduous and difficult job of "pulling," "running," and "sighting" a derrick, *i.e.*, building it, took Paul only one day, thereby saving two days of the usual time, as well as the labor of two men. The customary hatchet was too light for him; his weighed eight pounds and drove any nail to the head at a single blow. He could build a pair of the great wooden "bull wheels" in half a day, hang the massive "walking-beam" by himself, and "skid a rig" (the whole derrick) several yards over by hand. If any timbers, or even the crown block, fell off the structure in the process of building, Paul, who worked below, caught them in his hands to save the lumber as well as the heads of those who might be underneath.

Bunyan was such a powerful and tireless worker, and so considerate of his men, that he used to let them sleep half the tour while he did alone the work of the crew of five. His childish pride in his own ability led him to perform many stunts. One day without help he built a rig and "spudded in" the hole with a Ford motor. He boasted that he could dig faster with a "sharp-shooter" than any crew could drill, but since he could never find anyone to call his bet, he did not try this feat. It was not uncommon for him, whenever he grew impatient in building a rig, to drive a sixteen-pound hammer into the ground so deep that the oil came to the surface without drilling. This practice was deplored by the operators because it called for the very inconvenient and wasteful task of dipping the oil out of the hole.

Sometimes Paul's fiery nature caused even greater losses. The visits of officious "high-powers" often made him lose control of his hot temper. At these times the crew ran frantically for cover and left him to vent his rage in a wholesale smashing of derricks for a mile around. The most violent manifestation of this weakness brought him a fortune. One day while up in the derrick, he grew terribly angry at one of his crew who was below. Paul hurled his hatchet at the man with such force that, missing its aim, it penetrated the ground so far that oil gushed up. Quickly forgetting his anger, Paul and his crew set about casing and cementing the hole. The well brought him a million dollars, every cent of which he spent for Mail Pouch tobacco. He had conceived the scheme of soaking his tobacco in corn whiskey and making a "clean-up" by selling it to the oil-field "bullies." His own appetite got the better of him, however, and he chewed it all himself.

Paul did not waste his time with derricks of the usual size. His structures towered far above their conventional neighbors and had telephone connections for each member of the crew. After drilling started, the derrick man was able to come down only twice a month, for pay-day. On one occasion Paul determined to break his record for height. He built the structure up, up, up until it became so tall that he and his crew moved to Heaven and lived there while they finished their work. Paul determined to drill a well worthy of his derrick. He penetrated to China before he stopped drilling.

While building another tall rig, at Bakersfield, California, Paul had a remarkable experience. He was up on the derrick at work when a terrific wind storm carried him out to sea. His first conscious moment found him alone in the Pacific 500 miles from land with his hatchet in his hand, astride a board. A whale appeared and attacked him. Paul fell into the water, killed the big fish with a single blow of his hatchet, and, mounting the dead whale, paddled with his plank back to California.

As a driller Paul Bunyan is quite as striking a figure. He was equally at home on a rotary or on a standard rig; in fact, he devised most of the implements and practices of the trade. His naive humor is seen in the names used by every driller, toolie, and rough-neck: the "head-ache post"; "Maud," the heavy break-out tongs; "bull-wheel" and "calf-wheel"; the "lazy-bench," and many other names. On his own rig, when he was using a rotary, he did not unjoint the drill-stem in small sections, to be stacked in the derrick, but simply ran the 2,000 feet of steel pipe up into the air and held it in his hands until the bit was changed. For his own convenience, to allow him to leave the rig, he invented a way of winding the drillpipe around a big drum. He thus saved many days of the time usually required to drill a well. His boilers were so big that anyone who carelessly went near the injectors was sucked up inside. If a boiler blew up, Paul jumped astride it and rode it back safely to earth; he would not be baffled by such annoyances as that.

His experiences on a standard tool rig were often bizarre and colorful. One time while drilling in a mountainous country, he ran on to a "granite-rock" and pounded for a week without making any apparent progress. He put on an extra set of jars without any effect; a third and a fourth set of jars did not help materially, and he finally put on fifteen sets in a desperate effort to save the hole. The terrific pounding jarred the whole lease up fifty feet above the surrounding land before he broke through the rock. On another mountain-side location Paul drilled what seemed to be a very deep hole. Finally he ran into "soft diggin'" and decided to set casing before going any farther. He started putting in the casing; it kept going down until it seemed that it wouldn't stop. At last one of the crew who had gone over to another location on an errand came running back to tell him that the pipe was coming out the other side of the mountain. Paul discovered that the "tough diggin'" had deflected the tools; he had drilled through the mountain; the casing had run out and made a pipe-line for two miles down the valley. Another experience was more tragic. Paul was drilling in Mexico this time. There was a heavy flow of rubber that drenched the whole rig and cooled before it could be washed off. The poor toolie, who was up in the derrick, could not keep his hold on the slippery boards and fell. He hit the rubber-covered floor and bounced for three days and nights. They finally had to shoot him to keep him from starving to death.

Paul Bunyan's Wife

Research into the Bunyan saga has to be pursued with caution. Lumberjacks have a keen sense of humor which they are apt to exercise at the expense of the tenderfoot inquirer. They sometimes relate a series of Bunyan yarns to try the credulity of the listener and then confess that they never actually heard these stories in the camps. One may even have the experience of the young and earnest inquirer who walked up to an old jack and without preliminaries asked if he had ever heard of Paul Bunyan. The old lumberjack squinted for a moment, paused in his whittling, shifted his cud of chewing tobacco, and said: "Yes, I knew Paul and his wife. She had a double row of teats and used to give milk for our camp."

THE SAGA OF PECOS BILL

According to the most veracious historians, Bill was born about the time Sam Houston discovered Texas. His mother was a sturdy pioneer woman who once killed forty-five Indians with a broom-handle, and weaned him on moonshine liquor when he was three days old. He cut his teeth on a bowie-knife, and his earliest playfellows were the bears and catamounts of east Texas.

When Bill was about a year old, another family moved into the country, and located about fifty miles down the river. His father decided the place was gettin' too crowded, and packed his family in a wagon and headed west.

One day after they crossed the Pecos River, Bill fell out of the wagon. As there were sixteen or seventeen other children in the family, his parents didn't miss him for four or five weeks, and then it was too late to try to find him.

That's how Bill came to grow up with the coyotes along the Pecos. He soon learned the coyote language, and used to hunt with them and sit on the hills and howl at night. Being so young when he got lost, he always thought he was a coyote. That's where he learned to kill deer by runnin' them to death.

One day when he was about ten years old a cow-boy came along just when Bill had matched a fight with two grizzly bears. Bill hugged the bears to death, tore off a hind leg, and was just settin' down to breakfast when this cow-boy loped up and asked him what he meant by runnin' around naked that way among the var-mints.

"Why, because I am a varmint," Bill told him. "I'm a coyote."

The cow-boy argued with him that he was a human, but Bill wouldn't believe him.

"Ain't I got fleas?" he insisted. "And don't I howl around all night, like a respectable coyote should do?"

"That don't prove nothin'," the cow-boy answered. "All Texans have fleas, and most of them howl. Did you ever see a coyote that didn't have a tail? Well, you ain't got no tail; so that proves you ain't a varmint."

Bill looked, and, sure enough, he didn't have a tail.

"You sure' got me out on a limb," says Bill. "I never noticed that before. It shows what higher education will do for a man. I believe you're right. Lead me to them humans, and I'll throw in with them."

Bill went to town with this cow-hand, and in due time he got to enjoyin' all the pleasant vices of mankind, and decided that he certainly was a human. He got to runnin' with the wild bunch, and sunk lower and lower, until finally he became a cow-boy.

It wasn't long until he was famous as a bad man. He invented the six-shooter and train-robbin' and most of the crimes popular in the old days of the West. He didn't invent cow-stealin'. That was discovered by King David in the Bible, but Bill improved on it.

There is no way of tellin' just how many men Bill did kill. Deep down he had a tender heart, however, and never killed women or children, or tourists out of season. He never scalped his victims; he was too civilized for that. He used to skin them gently and tan their hides.

It wasn't long before Bill had killed all the bad men in west Texas, massacred all the Indians, and eat all the buffalo. So he decided to migrate to a new country where hard men still thrived and a man could pass the time away.

He saddled up his horse and hit for the West. One day he met an old trapper and told him what he was lookin' for.

"I want the hardest cow outfit in the world," he says. "Not one of these ordinary cow-stealin', Mexican-shootin' bunches of amateurs, but a real hard herd of hand-picked hellions that make murder a fine art and take some proper pride in their slaughter."

"Stranger, you're headed in the right direction," answers the trapper. "Keep right on down this draw for a couple of hundred miles, and you'll find that very outfit. They're so hard they can kick fire out of a flint rock with their bare toes."

Bill single-footed down that draw for about a hundred miles that afternoon; then he met with an accident. His horse stubbed his toe on a mountain and broke his leg, leavin' Bill afoot.

He slung his saddle over his shoulder and set off hikin' down that draw, cussin' and a-swearin'. Profanity was a gift with Bill.

All at once a big ten-foot rattlesnake quiled up in his path, set his tail to singin', and allowed he'd like to match a fight. Bill laid down his saddle, and just to be fair about it, he gave the snake the first three bites. Then he waded into that reptile and everlastingly frailed the pizen out of him.

By and by that old rattler yelled for mercy, and admitted that when it came to fightin', Bill started where he left off. So Bill picked up his saddle and started on, carryin' the snake in his hand and spinnin' it in short loops at the Gila monsters.

About fifty miles further on, a big old mountain-lion jumped off a cliff and lit all spraddled out on Bill's neck. This was no ordinary lion. It weighed more than three steers and a yearlin', and was the very same lion the State of Nuevo León was named after down in old Mexico.

Kind of chucklin' to himself, Bill laid down his saddle and his snake and went into action. In a minute the fur was flyin' down the cañon until it darkened the sun. The way Bill knocked the animosity out of that lion was a shame. In about three minutes that lion hollered:

"I'll give up, Bill. Can't you take a joke?"

Bill let him up, and then he cinched the saddle on him and went down that cañon whoopin' and yellin', ridin' that lion a hundred feet at a jump, and quirtin' him down the flank with the rattlesnake.

It wasn't long before he saw a chuck-wagon, with a bunch of cow-boys squattin' around it. He rode up to that wagon, splittin' the air with his war-whoops, with that old lion a screechin', and that snake singin' his rattles.

When he came to the fire he grabbed the old cougar by the ear, jerked him back on his haunches, stepped off him, hung his snake around his neck, and looked the outfit over. Them cow-boys sat there sayin' less than nothin'.

Bill was hungry, and seein' a boilerful of beans cookin' on the fire, he scooped up a few handfuls and swallowed them, washin' them down with a few gallons of boilin' coffee out of the pot. Wipin' his mouth on a handful of prickly-pear cactus, Bill turned to the cow-boys and asked:

"Who the hell is boss around here?"

A big fellow about eight feet tall, with seven pistols and nine bowie-knives in his belt, rose up and, takin' off his hat, said:

"Stranger, I was; but you be."

Bill had many adventures with this outfit. It was about this time he staked out New Mexico, and used Arizona for a calf-pasture. It was here that he found his noted horse Widow-Maker. He raised him from a colt on nitroglycerin and dynamite, and Bill was the only man that could throw a leg over him.

There wasn't anythin' that Bill couldn't ride, although I have heard of one occasion when he was thrown. He made a bet that he could ride an Oklahoma cyclone slick-heeled, without a saddle.

He met the cyclone, the worst that was ever known, up on the Kansas line. Bill eared that tornado down and climbed on its back. That cyclone did some pitchin' that is unbelievable, if it were not vouched for by many reliable witnesses.

Down across Texas it went sunfishin', back-flippin', side-windin', knockin' down mountains, blowin' the holes out of the ground, and tyin' rivers into knots. The Staked Plains used to be heavily timbered until that big wind swiped the trees off and left it a bare prairie.

Bill just sat up there, thumbin' that cyclone in the withers, floppin' it across the ears with his hat, and rollin' a cigarette with one hand. He rode it through three States, but over in Arizona it got him.

When it saw it couldn't throw him, it rained out from under him. This is proved by the fact that it washed out the Grand Cañon. Bill came down over in California. The spot where he lit is now known as Death Valley, a hole in the ground more than one hundred feet below sea-level, and the print of his hip-pockets can still be seen in the granite.

I have heard this story disputed in some of its details. Some historians claim that Bill wasn't thrown; that he slid down on a streak of lightnin' without knockin' the ashes off his cigarette. It is also claimed that the Grand Cañon was dug by Bill one week when he went prospectin'; but the best authorities insist on the first version. They argue that that streak of lightnin' story comes from the habit he always had of usin' one to light his cigarette.

Bill was a great roper. In fact, he invented ropin'. Old-timers who admit they knew him say that his rope was as long as the equator, although the more conservative say that it was at least two feet shorter on one end. He used to rope a herd of cattle at one throw.

This skill once saved the life of a friend. The friend had tried to ride Widow-Maker one day, and was thrown so high he came down on top of Pike's Peak. He was in the middle of a bad fix, because he couldn't get down, and seemed doomed to a lingerin' death on high.

Bill came to the rescue, and usin' only a short calf-loop, he roped his friend around the neck and jerked him down to safety in the valley, twenty thousand feet below. This man was always grateful, and became Bill's horse-wrangler at the time he staked out New Mexico.

In his idle moments in New Mexico Bill amused himself puttin' thorns on the trees and horns on the toads. It was on this ranch he dug the Rio Grande and invented the centiped and the tarantula as a joke on his friends.

When the cow business was dull, Pecos Bill occasionally embarked in other ventures; for instance, at one time he took a contract to supply the S. P. Railroad with wood. He hired a few hundred Mexicans to chop and haul the wood to the railroad line. As pay for the job, Bill gave each Mexican one fourth of the wood he hauled.

These Mexicans are funny people. After they received their

share of the wood they didn't know what to do with it; so Bill took it off their hands and never charged them a cent.

On another occasion Bill took the job of buildin' the line fence that forms the boundary from El Paso across to the Pacific. He rounded up a herd of prairie-dogs and set them to dig holes, which by nature a prairie-dog likes to do.

Whenever one of them finished a nice hole and settled down to live in it, Bill evicted him and stuck a fence-post in the hole. Everybody admired his foresight except the prairie-dogs, and who cares what a prairie-dog thinks?

Old Bill was always a very truthful man. To prove this, the cowboys repeat one of his stories, which Bill claimed happened to him. Nobody ever disputed him; that is, no one who is alive now.

He threw in with a bunch of Kiowa Indians one time on a little huntin'-trip. It was about the time the buffalo were getting scarce, and Bill was huntin' with his famous squatter-hound named Norther.

Norther would run down a buffalo and hold him by the ear until Bill came up and skinned him alive. Then he would turn it loose to grow a new hide. The scheme worked all right in the summer, but in the winter most of them caught colds and died.

The stories of Bill's love-affairs are especially numerous. One of them may be told. It is the sad tale of the fate of his bride, a winsome little maiden called Slue-Foot Sue. She was a famous rider herself, and Bill lost his heart when he saw her riding a catfish down the Rio Grande with only a surcingle. You must remember that the catfish in the Rio Grande are bigger than whales and twice as active.

Sue made a sad mistake, however, when she insisted on ridin' Widow-Maker on her weddin'-day. The old horse threw her so high she had to duck her head to let the moon go by. Unfortunately, she was wearin' her weddin'-gown, and in those days the women wore those big steel-spring bustles.

Well, when Sue lit, she naturally bounced, and every time she came down she bounced again. It was an awful' sad sight to see Bill implorin' her to quit her bouncin' and not be so nervous; but

Sue kept right on, up and down, weepin', and throwin' kisses to her distracted lover, and carryin' on as a bride naturally would do under those circumstances.

She bounced for three days and four nights, and Bill finally had to shoot her to keep her from starvin' to death. It was mighty tragic. Bill never got over it. Of course he married lots of women after that. In fact, it was one of his weaknesses; but none of them filled the place in his heart once held by Slue-Foot Sue, his bouncin' bride.

There is a great difference of opinion as to the manner of Bill's demise. Many claim that it was his drinkin' habits that killed him. You see, Bill got so that liquor didn't have any kick for him, and he fell into the habit of drinkin' strychnine and other forms of wolf pisen.

Even the wolf bait lost its effect, and he got to puttin' fish-hooks and barbed wire in his toddy. It was the barbed wire that finally killed him. It rusted his interior and gave him indigestion. He wasted away to a mere skeleton, weighin' not more than two tons; then up and died, and went to his infernal reward.

Many of the border bards who knew Pecos Bill at his best have a different account of his death.

They say that he met a man from Boston one day, wearing a mail-order cow-boy outfit, and askin' fool questions about the West; and poor old Bill laid down and laughed himself to death.

THE SAGA OF JOE MAGARAC, STEELMAN

While working in the steel mills along the Monongahela valley of Pennsylvania, I often heard one of the many Slavs who worked in the mills call one of his fellow-workers "*magarac*." Knowing that literally translated the word *magarac* meant jackass, but knowing also, from the tone of voice and the manner in which it was used, that it was seldom used derisively, I questioned my Hunkie leverman as to its meaning as understood by the Hunkie workers. He gave me a vivid explanation. He said:

"Magarac! Dat is mans who is joost same lak jackass donkey. Dat is mans what joost lak eatit and workit, dats all."

Pointing a finger toward another of his race, a huge Hunkie by the name of Mike, who was walking from the open hearth, he yelled:

"Hay! Magarac!"

At once, Mike's thumbs went to his ears, and with palms outspread his hands waved back and forth while he brayed lustily in the best imitation of a donkey that he could give.

"See," my leverman said, "dere is *magarac*. Dat is Joe Magarac for sure."

Then they both laughed and spoke in their mother tongue, which I did not understand.

It was evident enough there was some definite reason for the use of the word, and obviously that reason was, to their way of thinking, very humorous.

By working for a considerable number of years with a Hunkie on my either side, by sitting many evenings in their homes, and, since turning my thoughts to writing, by spending a good deal of my time with them, I have been fortunate enough to hear considerably more about Mr. Joe Magarac.

I find that Joe Magarac is a man living only in the imagination of the Hunkie steel-mill worker. He is to the Hunkie what Paul Bunyan is to the woodsman and Old Stormalong is to the men of the sea. With his active imagination and his childlike delight in tales of greatness, the Hunkie has created stories with Joe Magarac as the hero that may in the future become folklore of our country. Conceived in the minds of Hunkie steel-mill workers, he belongs to the mills as do the furnaces and the rolling-mills. Although the stories of Joe Magarac are sagas, they have no tangible connection, so far as I have been able to find, with the folklore of any of the countries which sent the Hunkie to these United States. It seems that the Hunkie, with the same adaptability that has made him into the best worker within our shores, has created a character and has woven about him a legend which admirably fits the environment in which he, the Hunkie, has been placed. Basically, the stories of Joe Magarac are as much a part of the American scene as steel itself.

The Marriage of Mary Mestrovich

One time long time ago, mebbe one, two hundred years, dere was living by Hunkietown, Steve Mestrovich. Steve he workit by open-hearth and he have daughter Mary. Oh, my, Mary was pretty girls: she have big, blue eyes, hairs yellow lak hot steel, hands so little lak lady, and big strong teeths. She was prettier as Hunkie girls from any place and all fellows what workit for mill comit around and say for Steve:

"Mebbe pretty soon now be plenty good ting Mary gone catch hoosband."

Den Steve he always laughit and he say:

"Gone on home little mans. Mary no gone marry some one lak you who not catch much steam dis time. Mary gone marry only strongest mans what ever lived, ya betcha."

Mary say nothing. She joost sit around and hope dat pretty soon mans who be all right comit, for she was seventeen year old already and she no lak dat business of wait around. Steve get sick too from wait around and nobody comit. Steve say:

"What the hells kind business is dat. I catch best young girls as anybody: she pretty lak hell, she wanit mans, she wanit be good for mans and joost stay home and raise kids and no say nothing, dats all. And, by God, I catch two hundred dollar I give myself for wedding present and I no find mans for her. By God, I tink gone have party dis time and ask everybody comit and den we see who is best mans for Mary, ya damn right.

"So, Old Womans, next Sunday we gone have party. You makit plenty prune-jack and I gone to Pittsburgh and gone have two barrel beer sent out on truck."

Well, Steve's old lady she makit plenty prune-jack and all week she workit makit cake and Mary she help and she was glad lak anyting because Sunday gone be party and she tink mebbe she gone catch mans lak 'nother Hunkie girls who have mans who workit in mills. Steve tell everybody what gone be on Sunday and all dem young fellows start lift 'em up dolly bars in eighteen-inch mill, its big hunk steel what is heavy lak anyting, so dat dey strong for Sunday. Some peoples say dey betcha dat Pete Pussick be strongest mans for Pete lift 'em up dolly bars same lak it was toothpicks; other peoples tink maybe Eli Stanoski be better mans and he gone catch fine girls lak Mary for *frau*. But everybody wish it gone be him who is best mans and everybody dey lookit at Mary and dey feel strong lak anyting.

So pretty soon next Sunday be dere and Hunkie mans comit from Monesson, comit from Homestead, comit from Duquesne, comit from every place along Monongahela River and dey gone show everybody how strong dey be dis time. Steve have everything fix 'em up: in big field down by river bank he put two barrel beer what comit from brewery, he put table what he makit where Old Lady gone put prune-jack and cakes, and he have three dolly bar what he get from mill.

One dose dolly bar its joost little one what weigh three hundred fifty pound, 'nother dolly bars weigh five hundred pounds, and big ones she weigh more as 'nother two put together. On side of field Steve has fixed 'em up benches where womans can sit and nurse baby and see what gone happen and right by dere is platform lak have on Fourth July with red paper and flags and everyting. Mary she sit on platform where all young fellow can see good and see what dey gone get after dey lift 'em up dolly bars. Mary was dressed up lak dere was big funeral: she have on dress what mudder had made from wedding dress and it was pretty I tell you. It was all red and green, silk too, and on front was big bunch lace what *Groszmuter* in old country makit. On finger was ring with nice red stone what Steve buy from company store and on head was nice scarf. Oh, sure, when Mary go on platform everybody say she was prettier as Queen.

Steve was happy mans dat day, I tell you. He was dressed up with sleeves down and tie on his neck and he walkit 'round lak he was Boss everyting and he yell lak dis:

"Hi, yah, Pete. You tink you feelit all right to-day? By Gods, better you no be sick and have lots steam. It take plenty strong mans to lift 'em up dolly bars."

And den he say:

"Hi, yah, Eli. What matter you? Mebbe better you take 'nother drink prune-jack. You lookit little bit white in face lak you was 'fraid Pete nor Sam gone be stronger as you. By Gods, was I young mans same as you I lift 'em up whole damn three bars one time to catch fine girls lak Mary."

Den he laughit and pull mustache and walkit up and down same lak nigger mans on pay day.

After everybody visit 'round little bit and everybody havit one, two, three drink all around, Steve get on platform for makit speech. He say:

"For coople year now everybody what is young mans and feelit pretty good dey comit for me and dey say: 'Pretty soon Mary gone lookit for mans. Me! I catch good job for blast furnace. Me, I be best mans what workit for mills, best mans what ever poke 'em out tap hole. Sure I be strong lak anyting. Whats matter Mary no be *frau* for me?'"

Den Steve he stopit speech and he stickit out tongue lak he was not feelit so good for stomach and he say:

"By God, I hear so many mans talk lak dat dat it makit me sick. So I fix 'em up plan and now we gone see who be good mans for marry Mary, daughter of Steve Mestrovich, me, by God, what is best mans who was cinderman for open hearth any place. First, everybody gone lift 'em up small dolly bars. If anybody no lift 'em up dat little one den he joost go and play with little kids, dats all. Next, everybody gone to lift 'em up second dolly bars. Anybody no lift 'em up dat second dolly bars den dey go and sit with womans and stay out road of strong mans while strong mans gone show him something. Den, everybody gone lift 'em up last dolly bars. By Gods, dis dolly bar she be from bloomer mill and she is so heavy dis time dat I no can lift him myself. Somebody gone lift 'em up dat hunk steel den by Jezus, dats mans what gone marry Mary, ya damn right, ya betcha."

So all young fellows pull off shirt and get ready to lift dolly bars. First mans was Pete. Pete he walkit over by dolly bars and he lookit 'round for make sure everybody see and den he reach down and lift 'em up easy lak anyting. Everybody holler:

"Dats big mans, you Pete! Dats good fellow!"

Pete he no say nothing. He joost walkit away and he laughit lak he feel sure he gone be plenty strong dis time. Den Eli gone over by dolly bars and he lift 'em up easier as Pete and everybody yell some more. Two fellows what comit from Homestead try and lift 'em up and dey no can move dolly bars from ground. Den everybody laughit and say:

"Ho! Ho! Ho! What kinds mans you have dat place, Homestead? At home I got boy joost two year old and I tink mebbe I better send him over by your mill to help you out little bit. Better you go and play with kids little mans so dat you no monkey 'round with big mans and get hurt dis time."

Well, after dat dey lift 'em up second dolly bars and what you tink? Only three mans catch enough steam to do dat. Dat was Pete, dat was Eli, and dat was 'nother mans from Johnstown. Dis fellow from Johnstown was plenty big mans all right and he catch plenty steam to lift 'em up dolly bars. He do dat easy as anyting. Den all his friends dey yell hoorah for him and dey make face at Pete and Eli same lak dey was sure dat dis fellow was gone be strongest mans and take Mary Mestrovich back to Johnstown with him. People from dis place no lak dat business. Dey lak much better Pete nor Eli gone be strongest and den Mary Mestrovich stay dis place which have better mills as Johnstown anytime. Dat mills at Johnstown is joost little place what when do best she can no makit more as one, two hundred tons steel a day. So peoples get mad at dese peoples from Johnstown and dey gone makit bet dat Pete nor Eli gone be stronger as dis fellow. Pete say dat is good business and nobody gone worry nothing, he gone lift 'em up big dolly bars joost same lak he lift 'em up little ones. Den Pete he gone over take big, big drink prune-jack and he spit on hands. Den he reach down and grab hold dat big dolly bars. His arm crack like paper bag, his eye stick out from head lak apple, sweat run down face same lak he was workit in front furnace in July. By Jezus, dat dolly bars no moveit one inch from ground. Den Eli try it and he was no good dis time. Peoples from dis place groan lak somebody kick in stomach when dey see dat. Dey tink for sure now dey gone lose Mary Mestrovich, dey gone lose money, and den dey must listen when peoples from Johnstown say:

"Ho! Ho! Ho! Over by dis place mans is joost same lak old womans who talkit all time and no doit nothing. Comit over by Johnstown where mans so strong dat dey tear down mill and fix 'em up again every day joost for fun."

Den dis fellow from Johnstown takit two big, big drinks prune-jack, he twist mustache so she look lak King, and he wave hand for everybody. Den he fixit his feets so he no be shaky and bend down and grabit dat dolly bars. He give big pull, and den another big pull and he grunt all time lak pig at dinner time. He pullit so damn hard on dat dolly bars dat his hand come loose and he fallit down on ground.

Peoples from dis place feelit much better: she is not so easy as dis fellow tink. Johnstown fellow mad lak *frau* when hoosband get drunk and spend all money on pay days. He joomp up from ground and he cuss lak hell and he grabit dolly bars again. No good dis time neither.

"Ho! Ho! HO!"

A laugh lak dat comit from somebody in crowd. Everybody lookit 'round to see who laughit lak dat; mans from Johnstown straighten back and he say:

"Who laughit for me? By Jezus Christ a Mighty, if dat fellow who laughit tink he be so strong mans whats matter he no comit here and pick 'em up dolly bars? Den after he do dat I gone broke his neck."

Den out from crowd walkit biggest mans whatever I see: he have back bigger as door, hands bigger as Pete nor Eli together, neck lak big bulls, and arm bigger as somebodys round waist. I betcha my life he was more as seven feets tall. Oh, he was prettiest mans whatever anybody ever see. Everybody lookit everybody and everybody say:

"Who is dat fellow anyhow?"

And everybody shake heads no dey never see before.

Dat fellow he walkit over to dolly bars and he was laughit so hard he have to holdit his belly so dat he can stand on feet. Dat fellow from Johnstown he takit pull at trousers, he spit on hands and he gone take slug at dat fellow. But dat mans he grabit fellow from Johnstown with one hands and with 'nother he pick 'em up dolly bars. Den he hold 'em out and shake until mans from Johnstown yell he was so 'fraid.

By Gods, everybody was white lak sheet. Dey never see before mans what was so strong lak dat. But dat fellow put dat fellow from Johnstown down so easy as little baby by mudder and he say:

"Nobody be 'fraid nothing. I no wanit hurt nobody, no wanit makit trooble. Joost havit little bit fun, dats all."

Steve Mestrovich walkit over and he say:

"What kind mans you are? Which place you comit from?"

And dat fellow answer:

"My name is Joe Magarac, what you tink of dat, eh?"

Everybody laughit for dat for *magarac* in Hunkie mean jackass donkey. Dey know dis fellow is fine fellow all right when he say his name is Joe Jackass. Den dis fellow say:

"Sure! Magarac, Joe. Dats me. All I do is eatit and workit same lak jackass donkey. Me, I be only steelmans in whole world, ya damn right. Lookit for me; I show you something."

He pull 'em off shirt and everybody lookit. By Gods, he no tell lie. He was steelmans all right: all over he was steel same lak is from open hearth, steel hands, steel body, steel everything. Everybody say:

"What the hells you tink of dat?"

Joe Magarac say:

"Dats all right, dats good business for me. Me, I was born inside ore mountain many year ago. To-day I comit down from mountain in ore train and was over in ore pile by blast furnace."

Den he laughit and twist dolly bars in two with hands.

Steve Mestrovich smile lak somebody givit him cold beer on hot day and he takit Mary by hand and leadit her over to Joe Magarac: dis time he gone catch best hoosband for Mary dat was in whole country. Joe Magarac takit long look at Mary and he say:

"Oh, boy, I never see such pretty girls as dat. You makit fine *frau* for anybodies. But dat is no business for me. What you tink, I catch time for sit around house with womans? No, by Gods, not me. I joost catch time for workit dats all. Be better all right if Mary have hoosband and I tink I see her get little bit dizzy in head when she lookit for Pete. Dats good, for after me dis Pete is best mans in country."

Joe Magarac close one eyes for Steve and Steve close one eyes for Joe Magarac and Mary was happy lak anyting for she lak dat Pete all right better as anybody. Fellow from Johnstown get black in face and he stomp 'round mad lak anyting, but he 'fraid say anyting for fellow who was made out of steel and who comit from ore mountain. So he go away.

Everyting was fixed 'em up all right den: Priest comit with altar boy and Pete and Mary kneel down and pretty soon dey was hoosband and *frau*. First one to dancit with bride was Joe Magarac. Den everybody get drunk, have big time and was happy as anyting.

Joe Magarac Makes Steel

Joe Magarac was workit every day and every night at mill and same lak before he was makit rails with hands. Pretty soon dat pile of rails in yard get bigger and bigger for Joe Magarac is workit so hard and after coople months yard was full, everyplace was rails. When Joe Magarac see dat he joost laughit and workit harder as ever. So one day roller-boss he comit up from down by finishing mills and he say to Joe Magarac who was workit by his furnace in open hearth. Roller-boss he say:

"Well, Joe Magarac, I guess we gone shut mill down early dis week. Dis time we catch plenty rails everyplace and we no catch many orders. So by Gods, we gone shut mill down Thursday night and we no start 'em up again until Monday morning. Mebbe you gone put slow heat in furnace: you tell stockman give you fifty-ton stock. You put 'em in stock and give furnace slow fire so dat she keepit warm and be ready for start 'em up on Monday."

Joe Magarac he act lak he gone say something and den he no say nothing and roller-boss tink everyting gone be all right dis time and he gone away.

When next Monday comit mans gone back to work for open hearth. Den dey see dat Joe Magarac is not workit on furnace dat morning. Everyplace dey lookit and dey no see Joe anyplace. 'Nother mans was workit on Noomber Seven and pretty soon when Noomber Seven was ready for tap 'em out melter-boss gone down to platform to see what kind steel dat slow heat makit. He was standit by ingot mould and pretty soon he heard voice what say:

"How she lookit dis time?"

Melter-boss lookit 'round and he no see nobody and den dat voice say again:

"It's me, Joe Magarac. I'm inside ladle."

Melter-boss turn around and he lookit inside ladle and he see Joe. Joe was sitting inside ladle with hot steel boiling up around neck. Melter boss was scared lak anyting and he say:

"What the hells you do in dere, Joe Magarac? Better you gone crawl out dat ladle right 'way or I tink maybe for sure dat she gone melt you up."

Joe Magarac close one eyes for melter-boss and he say:

"Dats fine. Dats good business, dats joost what I wanit. By Gods, I be sick dis time of mill what shut down on Thursday and no start 'em up again until Monday. What the hells I gone do all time mill is shut down anyway? I hear big boss say dat he was gone makit two, three good heats steel so dat he gone have best steel what we can makit for buildit new mill dis place. Dey gone tear down dis old mills and makit new ones what is gone be best mills in whole Monongahela valley, what gone be best mills in whole world. Den by God, I get plan: I gone joomp in furnace when steel is melted down and dey gone melt 'em up me, who was made from steel, to makit steel to makit dat mills. Now Mr. Boss you gone listen for me and I gone tell you someting. You gone take dis ladle steel what has me inside and you gone pour 'em out in ingot mould and den you gone roll 'em out and makit beam, channel, and maybe one, two piece angle and you gone take dat steel and makit new mills. You do lak I say for you and you gone see you gone have best mills for anyplace. Good-by."

Den Joe Magarac sit back down in ladle and hold his chin down in boiling steel until he was all melted up. Pretty soon dey pour him out in ingot mould.

Well, after dey roll 'em out dat heat and dey cut 'em up dey see dat dis time dey have best steel what was ever made. Oh, my, dat steel was smooth and straight and it no have seam or pipe nothing. Den melter-boss he gone 'round for everybody and he say:

"Now we gone have best mills for sure. You see dat steel? By Gods, nobody ever see steel lak dat before and dats joost because Joe Magarac he makit dat steel. Sure, he's inside and now we gone takit dat beam and dat channel and we gone build finest mills what ever was."

Dey do lak melter-boss say and dat is why all young boys want to go for mill, and dat is why when somebody call Hunkie *magarac* he only laughit and feel proud as anything, and dat is why we catch the best mill for anyplace, ya damn right!

Is Joe Magarac Folklore?

Is there any folklore content to be found in the Magarac story? Of course there is. [Owen] Francis obviously knew something about steel mills. A number of the embellishments might very possibly be authentic. Magarac is credited with squeezing out rails bare-handed and making cannon balls with his bare hands as you would make snowballs. He catches fifty-ton ladles when the crane-chain has broken. He scoops up molten steel in his hands to see whether it is hot enough for pouring. He makes horseshoes out of steel bars with little effort. My interviews indicated the strong probability that these feats are part of the lore of the mills. Joe McKay, who started to work in the McKeesport mills at the turn of the century, told me about Henny Palm, a big Swede, who could make horseshoes and pretzels out of bar stock with his bare hands. Andy Hurdick, a barber opposite the Edgar Thompson Works in Braddock for over forty years, told me about a man remembered as "Armstrong Joe" who made neckties out of thick bars. Albert Stolpe of Duquesne told about a Mike Lesnovich who could do the same. These tall tales refer to a personal hero. Joe Magarac was never mentioned. This seems to indicate that Francis took his manufactured tale, added a few local tall tales, and wrapped them up in the Magarac bundle.

The Last Word on "Magarac"

The word *magarac* is to be found in Croatian and Serbian only. In spite of this, it is applied to a hero who, when identified with any particular group, is identified as a Hungarian. If Magarac had been identified with another Slavic group, one might argue that the name was borrowed because of language similarities. But Hungarian is not a Slavic language and is entirely different from it. *Magarac* is not a Hungarian word and cannot be found anywhere in the language. Yet, the authors give us a Hungarian steel hero but reach over to give him a Slavic name. This error can easily be made by someone who is manufacturing a "hero" and who has no understanding of the cultural and language differences between the Slavs and Hungarians.

The word *magarac* means "jackass" in Croatian and Serbian. While it would be inconceivable for us to think of an Anglo-Saxon folk hero with such a name, we have unquestionably accepted it as proper for a hero of the Slavs and Hungarians. The only possible remaining claim to its authenticity then was that there may have existed positive connotations in the minds of the people who used it. . . .

The attitude of the people towards the word *magarac* was exactly the opposite. No matter what the national roots of the informants, everyone knew its meaning. There was absolute unanimity as to its connotation. *Magarac* is a word that is never used without spit and a sneer. In fact, I had to be careful in discussing it with my informants so that I would not be misunderstood. I spoke to Paul Blazek, prominent editor, publisher, and printer of Slavic publications and asked him what it meant to call someone a *magarac*. He said, "To call him that is to lower a man to dirt that is worse than after pigs pass over it." When I mentioned it to Leo Skoda, an old-time resident of the mill town of Clairton, he was embarrassed because I was using the word in front of his wife and daughter. Steve Berko, a moulder at one of the U.S. Steel foundries, put it even more directly. He said, "You call someone that and he'll beat your head in." When I asked Eli Strenich, a millworker for more than forty years, about the sort of person he would call a *magarac*, he told me this story in point:

He described a man in the old country, riding along the road on a *magarac*, smoking a long-stemmed pipe. The *magarac* stopped and refused to go on. "Then," says Strenich, "this man takes the pipe out of his mouth, and jabs the *magarac* in the behind with its stem. The *magarac* starts to move and the man puts the pipe *back in his mouth*. Now, which one is the *magarac*?"

FEBOLD FEBOLDSON, PRAIRIE BUNYAN

Originally the protagonist of a number of yarns, by known authors, in Gothenburg, Nebraska, newspapers, Febold made his debut before the general public in an article "Paul Bunyan and Febold" published by Paul Robert Beath in the *Prairie Schooner* (VI, 59–61) in 1932. Mr. Beath's yarn narrates "How Paul Bunyan and Febold Became Acquainted." It is supposed to be told by Bergstrom Stromberg, who is "over 90" and who is a "grand-nephew of Febold"; "Bergstrom remembers both men well." Febold's deeds were selected and written up or edited by Mr. Beath for the Nebraska Folklore pamphlets of the Writers' Project in 1937. . . . The stories of Febold published in the Writers' Project pamphlet do not name the tellers or give place and date. They are not "documented" in scholarly fashion. The fact is that Febold, the prairie hero, originated as a flight of fancy, patterned after Paul Bunyan, and he owes most of his fame, I think, to Mr. Paul Beath, who though not his creator, has spun many stories about him and floated him into fame. . . .

The character Febold, the strong man, and his name, seem to have been created by Wayne Carroll, a local lumber dealer, who wrote a column under the name of Watt Tell in the now defunct Gothenburg, Nebraska, *Independent*. This series began about 1923. Later Carroll used Febold in advertising that he wrote for his lumber company. Febold could never have been made a lumber hero like Paul Bunyan, for there are no trees on the great plains. So he became a hero wrestling with the adversities of the prairie region, tornadoes, droughts, extreme heat and cold, Indians, politicians, and disease. Later matter, concerning Febold, from the pens of Carroll and Don Holmes and other contributors, appeared in the Gothenburg *Times*, 1928–33, and sporadically since. . . .

But for Paul R. Beath I fear Febold might have died with the early newspaper yarns about him. . . . In answer to inquiries from me he wrote:

> I first became aware of Febold when stories of him were appearing in the Gothenburg *Times*. About this time I read James Stevens' *Paul Bunyan* (1925). I recognized the resemblance of Febold to Paul. . . . It was during this period that I started contributing an occasional story to the *Times*. . . . My stories were mostly adaptations of those I heard about town, yarns of various types, not however Febold yarns. These I elaborated and embellished to fit Febold and what I conceived to be his character, i.e., an indomitable Swedish pioneer who could surmount any difficulty. As a boy and young man I worked my way as a night clerk in a hotel in Gothenburg where I heard literally thousands of stories told by traveling salesmen and other garrulous wayfarers. I suppose I received clues to many of the stories from this ever-flowing stream.

As a contemporary instance of the type of yarning to which he refers, Mr. Beath tells that when he was traveling by bus from Schuyler to Grand Island, Nebraska, recently, a passenger exclaimed that he saw a rabbit. Another passenger promptly said, "That is no rabbit but a Kansas grasshopper." Asked how he knew, he answered that rabbits are as big as coyotes in the Nebraska region. This bantering and yarning was continuing when Mr. Beath left the bus at Grand Island.

Paul Bunyan and Febold Become Acquainted

Bergstrom always begins by telling you how Paul and Febold became acquainted. It was the year they were appointed by the Federal Government to re-establish the Kansas-Nebraska State Line. That was right after Paul had leveled Kansas. Before that time the State had been the most mountainous in the country. Then Paul, with the aid of Babe, had turned the mountains over and had found them flat on the bottom. But in levelling Kansas he had accidentally erased the northern boundary, so that no one could tell where Kansas ended and Nebraska began.

Since neither Paul nor Febold could read, write, figure, or operate surveying instruments, they were forced to rely on their wits. The giant logger made a mess of the job by trying to plow a furrow from Colorado to Missouri with his Blue Ox. The result is the channel of the Republican River which is nearly parallel to the State Line, but which is very crooked and too far north. Febold accused Paul of being drunk, but after it was explained that Kansas was a dry State at that time, he was almost forced to admit that a man cannot make a straight line without mechnical aids.

Almost, but not quite. Febold would never admit that anything was impossible. He began to experiment with eagles and bumble bees. It took fifteen years, but he finally succeeded in breeding bees as large as eagles. He hitched one of his best specimens to a plow. This bee made a bee-line, the straightest thing in nature, directly between Kansas and Nebraska. Thus the State Line was re-established and Febold again proved to the world that nothing is impossible.

Febold's Post Holes

When Febold first came west in the early days there was no need of posts or post holes, because there was no cattle or cultivated land. But as the frontier pushed across the Mississippi and onto the plains the pioneers began to feel the need of fences. They were familiar with only the two kinds which they had used back east, the rail fence and the stone fence. Since there were no stones or trees on the plains the early settlers were stumped. And they would be sucking their thumbs yet if it hadn't been for Febold and his post holes.

Just about this time barbed wire was invented and Febold got busy and bought a few thousand miles of it. His problem now was to get posts to put the wire on. This he did by digging post holes in the fall and letting them freeze all winter. Just before the first spring thaw he would dig up the holes and varnish them. Then he would put them partially back in the ground and string the wire. In time the varnish would wear off and leave the bare poles standing.

JOHNNY KAW, PAUL BUNYAN'S LATEST OFFSPRING

My acquaintance with the Kaw stories began in July 1970, when I visited the Agricultural Hall of Fame at Bonner Springs, just west of Kansas City. "Ag Hall" is an imperfect but promising American counterpart of the European folk museum, displaying all manner of domestic antiques and historical machines and implements, and putting on old-time "threshing bees" for summer visitors. At the end of a row of ancient sewing machines and butter churns, next to a hand-crank washing machine, stood a five-foot wooden statue of "Johnny Kaw," a stout blond farmer with his wheat cradle at the ready. I was curious about the statue as an interesting bit of handiwork, so I asked a museum employee for an explanation and was told that it was indeed Johnny Kaw, "the wheat farmer's Paul Bunyan."

No one at the museum seemed to know much about the fellow, but the director generously gave me two copies of the Johnny Kaw pamphlet, the only written source he knew containing the Kaw "legends." After I examined the twenty-eight page booklet, I became more interested in Kaw. My wife and I spent the summer with her parents in Hiawatha, Kansas, and I questioned a number of farmers and acquaintances about Johnny Kaw. However, none of the farmers had ever heard of him. These potential informants included many descendents of 19th century pioneer Kansas wheat-farmers in "Kaw's wheat country." Furthermore, the Kaw narratives in Dr. George Filinger's book were more like folk tales than legends, in that they had a logical structure, sensible endings, specific geographic settings, and morals which were implicit or explicit. What had seemed on the surface to be a legitimate compilation and rewriting of connected tales and legends began to suggest what Richard Dorson has called "fakelore." All my efforts to collect relevant tales and information proved unsuccessful, and I could find no publications except Dr. Filinger's pamphlet and a handful of newspaper articles. Kaw seemed to be a "fake hero," and Filinger seemed to have created him as W. B. Laughead created Paul Bunyan. I surmised that the Kaw legends were not folklore but rather "literature" with no known oral sources and no circulation in tradition.

Thus, on April 8, 1971, I drove to Manhattan, Kansas, to track down the essential facts of the Kaw phenomenon. The trip proved extremely successful. I first called on William E. Koch, a folklorist in the English Department at Kansas State University. His special interest is western folklore and folk life. Bill was very helpful and gave me his afternoon. Bill Koch and George Filinger are well acquainted, and Bill took me to meet Filinger. Dr. Filinger is a gentlemanly retired professor of horticulture (palmology), a mild-mannered and cordial hobbyist and local historian who has dedicated his energies to "establishing" Johnny Kaw as a local hero on the order of, but superior to, Paul Bunyan. *The Story of Johnny Kaw* is his only publication. His magazine subscriptions include *Good Old Days* and *True West*, and the furnishing and memorabilia about the house suggest a lively man with a keen interest in history, culture, and antiques. Dr. Filinger cares very much for his region of Kansas ("wheat country"), and he avidly peruses local history. In conversation, he stated that he did "cook up" Johnny Kaw, after he read about Paul Bunyan and was unhappy that there was no farmer's hero to challenge the prodigious lumberman from the north woods. The Manhattan town centennial in 1955 offered an opportunity for Filinger to write about the city's history; and a year earlier he and other local literati began writing periodic articles for the local newspaper. The articles based on historic events were not sufficiently popular, and friends requested something "more exciting" than the actual historical episodes which seemed dull and unromantic to an audience accustomed to such entertainment fare as "Gunsmoke," "Wyatt Earp," and "Tombstone Territory." . . .

At least half of this "ballad" is taken up with an account of how Johnny straightened out the Jayhawk. (The mascot of Kansas State University is the wildcat, and that of Kansas University at Lawrence is the jayhawk, and the two schools are long-time rivals in sports.)

Dr. Filinger maintains that there is a seed of genuine oral tradition supporting his tales "down south" of Manhattan, but Bill Koch doubts that such is the case. Neither Mr. Koch nor his folklore students have ever collected the Kaw stories. It is evident that Filinger did invent the "story" of Johnny Kaw, but with a scramble of other stories as a basis. The only problem is that Filinger neglected a clear statement that his story was fabricated by himself in his published booklet. He obviously did not set out to crib ideas from fugitive sources or to dupe readers; his motive seemed to have been pure and hearty patriotism. The problem is that readers cannot tell that the stories are in fact inventions, except by a very careful examination of the text. Filinger does not tell us in the book that he invented the stories, and no mention is made of his references or oral sources. His one-page preface does suggest the spurious nature of the story and his real intention in writing the book:

> Volumes have been written about many American and foreign heroes, some real, some mythical, and their many deeds of valor and/or rascality. Some were famous for their game hunting escapades like Davy Crockett of Tennessee. Others were great sailors who roamed the seven seas like John Buck of Wisconsin, the immortal Norwegian. You no doubt have read of wild Pecos Bill of Texas who was raised by coyotes and didn't see a human until he was ten years old. . . .
>
> Anyone around steel mills in Pennsylvania can tell you about Joe Magarac the steel worker, who stirred molten steel with his bare hands. Then there was Kemp Morgan, hero of Oklahoma oil fields. . . . And surely you

have heard of the Irish civil engineer, Finn MacCool who dug the Grand Canyon? Then there was Paul Bunyan. . . .

Have you noticed that there is not one Real Farmer on the list? You may well ask, "Why?" The answer is simple. Farmers are by nature modest and do not publicize their outstanding feats. For instance, Johnny Kaw the great wheat farmer of Kansas kept his exploits to himself. Since he never bragged about himself and Kansans are not wont to show off, no one has taken the trouble to tell the rest of the world about Johnny Kaw. He has always been accepted as a great pioneer and just taken for granted. Now that Kansas has attained the mature age of one hundred years, Johnny Kaw should be recognized because he was representative of the Spirit of Kansas.

What, then, are the Johnny Kaw "stories" all about? The following is a rough outline of the narrative which summarizes its basic elements. According to the story, the family of U.S. Kawmandokansan decided to move to Kansas from Michigan; U.S. heard that Bunyan had cleared the land of whiskey trees, and it looked inviting. After crossing the Missouri River, the two sons of U.S. (John B. and Jim F.) grew so strong and eager for work that they no longer needed the ox to pull the wagon—so the ox was turned loose to wander north where it was found in a blue lake during a blue snow storm by Paul Bunyan, who kept it and named it "Babe the Blue Ox." John B. pulled the wagon while lazy Jim F. sat on the back end and dragged his heels in the ground, in this way, Jim's boot heels dug the mighty Kaw River. The boys fought constantly and stirred up dust storms still visible today. U.S. decided to separate the boys and sent Jim F. south to settle the Neosho River area. The name Kawmandokansan was too long, so old U.S. changed John B. to "Johnny Kaw" and Jim F. to "Jim F. Kansan." Johnny's wheat cradle leveled the wheat country off to facilitate planting from the Missouri River to the

Rocky Mountains. Johnny thwarted tornadoes by cutting their
spouts with his cradle. Jim Kansan had a big fight with Paul
Bunyan down in the Gulf of Mexico, emerged victorious, tied
Paul's ears to Babe the Blue Ox, and plowed the Mississippi River
trench northward with Paul's nose. Johnny was a keen sportsman
and was capable of bagging a dozen prairie chickens with one
sweep of his flintlock rifle. Johnny invented the catfish. A "short
stack" of pancakes to Johnny measured 108 cubic feet (the actual
farmer's "stack" measurement.) Certainly, the Kaw cycle has elements of the Paul Bunyan bag of tricks, but it also contains tales
in which motifs and types of genuine folk tales are observable.

Since the publication of the original *Story of Johnny Kaw* at
the time of the Manhattan Centennial in 1955, a second edition
has appeared; and Dr. Filinger kindly gave me a copy. This new
edition is twice the length of the first booklet. The original stories
and illustrations have not been revised or altered, but another
batch of stories have been "cooked up" and added with more
drawings by Dr. Filinger's friend, Elmer Tomasch (art professor
at Kansas State University.) There has been only mild public acclaim or demand for the Kaw booklets since the Centennial cele-
bration, and Dr. Filinger has been the chief supporter and force
behind an attempt to popularize Johnny Kaw. The newly-written
Preface to Part II (page 29) of the new book states:

> Since the publication of Part I in 1955, many addi-
> tional "facts" have been discovered which justify the re-
> vision of this booklet. The stories continue to reveal the
> many contributions made by this great wheat grower to
> the growth and welfare of the State of Kansas. This ad-
> ditional information should further establish the authen-
> ticity of Johnny Kaw as an outstanding Kansas farmer. A
> statue to his memory has been erected in the city park in
> Manhattan, Kansas.

Included in those additional "facts" are stories testifying to
Kaw's skill as a politician (he invented the "polls" and began the

custom of "tossing a hat into the ring"). This edition also includes a "letter" to Johnny's Michigan cousins telling of the wonderful Kansas land and predicting the present agricultural situation, the fine wheat harvests, and the establishment of a great university. The letter also contains a map of "Kaw's Wheat Land" to assist the Michigan folks in locating Kansas. Other new tales involve Johnny as a shrewd businessman, the inventor of golf and the hot dog, and Filinger's comments on the present well-being of Johnny. After fifteen years, Filinger has realized his dream of a "memorial" to Kaw: a striking twenty-five foot tall concrete statue in the city park has recently been erected. The designers were careful to make the statue at least two feet taller than the statue of Paul Bunyan in Michigan. . . .

The seeds so carefully and diligently sown by Filinger have yielded a gratifying harvest. Johnny Kaw is believed to be a real folk hero by many area school children, and stories do circulate among them—but this situation is largely due to sympathetic school-teachers, and certainly not due to an authentic oral traditional transmission. A good reason why local teachers have picked Johnny Kaw up so readily is that the whole story cycle can be obtained "in the tin," without any problems of conflicting versions or attitudes.

When a folklorist fifty years from now asks the local citizens about the good old days of the 1970s, he will be delighted to find a folk hero in full maturity and circulation. Or will he? The question which only the passage of time may answer is whether or not Johnny Kaw will endure and continue to prosper, long after Filinger and associates have gone. In my opinion, the answer is a qualified yes; but only those stories are likely to prevail that clearly and harmoniously fit with the people's genuine history and heroic concepts and world view. The Kaw cycle is appealing, and much of it may well continue existence and one day rightly be considered as authentic folklore. One crucial test of folk tradition is its tenacity through time—its ability to remain in circulation after its first establishment. The theory that printed sources are injurious to folk tradition is a valid one, but it is of little use when considering material that is itself generated from printed sources. People may not believe that such a giant as Kaw ever existed, but they do believe in what Johnny represents—the perfect paragon of the aggressive, resourceful, tough pioneer spirit. Kaw stands for a concept of the "pioneer spirit" in Kansas, which for many immigrants and settlers was the "promised land" of new untilled soil and the expectation of a better existence.

SARA DeSOTO AND SARASOTA, FLORIDA

Perhaps no legend in all Florida is more popular than that of Sara DeSoto and Chichi-Okobee. . . .

Chichi-Okobee, a young Seminole brave, was held hostage by DeSoto. During his captivity, he fell in love with the explorer's daughter, Sara DeSoto. Chichi fell ill while he was confined to the Spaniard's camp, but the gentle Sara nursed him back to health. Then she fell prey to the tropical fever, whereupon the warrior begged permission to be allowed to return to his tribe for a medicine man. The leave was granted, but the ministrations of the "hex doctor" were futile. Chichi was prostrate with grief when Sara died. He confessed his love for Sara to her father and asked that he be permitted to select Sara's burial site. Aided by hundreds of armed warriors, Chichi-Okobee lowered the remains into Sarasota Bay, the place he thought most beautiful in all Florida. Then he and his braves slashed the bottoms of their war canoes and drowned themselves in the blue waters of the Bay.

WENONAH AND WINONA, MINNESOTA

Winona, Minnesota, received its name from an Indian Legend. Wenonah was the daughter of Wa-pah-sha, Chief of the Sioux Indian tribe, which had a village named Keoxa, standing between the Great River Kitchee Seebee and the blue water now called Lake Winona.

Wenonah, whose first name means "first-born-daughter," was so beautiful that she was often called "Wild Rose of the Prairie."

A young hunter played his reed flute to her and won her heart, but her father and brothers favored another suitor, a terrible warrior named Tamadoks, who was wealthy.

Time went on and the tribe paddled canoes up Lake Pepin many miles to a place where they could find clay for making pottery. Here Tamadoks again pressed his suit so that the father set the wedding day and prepared a great feast.

Wenonah, in despair, climbed to the top of a high rock where she was heard singing her death dirge. Her people below, realizing her purpose, hastened to stop her, the swift Tamadoks leading them all. Before they reached the cliff however, Wenonah had disappeared in the dark waters below.

Ever since, the place has been known as Maiden Rock or Lovers' Leap.

AS STRONG AS ANNIE CHRISTMAS

Annie Christmas, a white woman of prodigious strength, was said to be a real New Orleans product, having lived on Tchoupitoulas Street, Jackson Square, and on the river docks along the edges of the French Quarter. She could sport a black mustache and pass easily for a man with her height of eight feet six inches and her two hundred fifty pounds avoirdupois. She was said to be fearless and took an especial pride in whipping "bullies." "As strong as Annie Christmas" became a popular phrase along the river. She is said to have had, at her death, a string of beads measuring thirty feet to which she had added a bead every time she bit off an ear or nose or gouged an eye out of a cheek. The story goes that she sent word to Mike Fink, one of the bullies of the upper Mississippi, if he ever came her way, she would send him home lashed to a keel-boat.

Many stories developed about Annie's strength, up and down the river between New Orleans and Natchez, adding to her accomplishments. One was that, when the river was high and about to flood the country, she threw up a levee all by herself. She worked as a stevedore along the river and had such great luck at fighting and gambling that she impressed the Negroes to the extent that they claimed her as one of their color. In their stories they glamorized her in life, surrounded her death with romance and her burial with mysticism. They considered her a demi-god and placed her in their pantheon-clan.

"THE RENEGADE"

[To introduce a new product, Heublein, Inc., engaged the advertising agency of Wayne Jervis, Jr., & Associates, Inc. The Agency "created," which is to say invented, "The Renegade Legend," and produced an advertising layout that appeared nationally. It is printed below, followed by a statement from the agency on how the "legend" was generated and why it was believed to be an effective means for promoting the sale of a rum liqueur.]

The Legend.

In the year 1774, a brash, hot-blooded young English officer, in the service of King George the Third, was peremptorily denied his rum rations for presuming to admire his Captain's daughter as she admired her father's ship. In a rebellious rage, the young upstart seized the lugger and the lovely both for himself. Thereby embarking on a sinfully successful career as a privateer, specializing in the pursuit of an exceptionally fine, dark, golden-hued rum that was much sought after by the American Revolutionaries as well as their British counterparts. However, our Renegade would only sell to the Continentals. Thus, the term and the name "Renegade, the Spirit of Rebellion!"

The Facts.

Renegade is indeed a dark, golden-hued, highly select, very different kind of rum-based drink that could well have inspired rivalry between the English and American officers.

Pour it over ice and find out for yourself why Renegade is the legendary rum taste of the New World.

How to Create a Legend

The Renegade Legend was totally created by Barbara Lui, the Creative Director of Wayne Jervis, Jr. & Associates, Inc.

It has no basis in historical fact, although it was carefully researched to accurately reflect the era and locale that is its frame of reference.

The product concept of a rum liqueur was conceived first. Then, in reviewing the history of liquor advertising, it was concluded that stories, narratives and legends were a most effective tool in liquor communication-positionings and could be most dramatically used in a rum project.

In finessing and editing the legend, Ms. Lui used the word "renegade" as part of the copy.

Its use as a name for the product was the next natural order of events. And finally, its full acceptance by the entire group at Wayne Jervis, Jr. & Associates and, our client, Heublein, Inc. completed the cycle.

To our knowledge no one has challenged the legend or, contrariwise, stated that they have ever heard it before.

NOTES

Abbreviations Used in Notes and Index

Child   Child, Francis James. *The Eng-
                                       lish and Scottish Popular Bal-
                                       lads*. 5 vols. Boston, 1882–98.

Folklore in America   Coffin, Tristram Potter, and
                                       Cohen, Hennig, eds. *Folklore
                                       in America*. Garden City, N.Y.:
                                       Doubleday & Co., 1966.

Folklore from the Working Folk   Coffin, Tristram Potter, and
                                       Cohen, Hennig, eds. *Folklore
                                       from the Working Folk of
                                       America*. Garden City, N.Y.:
                                       Anchor Press/Doubleday, 1973.

Laws, *NAB*   Laws, G. Malcolm, Jr. *Native
                                       American Balladry*. Philadel-
                                       phia: American Folklore Soci-
                                       ety, 1964. Rev. ed.

Motif   Thompson, Stith. *Motif-Index
                                       of Folk Literature*. 6 vols.
                                       Bloomington: Indiana Univer-
                                       sity Press, 1955.

Type   Aarne, Antti and Thompson,
                                       Stith. *The Types of the Folk-
                                       tale*. Helsinki, 1961. Rev. ed.

I. GODS, DEMIGODS, AND SUPERMEN

Culture Heroes

"Manabozho, Creator of the Earth": *Journal of American Folklore* (1903), 229, 231.

Collected by James Cleland Hamilton from Alexander Henry's *Travels and Adventures* (1809) and the reports of Assikinack, who died in 1861, "the most famous Ottawa orator of his day." Manabozho, or Nanabozha among the East Central and Central Algonquins, was the most powerful of their supernatural beings. He was the creator of the earth, bringer of fire, preserver from the flood, and founder of the most sacred rites. He was also the Messenger of the Great Spirit and grandson of Nokomis, the Earth. His was a contradictory character and sometimes he was the object of crude jokes and a victim of his own stupidity. Counterparts of Manabozho appear, for example, as Gluskap among the Micmac (see p. 8), Wisaketchak among the Cree, and Wisaka among the Sacs and Foxes.

"Gluskap Tested": *Journal of American Folklore* (1915), 60–61.

From a collection of tales of Gluskap, or Glooscap, dictated to F. G. Speck by Joe Julian and John Joe, Micmac Indians, of Cape Breton Island, Nova Scotia, Canada. Speck states that "they represent local versions of some myths [common] among the northern Algonkin in general."

"Songs of Elder Brother, the 'Papago Christ'": *Bureau of American Ethnology, Bulletin* No. 90 (1929), 15–26.

Frances Densmore made phonograph recordings of the Papago origin myth, the first part of which includes the flood, the death and revival of Elder Brother (Ithoi or I'itoi), and his guiding the Papago people to their lands. The performance combines narrative and songs. She made the recordings "at Vomari village . . . on the Papago Reservation in Arizona, during the spring of 1920 and the following winter." Her main assistant and an important informant was Mattias Hendricks, the chief of the village. Other singers were José Hendricks, José Ascencio, and Rafael Mendez. Ruth Underhill summarizes the Elder Brother origin myth in *Papago Indian Religion* (New York, 1946), 6–14. She observes that the "influence of Christianity has had the effect in raising I'itoi's status as the supreme supernatural, and many now speak of him as the Papago Christ" (p. 315). Elder Brother is so called because of his claim to be the first to emerge after the flood.

"The Three Nephites, Mormon Immortals": *Southern Folklore Quarterly* (1938), 123–29.

Wayland D. Hand has obtained, mainly from periodicals designed for members of the Church of Jesus Christ of Latter-day Saints and from the collectanea of M. Wilford Poulson, references and tales of the Three Nephites in popular tradition. His analysis and description of this material is fully documented. The story of Robert Edge, which he summarizes, was published by Hyrum Belnap under the title "A Mysterious Preacher" in the *Juvenile Instructor*, Vol. 21 (1886), of Salt Lake City. Hand states that "in the vicinity of Lexington [Tennessee] there are still circulating many stories attesting the legendary character of Robert Edge." Hand uses "the term 'legend' . . . in the technical sense, viz., a tale referring to the deeds of saints or stories about religious characters."

For further information, see Hector Lee, *The Three Nephites: The Substance and Significance of the Legend in Folklore*, University of New Mexico, Publications in Language and Literature, No. 2 (1949).

"A Nephite Brings a Spiritual Message": *Journal of American Folklore* (1940), 23–25.

Collected by A. E. Fife in 1939 from Joseph Wood, age eighty-two, of Woods Cross, Utah. Fife provides a background discussion of the basis of the legend of the Three Nephites, its position as a phenomenon of American folklore, and its relation to the legend of the Wandering Jew (see p. 225–30). *Type 777*.

"Pele, Goddess of the Volcano, and the Fisherman": *Journal of American Folklore* (1929), 73–75.

Reported by Melville J. Herskovits and Morris J. Rogers, Jr., from events related by Emily Warrender of Hawaii "who was an eyewitness of many of the incidents recorded in the latter part of our account, and was told the interpretations of them given here." They call attention to the seriousness with which a Hawaiian myth is taken by alien ethnic elements such as the Japanese taxi driver and perhaps even the American geologist. Pele is the powerful Hawaiian fire goddess, closely associated with volcanoes. She appears in various forms, including that of a hag. Note the presence of *Motif* E332.3.3.1 (Vanishing hitchhiker) in this tale. See also the Nephite tale immediately preceding.

"Davy Crockett as Demigod": *Scribner's Magazine* (July 1936), 10.

Max Eastman, in an essay-review titled "Humor and America," reprints this passage from Constance Rourke's *American Humor: A Study of the National Character* (New York, 1931) to support his argument that ultimately Crockett "became a demigod and spoke in his own person." Rourke is quoting from an unspecified *Davy Crockett Almanac*. She states in her biography *Davy Crockett* (New York, 1934) that "the story belongs to the Winter of the Big Snow of 1835, when Crockett set out for Texas" (p. 241). The protagonist of the story is a historical personage, the writing is that of a professional, the medium is print directed toward a mass readership; but the language is informed by the vernacular and the impetus for the imaginative flight is the folk. In America, where the Judeo-Christian tradition prevails, biblical figures such as Jehovah and Jesus are the culture heroes—creating and peopling the world, establishing institutions, and laying down codes of conduct. In this case, however, an unknown writer has transferred certain of these functions to a native American hero, the historical figure Davy Crockett. He is given godlike powers that of course he never had. He frees the frozen sun, a world disaster common in mythologies and similar to the "Sun-snare" *Motif* A728, and related to the myths of the Flood. Thus Crockett becomes a hero akin to Noah, who ensured the survival of mankind during the Flood.

Of course, the Crockett tale, unlike the biblical story of Noah and the Flood, was not believed by the man who wrote it or his readers. For related Crockett material, see pp. 431–36.

Tricksters

"A Trickster Tricked": *Journal of American Folklore* (1925), 484–85.

Among tales collected by Alanson Skinner from Indian informants of the Iowa tribe in Oklahoma in 1914 and 1924. He lists their names but does not indicate which particular tales each tells. The Iowas are of Siouan stock.

The name *Ishjinki* means "trickster." He appears in the form of a rabbit and as such is similar to Manabozho, who, as the Great Hare, sometimes assumes the role of trickster and is himself occasionally tricked (see p. 5). The story is well known among American Indians. See *Motif* K826 (The hoodwinked dancers).

"Hare Rides Coyote": Ibid., 495.

From the Skinner collection, above. This is a variant of the European, *Type* 72 (Rabbit rides fox a-courting).

"Br'er Rabbit and His Tricks": *Journal of American Folklore* (1927), 216–17, 220, 222, 233–34, 236.

Collected by Arthur Huff Fauset. He supplies only sparse information on his sources, as follows: "Br'er Rabbit Fools Br'er Buzzard," from Plateau, Alabama; "No Tracks Coming Back," from Kowalinga, Alabama, and Natchez, Mississippi; "Fox and the Dead Horse," from Jackson, Mississippi; "Baby Rabbits," from Greenwood, Alabama; "Toad Loses His Tail," from "Pappy" Jackson, railroad porter, age about sixty, born St. James Parish, Louisiana; "Toad Loses His Tail: Another Version," from Natchez, Mississippi. These are typical Br'er Rabbit adventures deriving from medieval European and African sources. "Baby Rabbits" is the famous *Type* 15, usually called "Just started, Half done, All gone."

Br'er Rabbit was first popularized through the Uncle Remus stories of Joel Chandler Harris in the late nineteenth century and later the cartoon films of Walt Disney.

"Br'er Rabbit Song": *Journal of American Folklore* (1911), 356.

Collected by Howard W. Odum from unspecified black singers "of the Carolinas." He does not supply a melody.

"Konsti Koponen, the Eyeturner": *Midwest Folklore* (1955), 6–10.

Collected by Aili Kolehmainen Johnson from members of her family in 1946, as indicated in her discussion. They are, respectively, her grandfather, Henry Hankila, Mass, Michigan, an immigrant from Kärsämäki, Oulunlääni, Finland, and fifty-six years old in 1920 when Johnson recalls first hearing his tale; her aunt, Hilja Hankila, Republic, Michigan, age fifty-seven, whose parents were from Finland; her mother, Hilda Hankila Kolehmainen, age fifty-five, whose parents were from Finland; and her father, Theodore Kolehmainen, age sixty-two, who emigrated from Finland. Johnson distinguishes between a *noita*, or wizard capable of actual transformation, and the *silmän-käätäjä*, or eyeturner, who has the power to "turn men's eyes" so that they see whatever he wants them to see. See "A Finnish Eye-turner in Northern Michigan" (p. 237). Cf. *Motif* D921.

"Konsti Cures a Horse": Ibid., 8.

Cf. *Motif* K1036.1.

"Konsti Passes Through a Log": Ibid., 8.

Cf. *Motifs* D216 and D1382.5.

"Konsti and the High-toned Miss": Ibid., 8–9.

A *haituuni neiti*, Johnson explains, is a " 'Finn-English' term meaning 'high-toned miss.' " Cf. *Motifs* D2031.2 and D2031.1.

"Konsti Helps a Poor Farmer": Ibid., 9.

Johnson explains that in Finnish, the word for "leaf" is *lehti*, which also means "newspaper" and "page," as of a book. In a Finnish variant, pages of an almanac are seemingly turned to gold. Cf. *Motifs* D475.2 and D479.

"Old John Tricks the Master": *Southern Folklore Quarterly* (1961), 195–96.

Collected by John Q. Anderson from a student, William H. Little, who heard these "anecdotes about a faithful old slave and his master" from his father, Van Allen Little, a professor of entomology at Texas A & M University. Professor Little remembered them from his boyhood in Northeast Texas. Anderson identifies them as "survivals of African trickster tales" that were adapted to the master-slave relationship of the ante bellum South, but many of them are similar to the "clever servant" motifs known throughout Europe, Asia, and South America. Arthur Huff Fauset prints a version of the coon story from Philadelphia, Mississippi, in *Journal of American Folklore* (1927), 265–66.

"Tom and the Master": *Journal of American Folklore* (1970), 235.

Collected by Roger D. Abrahams from Arlette Jones of Houston, Texas, in 1965. He cites it as an example of a type of story showing extreme aggression, which "commonly turns on some kind of obscene reference in which Marster [*sic*] is not only made the fool but his masculinity is placed in question."

Prowess Heroes

"Mejewedah, Gifted in Magic": *Journal of American Folklore* (1906), 220–22.

Collected by Harlan V. Smith: "Monday evening, October 22, 1894, Kinneoba told me a story, which was interpreted by Quewis." Mejewedah, or Midgewida, is an Ojibwa hero. His name is probably derived from "a term applied to a warrior who has taken scalps or has counted coup or who has done both." For another supernatural bear provoked by a foolish brave, see "The Greatest of the Grizzlies" (p. 461). The transformation flight is common to folk tales all over the world. See *Type* 313.

"Giant Joe Call": *New York Folklore Quarterly* (1953), 5–7.

C. Eleanor Hall has collected the facts and legends about Joe Call, who was born in Woodstock, Vermont, in 1781 and died in Westport, New York. She does not specify her sources for the legendary stories related here, but the motifs are widespread in folklore. In fact, Call seems to have been best known as a wrestler. See *Motif* F617 (Mighty wrestler) and related strong-man motifs in connection with Joe Call and his sister, below.

"Joe Call's Sister": Ibid., 9–10.

Hall records the story of Joe Call's nameless sister but not the names of the informants. Cf. "Francisco as Frontier Strong Man" (p. 196) and Richard M. Dorson, *Jonathan Draws the Long Bow* (Cambridge, Mass., 1946), 125, 126n.

"Clay Allison, Gunfighter": *Southwest Review* (1929–30), 193–94, 197–200.

Retold by Maurice G. Fulton from "stories about Clay Allison . . . discovered among old-timers of New Mexico." Apparently Allison was born in Tennessee about 1840, grew up on a farm, joined the Confederate Army, and took part in the irregular warfare against Union troops attempting to keep order in the West. He then drifted on to the Indian Territory, Texas, and New Mexico. His later years were prosaic: he married, cut down on his drinking, and died in the 1880s of a fall from his wagon.

"Lamar Fontaine, Confederate Sharpshooter": *Tennessee Folklore Society Bulletin* (December 1973), 108–9.

James H. Stone reprints, with an introduction and notes, extracts from an interview of Lamar Fontaine (1829–1921) of Lyon, Mississippi, by a reporter from the New York *Sun* in Memphis, Tennessee, in 1896. Stone writes "that Fontaine was an authentic Confederate hero" but that his stories "improved considerably with age, particularly those dealing with his own heroics." Fontaine's story of how he indicated which enemy soldier he would pick off has a parallel in Babe Ruth's "indicator home run" in the World Series of 1932 between the Chicago Cubs and the Yankees. There is an apocryphal tale that, with a 4–4 score, Babe walked up to the plate, accepted the umpire's call of two strikes, and then pointed his finger toward a spot far out in center field to indicate where he intended to slam the ball, and put it there. Eyewitnesses dispute what happened, but the story persists. See also *Motif* F661 (Skillful marksman).

"Antoine Barada and the Pile Driver": *Southern Folklore Quarterly* (1943), 140–41.

Collected by Louise Pound for an article on "Nebraska Strong Men." Her source was Mari Sandoz, the regional novelist and historian, who "testifies that she knew stories of him when she was a child" and describes him as "a half-breed" whose father was supposed to be "of royal connections in Spain." In "Nebraska's Antoine Barada Again," *Nebraska History* (1949), 286–94, Pound writes that he was born in 1807 near Fort Calhoun, Washington County, Nebraska, and died ca. 1886. Although there are stories "that his father Michael was a Parisian Count" or "a Spanish grandee," this is unlikely. He did serve as representative of the Omaha Indians and was married to "a full-blooded Indian woman."

"John Henry Hammer Songs": *Journal of American Folklore* (1892), 163–64.

Collected by E. C. Perrow. In his famous steel-driving contest with a steam drill, John Henry, the hero of a cycle of tales and ballads, "died with his hammer in his hand" (cf. "Moe Stanley," p. 69). Guy B. Johnson calls him "the Negro's greatest folk character and argues that the fatal contest took place in the 1870s (see *John Henry: Tracking Down a Legend* [Chapel Hill, N.C., 1929]), but the facts of the matter are disputed.

A hammer song is a work song used by laborers as they drive their drill into rock, the rhythm marking the time of the hammer strokes.

Perrow obtained the first of the hammer songs in 1905 from the memory of an East Tennessee mountain white. His other verses are from the undated manuscript of a Mr. Davidson of Indiana and from the manuscript of R. J. Slay, of Mississippi, dated 1909.

"Moe Stanley": University of Pennsylvania Folklore Archive (1973). Unclassified.

Collected by Stephanie Urchich, University of Pennsylvania student, in 1973 from Algie Link of Monessen, Pennsylvania, employed for seventeen years on the rail crew of the Clairton works of the United States Steel Company and then recently retired. He learned it from members of the rail crew. Link was familiar with other versions of the John Henry ballad (Laws, NAB, I, 1) and suggested that the name Moe Stanley was taken from another favorite of Clairton steel mill workers, "Monongahela Sal," about a young girl who is in love with a river pilot of that name.

"John L. Sullivan and Jim Corbett": *Folklore and Folk Music Archivist* (1965), 10–12.

Collected by Richard M. Dorson of Indiana University from Lorry Grant at Columbia Falls, Maine, in July 1956, who first heard it "when I was young." The account of the heavyweight championship bout, the first to be fought under the Marquis of Queensberry rules, is accurate. Sullivan (1858–1918), who had held the title since 1882, was an enormously popular champion for such feats as winning the last bare-knuckles heavyweight championship by defeating Jake Kilrain in seventy-five rounds. James J. Corbett (1866–1933) held the title from his bout with Sullivan in 1892 until his defeat by Robert Fitzsimmons in 1897.

"Babe Ruth: The Body Behind the Bat": *New York Folklore Quarterly* (1975), 99.

Bonnie McGuire has investigated the dimensions of the "heroic stature" of George Herman Ruth (1895–1948), relying heavily on anecdotes reported by sports writers, many of them from clipping folders at the National Baseball Library, Cooperstown, New York. Cf. the prodigious appetite of Charlie Parker (pp. 76–77), and *Motifs* F632, J1468, and X931.

"Charlie 'Bird' Parker": *Keystone Folklore Quarterly* (1972), 54–55.

William E. Lightfoot examines and cites examples of "some of the lore existing, or which has existed, in active, oral tradition concerning the life of jazz musician Charlie Parker" (1920–55), citing Robert Reisner, *Bird: The Legend of Charlie Parker* (New York, 1962) and other printed sources as well as his own taped interviews. He argues that Parker's career fits the pattern described by Orrin E. Klapp whereby "historical personages become legendary" and "even popular heroes of the present day are subject to the myth-making process" (*Journal of American Folklore*, [1949], 11). Here Lightfoot quotes jazz musicians and critics on Parker's mythic stature.

"The Feats of Charlie Parker": Ibid., 53–54.

Cf. "Babe Ruth" (p. 73).

"How 'Bird' Got His Nickname": Ibid., 51–52.

"The Prophet of Pond River Bottoms": *Kentucky Folklore Record* (1975), 41–42.

The nameless prophet is recalled from childhood and described by Mel Tharp of Crossville, Tennessee. The Pond River bottoms are in northwest Kentucky. The power of clairvoyance has long been revered at the folk level, as the legends of Cassandra and Thomas Rymer testify.

Ethical Heroes

"Hiawatha Founds the Iroquois Confederacy": *Journal of American Folklore* (1895), 214–15.

Reprinted by W. M. Beauchamp from William Dunlap's *History of New Netherlands* (New York, 1839), II, 29–30. Ephraim Webster, an interpreter, lived among the Indians and had an Indian wife.

Dunlap knew him in 1815. Horatio Hale (1817–96), the ethnologist, was an authority on the Iroquois. Hiawatha, the Indian statesman and magician, flourished about 1590.

"A Drunken God and a Pious King": Bureau of American Ethnology, *Bulletin* No. 38 (1909), 130–31.

In a monograph on *The Unwritten Literature of Hawaii: The Sacred Songs of the Hula*, Nathaniel B. Emerson published a *mele* or song "cantillated with an accompaniment of expressive gesture . . . given at an awa-drinking bout indulged in by hula-folk" and then summarizes the legend that explains it. Awa, or kava, made from the root of *Piper methysticum*, is an intoxicating drink. Lani-kaula, Emerson notes, was a prophet who lived on Molokai in the midst of a grove of kukui trees, the nuts of which were used as torches to illuminate the revelries of Kane and his fellows. Emerson states that this mele was sung and danced in 1849 at Kahuku on the island of Oahu on the occasion of a visit by King Kamehameha III. In his opinion it is "an admirable specimen of Hawaiian poetry, and may be taken as representative of the best product of Hawaii's classical period."

"Benjamin Franklin's Proverbial Ethics": *Journal of English and Germanic Philology* (1949), 229, 232–33.

Stuart A. Gallacher establishes the "popular currency" of the proverbial sayings that Franklin "form'd into a connected discourse" and published as "The Way to Wealth" by identifying earlier parallels in such collections as Thomas Fuller's *Gnomologia* (London, 1732), Randle Cotgrave's *Dictionary of French and English* (London, 1611), and Henry C. Bohn's *Hand-Book of Proverbs* (London, 1915), which includes John Ray's *English Proverbs* (Cambridge, 1670). Franklin had refined traditional proverbs and used them throughout his *Poor Richard's Almanacs*. To preface the last almanac in this popular series, he presented them as admonitions from a patriarchal figure, Father Abraham, to a crowd at a country fair. Father Abraham's theme is how to get ahead in the world. For Franklin's literary techniques as a purveyor of ethics, particularly the Protestant ethic, through traditional proverbs, see Charles W. Meister, "Franklin as a Proverb Stylist," *American Literature* (1952), 157–66, and Edmund J. Gallagher, "The Rhetorical Strategy of Franklin's 'Way to Wealth,'" *Eighteenth-Century Studies* (1973), 475–85.

"A New York Merchant's Way to Wealth": *New York Folklore Quarterly* (1962), 125–26, 130–35.

Harry E. Resseguie collected legends and superstitions associated with the career of the fabulously successful merchant Alexander Turney Stewart (1801–76). His sources are contemporary newspaper files and memoirs. He provides full documentation. The Stewart version of the rags-to-riches legend reflects the American myth of social mobility. The democratic political system is helped by the belief that an unknown, unpromising individual can make his way from nowhere to the top. The career of Elvis Presley, the "Hillbilly Cat who became the King," is another version of the same story. See pp. 424–26).

"Preacher Dow Raises the Devil": *New York Folklore Quarterly* (1947), 237–40.

Harry M. MacDougal recounts a version from family tradition of a familiar tale about Lorenzo Dow (1777–1834), itinerant evangelical preacher, as famous for his Yankee wit and oddity as for his moral fervor and evangelical zeal. Elizabethtown, Essex County, is in northwest New York.

"Preacher Dow Catches a Thief": *New York Folklore Quarterly* (1948), 47–48.

Henry Charlton Beck reports tales of Lorenzo Dow current in lower Burlington County, New Jersey. They were recorded by Hollis Koster of Greek Bank, whose source, Harvey Ford, "holds memory links with his Granny and uncles, remembering what they told him." Cf. "Recovering Stolen Property" (p. 199). The motifs are ones traditionally associated with parsons and priests. See *Types* 1832f.

"Marie Leveau, Hoodoo Queen": *Journal of American Folklore* (1931), 326–27.

Zora Neale Hurston, the novelist and anthropologist, wrote this sketch of Marie Leveau, based on traditional New Orleans lore, to introduce a section of her collections and study of "Hoodoo in America." She does not cite her sources. For a comparison of Marie Leveau's supernatural powers with those of witches, see *Motifs* G200–299. The reference to the rattlesnake suggests the incorporation of African snake worship and tales of voodoo sorcerers' transformation into snakes brought to Louisiana by Haitian voodoo. See *Journal of American Folklore* (1942), 219 and especially 224–25, and (1954), 395–403.

"A Gambler's Petition and a God's Reply": Ibid., 328–29.

Hurston learned this ritual from Samuel Thomas, "in his seventies, a Catholic hoodoo doctor of New Orleans" (p. 357), who claimed to be Marie Leveau's grandnephew. She states that "practically all of the hoodoo doctors of Louisiana knew the Leveau routines, though most of them have developed also techniques of their own."

In the ritual, the "supplicant" addresses the "god" according to a traditional "routine" and the "god" replies through the "doctor."

"Hasnohanna," or "Has-no-harra," is a jasmine lotion, believed to bring luck to gamblers.

"A Puerto Rican *Décima* on the Death of Franklin Delano Roosevelt": *Folk Music of the Americas* from the Collections of the Archive of American Folk Song, Music Division, Library of Congress, Notes to Album XVIII, 10–11.

Richard A. Waterman recorded this elegy on the death of President Roosevelt as sung by Timoteo Quinones, "a boy of Arecibo who sings in purest *jíbaro* style," accompanied by Manuél Rodriguez Robles of Barrio Sabana, Luquillo, Puerto Rico, on July 16, 1946, at a 4-H Club near Luquillo. The décima is a verse form common in Puerto Rico and Mexico, but rare in folk music elsewhere in Latin America, which was popular in seventeenth-century Spain. Waterman explains that in Puerto Rico "it is the mainstay of folk song, and the *jíbaros*, or countrymen of the interior have developed amazing proficiency in improvising décimas on any given theme." The name is derived from its ten-line stanza, usually octosyllabic and rhyming *abbaaccddc*. For a "Corrido de Presidente Roosevelt," written the day after his death, see *New Mexico Folklore Record* (1946), 7–8. A corrido, in Mexican tradition, is a ballad on current happenings or historical personages. The transcription of the recording is by Thomas Brothers.

"The Purim *Shpil* of Abraham and Isaac": Collection of Shifra Epstein (1976).

Shifra Epstein, a fellow of the Max Weinreich Center, YIVO Institute for Jewish Research, describes the background, production, and performance of a Purim play that was presented on March 16, 1976, at the Bobover *Shul*, Forty-eighth Street and Fifteenth Avenue, Borough Park, Brooklyn, New York (all Yiddish terms have been transliterated according to standard YIVO usage and not according to the dialect of the Bobover Hasidim). Her study of the Purim festival as observed by the Bobover Hassidic community is part of her research as a doctoral candidate in folklore at the University of Texas. For the biblical origin of Purim, see *Esther*, III, 1–13, and IX, 24–26.

II. WORK, PLACES, PEOPLES

Workers

"James Bird, Hero Shot as a Deserter": *Keystone Folklore Quarterly* (1961), 3–7.

Charles A. McCarthy, a resident of Luzerne County, Pennsylvania, has written a sketch of James Bird based on "history as it has been preserved in Luzerne County, his native home." Aware that "many versions of Bird's biography are in circulation orally and in print," he attempts to set the record straight. But he appears to err in following the Luzerne County tradition of the extenuating circumstances of Bird's plan to join General Jackson at New Orleans. In June 1814 Jackson was engaged in a campaign against the Creeks, and as late as November was invading Spanish Florida.

"The Ballad of James Bird": Ibid., 8–12.

George Swetnam reprints "the original text" as it appears in C. F. Richardson and Elizabeth Miner Richardson, *Charles Miner, A Pennsylvania Pioneer* (Wilkes-Barre, Pa., 1916), 67–71. He states that the tune is "The Glooms of Autumn," to be found in William Walker's *Southern Harmony* (Spartanburg, S.C., 1854). See Laws, NAB, 121–22, A 6, for bibliography and discussion.

"Cherry Tree Joe, Raftsman": *Keystone Folklore Quarterly* (1962), 15–30.

George Swetnam began his search for facts, stories, and songs about Cherry Tree Joe McCreery in the late 1950s. Among his most helpful informants was Joseph Dudley Tonkin, a lumberman from Cherry Tree, Pennsylvania, "who clearly recalled knowing Joe McCreery" and showed him "the folk hero's grave, where the stone revealed that he died on Nov. 23, 1895, 'past 90 years of age.'" Swetnam collected the song from Mrs. Jasper Estep, McCreery's great-granddaughter, in Marianna, Pennsylvania. She "remembered how my great-grandfather used to sing that song about himself." The tune was transcribed by Jacob A. Evanson. Swetnam identifies persons and places and explains rafting terms.

"Charlie Glass and the Sheepherders": *Colorado Magazine* (1969), 40–47, 50–51.

Walker D. Wyman and John D. Hart base this "legend" (the term is theirs) of the range war between the cattlemen and sheepherders "largely on interviews conducted . . . with persons who knew Charlie Glass," discreetly unnamed, and newspaper accounts. Glass was "about 65" when he died.

"The Best Straight-edge Man in the World": *Western Folklore* (1961), 23–25.

Collected by William M. Jones from barbers, names and dates not provided. Rocheport was a Missouri River town of about 350 people when the stories of Hugo's prowess with a razor were collected. His clientele included transient railroad men, rivermen, and retired farmers. He seems to have plied his trade there from about 1900 until some time after World War I. See *Motif* F665 (The skillful barber).

"The Tattoo Lady of the Bowery": *New York Folklore Quarterly* (1967), 196, 198–200.

A. S. Bernstein has reconstructed an interview he had with Millie Hull, known as the "Queen of the Bowery," in 1939. By virtue of her personality, reputation, vocation, and to some extent her Bowery life, she exists in the twilight zone between folk and popular art.

"Big Max": *West Virginia Folklore* (1959), 8–10.

Contributed by Carl McKinney of Jackson Addition, West Virginia, to a collection of "Ghost Stories and Devil Stories as told by Fairmont College Students." Similar motifs are found in the E334–336 group.

"Why Students Call Pedro": *Western Folklore* (1947), 228–30.

Collected by Archer Taylor. His student informants were (1) Martha Long; (2), (3), and (4), Kate Ware; and (5) Betty Suffern. Harbison Parker provided information describing the practice. For further information see "Calling Pedro: With Various Explanations" in *Folklore from the Working Folk*, 289–93.

"Perry Martin's Moonshine": *Mid-South Folklore* (1974), 3–6.

William A. Sullivan reports on Perry Martin, a Mississippi Delta folk hero of the recent past. His sources are interviews and "surviving oral narratives." Sullivan defines a folk hero as a "person who best represents and embodies the values of a particular group of people." In this case the "people" are "the river rat folk who live within a twenty-five mile radius of Rosedale [Mississippi]." He quotes William Alexander Percy's description of the river rat from *Lanterns on the Levee* (New York, 1941): "Illiterate, suspicious, intensely clannish, blond, and usually ugly, river-rats make ideal bootleggers. The brand of corn or white mule they make has received nation-wide acclaim. They lead a life apart, unclean, lawless, vaguely alluring." Sullivan states that "to this day the river rat has resisted assimilation into American society. . . ." For a description of moonshine making, see "Moonshining as a Fine Art" in *The Foxfire Book*, edited by Eliot Wigginton (Garden City, N.Y., 1972), 301–45.

Local Characters

The Character of Strap Buckner": *Publications of the Texas Folk-Lore Society* (1930), 143–49.

Florence Elberta Barns "summarizes" these stories about Strap Buckner from *The Coming Empire, or Two Thousand Miles in Texas on Horseback* (New York, 1877) by N. A. Taylor and H. F. McDaniel. Taylor heard them from "a dapper young man" living near La Grange, Texas. Barns identifies the prototype of the legendary Strap as Captain Aylett C. Buckner, an adventurer and a soldier of fortune in Texas by 1812, a member of the Stephen Austin colony who eventually settled on the Colorado River near La Grange. He was killed in the battle of Velasco in 1832. The stories are variations on and reworkings of motifs used about other American brawlers and strong men such as Ethan Allen and Davy Crockett.

"Strap Meets His Match": *Publications of the Texas Folk-Lore Society* (1932), 128–29.

Collected by Florence Elberta Barns from H. B. Parks of San Antonio, Texas, who told her he heard the story from "a Mr. Stephens of San Gabriel, in Milam County."

"Judge Bean Serves as Coroner": *Publications of the Texas Folk-Lore Society* (1938), 254–56.

Told by J. Marvin Hunter, date and informant not given. Roy Bean (ca. 1825–1903), a Kentucky adventurer, went to California in 1847, wandered about Mexico, and eventually became a self-appointed justice of the peace in Texas, who called himself "the law west of the Pecos." He set up his court in his saloon, "The Jersey Lily," in the camp town of Langtry, administering justice whimsically, with the aid of a single law book, a six-shooter, and plenty of liquor.

" 'Big Shot' Bill Greenfield, Adirondack Münchausen": *New York Folklore Quarterly* (1956), 216–19.

Eugenia L. Millard collected tall tales about William Greenfield (ca. 1833–1903) from Walter B. Edwards, a farmer, of Edinburg, Saratoga County, New York, "some years ago." Her informant on "Big Shot Bill's" checker games was Elwyn Tenant, "who operated a garage in Northville" and whose father "often played checkers with the champion." Cf. "Swapping Work: A Country Custom," *Folklore from the Working Folk of America*, 225–28. The split-dog story is common in America. See *Motif* X1215.11.

"Eel Olive's Fall from Grace": *North Carolina Folklore Journal* (1948), 5.

Collected by T. Pat Matthews and Edwin Massengill for the Federal Writers' Project in North Carolina. It is based on a story told by

Z. D. Matthews of Angier, Harnett County, "about a legendary prankster of post–Civil War days." Other Eel Oliver pranks are recorded in *North Carolina Folklore Journal* (1971), 28–32.

"Nick the Fiddler": *New York Folklore Quarterly* (1952), 99–101.

Dean Frederick Bock obtained most of the information for his account of Nick Goodall from Watertown, New York, newspapers. He states that Goodall "died in the eighteen-eighties at the age of thirty-five," but that stories about him "are still on the lips of the inhabitants of this vicinity."

"The Leather Man": *New York Folklore Quarterly* (1953), 201–5, 207.

Jean Cowles's informants included Harry Disbrow, of Wilton, Connecticut, grandson of James Moriarity; and Seymour Matthews, of Scarsdale, New York, and J. H. Cowles, of Waterbury, Connecticut, both of whom "saw 'The Leather Man.'" Dates are not given. She also used newspaper clipping files and supplies a bibliography of published sources. A bronze plaque placed "near the iron pipe" in 1953 by local historians marks the "Final Resting Place of Jules Bourglay of Lyons, France 'The Leather Man' who regularly walked a 365 mile route . . . from the Connecticut River to the Hudson living in caves, in the years 1858–1889." As is often the case, Bourglay's story is a blend of demonstrable fact, lore in oral tradition, and influences of the mass media ranging from newspapers to postcards, to exhibition halls like the Eden Musée and the Globe Museum of New York, which exploited popular interest in the macabre.

"Who Was the Leather Man?": *Westchester Historian* (1937), 90–91, 101–2, 103–4.

Allison Albee posed the question "Who was 'The Leather Man'?" and in seeking an answer assembled the basic information. He used interviews, newspaper files, and legal records and was equally interested in establishing the facts and collecting the legends circulating in the mass media and oral tradition.

"'Coxey' Bivens Lived in a Cave": *New York Folklore Quarterly* (1963), 197–200.

Arthur N. Myers does not detail his sources but does reprint an obituary notice documenting "Coxey" Bivens' local notoriety. He was born Joseph Bivens and was nicknamed because of his enthusiasm for "General" Jacob S. Coxey, who led an "army" of unemployed to Washington in 1894 advocating public works projects. The cave is on the Pennsylvania side of the Delaware River and is known as Coxey's Cave.

"Bone Mizell, Florida Cowpuncher": *Southern Folklore Quarterly* (1971), 34–41.

Merlin P. Mitchell obtained background information on Bone Mizell from his cousin Olin Mizell, interviewed in Moore Haven, Florida, December 19, 1949; from Florida newspapers; and from stories "told around swamp-country campfires for years." Informants for "Bone Goes to the Circus" were Cecil Farabee, restaurant owner, Moore Haven, Florida, and "several 'crackers' in the bar next door." For "Bone Buries a Friend," which "has much currency among Florida cowboys," Mitchell reprints a version from Stephen Trumbull of the *Miami Herald*, date not given. The traditional nature of some of this material is evident when it is compared with stories like that of the substituted corpse, *Motif* J1959.2.

Ethnics

"Peter Francisco, Revolutionary War Hero": *Southern Folklore Quarterly* (1963), 141–42.

George Monteiro examines the history and legends associated with Peter Francisco and the "unhistorical uses" of this material in the mass media "in an attempt to fill out artificially some national image or to give design to a heroic past." He cites the historical documents, shows how Francisco's "folk and popular biography" in many details parallels folk motifs and how Francisco attracted familiar folk anecdotes, and argues that the publication of sketches in mass-circulation magazines transformed Francisco from historical hero and folk hero into "popularized" hero.

"Francisco as Folk Hero": Ibid., 142–43.

"Francisco as Frontier Strong Man": Ibid., 148–49.

Monteiro reprints this tale quoted from the Georgia *Courier* in the Wheeling, Virginia, *Gazette* of February 7, 1829. It uses the idiom of the tall tales of the Old Southwest and an anecdote told of many strong men. Cf. "Joe Call's Sister" (p. 57).

"Francisco in the Portugese-language Press": Ibid., 157.

"The Welsh Wizard": *New York Folklore Quarterly* (1947), 41–46.

Millard F. Roberts is the author of *A Narrative History of Remsen, N.Y.* (Syracuse, 1914), from which the tales of Dr. Daniel Roberts are taken. Remsen, where Dr. Roberts practiced medicine and magic, attracted many Welsh settlers. For similar folk tales of magic used to thwart thieves, cf. "Preacher Dow Catches a Thief" (p. 99) and *Motifs* Q551.2.3 (Thieves rendered unable to remove stolen goods) and D2072.5 (Thieves petrified when they enter house).

A "medicamentum" is a potion or remedy. *The Narrative History* has this quote on Dr. Roberts from the "brief reminiscences" of Simon Fuller, Jr. (1791–1862?): "He had such wonderful success that the superstitiously inclined believed that the evil one was in league with him, and he rather encouraged the belief. . . . Some days the fences on the roadside were lined with teams for long distances, and his house was filled with patients, and he dealing out Medicamentum from a little bar in one corner of the room" (p. 186).

"An Absent-minded Scholar": *New York Folklore Quarterly* (1956), 189–90.

Robert Anderson gives as his source "John F. Seymour's *Centennial Address*, 1877." He concludes that the stories about Van der Kemp show the tendency "to accept the notion that a scholar should be impractical and absent-minded, and to attach that conception to the most available man who had some pretensions to scholarship." Cf. *Motifs* J2000–2049. For a latter-day absent-minded scholar, see stories of Norbert Wiener (p. 368–71).

"Pat Casey Who Struck It Rich": *California Folklore Quarterly* (1946), 345, 348.

Reprinted by Levette Jay Davidson from "an 1864 pamphlet published in New York by Edward Bliss, 'Agent of the Colorado Emigration Office, and Late Editor of the Rocky Mountain News.'" Davidson's other sources are Alice Polk Hill, *Tales of the Colorado Pioneers* (Denver, 1884), and *Glimpses of Golden Gilpin*, published by the Gilpin County, Colorado, Chamber of Commerce, ca. 1908. The anecdotes are literary rather than traditional except for the discovery of treasure on a grave, *Motif* N545.

"Zishe, the Yiddish Samson": Collection of Toby Blum-Dobkin (1973).

Toby Blum-Dobkin, a fellow in the Max Weinreich Center, YIVO Institute for Jewish Research, New York, recorded the song about Zishe Breitbart as sung by Yitskhak Milstein, and provides the commentary and translation. The transcription is by Thomas Brothers. Mr. Milstein is a tailor who lives in Brooklyn, New York. He survived the Nazi concentration camps and came to the United States in 1950. Blum-Dobkin showed her original text to Mr. Milstein and he requested several minor changes, which she made. In preparing the transliteration from Yiddish, Blum-Dobkin follows the guidelines suggested by the YIVO Institute "with some adjustments to Mr. Milstein's Central Yiddish dialect." For example, the Yiddish word for *years* would in Standard Yiddish be pronounced *yorn*, and the word for *chains* would be *keytn*. The Central Yiddish pronunciations, used here, are *yurn* and *kaytn*. Of her translation, she says: "I have tried to keep as close as possible to the Yiddish . . . it sounds somehow as if I'm trying to rhyme and not quite succeeding. In fact, I did the opposite—even in cases in which obvious rhymes suggested themselves, I did not use them if they distorted the meaning."

Another version of the Zishe song from an informant in Los Angeles was printed in 1973 by Eleanor Gordon Mlotek in the *Forverts* column headed "Perl fun der yidisher poezye." Although this is a European broadside ballad that rather recently entered oral tradition, it shares with the medieval ballad an aura of fatality. The boy who leaves home despite the protest of his mother somehow brings upon himself the punishment he receives, and because he is so outstanding he is especially vulnerable. This song is not simply an instance of how easily folklore is transported. The fact that Zishe Breitbart was a success in show business in the United States certainly helped to keep alive songs and stories about him here.

"A Poet Turns the Tables on the King of Bagdad": *Journal of American Folklore* (1903), 142–44.

Collected by Howard Barrett Wilson from a native of Syria living in Boston, ca. 1900. Exact date, place of birth, and name not given. Abu Nuwas or Abu'n-Nuwâs (ca. 756–810) spent most of his life in Bagdad, where he enjoyed the favor of Caliph Harun al-Rashid. He "is recognized as the greatest poet of his time" (*Encyclopedia Britannica*, 11th edition). Another version of this tale is recorded in the dialect of Christians of Beirut by H. M. Huxley in the *Journal of the American Oriental Society* (1902), 234–37. Also see Motif J1115.6 (The clever peasant). In "The Story of the Barber's Sixth Brother" from *Arabian Nights*, a prince of the Barmecide family of Bagdad serves empty dishes to a hungry man to test his sense of humor; hence the phrase "Barmecide Feast," meaning an imaginary banquet or an illusion.

"Stratouhotdas, Biggest Thief That Ever Lived": *New York Folklore Quarterly* (1949), 268–72, 274–75.

Ernest S. Mathews heard these stories from Anna Christ of Buffalo, New York, a native of Greece, age about fifty, who "speaks rather broken English" and "is quite well established financially." He notes: "She wanted an explanation as to what type of material I was seeking. . . . As I ran through my list, I came upon folk heroes, and she stopped me. She told me that she had many a story about a famous folk hero of her land." They are typical of thousands of anecdotes about deception, wise and foolish conduct, and sly verbal response known throughout Europe.

"King Matt's Riddle": *West Virginia Folklore* (1955), 45–46.

Collected by Raymond Kalozy "as told to him by his grandmother, who came from Hungary." Her name and age not given. "King Matt" is Matthias I, Hunyadi (1440–90), king of Hungary, "indisputably the greatest man of his day, and one of the greatest monarchs who ever reigned" (*Encyclopedia Britannica*, 11th edition). He is the central figure in a cycle of legends and folk tales, often jocular, and in various proverbs and folk sayings still current in Hungary. See *Type* 922 (The king and the abbot).

Old World Heroes in the New World

"King Arthur's Grave": University of Pennsylvania Folklore Archive (1963). Unclassified.

Collected by MacEdward Leach from Hiram Cranmer, age seventy-five, a lumberman and hunter of Clinton County in the western Pennsylvania mountains, January 1963. Cranmer said he had visited the grave many times. He claimed the story was of Indian origin and that he learned it from his grandfather who "had it from a man married to a squaw who had the story from her people." Leach reports that similar stories of Arthur's death are widespread in Western Europe, though previously unrecorded in the United States. See *Motifs* H1321.2 and H1324 for quest of wounded hero for healing waters; unusual burial in stone coffin, *F852.5; and cairn marks burial, A988. The tale is discussed fully by Leach in *Two Penny Ballads and Four Dollar Whiskey*, edited by Robert H. Byington and Kenneth S. Goldstein (Hatboro, Pa., 1966).

"The Wandering Jew in Louisiana": *Louisiana Folklore Miscellany* (1970), 46–47, 49–52.

George F. Reinecke discusses the Wandering Jew legend (*Type* 777) in French-speaking Louisiana; summarizes its European background;

and presents a French text (his translation) and a tune collected by Dr. Corinne Saucier of Natchitoches, Louisiana, from a Mrs. Lacour of Simmesport, Avoyelles Parish, Louisiana, in 1949.

"The Wandering Jew in the Utah Desert": *Journal of American Folklore* (1940), 30–31.

Collected by A. E. Fife, who was seeking information on the Three Nephites (see pp. 22–28) from Mormon informants. He obtained this tale from Charley Seegmiller, age ninety-three, of St. George, Utah, interviewed in 1939. Seegmiller was a native of Germany. Fife estimates that the events described took place about 1870.

"Marshal Ney, Napoleonic Hero in America": *North Carolina Folklore Journal* (1975), 67–69.

Harry C. West writes a brief account of the conjectures surrounding the last years of Michel Ney (1769–1815), Marshal of France, dubbed by Napoleon and popularly known as "the bravest of the brave." A trusted subordinate of Bonaparte, he attached himself to the Bourbon king after the restoration, but when he was sent to seize Napoleon on his return from Elba, he joined him instead and played a commanding role in the Waterloo campaign. Ney was condemned for treason and shot, though the Duke of Wellington is said to have sought to mitigate the sentence. West bases his account on a biography of LeGette Blythe, *Marshal Ney: A Dual Life* (New York, 1937) and North Carolina "legends." Cf. *Motifs* A571 (Culture hero still lives) and A580 (Culture hero's expected return).

"An Ozark Fiddler Plays Napoleon's Battle Tunes": *Mid-South Folklore* (1975), 95.

Judith McCulloch taped the tunes and comments of Uncle Absie Morrison (1876–1964) in 1962 at Landis, Arkansas, and in 1963 at Eureka Springs, Arkansas. Her tapes are on deposit in the Archives of Traditional Music of Indiana University. With his twin brother, Abbie, Absie began to play the fiddle when he was twelve. They were much in demand at dances and veterans' reunions and formed a nucleus of a family string band.

"Dry and Dusty": Ibid., 97.

Uncle Absie Morrison's claim that "Dry and Dusty" was "Bonaparte's charge piece" is dubious, according to Samuel Preston Bayard, who informed us in a letter dated February 10, 1977, that the tune is probably Scottish: "It is an air called 'Willie Winkie' or 'Willie Winkie's Testament' and is to be found in James Oswald's *Caledonian Pocket Companion*, published in several editions beginning early in the eighteenth century. The earliest-appearing and simplest set of this 'Winkie' tune I've seen is one called 'Willey Wilkey' in John Walsh, *Caledonian Country Dances*, London, ca. 1752, p. 17."

The Morrison family string band recorded "Dry and Dusty" for Victor in 1930.

"Bonaparte's Retreat": Ibid., 98.

Although Uncle Absie states flatly that "Bonaparte's Retreat" is "French music," it is more likely a version of an old Irish marching tune usually known as "The Eagle's Whistle" ("Fead an Iolair"). See Samuel Preston Bayard, *Hill Country Tunes* (Philadelphia, 1944), Number 87, for a discussion and a version he collected in western Pennsylvania in 1943 as a fife tune from an informant who learned it from a fifer who had "played it as a retreat in Civil War days." Bayard informed us by letter (see above) that the title serves for several tunes current in North America, of which Absie Morrison's is a common one, and he adds: "This is quite a characteristic set from down South. In order to see the relations between sets of this 'Bonaparte' piece and 'The Eagle's Whistle,' it is usually necessary to reverse the parts, and read the second part first, and the first part second."

"A Finnish Eyeturner in Northern Michigan": *Midwest Folklore* (1955), 9.

Selected from a cycle of Finnish wizard tales from the Upper Peninsula of Michigan, which are reported and discussed by Aili Kolehmainen Johnson. She collected Finnish tales with Richard M. Dorson in 1946. For another example of the occult powers of August Sunnell [*sic*], see Dorson's *Bloodstoppers and Bearwalkers* (Cambridge, Mass., 1952), 134. For other tales of eyeturners collected in America, see "Konsti Koponen, the Eyeturner" (pp. 45 and 540). *Motif* D479.

III. A PARADE OF HEROES

Frontiersmen and Pioneers

"The Man Who Killed General Braddock": *Keystone Folklore Quarterly* (1962), 33-35.

Lillian McCahan first heard, and disbelieved, this legend when she moved to Ohiopyle, Pennsylvania, about 1932. As she talked to a local historian, Felix F. Robinson of Oakland, Maryland, and to Tilghman Mitchell and other members of the Mitchell family of Ohiopyle, she became convinced of its authenticity: "I remembered that Tilghman Mitchell, who has been dead these many years, was a very old man when he died and could have had a grandfather who fought in the Revolution. And that a man who fought in the French and Indian War could have lived then." General Edward Braddock (1695-1755), reputedly a harsh disciplinarian skilled in European military tactics, was ambushed while commanding an expedition against the French military post Fort Duquesne (now Pittsburgh). Braddock fought bravely. The persistent story that he was shot by a colonial soldier has been called "absurd" (Columbia Encyclopedia, 3rd edition, 1963).

"The Courtship of Daniel Boone": *North Carolina Folklore Journal* (1948), 5-6.

Collected by Furman Bisher in Denton, North Carolina, for the Federal Writers' Project. Date and informant not given. The story of Daniel Boone (1734-1820), the pre-eminent frontiersman, begins with his life as a backwoods trail blazer, an agent for the Transylvania Company in Kentucky and a land speculator himself who lost title to his holdings there and moved westward to Missouri, then Spanish territory, where he died. He came to represent, in his own lifetime, the progress of civilization, especially its spirit of enterprise, and the opposite, a need to escape from society's corrupting influence to the freedom of the open frontier. A supposedly autobiographical account of Boone appeared in John Filson's *Discovery, Settlement and Present State of Kentucke* (1784), which launched him into legend as a trail blazer, and he became internationally known through references by Byron in *Don Juan* (1823) as one of nature's noblemen. Subsequently, the mass media, the media of the higher arts, and folklore together made Boone the most famous American pioneer. Born near Reading, Pennsylvania, of English Quaker parentage, he moved to the Yadkin Valley of North Carolina in 1750 and married Rebecca Bryant there in 1756.

An early version of Boone's fire-hunt appears in Timothy Flint's very popular *Biographical Memoir of Daniel Boone* (1833). A fire-hunt is a night hunt by torch or firelight, which is reflected by the eyes of the game. Boone's fire-hunt is analyzed by Richard Slotkin in *Regeneration Through Violence* (1973). He argues that the legend "clarifies the symbolic relationship between Boone and his wilderness world," which is that "of hunter to prey." In marrying Rebecca, Boone achieves a "symbolic marriage with the female spirit of the wilds" (p. 425). For a fire-hunt tale from North Carolina, ca. 1820, see *Folklore in America*, 36–37, and the *Journal of American Folklore* (1934), 270 and 318.

"The Last Days of Daniel Boone": *New Monthly Magazine and Literary Journal* (1823), 524–26.

The *New Monthly Magazine* was published in London and republished in Boston by Oliver Everett. The extract used here is from the concluding passage of an essay signed "I.Y." He indicates his main concern in the title, "Social and Savage Life: Daniel Boon," using the example of Boone to argue in favor of "that state of society which approaches nearest to the simplicity of Nature." Such essays suggest the contribution of the popular literary magazine to the development of the Boone legend at the time of his death and the international emergence of Boone as an archetypal figure. Much of the accumulating legend was pure invention. For example, Boone did not die alone and forgotten. He departed this life in the bosom of his family, and the state legislature of Missouri expressed its "distinguished respect" by wearing mourning crepe for twenty days. Certain details of this account have a folkloristic quality, such as the statement that "he was found dead . . . his rifle cocked. . . ."

Henry Nash Smith discusses the symbolic aspects of the Boone legend as it developed in the literature, mass-media publications, and fine arts to the mid-nineteenth century. See *Virgin Land* (Cambridge, Mass., 1950), 53–58.

"Johnny Appleseed and the Bewitched Cow": *West Virginia Folklore* (1951), 2–3.

Contributed by Laura Rector of Mineralwells, West Virginia, from material she has collected on West Virginia legendary figures for a master's thesis at Fairmont State University. Her source, which she quotes almost verbatim, is Henry A. Pershing, *Johnny Appleseed and His Times* (Strasburg, Va., 1930). For tales of John Chapman (1774–1847), better known as Johnny Appleseed, among the Indians and as a planter of fruit trees and frontier preacher in Pennsylvania and the Ohio River Valley, see *Folklore from the Working Folk*, 409–16.

"Hugh Glass Fights a Bear": *Colorado Magazine* (1941), 5.

Summarized by Levette Jay Davidson from Hiram M. Chittenden, *The Yellowstone Park* (Cincinnati, 1895), 689–97. Glass was badly mangled by a grizzly in 1823 when employed as a trapper. The oft-told story of his survival made its initial appearance in print as an unsigned sketch in *Portfolio* (Philadelphia, March, 1825). Edgeley W. Todd identifies the author as James Hall, then a young frontier lawyer, and suggests plausibly that Hall heard it told "around the campfires of backwoodsmen and hunters" (*American Quarterly* [1955], 364). Glass is thought to have been killed by Indians in 1833.

"Scalping Grizzlies": Ibid., 5.

Taken by Levette Jay Davidson from Lewis H. Garrard's autobiographical *Wah-to'-yah, and the Taos Trail* (Cincinnati, 1850), Chap. xix. James Bridger (1804–81), mountain man, born in Virginia, is supposedly the first white to have seen the Great Salt Lake and was an early explorer of the Yellowstone. In 1843 he established Fort Bridger in Wyoming, a famous supply post on the Oregon Trail.

"Kit Carson Shoots a Bully": Ibid., 6.

Taken by Levette Jay Davidson from Samuel Parker's *Journal of an Exploring Trip Beyond the Rocky Mountains* (1838), 75–81. Christopher Carson (1809–68) was born in Madison County, Kentucky. By 1826 he had made his way to Taos, New Mexico, where he was a scout, trapper, and meat-hunter. He became famous as a guide for the Frémont expeditions of the 1840s and as a scout during the Mexican War and Civil War. See Henry Nash Smith's chapter "The Mountain Man as Western Hero: Kit Carson" in *Virgin Land* (Cambridge, Mass., 1950), 81–89, for an account of his elevation to the role of popular hero.

"Grandma Doctor Emma French": *Arizona Friends of Folklore* (1972), 1–2.

Vada F. Carlson of Winslow, Arizona, is the author of this brief sketch of a heroic Winslow pioneer. She does not give the sources of her information.

Indians

"Watkuese Saves Lewis and Clark": *Western Folklore* (1953), 175.

Collected by Ella E. Clark in 1952. The story was recorded by Kate McBeth, a missionary among the Nez Percé in 1879, who reported the survival of "evidences of Nez Percé affection for their first white visitors." The journals of Lewis and Clark do not mention Watkuese or indicate Nez Percé hostility. They do state that on September 20, 1805, Captain Clark and his party, weak and sick from lack of food, encountered three Indian boys near the present site of Weippe, Idaho, who led them to a Nez Percé village where they were befriended. Captain Lewis, "very sick," arrived two days later.

"Black Hawk Remembered": *Journal of American Folklore* (1911), 235–37.

Published posthumously by Franz Boas from the field notes of William Jones's "extended observations of the Fox Indians." Black-hawk (1767–1838) was a minor Sauk-Fox chief who fought for the British in the War of 1812. He gained renown as a warrior and be-came a major force in the so-called Black Hawk War (1832), which was caused by disputed land treaties with American settlers. Captured, he was imprisoned and then paraded before curious crowds in various eastern cities. Eventually he returned to Iowa to die among the rem-nants of his tribe. His remains were stolen, exhibited, and destroyed in a fire. The account Jones collected from an unknown Indian source is essentially accurate.

"The Last Day of Tecumseh's Life": *Journal of American Folklore* (1931), 191–92.

Collected by Lilian Walker "many years ago" near Mount Pleasant, Michigan, from an Ottawa informant who heard it from "a very old man, twenty-seven years ago, whose name I will give, Na-be-na-yak-nee-kodwa-bi (Sitting on Half the Sky), who died at the age of ninety-one." Lilian Walker recorded the tale in Ottawa and provided an English paraphrase, which is given here as modified by Truman Michelson. It is printed with the permission of the Smithsonian Insti-tution. Tecumseh (1768?–1813), Shawnee chief, organized a confed-eracy emphasizing communal land ownership, a movement crushed at the battle of Tippecanoe in 1811. In the War of 1812 he held a com-mission as brigadier general in the British Army and was killed in ac-tion.

"Tecumseh at the Naval Academy": Bureau of Navigation *Bulletin* No. 134 (June 28, 1930), 4.

The Bureau of Navigation issued, anonymously, a "Tecumseh Num-ber" occasioned by the presentation to the United States Naval Acad-emy on May 31, 1930, of "a bronze statue of Tamenend, to replace the old wooden figure of the U.S.S. *Delaware*, known to thousands as Tecumseh." The figurehead, and subsequently the statue, have been central to rituals and legends among generations of midshipmen. For example, Kendall Banning in *Annapolis Today* (Annapolis: U. S.

Naval Institute, 1963), 54, writes: "This custom of paying homage to the old warrior, accompanied by a left-hand salute, originated somewhere in the dim past. . . . It has been surmised by competent surmisers that the wooden midshipmen found a kinship with this wooden Indian, and paid their compliments to him in their hours of need in the primitive manner of superstitious man since the first Medicine Man pranced about in his war feathers to scare away the spirits of evil." A reference librarian at the Naval Academy Library recently recorded "a new tradition" involving Tecumseh's nose. A contest has grown up between the first class and the fourth class: "Plebes keep it polished; first class tries to catch them doing it."

"Tecumseh in Bronze": Ibid., 5, 9–10.

The importance to the naval service of the function of the Tecumseh as a bearer of unifying lore is evident in the dignity of the ceremonies which developed around the casting of the statue and its formal presentation.

"Tsali and the Cherokee Removal": *Ethnohistory* (1963), 330.

Paul Kutsche collected and analyzed data associated with the Eastern Cherokee hero Tsali, and with Indian efforts "to escape exile from the Southern Appalachian Mountains to Indian Territory in 1838. . . ." He compares several versions of the Tsali legend—contemporary United States Army reports; the account of the artist and journalist Charles Lanman a decade later; the account of the anthropologist James Mooney; and a transcript of the telling of Molly Sequoyah, an Eastern Cherokee informant, in 1961. That the Tsali legend is exceptionally well documented provides Kutsche with an opportunity to focus on "the cultural bias of each teller of the tale." He finds factual discrepancies "few and inconsequential" and concludes that the persistence of the story "so warmly, and in so much detail is explained by the importance of Tsali to the present Eastern Cherokees. Tsali is for them a principal culture hero, a combination of the attributes of George Washington in making possible the founding of his state, and Jesus Christ in dying as a martyr to the foreigner so that others might live" (p. 343). Kutsche's analysis is sensitive and fully documented.

"The Army Version": Ibid., 331–32.

Kutsche's source is a copy of a report of November 5 from Lieutenant Smith to his immediate superior, First Lieutenant C. H. Larned. On the same date Lieutenant Larned transmitted a report to Major General Winfield Scott, who was in command of the Cherokee removal. General Scott then set in motion a military operation and negotiations to recapture Tsali and his band. These official records are deposited in the National Archives, Washington, D.C. According to Kutsche, the military reports "give us a picture of the virtuous Army rounding up recalcitrant Indians," acting mercifully by "giving up its horses to Indian children" while the "Indians are treacherous, plotting to murder the soldiers without any provocation beyond their desire to escape."

"A Journalist's Sketch": Ibid., 336–38.

Charles Lanman (1819–95), an artist, contributed colorful travel letters to the *National Intelligencer*, a Whig journal sympathetic to the Cherokees. They were later collected in *Letters from the Allegheny Mountains* (New York, 1849), 112–14, Kutsche's source. Lanman's information was obtained from William H. Thomas, mentioned in the report of Lieutenant Smith, with whom he stayed at Qualla Town, now Cherokee, North Carolina, for about two weeks. Thomas was an Indian trader and an adopted son of a Cherokee chief. James Mooney of the Bureau of American Ethnology wrote in 1900 that "the East Cherokee of to-day owe their existence as a people" to him. Kutsche concurs.

"A Cherokee Recollection": Ibid., 34–43.

Kutsche tape-recorded the Tsali legend in 1961 as remembered by Mollie Sequoyah. He describes her as "an aged and much-respected grandmother and great-grandmother of the Big Cove community on the Qualla Reservation" who has been an informant "for at least two generations of ethnographers." Her version "is the only one which relies entirely on a Cherokee source [Tsali's son, Washington], and is the only one told by a Cherokee."

"Deluvina, Friend of Billy the Kid": *New Mexico Folklore Record* (1949–50), 15–16.

Collected by Rose P. White. Her source was a letter from Colonel Jack M. Potter of Clayton, New Mexico, dated February 15, 1949. Potter lived in Fort Sumner, New Mexico, 1885–90. See "An Obituary for Billy the Kid" (p. 304).

Badmen

"Jean Lafitte's Treasure": *Publications of the Texas Folk-Lore Society* (1924), 185.

"Adapted" by E. G. Littlejohn from a story in the Galveston, Texas, *News* of October 27, 1908. Jean Lafitte (1782–1854), the French pirate leader, black market operator, and sometimes patriot, had a hideout on the Baratarian coast south of New Orleans and later on an island near Galveston.

"Lafitte's Lieutenants": Ibid., 189–91.

Collected by J. W. Morris. Informants cited in text.

"The Iron Box": *Journal of American Folklore* (1915), 291.

Recalled by Walter Prescott Webb, the Texas historian. He does not give date or name of informant.

"Mustang Gray, Horse Thief and Horseman": *Publications of the Texas Folk-Lore Society* (1932), 115.

J. Frank Dobie collected "Fact, Tradition, and a Song" about Mabry B. Gray who "came to Texas from South Carolina in January, 1835, aged twenty-two," who fought at the battle of San Jacinto, and who "was a leader among those bold, daring, and ruthless raiders who preyed on the Mexican ranches between the Nueces and the Rio Grande. . . ."

"How Mustang Gray Won His Name": Ibid., 116–18.

Dobie cites as his source Dolp Quinn of Beesville, Texas, "whose father was such an ardent Mustang Gray man that he named his first-born son Mabry Gray." Quinn's age is not given and he is not directly quoted.

"The Curse on Goliad": Ibid., 119.

Dobie retells this tale, which he heard from Kate Stoner O'Connor of Victoria, Texas, who got it from an "Old Mexican woman living in Goliad, whose ancestors were there long before Moses Austin secured permission to bring English-speaking colonists to Texas. . . ." He does not reveal the age of his informants.

"The Song of Mustang Gray": Ibid., 122–23.

Collected by Dobie, who conjectures that the author was James T. Lytle, a Texas Ranger. Dobie obtained the tune from "a veteran Texian and trail-driver named James Hatch, of San Antonio."

"James Copeland of the Murrell Gang": *Southern Folklore Quarterly* (1961), 126–28.

Collected by Margaret Gillis Figh from D. C. Matthews, Grove Hill, Alabama, in April, 1951. She states that her informant's "great-grandmother's sister was Elizabeth who married James Copeland." John Murrell (fl. 1804–44) was the leader of a gang of "land pirates" supposedly numbering in the hundreds. He operated in the Old Southwest, especially along the Natchez Trace.

"The Gold Cap of Joaquin Murieta": *Western Folklore* (1954), 99–100.

Collected by Mary Jean Kennedy from Mary Pohot, "an elderly Yokuts Indian woman of Woodlake, California, in the summer of 1949." The meeting with the mistress of Joaquin Murieta (ca. 1832–53) "must have taken place fifty or sixty years earlier." The transformation of Murieta from a bandit leader during the Gold Rush period into a legendary figure of the Robin Hood type began with the publication of *The Life and Adventures of Joaquin Murieta* (1854) by John R. Ridge, a San Francisco journalist.

"My Kin Knew Jesse James": *Arizona Friends of Folklore* (1971), 18–20.

Colleen Quiner, as a student at Northern Arizona University in the late 1960s, interviewed Della Lundman, then more than sixty years old. Mrs. Lundman's account differs from the equally sympathetic Ozark tradition that blames the brutality of Union soldiers, not the railroad officials, for provoking the James brothers into a life of crime. The portrayal of Jesse James as a friend of the poor is common to most versions. See "Generous Jesse James" (p. 301).

"Jesse James Robs a Bank": *Southern Folklore Quarterly* (1961), 129–30.

Collected by Margaret Gillis Figh from William Phillips of Huntsville, Alabama, in February 1948. The most notorious American outlaw, Jesse James (1847–82) joined the guerrillas led by William Quantrill at fifteen, taking part in the civil warfare in Kansas and Missouri. During the 1870s he and his brother, Frank, led a gang that robbed trains and banks. Despite his murderous career, he attracted public sympathy and became the central figure in a number of folk tales, songs, and dime novels. He was killed for a reward by Robert Ford, who had joined his gang for that purpose.

"Generous Jesse James": Ibid., 130.

Collected by Margaret Gillis Figh from L. C. Rogers of Montgomery, Alabama, in March 1948. Jesse James in this Alabama tale appears as a Robin Hood figure with a touch of Yankee cunning that allows him to prove generous at no sacrifice. The story is an old one told about many outlaws such as Heraclío Bernal and Pretty Boy Floyd. Cf. "Stagolee and the Widow" (p. 308).

"El Tejano": University of Arizona Folklore Archive.

Collected by Edna Barnes from Mrs. C. N. Barnes, place and date not supplied. Reprinted, with background and analysis, in *Western Folklore* (1968), 38, by Joyce Gibson Roach, who found no name, only the designation El Tejano (The Texan), in the tales she studied. She credits Carl Hartman of Tucson, Arizona, with translating the tales and supplying information leading to the probable identification of the prototype of her nameless outlaw. He may have been William Brazelton, "a minor badman hero who gained his reputation as a stage robber in the Tucson area in the 1870s." He wore a grotesque mask and his body was publicly displayed after he had been killed by a posse. But his generosity to the poor, his reversal of the horseshoes, his betrayal by a friend, and his hidden treasure are well-known outlaw motifs.

"All or Nothing": *Western Folklore* (1968), 36.

Collected and translated by Carl Hartman, who heard it from Lola Abad, about whom no information is supplied. See note above.

"An Obituary for Billy the Kid": *New Mexico Folklore Record* (1949–50), 14.

Collected by George Fitzpatrick. The obituary was printed originally in the Santa Fe *Weekly Democrat* of July 21, 1881. William H. Bonney (1859–81), desperado and a leading figure in the Lincoln County cattle war, was not universally admired at the time of his death. Rose P. White (see "Deluvina, Friend of Billy the Kid," p. 277) states that "any old cowboy who lived in Eastern New Mexico in the days prior to 1900" would say: "He was nothing but a cattle thief and a murderer. He wasn't no hero—not in the days when he was livin' and not in the twenty years after he was killed."

"Billy the Kid and the Biscuits": Ibid., 14.

Collected by George Fitzpatrick. His source was "a recent letter" from Colonel Jack M. Potter, "the old time trail driver," of Clayton, New Mexico.

"Stagolee": *Journal of American Folklore*, 1911, 289.

Howard W. Odum was the first to record this powerful murder ballad, which he described as "common in Georgia." Exact date, informant, and place not given. Stagolee or Stackalee is the hero of more than forty ballads as well as tales and toasts (bawdy narrative poems). In several versions he shoots Billy the Lion, sometimes Bully or Billy Lyons, for stealing his magic hat. In others they quarrel over a gambling game. There is an element of fact behind these stories, or at least behind the name of the hero. A Samuel Stacker Lee (1848–90) was an ex-Confederate soldier and steamboat captain for the Lee Line on the Mississippi. A Lee Line steamer was named for him in 1906. This Lee was white, but may have given his name to Stagolee.

"Stagolee Blues": Louisiana Folklore Society, 1959.

From a collection of "Angola Prisoners' Blues" recorded by Harry Oster and Richard B. Allen at Camp H, a prison farm, at Angola, Louisiana, in 1959. The performer is Hogman (Matthew) Maxey, a black prisoner born in Haynesville, Louisiana, in 1917. Maxey learned this variant about 1939. A blues singer, he frequently used F natural, the "blue" note for D major, in his bass accompaniment on the twelve-string guitar. He changed meter capriciously throughout and this has not been indicated; also, the song should be performed in a free rhythmic style, without rigid syncopation. The transcription is by Thomas Brothers.

"Stagolee and the Widow": *Southern Folklore Quarterly* (1965), 191–92.

Bruce Jackson heard this tale from John Hurt, the black folk singer, in October 1964 at Cambridge, Massachusetts. Hurt had made a recording of "Stack O'Lee Blues" in 1928, released by Okeh, but had dropped out of sight until the 1960s. Jackson notes that in Hurt's stories the Negro folk hero, who usually appears in the role of badman or trickster, is cast as a more gentle figure. Cf. "Generous Jesse James" (p. 301). In some tales and songs, Stagolee is associated with James.

Sharp Operators

"Jemima Wilkinson, 'Publick Universal Friend'": *New York Folklore Quarterly* (1964), 6, 8–10.

Herbert A. Wisbey, Jr., has studied "the folk image" of Jemima Wilkinson (1752–1819), an antecedent of Aimee Semple McPherson, and collected "anecdotes handed down from one generation to another" about her. He does not name his sources but notes that in Yates County, New York, she is depicted as "a sincere, kindly, benevolent women" while in her native New England her name "was synonomous with fraud and delusion." About 1790 Jemima Wilkinson founded a colony, "Jerusalem," in Yates County. She advocated celibacy. Similar stories are told about Joseph Smith, founder of the Mormon religion, by his detractors.

"'Gassy' Thompson and His Mining Swindles": *California Folklore Quarterly* (1946), 339–41, 343.

Levette Jay Davidson collected tales of the metal miner and swindler, George "Gassy" Thompson, from both oral tradition and nineteenth-century newspapers. "An Easy Way to Sink a Shaft" is from the Georgetown, Colorado, *Courier* of February 18, 1886. The informant for "'Gassy' a Game Sport" was Mrs. Mamie Sturm, from whom Davidson obtained a version of the snow tunnel story. Other sources appear in the texts.

"How to Carry a Watch": *Midwest Folklore* (1954), 153.

Reminiscences of Dan'l Stamps and tall tales he told were gathered by Warren Stanley Walker, with the assistance of Richard Logan and Gordon MacLeod. They provide a list of their informants but few details about where and when and exactly from whom their information was obtained. The watch trade anecdote came from a resident in "the Home for the Aged in Hardin" (Illinois). It is in the tradition of tales told about sharp-trading Yankee peddlers and popularized by T. C. Halliburton in the 1840s through his books about Sam Slick, an itinerant clockmaker.

"Keeping an Odd Bargain": *Midwest Folklore* (1960), 129–32.

Published by Ruth Ann Musick as an example of a European trickster story retold in America. Her source was Violet Forchi, otherwise unidentified, who heard it from Joe Catania, born in Italy, and working as a miner in West Virginia in the early 1900s. Tale *Type* 1000 (Bargain not to become angry). It also includes *Type* 1002 (Dissipation of ogre's property) and *Type* 1004 (Hogs in the mud; Sheep in the air).

Quick Wits

"The Arkansas Traveler": *Century Magazine* (March 1896), 707–9.

Henry Mercer, a pioneer student of folk life, investigated the early history of this backwoods comedy routine, which combines fiddle tunes and dialogue. His findings reveal a blend of folklore and popular culture. The earliest recorded printing of the melody was in 1847 by W. C. Peters, without indication of composer or place of publication. The tune with dialogue was published in sheet music editions by Blodgett & Bradford of Buffalo, New York, 1858–63. The chief but not undisputed claimant to authorship of the tune and dialogue is Colonel Sandford C. Faulkner (1806–74), whose name first appeared on a sheet music version with an 1859 copyright. Another possibility is Mose Case of Charlestown, Indiana, a black guitarist, who is named as the composer on a sheet music version published by Oliver Ditson in 1863. A third is José Tosso, a Cincinnati violinist, for whom credit is claimed in his 1887 obituary.

Currier & Ives published a pair of lithographs in 1870 titled "The Arkansas Traveler" and "The Turn of the Tune." There were also theatrical skits based on "The Arkansas Traveler," the earliest said to have been performed in Salem, Ohio, in 1852, and there are many nineteenth-century references to the dance tune in southwestern and sporting publications such as the *Spirit of the Times*. See James Masterson, *Tall Tales of Arkansaw* (Boston, 1943), for a full study and Mary D. Hudgins, "Arkansas Traveler—A Multi-Parented Wayfarer," *Arkansas Historical Quarterly* (1971), 145–60, for a recent summary.

On the matter of parentage, Hudgins states that the "tune and legend were already quite old" and thus Faulkner, Case, and Tosso merely arranged the music and adapted the dialogue. In " 'The Arkansas Traveler' and the Strategy of American Humor," *Western Folklore* (1962), 153–60, Gene Bluestein sees the contest between the squatter and the traveler as a typically American comic clash based on tensions between urban and rural life.

"The Lock Boat after the Scow": Ibid., 709.

Henry Mercer reports that he heard this story before 1880, told him by George Long of Doylestown, Pennsylvania, who played the tune for him on the violin.

"Ol Gallagher, Homespun Orator": *West Virginia Folklore* (1963), 48–49.

Reported by Terry Ann Bradley, a student at Fairmont State College, West Virginia, in 1962–63, whose source was her father. He was once a teacher in "a country school on Lowman Ridge" and personally acquainted with "Oliver Gallagher who likewise resided there." After completing his education, Gallagher returned to Wetzel County, to live "in a little plank house on a little farm, with a patch of beans and corn, and a few hounds at his side," according to Terry Ann Bradley. His speech at the opera house is preserved in Sylvester Myers, *History of West Virginia* (New Martinville, W.Va., 1915), II, 280–82. Natural gas was discovered in Wetzel County in 1898.

"Ol Gallagher on the Other Side of the Question": Ibid., 50–51.

Reported by Terry Ann Bradley. Gallagher was something of a public figure, serving many years as a justice of the peace and a term in the West Virginia legislature.

"Is Uncle Billy Dead?": *Keystone Folklore Quarterly* (1971), 86.

Collected by William Hugh Jansen from an unnamed county judge in Kentucky, a breed traditionally noted as storytellers. Jansen is concerned with what he calls "semi-legends" or "narratives which had not yet made it . . . because they have not been circulated sufficiently to have been molded by oral transmission." He states that this anecdote belongs to a group which depends upon "the memorable or witty statement." The unconventional response to death also turns up on "cruel jokes" (see pp. 365–67), and in frontier humor. For examples, see "The Consolate Widow" by Sol Smith, reprinted in *Humor of the Old Southwest* (Athens, Ga., 1975), edited by Hennig Cohen and William B. Dillingham, and "Well! Dad's Dead" in *Sut Lovingood's Yarns* (New Haven, Conn., 1966), edited by M. Thomas Inge.

"Jones Tracy and the Game Warden": *Northeast Folklore* (1968), 20.

Collected by C. Richard K. Lunt from Farnham Butler of Mount Desert Island, Maine, in 1963. See note below on Jones Tracy (pp. 588–89). This story is also associated with B. F. Finn of western Oregon. See Susan Mullin, *Northwest Folklore* (1966), 21. For an analogue collected in Alabama by Ray B. Browne in 1951 from "a Negro Methodist minister, aged 66," see *Southern Folklore Quarterly* (1954), 130–31.

"Jones Tracy Washes His Hands": Ibid., 20–21.

Collected by Lunt from Clark Manring, Tracy's grandson, of Northeast Harbor, Maine, in 1964. See note on Jones Tracy (pp. 588–89).

"A Mind Like a Computer": *Mississippi Folklore Register* (1969), 105–6.

Ben Gray Lumpkin recalls an academic tall tale told by a memorable college professor to his graduate students. Professor Kennon's purpose was clearly didactic. Lumpkin reports that his widow believed the story "was no idle jest." She said that he often told it "to his students to emphasize the importance of taking all the facts into consideration and handling them accurately." The "facts" may or may not be entirely accurate, though Professor Kennon asserted that they were. This sort of story is well known in oral tradition: cf. *Motifs* F660–769, on persons of remarkable skills, and X980–1010.

Dim Wits

" 'Boots' Van Steenburgh and Jenny Lind": *New York Folklore Quarterly* (1959), 24–27.

Pauline Hommell calls Van Steenburgh "one of our local celebrities" and retells stories associated with him. He lived in Saugerties, New York. She reports that the "older generation can remember him as a very old man," but she does not provide documentation or names of her informants, and she has diminished the vernacular strength of the legend in her pursuit of literary effects. "Boots" was so called because, according to Hommell, "Winter and summer, year in and year out, he wore high leather boots." Jenny Lind, the coloratura soprano, toured the United States with stunning success in 1850–52 under the management of P. T. Barnum.

"Hard on the Horses": *Northeast Folklore* (1968), 27.

Collected by C. Richard K. Lunt from Clark Manring, Jones Tracy's grandson, of Northeast Harbor, Maine, in 1964. Lunt collected four versions of this common type, including one from another grandson. In each case the informant professed that the tale was true and assigned it to someone he knew personally, but it is *Type* 1242A (Carrying part of the load).

"Foolish John": *Southern Folklore Quarterly* (1948), 151.

Calvin Claudel has collected and studied Louisiana French folk tales from Avoyelles Parish, including a group centering on a simpleton, Foolish John. He is often set in motion by his mother, who assigns him tasks, attempts to correct him, and in general serves as a foil for his comic antics. A literal-minded dim wit, he is sometimes called Jack in English-language tales, Jean Sot or Sotte in French, and Juan Bobo or Juan Sonso in Spanish, and his Italian counterpart, contracted to Zanni, gives us the English word *zany*, meaning "clown" or "silly person." See *Type* 1291B.

"Foolish John and the Errands": Ibid., 157–59.

Collected on phonograph recordings in 1944 by Calvin Claudel from Mrs. A. E. Claudel of Avoyelles Parish, Louisiana. He translated the text from Louisiana French and retains the recordings and full data on informant. See *Type* 1685.

"Foolish John and the Washpot": Ibid., 163–64.

Collected on phonograph recordings in 1944 by Calvin Claudel from Manuel Maurace of Avoyelles Parish, Louisiana. Claudel translates the text and retains the recordings and full data on informant. Note that this tale incorporates the episodes of throwing objects to the frogs and greasing the cracks in the dried ground also occurring in "Foolish John and the Errands" (p. 342). See *Types* 1218 and 1291A and B.

"Jean Sotte Gets Drunk": *Journal of American Folklore* (1908), 364.

The tale of Jean Sotte (or Foolish John, see above) was reported anonymously, collected from Marie Ray of Avery Island, Louisiana. She told four stories about "an old woman who had two sons—one so simple that he received the name Jean Sotte, and the other so bright and intelligent that he was known as Jean Esprit." But in her stories Jean Esprit does not demonstrate his intelligence. He merely serves as a foil for the dim-witted doings of his brother. See *Type* 1218.

"Grandpa Weemish and His Pumpkin Rock": *Tennessee Folklore Society Bulletin* (December 1964), 128.

Told by L. A. Wallace of Soddy, Tennessee, who does not name his source.

Big Men Put Down

"George Washington in Texas": *Western Folklore* (1955), 269–70.

Heard by George D. Hendricks, who does not cite his source. His main interest is in pointing out that it "seems to be the technique of the folk yarn spinner to take some famous saying out of context, out of its proper setting in time and place, and twist it"—with humorous results.

"George Washington and the Outhouse": Ibid., 269–70.

A Pennsylvania German variant is reported by Albert F. Buffington, in *Keystone Folklore Quarterly* (1963), 78–80.

"Jimmy Carter and the Bamboo Tree": University of Pennsylvania Folklore Archive (1977). Unclassified.

Collected by John Eilertsen, a graduate student at the University of Pennsylvania, in January 1977, from Peter Crane of Boston, also a University of Pennsylvania student, who heard it from his father in the fall of 1976.

"A John Brown Ballad": *New York Folklore Quarterly* (1953), 48–49.

Collected by Israel Kaplan from E. R. Safford of Potsdam, New York. He recalled "four stanzas and the tune . . . from the singing of Mr. Fred Haywood's uncle" (see below). Music transcribed by Francis S. Fox. John Brown (1800–59), the Abolitionist, was known as "Osawatomie" Brown for his residence in Osawatomie, Kansas, where he deliberately murdered five of his pro-slavery neighbors. "Judge Wise" is probably Governor Wise of Virginia, who declined to pardon Brown after his conviction for treason and inciting the slave uprising at Harpers Ferry. The ballad fragment may be a political lampoon, but the name alone invited vulgar wordplay. Safford believed the concluding stanza, which he could not remember, concerns Brown's execution and burial at North Elba, New York.

"Old Ass Waterbee Brown": *New York Folklore Quarterly* (1953), 47–48.

Collected by Israel Kaplan from Fred R. Haywood of Potsdam, New York, who called it "a parody song." Haywood learned it from an uncle who knew the ballad in full but thought it "was too coarse for preservation, and died without setting it down on paper." Haywood said that John Brown was known to the Indians as "Asa Mah Water-bee."

"Republicans Taunt Cleveland": *Western Folklore* (1964), 199.

Collected by Alice O'Brian in 1960 from Dr. Clive Warner of Santa Monica, California, who recalled it from childhood. In the presidential campaign of 1884 the Republicans discovered that the Democratic candidate, Grover Cleveland, a bachelor, was the father of an illegitimate child. At their political rallies, they shouted in chorus their taunting question, to which Democratic supporters replied. The resulting rhyme passed into oral tradition.

"McKinley and Bryan": Ibid., 199.

Contributed by Ed Cray to a note on election rhymes. Source not cited. Republican William McKinley defeated William Jennings Bryan in the presidential elections of 1896 and 1900. Bryan became a popular hero at the age of thirty-six with his "Cross of Gold" speech to the Democratic convention. He favored Prohibition, but the image of respectability fostered by the Republicans and unrest evident in such movements as Coxey's "army" (see p. 555), reflected in this rhyme, contributed to his defeat.

"Goldwater and Johnson": *Tennessee Folklore Society Bulletin* (December 1965), 108–9, 111–12.

Collected and discussed by Raymond Varisco. Informants and exact dates not supplied, but the material is associated with the presidential election of 1964.

"Nixon and Ford": *North Carolina Folklore Journal* (1975), 78.

The Nixon joke was collected by Mac E. Barrick at a conference of scholars at Duke University from a "Professor from Los Angeles, July 16, 1974." Also heard in a shorter version on July 31 from a Duke faculty member. Cf. the Ford joke with Louie W. Attebery, "Governor Jokes," *Southern Folklore Quarterly* (1969), 350–51. Barrick's primary interest was "folk narratives drawn from oral tradition" circulating "even in the most sophisticated cultures."

"The Presidential Psalm": *Folklore Forum* (1975), 357–58.

Collected and discussed by Mac E. Barrick. Ray B. Browne's version was first printed in the *Journal of American Folklore* (1959), 94. Michael J. Preston's versions are in *Keystone Folklore* (1974), 24, and *Western Folklore* (1975), 239–40. George McGovern is the subject of a psalm parody collected during the 1972 campaign and reprinted in *Folklore Forum* (July 1974), 203–5, by Gary Fine. See note below.

"The President's Statue": Ibid., 358–59.

Collected and discussed by Mac E. Barrick. The example collected by Alan Dundes appears in the *Journal of the Midcontinent American Studies Association* (1963), 52–55. Barrick notes that such examples of political satire as "The Presidential Psalm" and "The President's Statue" generally circulate "surreptitiously in typed or Xeroxed copies." Thus they exist in an uncertain area between folk material orally transmitted and popular material circulated through the mass media. Their folkloristic nature is clear, for example, from the fact the text is not fixed as a result of being written down but in a sense re-created as it is passed along in a subterranean fashion. This "surreptitious" circulation seems analogous to the *samizdat*, publication in typescript of unauthorized material, often of a political or literary nature, in the Soviet Union.

"Lydia Pinkham Rhymes": University of Pennsylvania Folklore Archive (1975). Unclassified.

Collected by Tristram P. Coffin from Dr. Clarence Gallagher of Columbus, Ohio, in the summer of 1975. Dr. Gallagher has known the rhymes since "YMCA days" about forty-five years ago. Lydia Estes Pinkham (1819–83) was a Quaker housewife from Lynn, Massachusetts, whose husband, Isaac Pinkham, was ruined in the depression of 1873. She organized her family and began brewing and selling a home remedy, her Vegetable Compound. Aided by its high alcoholic content, by a "Guide for Women" dispensed free with it, and by the progressive advertising methods of son Dan Pinkham, the "old squaw remedy" quickly became the leading women's medicine in the nation and Lydia Pinkham's name a household word. Many rhymes and jokes developed out of the supposedly miraculous cures the compound worked on all parts of the female body. Nonetheless, Mrs. Pinkham has long been recognized as a pioneer in women's medicine of the late nineteenth century.

"Gus Bailey and the Boss's Daughter": University of Pennsylvania Folklore Archive (1976). Unclassified.

Collected by Horace P. Beck from Dale Potter of Kingman, Maine, in February 1947. Gus Bailey is a genuine folk figure of Bunyanesque stature. He flourished in Aroostook County, Maine, working local lumber camps at the turn of the century. Although his birth and death dates are not known, he is recalled by loggers as active from around 1890 until 1915. Quick as a cat, afraid of nothing, he was supposedly impervious to heat and cold, with hair all over his body that made him as comfortable as a beaver in freezing water. He is typical of the actual logging heroes upon whom the Paul Bunyan legends were modeled. Beck included a variant of the text given here in his *Folklore of Maine* (Philadelphia, 1957), 143. The present text was the way he told the story in Philadelphia in 1976.

"Sick Jokes on the Death of Kennedy": *Tennessee Folklore Society Bulletin* (December 1964), 127–28; December 1965, 112.

The first four items were collected by Alan Dundes and Roger D. Abrahams shortly after the assassination of President Kennedy. The fifth, a variant of the fourth, was collected by Raymond Varisco in Austin, Texas, from an informant from Dallas. He did not supply the date, place, or informant. These items are a subspecies of the sick joke, collected and analyzed by Brian Sutton-Smith. See *Folklore from the Working Folk*, 41–45, 424–25. Sick jokes often involve gestures, perhaps because gestures are more primitive and dramatic and somehow seem less self-contaminating as a way of expressing taboo subjects than words.

"Cruel Jokes on Famous People": *Midwest Folklore* (1960), 21.

Chosen from a collection of 155 "cruel jokes" made by Brian Sutton-Smith in 1958. His informants were high school and college students in Ohio, described in detail in the article cited above. Sutton-Smith suggests that cruel jokes disregard sentiments that society takes seriously, including the suffering of others. They are heartlessly disrespectful of historical figures and mass media celebrities caught in tragic situations.

" 'I Don't Care . . .' ": Ibid., 21.

In a milder form, such as the reference to President Eisenhower's notorious preoccupation with golf or Napoleon's itch, cruel jokes deflate sacrosanct figures, thus performing a democratizing function.

"Norbert Wiener, the Great Mathematician": *Western Folklore* (1972), 1.

Collected and discussed by Bruce Jackson. Norbert Wiener (1894–1964) originated the theory of cybernetics and contributed to the development of electronic computors. Jackson remarks that some of the "stories are obviously folktales; others are cast in the form of personal reminiscence or anecdotes," which he considers "equally legitimate folklore forms" because the teller chooses to remember and transmit them.

"Wiener and the Little Girl": Ibid., 4.

Collected by Bruce Jackson. See *Motif* J2014 and, for absent-mindedness in general, J2040.

"Then I Had Lunch": Ibid., 5.

Collected by Bruce Jackson from Phil Spiro on tape, Cambridge, Massachusetts, January 2, 1965. Spiro was a student at MIT, 1958–61, and at the time of the recording was engaged in electronics research in Cambridge. See *Motifs* X120 and J2040.

"The Calculus Class": Ibid., 6.

Collected by Bruce Jackson from Phil Spiro, above. See *Motif* X370.

"The Right Answer": Ibid., 11.

Collected by Bruce Jackson from Phil Spiro, above. See *Motif* J1210.

"Where Is the Car?": Ibid., 6.

Collected by Bruce Jackson from Warren G. Bemis on tape at his home in Eggertsville, New York, September 11, 1970. Bemis was a graduate student at Massachusetts Institute of Technology, 1951–55, and a member of the faculty, 1959–67. The second version is from Norman Holland, an undergraduate at MIT in Electrical Engineering, 1944–47, and subsequently a professor of English at State University of New York, Buffalo, New York, where Jackson taped this on September 11, 1970. Cf. the absent-minded scholar who forgot his horse and rig (p. 202).

Storytellers

"Jim Bridger's Big Yarns": *Colorado Magazine* (1941), 7.

Summarized by Levette Jay Davidson from Hiram M. Chittenden, *The Yellowstone Park* (Cincinnati, 1895) and Mrs. Henry R. Carrington, *Ab-Sa-Ra-Ka; or Wyoming Opened* (Philadelphia, 1868), especially Chapter 12, 1896 edition. A longer version of the echo story is told by Len Henry (pp. 381–82). For information on Bridger, see pp. 565–66. Though he was illiterate, his knowledge of Indian languages and western geography was unmatched, as was his reputation as a storyteller.

"Hunter John Ellis": *Piscataquis County Historical Society Collections*, Dover, Maine (1910), 142–44.

Sarah A. Martin, who "as a little girl" in her "native town, Guilford," knew Ellis, collected lore about him locally from oral tradition and newspapers. She took the story of the trout from the Piscataquis *Observer* of November 15, 1860. Ellis died in 1867. Basil F. Kirtley in *Northeast Folklore*, 1958, 13–16, states that Ellis "seems to have first owed his local renown to his skill as a raconteur," telling tales "which in reality were traditional." He cites a parallel to the trout story in Rufus Jones, *Selected Stories of Maine Humor* (Clark University Library, 1945), and *Motif* B422, the helpful cat. See also *Motifs* X1156 (Lie; other unusual methods of catching fish) and J2300–2349 (Gullible fool series).

" 'Oregon' Smith of Indiana": *Southern Folklore Quarterly* (1942), 164–67.

Collected by Herbert Halpert and Emma Robinson, who provide a commentary and documentation. "Oregon" Smith was celebrated locally as a teller of tall travel tales, comparable to Jones Tracy of Maine (pp. 386–92) or Len Henry of Idaho (pp. 380–83). Halpert and Robinson point out that most of his stories were "part of the general stock of tall tales circulating in this country." The authoritative study is William Hugh Jansen, *Abraham "Oregon" Smith: Pioneer, Folk Hero, and Tale Teller* (New York, 1977).

"Buffalo-milk Butter": Ibid., 164.

Collected by Herbert Halpert from Emma Robinson, a student at Indiana University, Bloomington, who heard it from her grandfather, David Beswick. Cf. *Motif* H1361.6.

"The Peach Tree Deer": Ibid., 165.

Collected by Herbert Halpert from Emma Robinson, who heard it from her grandfather (see above). This is a Münchausen tale, *Type* 1889C, with a peach tree substituted for a cherry, but it is known in America with both peach and cherry pits.

" 'Oregon' Sheds a Barrel of Tears": Ibid., 166.

Collected by Herbert Halpert from Emma Robinson, who transcribed it from the dictation of her aunt, Mrs. Charles Fyffee. Cf. *Motif* F1051.1.

"Len Henry, Idaho Squawman": *Northwest Folklore* (1965), 11–14, 17–19.

Jan Harold Brunvand calls Len Henry a "regional Münchausen." He collected sixty-seven tales associated with him, about 80 per cent of them first-person and tall. Len Henry (his given name was Lorenzo), was born in Kansas City, Kansas, probably about 1852, though he claimed to have been born in 1841. He died in 1946. The informants for the five Len Henry "stretchers" presented here are, respectively: Mylie Lawyer, collected November 2, 1963; collected by letter from A. L. Perkins, formerly of the Lapwai, Idaho, area, by Mrs. Artylee Turnball, his daughter; collected by tape from Frank McIntire, Sweetwater, Idaho, October 12, 1963; "sent to me in a letter"; and Barney McGovern, age seventy-four, who "lived across the road from Len Henry from 1929 to 1934." Brunvand found parallels for the first three "stretchers" but not the last two and suggests that they "may be original with Len Henry." See *Types* 1889F and J.

"John Snyder of Slippery Rock": *Keystone Folklore Quarterly* (1962), 25–27.

Contributed by Mrs. Ruby Watson, whose source was William A. Ralston's pamphlet *Early Life Along the Slippery Rock* (1956). Lunt (see below) records a Jones Tracy version of *Type* 1882 (Man carrying a bed tick full of shot sinks into earth up to his hips). See also *Type* 1895 (Man wading in water catches many fish in boots).

"Jones Tracy of Mount Desert Island": *Northeast Folklore* (1968), 16–17, 28, 43, 45–46.

C. Richard K. Lunt has written a monograph on Jones Tracy (1856–1939), son of a lighthouse keeper and for most of his life a farmer on Mount Desert Island, Maine. Lunt's study of "the skill and repertoire of a master performer of exaggeration humor" includes chapters on Tracy's biography, his style as a storyteller, a collection of Tracy's tales and their analysis, and a discussion of his role "as a Tall-Tale Hero." He provided full information on his informants, circumstances of his interviews, and motifs. Tales and informants presented here are: "Jones Tracy of Mount Desert Island": Clark Manring, age fifty-seven, Tracy's grandson, of Northeast Harbor, interviewed January 1, 1964, and John Carroll, age eighty-eight, Tracy's son-in-law, of Southwest Harbor, interviewed September 28, 1963. "A Heavy Fog in Maine": collected from Augustus Phillips, age sixty, a retired carpenter and wood carver, of Northeast Harbor, on January 2, 1964; "The Snakes That Ate Themselves": collected from Ralph Tracy, age sixty, Jones Tracy's son, on September 22, 1963; "Keeping Dry," collected from Chauncey Somes of Somesville, "a noted Island story teller," age sixty, a ship's carpenter, on September 21, 1963; and "Saving the Powder," collected from Chauncey Somes, same date. The Tracy stories are typical of traditional lies and exaggerations. See, for example, Type 1889B (Hunter turns animal inside out) and "A Bear Turned Inside Out" (p. 391).

"Jones Tracy Goes Hunting": Ibid., 33, 38, 44, 47, 49.

Lunt's informants in this grouping are: "The Bunghole Story": from John Carroll, described above, September 28, 1963; "Speeding Up a Slow Bullet": from Ralph Tracy, described above, September 22, 1963; "A Bear Turned Inside Out," from Clark Manring, described above, January 1, 1964; "Double-jumping a Brook," from John Carroll, September 28, 1963; and "Lifelike Decoys," collected from Lindsey Smallidge of Northeast Harbor, who had run a dry cleaning business since 1920, did not know Jones Tracy directly, but had heard about him as a young man.

Song Makers

"Larry Gorman, 'The Man Who Makes the Songs'": *Western Folklore* (1960), 17–18, 22.

Edward D. Ives in this "Preliminary Report" does not include his specific sources, tunes, full text, or informants. "Billy Watts" appears in full, with a discussion, in his authoritative study *Larry Gorman: The Man Who Made the Songs*, Indiana University Folklore Series, No. 19 (Bloomington, 1964; reprinted New York, 1977), 91–92, 190–91. His informant was Alden F. Mace of Southwest Harbor, Maine.

"A Larry Gorman Cante Fable": *New England Quarterly* (1959), 228.

Collected by Edward D. Ives. A cante fable is an integral combination of prose tale with song or verse that may be chanted. In his monograph on Larry Gorman, cited above, Ives states that "Matt" was Larry's nephew, Matt Howard, and that his informant was Harry Thompson of Glengarry, Prince Edward Island. (See Ives, *Larry Gorman*, 37, 204.)

"Larry Gorman and 'Old Henry'": *Northeast Folklore* (1959), 40–41, 43–45.

Collected by Edward D. Ives, who supplied the following statement, by letter dated December 17, 1977: "This article represents an early version of what became the first half of Chapter Six in Edward D. Ives' *Larry Gorman: The Man Who Made the Songs* [cited above], pages 101–106. The reader is referred to that volume for a more detailed account, a far better transcription of the tune, a more accurate transcription of the words, more detailed notes on page 208, and complete archival references on page 193."

Ives obtained information on the Henrys from "several old woodsmen." If Larry Gorman became a legendary figure for his impudent songs and verse, "Old Henry," the butt of Larry's sass, was something of a legend, too.

"A Ballad Composer of the Nineties": *Tennessee Folklore Society Bulletin* (December 1953), 85, 87–90.

Maggie J. Lowe of Murfreesboro, Tennessee, has written a biographical sketch of William Pleasant Ewell, a country schoolteacher in Rutherford and Coffee counties from about 1875 to 1895, based upon interviews with her family, friends, and neighbors who remember him as a local character and composer of songs. She identifies her informants carefully in her footnotes, here omitted. The story behind the song "It's Hard Times Pore Boys" is retold from the recollections of J. W. Lowe and J. T. Earp, both of Murfreesboro. The song is apparently given as she knew it but "confirmed by all the people previously mentioned in the footnotes."

"An Angry Ozark Singer": *Studies in the Literary Imagination* (1970), 37–38.

Loman D. Cansler gives an account of the career of William Henry Scott (1868–1947), a Missouri folk composer noted for going his own way. He had a fine orchard in the 1920s and went about barefooted "peddling apples and other fruit" and, on occasion, hard cider. He was given to litigation, voted the Socialist ticket, and was reputed to be a powerful swimmer who saved at least one man from drowning.

"The Tie Maker": Ibid., 38–39.

Cansler recorded this song on August 4, 1957, as sung by Charlie D. Scott, eldest son of William Henry Scott, his principal source of biographical information and details about his father's songs. Music for this and the songs that follow was transcribed by June Walker and Curtis Surkamp of Kansas City, Missouri.

"Hominy Hoe Cake and an Old 'Possum's Head": Ibid., 43–45.

Recorded by Cansler from the singing of Charlie D. Scott on September 24, 1960. Cansler notes that a version of this song was collected by Vance Randolph at White Rock, Missouri; another by Roger D. Abrahams as sung by Almeda Riddle, a traditional singer "living in the White-Cleburn County area of Arkansas"; and a third version is in the Georgia Folklore Archives "as collected in north Georgia." Therefore, he says, "it is uncertain whether Scott actually composed the song."

"The Battle of Kudd": Ibid., 46–47.

Recorded by Cansler on March 27, 1959, from the singing of Charlie D. Scott.

"Aunt Molly Jackson Arrives in New York": *Kentucky Folklore Record* (1961), 134–39.

Abridged from a newspaper interview by Ben Robertson in the New York *Herald Tribune* of December 2, 1931, reprinted in an issue of the *Kentucky Folklore Record* dedicated to Molly Jackson. A native of Clay County, Kentucky, Aunt Molly went to New York to assist a committee of writers and intellectuals in rallying support for striking coal miners of Harlan County. Theodore Dreiser was a key figure on this committee. He had heard Aunt Molly sing earlier in 1931 at the Glendon Baptist Church in Arjay, Kentucky, where he had gone to investigate poverty and terrorism in the Kentucky mine fields. Aunt Molly eventually became one of the most famous informants in the history of American folklore. Alan Lomax wrote: "Her songs of protest can only be matched by those of Woody Guthrie."

"Aunt Molly Remembers Robin Hood": *Journal of American Folklore* (1956), 25–27.

The fame of Aunt Molly as a folk informant elicited studies of her repertory. John Greenway, who examined her version of "Robin Hood and Little John," found that she borrowed from the landmark collection of Francis James Child and calls attention to her modifications. He shows that Aunt Molly got the introductory stanza from "A True Tale of Robin Hood" (Child 154) and thereafter parallels closely "Robin Hood and Little John" (Child 125), except for dropping eight stanzas, mainly the christening episode, combining four others into two, and adding five stanzas—24, 28, 31, 34, and 35, marked with asterisks. Considering her political orientation and her family pride, it is no surprise that the stanzas she added are about taking from the rich and giving to the poor and enhance the role of the ancestor she claimed, Little John Garland, by having him present at the death of Robin Hood and helping to place his headstone. It is possible that Aunt Molly beguiled herself so readily, assuming she did not intend to deceive anyone else, because she did indeed have some vague recollection of Robin Hood ballads. But the claim of kinship to Little John recalls a readiness on her part, evidenced elsewhere, to tilt in her own direction. Aunt Molly's folk credentials were impeccable, but she was responsive to urban, literate culture. An instinctive though unsophisticated radical, she absorbed doctrinaire Marxism without dismay; and similarly, she was quick to seize on traditional material like the Robin Hood ballad, not in her original repertoire, and make it her own. For further information on Aunt Molly, see

Greenway's *American Folksongs of Protest* (Philadelphia, 1953), 252–74.

"Elvis Presley: A King Dies but a Legend Lives": University of Pennsylvania Folklore Archive (1977). Unclassified.

Jack Lloyd, by-lined as an "Entertainment Writer," contributed this "evaluation" of Elvis Presley to the Philadelphia *Inquirer*. It was printed on August 17, 1977, the day after he died. Summarizing his career, Lloyd concluded: "From 1956, when the world at large discovered what was dubbed rock 'n' roll, until the Beatles appeared about seven years later, there was no question that Presley was the unchallenged king of pop music."

"Some Myths and Facts": Ibid.

Marc Schogol wrote the front-page, streamer-headlined obituary of Presley published in the Philadelphia *Inquirer* of August 17, 1977, summing up the facts and recounting some of the legends. Seeking to explain Presley's phenomenal popularity, Schogol placed him in the "James Dean–Marlon Brando school of alienated young rebel without a cause," and described his style, "which integrated black rhythm & blues into the mainstream of white pop music," as "urgent and sexual and low-down."

"The Shrine": Ibid.

An Associated Press story in the Philadelphia *Inquirer* of August 20, 1977, reported the veneration of "thousands of pilgrims" at the "shrine" of Elvis Preseley. They knelt beside his tomb, wept, and sought souvenirs (holy relics?) as if he were a sacred being. The early death in 1926 of the silent film star Rudolph Valentino evoked a parallel response.

"The Sale": Ibid.

Like many another popular hero, Elvis Presley alive was packaged and sold to the public. Isabel Spencer, writing in the Philadelphia *Inquirer* of August 26, 1977, shows that the spirit of commerce transcends the grave.

"A Song Is Over": Ibid.

This excerpt from a syndicated column by Smith Hempstone clipped from the Philadelphia *Inquirer* of August 27, 1977, places Presley in the folk tradition of the rogue hero who dies young—or should have. Hempstone's acerbic comments on a Presley past his prime drew protesting letters.

Fantastics

"Davy Crockett, Fantasy and Horse Sense": *Southwest Review* (1939–40), 444–45, 461–62.

Walter Blair in an analytical essay found "six Davy Crocketts," or successive and conflicting images of the historical David Crockett (1786–1836), Tennessee hunter, congressman, and hero who died at the Alamo. He traces the Crockett progress as he moved from historical figure, through the nineteenth-century mass media—the newspapers, almanacs, and stage—and on into folk tradition. Blair suggests that the power of the Crockett legend comes from its blend of fantasy and common sense. Blair does not cite his sources in this essay. Today Davy Crockett still flourishes as a media hero.

"Davy Crockett Rides a Wild Stallion": *Southwest Review* (1933–34), 153–54.

In the discussion of the Crockett legend from which this extract is taken, Constance Rourke argues that Crockett "was unique, surely, in being a man of stature who even while living stepped straight into myth." She emphasizes the "legends clustered about his name," for example, the "white steed of the prairies," famed in western folklore for his beauty, strength, and cunning, and referred to in Melville's *Moby-Dick*, Chapter 42. She does not provide the source of her story of Crockett's ride.

Col. Crockett's Exploits . . . (1836) was a posthumously published biography.

"Pompey Smash: Davy Crockett on the Minstrel Stage": *Publications of the Texas Folk-Lore Society* (1927), 205–6.

Collected by Julia Beazley from a Mrs. Melton of Houston, Texas; date not given, but known previously in another version (of which the first stanza is given here) given to Miss Beazley from "some sailors on the Texas coast" in the years "before the advent of motor cars and motor boats." "Pompey Smash" was one of the most popular Negro minstrel songs of the 1850s. It incorporated topical allusions and references to celebrated figures. Fragmentary versions containing Crockett material had been reported previously. For a Virginia reel with similar words, titled "Colonel Crockett," see *Tennessee Folklore Society Bulletin* (December 1947), 81–82.

"The Fantastic Sam Patch": *New York Folklore Quarterly* (1945), 133–38.

Richard M. Dorson provides the basic study of Sam Patch (1807–29). He gives biographical information and examines the image of Patch in popular, folk tradition, and literary tradition. He also supplies a bibliographical note. Responding to the question of why Sam Patch captivated the American public in the decade of the 1830s, he suggests that Patch was "a natural": "With the squat name, the senseless bravado, the nonsense sayings, the common-man origin, the fondness for brag, antics, drink, and danger, and the death-in-action, the historic Patch possessed attributes for American apotheosis equalled by few folk-hero prototypes." Gerald Parsons (*New York Folklore Quarterly* [1969], 83–92) counters that the Patch material exists mainly in the mass media, in literate rather than folk tradition, and hence Patch is a popular rather than a folk hero. His spiritual heirs include Steve Brodie, who, to win a bet, jumped from Brooklyn Bridge in 1886, and more recently, the stunt motorcyclist Evel Knievel.

"An Elegy to Sam Patch": *New York Folklore Quarterly* (1972), 126.

Kathleen M. Kavanagh reprints the elegy from the Providence, Rhode Island, *Manufacturers' and Farmers' Journal* of November 26, 1829.

"Sam Patch's Epitaph": Ibid., 126.

Reprinted by Kavanagh from Dorson's "The Story of Sam Patch," *American Mercury* (June 1947), 745. It dates from the 1840s.

"Sam Patch's Last Leap": *New York Folklore Quarterly* (1945), 147.

This tall tale is quoted by Richard M. Dorson in his pioneering study of Sam Patch, but he does not cite his source. The author is T. C. Haliburton and the tale appears in his series about a comic Yankee peddler, *Sam Slick: The Clockmaker* (1837–40). Strictly speaking, it is not in the folk tradition.

"Sam Patch Lives": Ibid., 140–43.

Collected by Richard M. Dorson, who provides comment. Patch was killed on Friday, November 13, 1829, so this is a newspaper hoax about a suspected hoax that Patch was thought capable of perpetrating. At the time, his body had not been recovered. The reports of his having been seen after the fatal jump have many parallels in folklore. The newspaper hoax tended to encourage such rumors and, as it led off with Sam's famous sayings, helped to make these crazy boasts proverbial. Cf. *Motifs* A571 (Culture hero still lives) and A580 (Culture hero's expected return).

"Old Joe Clarke": *Southern Folklore Quarterly* (1959), 172–74.

F. W. Bradley published this synthetic version of "Old Joe Clarke," which he obtained from John Bennett of Charleston, South Carolina, who combined two songs he had "heard sung in West Virginia and North Carolina . . . into what is a complete story." Bennett seems to have used details from play-party songs. In these nonsense verses, Joe appears as a preacher or sheriff as often as he does an outlaw. The song is seldom found with a coherent story line. B. A. Botkin prints most of the stanzas in his *The American Play-Party Song* (Lincoln, Nebr., 1937), 269–85. See note below on "Ol' Joe Clark, Play-party Song."

"Ole Joe Clark, a Variant": *Journal of American Folklore* (1912), 152.

Collected by E. C. Perrow in 1905 in East Tennessee from the memory of unnamed "mountain whites." Cf. the first stanza of the John Bennett version above.

"Ol' Joe Clark, Play-party Song": *Journal of American Folklore* (1929), 222.

Collected by Vance Randolph from Mrs. Emma Chambliss as she heard it sung "by an old woman in McDonald County, Missouri." Randolph explains that the play-party was popular in the South and Southwest among religious groups who believed that dancing was immoral. They got around this ban by substituting "plays" or "games," actually dances with intricate steps, accompanied by songs, hand clapping, foot stamping, and skipping. Randolph states that he had heard the tune he gives also used for square dances. Play-party songs are characterized by attractive nonsense lines such as "Little red wagon painted blue" from the widely known "Skip to My Lou"; dramatic action such as choosing partners and singing in dialogue; and fragmentary, ballad-like storytelling such as "Ol' Joe Clark."

"The Pigs of the Love Mad Lopez": *California Folklore Quarterly* (1942), 369–71.

Transcribed by Frederick Morris of Los Angeles, California, who "heard it from a fellow named Daniel Boone, descended from Boone of Kentucky fame and the Lopez family of Arizona" and who describes the fantastic doings of "the Great Don Jose" as "partly true, partly folklore." The editor notes that he has retained Morris's "original style and spelling. The style is typical of the folk narrator and as such deserves to be preserved."

"Enter Joe Root and the Jeebies": *Keystone Folklore Quarterly* (1957), 43–46.

Herbert R. Spencer describes Joe Root (ca. 1860–1912) of Presque Isle, Maine, and his fantasies, drawing upon personal and local recollections. Root was born "probably in the County Poorhouse," spent his summers in a shack on Presque Isle that he had knocked together, and returned to the poorhouse for the winters. He died in the State Hospital at North Warren, Maine.

"Huckleberry Charlie and His Spiel": *New York Folklore Quarterly* (1952), 93–98.

Dean Frederick Bock's sources for the account of Charlie Sherman's verbal extravagances and antic behavior are mainly newspaper clippings from the "Morgue" of the Watertown *Daily Times* and the notes of Harold B. Johnson, former editor of this New York newspaper. Bock reports, however, that stories about Huckleberry Charlie were still current in the 1950s.

Fabulous Beasts

"The Greatest of the Grizzlies": *California Folklore Quarterly* (1944), 12–15.

Collected by J. Frank Dobie from Yellow Brow, a Crow, on the Crow Indian Reservation in Montana, in 1941. Yellow Brow, age seventy-nine, was described by Dobie as "a mighty man in frame, well over six feet tall, erect, his dark face pitted from smallpox." Cf. "Slue-foot, the Indestructible Bear," below. Also cf. the "foolish brave" who provoked the magical animal in "Mejewedah, Gifted in Magic" (p. 54).

"Slue-foot, the Indestructible Bear": *West Virginia Folklore* (1966), 16–18.

Retold by Pat Sloan, who heard it from her father, who "brought this story from his boyhood home in Pocahontas County," West Virginia.

She believes that the "story is true, for John Tallhorse told it to him personally." "Indestructible" bears abound in the tall tales of the Old Southwest. The best known, "The Big Bear of Arkansas," by T. B. Thorpe, is about "an unhuntable bear." The most famous example in modern literature is William Faulkner's *The Bear* (1942), in which Sam Fathers, a woodsman of Indian and black ancestry, has a role paralleling that of John Tallhouse. Faulkner's bear, "Old Ben," has "one trap-ruined foot." When Faulkner was asked about the sources of his story, he replied: "There used to be a bear like Big Ben [*sic*] in our county when I was a boy. He'd gotten one paw caught in a trap, and 'cause of that, folks used to call him Reel Foot, 'cause of the way he walked" (*Accent* [1956], 174).

"Gray Bess, the Horse that Trailed Comanches": *Publications of the Texas Folk-Lore Society* (1962), 38–40.

Recalled and retold by A. L. Bennett "somewhat as follows" from the original telling of Joe Sappington, as Joe Sapp, a writer for country weekly newspapers in central Texas and "a teller of tales by natural predilection." Sapp was best known in Bell, McLennan, and Coryell counties "around the turn of the century," but Bennett does not supply details about time and place.

"Murderous Mary, Circus Elephant": *Tennessee Folklore Society Bulletin* (March 1971), 1–5, 7.

Collected by Thomas G. Burton "from the oral and written tradition of the surrounding area." Names of informants and printed sources cited in the text. An analagous execution of a rogue elephant said to have occurred in Danville, Indiana, is reported in *Tennessee Folklore Bulletin*, March 1972, 4–5. The execution and ritual burial of animals convicted of capital offenses has biblical sanction in Leviticus 20:15. See William Bradford's *Of Plymouth Plantation* for the year 1642, in which he records an instance of bestiality and the execution of the animals involved. Cf. the execution of the "bewitched" dancing bear in Nathaniel Hawthorne's "The Maypole of Merry Mount."

For another aspect of the elephant in American folk, popular, and literary tradition, see Donald Yannella's discussion of a related proverbial phrase, "Seeing the Elephant in *Mardi*," in *Artful Thunder*

(Kent, Ohio, 1975), and J. Rea, "Seeing the Elephant," *Western Folklore* (1969), 21–26.

"Old Satan, the Miraculous Mule": *West Virginia Folklore* (1965), 22–23.

Collected by Mike Porter from Jeffrey Morgan of Carolina, West Virginia, a small, coal-mining town. There are thousands of exaggerations and lies about animals of all sorts in the folk literature of the world. For others about mules, see *Motif* X1242.

"The Leader of the Pack": *Keystone Folklore Quarterly* (1963), 129–30.

Reported by Russell Fluharty, who does not cite date or informant.

"Heigh-ho Silver": *Beloit Poetry Journal*, Vol. 6, Chapbook No. 4 (undated), 5.

Included by Marion Kingston in "A Folk Song Chapbook," issued by the *Beloit Poetry Journal*, this children's verse is based on heroes from the mass media who have found their way into oral tradition—the Lone Ranger; his Indian companion, Tonto; and his horse, Silver. Their radio series began in 1933 and moved on into film. The opening formula included the Lone Ranger's call, "Hi-yo, Silver." Kingston states that the rhymes in his chapbook were "collected from oral tradition." He obtained this one from Marjorie Kimmerle's archive, originally collected "by Alice Ingwersen in grade school, Illinois."

"Hi-O Silver, Jump-rope Rhyme": *Southern Folklore Quarterly* (1963), 205.

Selected by Roger D. Abrahams from the University of Texas Folklore Archives, Amarillo, Texas, undated, informant unspecified. Beginning with the Lone Ranger's call, it moves on to lines often found in another jump-rope rhyme, "Policeman, policeman, do your duty."

Paul Bunyan—and His Kin

"The Birth of Paul Bunyan": *Southern Folklore Quarterly* (1943), 138–39.

Louise Pound collected information on Paul Bunyan as background to her studies of legendary Nebraska strong men such as Febold Feboldson (p. 517) and Antoine Barada (p. 66). William Hutchinson diagnoses the case: "the Paul Bunyan anecdotes, legends, stories—call them what you will—simply did not have time to develop because they were delivered by Caesarean section before their gestation period had been accomplished. The scalpel in this operation was the power of advertising. The surgeon was the late W. B. Laughead . . ." (*Western Folklore* [1963], 1). Hutchinson taped interviews with Laughead September 17–19, 1957, in which Laughead repeated that he had "never heard anyone in the camps or anywhere else mention Paul Bunyan in a narrative form, that is, start out to tell you a story, something that Paul did" but he had first heard in 1901 "Paul Bunyan gags," which he thought originated "in the Saginaw River Country" of southern Michigan.

As a writer of advertising copy, Laughead's problem was to promote the sale of pine lumber from California sawmills for a market that needed to be assured that it was the equivalent of white pine from Minnesota, and the device he sought was "some kind of slogan or tie-up with the old traditions of eastern white pine." He credits the suggestion of Paul Bunyan, known "from the old white pine camps on New England out to the Lake States," as a means of making this connection, to Archie D. Walker, secretary of the Red River Lumber Company, and wrote a sales pamphlet titled *Introducing Mr. Paul Bunyan of Westwood, California* (Minneapolis, 1914). In fact, Paul Bunyan was not as well known in the lumber trade as Laughead and Walker assumed, but this disadvantage was overcome by an effective, continuing advertising campaign. Laughead told Hutchinson that he "exchanged quite a number of letters with Dan Hoffman," whose *Paul Bunyan, Last of the Frontier Demigods* (Philadelphia, 1952) is an authoritative study of the origins and permutations of this synthetic folk hero.

"Paul Bunyan in 1910: First Time in Print": *Journal of American Folklore* (1944), 188.

W. W. Charters collected and ascertained the authorship of the earliest published example so far found of a Paul Bunyan yarn, antedating W. B. Laughead's 1914 advertising pamphlet for the Red River Lumber Company. Max Gartenberg observes that this initial appearance in print reveals "artificial details and embellishments which are a parcel of the literary art," though it is "composed in a natural earthy prose which nicely approximates the speech of men in work gangs" (*Journal of American Folklore* [1950], 444). "The Round River Drive" was the subject of a lively doggerel poem, authorship uncertain, which was printed in a trade journal, *American Lumberman* (April 25, 1914). Gartenberg suggests this verse was the impetus of Archie D. Walker's suggestion to Laughead that he exploit the Paul Bunyan materials to promote the sale of western white pine (see note on "The Birth of Paul Bunyan," above).

At the same time that Paul Bunyan was making his literary debut, the first record in oral tradition was being noted (see Stith Thompson note below). Sol Smith, in *Theatrical Management in the West and South* (New York, 1868) tells an Old Southwest story similar to the Round River Drive about a Mississippi steamboat that spent the night circling back to refuel at the same woodyard.

"Paul Bunyan in 1910: The Oral Tradition": *Journal of American Folklore* (1946), 134–35.

Stith Thompson, in an attempt to determine whether the Paul Bunyan legend is "an old tradition in the American lumber camps which recent writers collected and perhaps elaborated" or whether it is "all essentially a literary concoction of the last thirty years stimulated by activities of the lumber companies," places on the record the 1910 diary of Edward O. Tabor, a Pittsburgh attorney. In the summer of 1910 he and Thompson worked as lumberjacks at Palmer Junction, eastern Oregon. This was prior to the publication of W. B. Laughead's advertising pamphlet, but Tabor's recollections in his letter to Thompson, though not in his diary, are to some extent touched by it;

for example, Laughead claims credit for naming Bunyan's blue ox "Babe" (see note above).

"Told at the Paul Bunyan Winter Carnival": *Western Folklore* (1956), 183–84.

Reprinted by Richard M. Dorson from a United Press article filed from Bemidji, Minnesota, during that town's annual winter carnival, date and author not given. Dissemination by the mass media in the context of the publicity and commercialization attending a winter sports carnival is consistent with the forces that initially popularized the Paul Bunyan tales. Dorson reports that the same stories, with some seasonal additions, were being written for the press months later when Bemidji held a Fourth of July Paul Bunyan Festival. The exaggerations are folk-like, but have the flavor of the lying contests and liars' clubs that belong to the pseudo-folklore of popular culture rather than to true oral tradition (e.g., see *Tennessee Folklore Society Bulletin* [March 1974,] 17–22). Cf. *Motifs* X900–1899 (Humor of lies and exaggeration), especially *Motifs* X1237.2f.

"Paul Bunyan in the Oil Fields": *Publications of the Texas Folk-Lore Society* (1928), 46, 48–52.

John Lee Brooks first encountered fragments of Paul Bunyan lore as an inexperienced workman in an oil field in Oklahoma in 1920 and again the following year at a field near Breckenridge, Texas. Two years later, he deliberately sought "to collect Bunyaniana," following "the trail of the oil development through [the Texas fields of] Ranger, Breckenridge, Eastland, Cisco, Big Lake, Best, and finally to McCamey, the latest frontier."
   Some oil field terms:
"boll-weevil"—new or clumsy worker
"bull wheel"—large reel on which the drilling cable, which drives the derrick, is wound
"walking-beam"—beam worked with a seesaw motion to raise and lower the tools in the hole for drilling
"crown block"—wooden block on top of the derrick holding pulley wheels over which the steel cables run
"spudded in"—started the hole

"sharp-shooter"—a long, narrow spade
"high-powers"—company officials controlling the drilling
"head-ache post"—a beam that moves up and down monotonously over a well as long as oil is being piped
"calf-wheel"—an auxiliary to the bull wheel
"lazy-bench"—a makeshift combination chair and bench upon which the fireman at the boiler, the power source, reclines
"jars"—two heavy steel links attached above the drill stem, which allow several inches of play and therefore increase the force of the blow
"soft diggin' "—soft rock
"tough diggin' "—hard rock

"Paul Bunyan's Wife": *Journal of American Folklore* (1951), 407.

Collected by Rodney C. Loehr from Alec Hodgon, University of Minnesota. No further information supplied. For another example in folk tradition about the wife of a hero, see "Moe Stanley" (p. 69) and versions of the "John Henry" ballad in which his wife "drives steel like a man" (Laws, *NAB* I, 1). See also "Joe Call's Sister" (p. 57).

"The Saga of Pecos Bill": *Century Magazine* (October 1923), 828–33.

Edward O'Reilly is the author, perhaps more accurately the fabricator, of the synthetic "saga" (to repeat O'Reilly's word) of Pecos Bill. Pecos Bill appears not to have existed in print or in oral tradition prior to the publication of O'Reilly's sketch. In a preamble O'Reilly calls attention to a sketch of Paul Bunyan in an earlier issue of *Century Magazine* and claims that he and "Pecos Bill, cow-boy hero of the Southwest, were blood brothers," who "can meet on one common ground: they were both fathered by a liar." True.

Brent Ashbranner, in an appraisal of Pecos Bill, observes that the "reading public want to believe in a sound folk basis for tall tale heroes," implying that literary types often oblige. He points out that O'Reilly's accomplishment was to attach a number of miscellaneous tall tales to Pecos Bill, unifying them around a single character (*Western Folklore* [1952], 20–24). He cites as an example a story "current in the early days of Oklahoma's cattle industry, telling of how a man arrived at a small Arkansas town one day driving a cart to which was hitched two huge catamounts. The man used a rattlesnake for a whip, and when he pulled up to the local saloon, he called for straight sulfuric acid as his refreshment. When asked what he was doing in Arkansas, he announced blandly that all sissies were being run out of Oklahoma!"

Pecos Bill material is also borrowed from the brags and tall talk of frontier roarers like Mike Fink and Davy Crockett. Cf. Bill's "bouncin' bride" and Paul Bunyan's oil field "toolie" (p. 497).

"The Saga of Joe Magarac, Steelman": *Scribner's Magazine* (November 1931), 505.

In his introduction, Owen Francis confesses that his inspiration and information were largely derived from the prune juice: "Some of it I heard in the mill; some of it while sitting on the hill above the mill; the most of it while sitting in Agnes's kitchen with Hunkie friends at my side and well-filled tin cups of prune-jack before us." He supplies no further details regarding informants. Like Edward O'Reilly, author of "The Saga of Pecos Bill" (see note above), Owen Francis fabricated the "saga" of a synthetic folk hero who is the center of various genuine folk motifs; published it in a popular magazine that featured American literary material; called his sketch a "saga"; and claimed kinship for his hero to Paul Bunyan. Hyman Richman, in an article also titled "The Saga of Joe Magarac" (*New York Folklore Quarterly* [1953], 282–93), reports after exhaustive research: "I . . . began with the premise that Joe Magarac was an authentic folk character and that I would try to uncover more about him . . . my research developed the entirely unexpected conclusion that Joe Magarac is an entirely manufactured legend . . . having no basis whatsoever in the lore of this area." Francis, who was the first to publish on Joe Magarac, is, according to Richman, "the only author who claims he got his account from an original source." Richman did not find Magarac tales in oral tradition.

"The Marriage of Mary Mestrovich": Ibid., 506–9.

Although Richman, above, found no Magarac stories in oral tradition, suitor contests are universal in both literature and traditional lore. Cf. *Motifs* H310–333. Also see note below for other literary and folk motifs in the Magarac "saga."

"Joe Magarac Makes Steel": Ibid., 510–11.

"The Saga of Joe Magarac" was published during the depression when the steel industry was hit by hard times, and Owen Francis, in describing Joe's sacrificial death, is conveying the conventional answer of the industry: a more efficient mill would increase production at lower cost, which would bring greater sales and more jobs. Hyman Richman observes that the notes on Joe Magarac collected for a *Federal Writers' Project Report* (1937) have a different slant. Joe leaves his job "because he is doing the work of many men and is depriving others of work." Topical economic theories are not exactly what one expects in genuine folk tales.

The episode contains *Motifs* A978.1 (Origin of minerals from the body of dead culture hero) and E630 (Reincarnation in object), but cf. another fictional treatment, "The Soul of the Great Bell" in Lafcadio Hearn's *Some Chinese Ghosts* (1887), in which the daughter of the bell caster immolates herself in molten metal so that the tone of his bell will be perfect and carry a great distance. For a Korean analogue, see "The Great Bell of Seoul," *Southern Folklore Quarterly* (1957), 146–48.

"Is Joe Magarac Folklore?": *New York Folklore Quarterly* (1953), 291.

Hyman Richman's informants, in addition to those specified in the text, numbered more than a hundred, including steelworkers who had been in the mills for fifty years, union officials, and mill supervisors. Representatives of more than a dozen ethnic groups were interviewed, with a heavy proportion of Slavic and Hungarian origin. He talked to men in the Pennyslvania steel towns of "Monessen, Braddock, Duquesne, McKeesport, Clairton, Homestead, Pittsburgh, Johnstown, and in other mill towns."

"The Last Word on 'Magarac' ": Ibid., 286–88.

Hyman Richman argues that "one of the strongest reasons for doubting this legend [of Joe Magarac], lies in the name of the hero himself" and reports that this was the point of "greatest comment and criticism" from his informants. His informants are cited in the text, and his research is documented by an array of dictionaries of the relevant languages. As a framing device (of an obviously literary sort), the name is notably inapposite. Richman points out that the repeated use of the word "Hunkie" also reveals ignorance or gross insensitivity.

"Febold Feboldson, Prairie Bunyan": *Southern Folklore Quarterly* (1943), 133–36.

Louise Pound establishes the origins of Febold Feboldson, who "looms largest" among Nebraska strong men, as a journalistic invention outside of folk tradition. It gained currency through skillful literary popularization at the hands of Paul R. Beath, Carl Carmer, B. A. Botkin, and others. According to Professor Pound, they did "not hesitate to admit that as a folk hero he is a successful hoax."

"Paul Bunyan and Febold Become Acquainted": *Nebraska Folklore Pamphlet Five* (July 1, 1937), 5–6.

The Federal Writers' Project in Nebraska published these "excerpts from a manuscript written by Mr. [Paul Robert] Beath concerning Nebraska's foremost legendary character." They are a slightly modified version of Beath's concoction about Feboldson and Bunyan in the *Prairie Schooner* (1932), 59–60. In the preface to the excerpts in the pamphlet, Beath affirms his original indebtedness to Feboldson tales "printed by Wayne Carroll in the *Independent* of Gothenburg, Nebraska" and to Don Holmes of the Gothenburg *Times*.

"Febold's Post Holes": Ibid., 4.

This story is unusual among the Feboldson material because it is a typical Münchausen exaggeration. See *Motifs* X1760f (Absurd disregard of the nature of holes). Most of the motifs in Feboldson tales are too arch and polished to have come directly from folk sources.

"Johnny Kaw, Paul Bunyan's Latest Offspring": *Arizona Friends of Folklore* (1971), 11–12, 14–18.

Howard W. Marshall has investigated, in the field and library, the origins of "the 'legendary' character of Johnny Kaw, the alleged folk hero of Kansas wheat farmers," whom he finds "important because he represents the values of his creator (which can be summarized by his conception of the 'pioneer spirit') and because he illustrates the current 'looking backward' which is so much a part of popular American culture." Although Marshall calls Johnny Kaw "a fake hero," he points to the presence of traditional folk motifs in the cycle such as Motifs D1652.1.3, X792, X1122.2, and X1611.

"Sara DeSoto and Sarasota, Florida": *Southern Folklore Quarterly* (1938), 220.

Collected by J. Frederick Doering during "several field trips among the folk of Florida" where "no legend is more popular." Doering expresses indebtedness to W. T. Wells of Sarasota "for information concerning this interesting story." The story is a traditional, but fabricated, explanation of the origin of a place name, but makes use of the same sort of motif as do many folk tales of tragic love. Cf. Motifs T80–89. The explorer Hernando DeSoto set out to conquer Florida in 1539. He had no daughter accompanying him and none named Sara. See Alton C. Morris, *Florida Place Names* (Coral Gables, 1974), 133.

"Wenonah and Winona, Minnesota": Winona County Historical Society, 1977.

This summary of the Winona legend, prepared in 1977 as a handout for visitors to the Winona County Historical Museum, Winona, Minnesota, was supplied by David N. Sterling of the museum staff. The legend, here associated with Maiden Rock overlooking Lake Pepin, Upper Mississippi River, was first recorded in 1805 by the explorer Zebulon Pike in his diary: "I was shown a point of rocks from which a Sioux maiden cast herself. . . . She had been informed that her friends intended matching her to a man she despised . . . and before they could overtake her and obviate her purpose she took the lover's leap!" For a summary of its many versions and their authenticity, see G. Herbert Smith, "The Winona Legend," *Minnesota History* (1932), 367–76. Similar place-name legends about lovers' leaps dot the American landscape.

"As Strong as Annie Christmas": *Tennessee Folklore Society Bulletin* (September 1945), 6–7.

Contributed anonymously as a preface to excerpts from a poem, "Mighty Annie Christmas of New Orleans," the "facts of the poem" being credited to Herbert Asbury's *The French Quarter* (New York, 1936). B. A. Botkin prints in *Mississippi River Folklore* (New York, 1955) a letter from Mrs. Roark Bradford dated December 29, 1954, describing the origin of Annie Christmas. She was conceived by Roark Bradford and Lyle Saxon on the sidewalk in front of a Decatur Street dive. Mrs. Bradford writes: "Together B. and L. made up a story of a large, Tug-Boat Annie type of woman who ran one of the dives" (p. 35). Her seven sons were bouncers who rolled sailors and dumped them into the Mississippi. Lyle Saxon suggested calling her "Mary Christmas" but Bradford opined that the name was incredible, and they agreed on "Annie." Bradford was feature editor of the New Orleans *Times-Picayune*, for which Saxon wrote his first Annie Christmas story, "faking that he had found it in some old ms." Saxon includes an account of Annie Christmas in his book of New Orleans local color and lore, *Gumbo Ya-Ya* (Boston, 1945), 376–77.

"The Renegade": University of Pennsylvania Folklore Archive, 1977. Unclassified.

Collected by Hennig Cohen from Gail Danyluk of Heublein, Inc., in February 1977. Gail Danyluk also supplied the statement on how the advertising agency "created" the "legend."

INDEX

STATES

ETHNIC AND SPECIAL GROUPS

TALE TYPES OF THE TEXTS

MOTIFS FOR THE TEXTS

SONG TITLES AND FIRST LINES